The Life of Saint Alban
by Matthew Paris

MEDIEVAL AND RENAISSANCE
TEXTS AND STUDIES
VOLUME 342

THE FRENCH OF ENGLAND TRANSLATION SERIES
(FRETS)
VOLUME 2

The Life of Saint Alban
by Matthew Paris

Translated and Introduced by
Jocelyn Wogan-Browne and
Thelma S. Fenster

with

The Passion of Saint Alban
by William of St. Albans

Translated and Introduced by
Thomas O'Donnell and Margaret Lamont

and

Studies of the Manuscript
by Christopher Baswell and Patricia Quinn

FRETS Series Editors
Thelma Fenster and
Jocelyn Wogan-Browne

ACMRS
(Arizona Center for Medieval and Renaissance Studies)
Tempe, Arizona
2010

Published with the assistance of Fordham University.

Published by ACMRS (Arizona Center for Medieval and Renaissance Studies)
Tempe, Arizona
© 2010 Arizona Board of Regents for Arizona State University.
All Rights Reserved.

Library of Congress Cataloging-in-Publication Data

Paris, Matthew, 1200-1259.
   [Vie de Seint Auban. English]
   The life of Saint Alban / by Matthew Paris ; translated and introduced by Jocelyn Wogan-Browne and Thelma S. Fenster. With The passion of Saint Alban / by William of St. Albans ; translated and introduced by Thomas O'Donnell and Margaret Lamont ; and studies of the manuscript by Christopher Baswell and Patricia Quinn.
       p. cm. -- (Medieval and Renaissance texts and studies ; v. 342) (The French of England translation series (FRETS) ; v. 2)
   Includes bibliographical references and index.
   ISBN 978-0-86698-390-7 (alk. paper)
   1. Alban, Saint, d. 304?--Poetry. 2. Christian saints--Poetry. 3. Paris, Matthew, 1200-1259. Vie de Seint Auban. I. Wogan-Browne, Jocelyn. II. Fenster, Thelma S. III. O'Donnell, Thomas (Thomas Joseph) IV. Lamont, Margaret. V. Baswell, Christopher. VI. Quinn, Patricia A., 1948- VII. Title.
   PQ1501.P18V5313 2010
   843'.1--dc22
                                                                                      2010027183

Cover Art:
The Execution of St. Alban, Trinity College Dublin, MS. 177, fol. 38r.
Reproduced by permission of the Board of Trinity College, to whom it remains copyrighted.

∞
This book is made to last. It is set in Adobe Caslon Pro,
smyth-sewn and printed on acid-free paper to library specifications.
Printed in the United States of America

Contents

List of Plates and Figures	*viii*
Series Editors' Preface	*ix*
Acknowledgments	*xi*
Abbreviations	*xiii*

1. The *Life of Saint Alban* by Matthew Paris
by Jocelyn Wogan-Browne and Thelma Fenster

Introduction	
Matthew Paris and the *Life of Saint Alban*	1
Alban's Story	4
Inventing St. Albans: Cult, Place, and Book	11
The Book of St. Albans	15
Dating the Book	19
The Saint and the City	20
Mirrors and Shadows: Romans, Saracens, and Others in the *Life of Saint Alban*	23
Lordship and Conversion	29
Women Readers	32
Blood Matters	36
The Burial of the Dead	39
Language and Versification	41
Speaking and Writing French	41
Verse Form	42
Syllable Count	44
Enjambement	49
Rhyme	50
Style and Treatment of the Source	51

Suggested Further Reading	59
Note on the Treatment of the Text and Rubrics	65
MATTHEW PARIS, *THE LIFE OF SAINT ALBAN*	67
Notes	107

2. The Passion of Saint Alban by William of St. Albans
by Thomas O'Donnell and Margaret Lamont

Introduction	133
Note on the Text and Translation	136
WILLIAM OF ST. ALBANS, *THE PASSION OF SAINT ALBAN*	139
Notes	161

3. The Manuscript
(Dublin, Trinity College MS. 177 [E. I. 40])

The Manuscript Context	169
by Christopher Baswell	
A Work in Progress? The Making of the Manuscript	169
Date of the Manuscript	171
Format	173
Rubrics	174
The Order of Writing and Illustrations	176
Scribal Confusion at Fols. 63r-66r	177
An Evolving, Unfinished Manuscript	179
A Maquette for Later Fair Copies?	181
Reading the Manuscript	182
A Dossier of Abbatial Antiquity and Rights	182
Mixed, Evolving Audiences of Monks and Aristocrats	184
The Aristocratic Arc of Narrative and Illustration	186
The Translation of Dominion: Roman Prince, English King, and Converted Knights	187
Appendix: The Hands of TCD MS. 177	191

Alban Disbound: Codicological Remarks on Matthew Paris's *Life of St. Alban* by Patricia Quinn	**195**
Introduction	195
Contents	196
Structure and Collation	197
Marginalia	201
Missing Illustrations	203
Skins Used	204
Pigments	206
Conservation and Binding Note	207
Appendix: Collation Maps	209
Appendix: Passages from *La Vie de seint Auban*	213
List of Proper Names in the *Life of Saint Alban*	221
List of Proper Names in the *Passion of Saint Alban*	223

List of Plates and Figures

Cover.	Alban's execution, Trinity College Dublin MS 177, fol. 38r
Plate 1.	Alban's dream, TCD MS 177, fol. 30v
Plates 2–3.	Alban and Amphibalus spied on by a Saracen, TCD MS 177, fols. 31v–32r
Plate 4.	The exchange of cloaks between Alban and Amphibalus, TCD MS 177, fol. 33r
Plate 5.	Alban venerates Amphibalus's cross as the pagans burst in on him, TCD MS 177, fol. 33v
Plate 6.	Alban in the pagan temple, TCD MS 177, fol. 34v
Plate 7.	Alban's banishment from Verulamium, TCD MS 177, fol. 36r
Plate 8.	Heraclius's conversion and beating, TCD MS 177, fol. 37r
Plate 9.	Amphibalus's martyrdom, TCD MS 177, fol. 45r
Plate 10.	God punishes the pagans, TCD MS 177, fol. 49r
Plate 11.	The first image of King Offa, TCD MS 177, fol. 55v
Plate 12.	The final image of King Offa, TCD MS 177, fol. 63r
Figure 3a.1.	Hand 2, TCD MS 177, fol. 60v, col. A, lines 1–5
Figure 3a.2.	Hand 3, TCD MS 177, fol. 63r, col. A, lines 1–7
Figure 3a.3.	Hand 4, TCD MS 177, fol. 66r, col. A, last 5 lines
Figure 3b.1.	TCD MS 177, fol. 31r
Figure 3b.2.	TCD MS 177, fol. 13r (detail)
Figure 3b.3.	TCD MS 177, fol. 49r (detail)
Figure 3b.4	TCD MS 177, fol. 60r (detail)

All plates and figures are reproduced by permission of the Board of Trinity College, to whom they remain copyrighted.

Series Editors' Preface

The French of England Translation Series (FRETS) has been designed to make more readily available works composed in French in medieval England over the twelfth to fifteenth centuries. Although many such texts have been given excellent editions by the Anglo-Norman Text Society, more general awareness of the large French literary corpus (nearly a thousand works) and extensive documentary records of England has often fallen between continental French scholarship and scholarship in medieval English. The works composed in the French of England include a number of important texts that deserve attention in their own right, while medieval English and Latin literature and historiography need to be studied in the context of the multilingual culture of medieval Britain.

Matthew Paris is well known for his Latin chronicles, manuscript illustration, and map-making, but his French works have received less attention. FRETS volume 1 is a translation of Paris's *History of Saint Edward the King (La Estoire de seint Aedword le rei)*, dedicated to Eleanor of Provence, queen of Henry III. The current volume, FRETS volume 2, is the first translation into English of the French text and rubrics of Paris's *Life of Saint Alban (Vie de seint Auban)*, a life of the patron saint of Paris's own monastery, St. Albans Abbey. This life is extant in a manuscript largely copied and illustrated by Paris himself (Dublin, Trinity College MS. 177 [formerly E. I. 40]), and there are many indications in both the text and the manuscript that, in its vigorous promotion of St. Alban's cult, the life was designed to appeal to lay patrons of the monastery and to members of Henry and Eleanor's court. In Paris's reworking of his Latin source, the *Life of Saint Alban* becomes, among other things, a text in the literature of holy violence — the *chansons de geste*, romances, saints' lives, and crusading histories of the "vengeance of our Lord." At the same time, the *Life* needs to be seen in its particular context as a St. Albans manuscript whose illustrations, layout, and texts are largely from Matthew Paris's own hand.

This volume includes both the first translation of Paris's French life of Alban and a new translation of Paris's source (which he himself copied into the manuscript directly before his French *Alban*). This gives every opportunity of observing how Paris, a highly original artist in textual as well as visual media, creates his French text. The manuscript context is indispensable for understanding Paris's work, and this volume includes a study of the manuscript by Christopher Baswell, and a study of its codicology by Patricia Quinn, made at the time of conservation work on the manuscript in 1983–1984 but never previously published. The *Alban* manuscript is not yet digitized, but meanwhile we hope that FRETS 2 may help raise awareness of this important manuscript as well as facilitating study of a fascinating text.

Thelma Fenster
Jocelyn Wogan-Browne

Acknowledgments

For their support of our work on the French of England, we are grateful to the National Endowment for the Humanities, USA; to Fordham University, New York; and to the University of York, UK. We thank Fordham's former Vice President for Academic Affairs, Dr. John Hollwitz, for his initial encouragement, and we remain very grateful to Dr. Nancy Busch, Associate Vice President for Academic Affairs at Fordham, for her continuing strong support. Our special thanks go to Maryanne Kowaleski, the Joseph Fitzpatrick, S.J. Distinguished Professor of History and Director of Fordham's Center for Medieval Studies, for her continuing expert help and generous support.

We are deeply indebted to the generosity of Dr. Bernard Meehan, Keeper of Manuscripts at Trinity College, Dublin, and the library staff. Dr. Meehan permitted access to this rare manuscript, arranged for the inclusion of Patricia Quinn's essay on its codicology, and made possible all the beautiful reproductions from the manuscript we are privileged to include here.

In addition to his own essay on the manuscript, Christopher Baswell has been a tireless and acute reader of the rest of the volume, and we are very grateful. His former graduate students Thomas O'Donnell and Margaret Lamont have contributed a new translation of William of Alban's *Passio sancti Albani*, and we thank them for their excellent work and fresh ideas. Paul Hyams has responded graciously and helpfully to queries about legal terminology, and Rodney Thomson has generously allowed the use of some unpublished papers. Seminars and papers at the University of California at Los Angeles and at Santa Barbara, Mount Holyoke College, and at the King's College, University of London and Westminster Abbey 2007 celebration of Henry III, helped to develop the material for the Introduction: for these invitations we thank Christopher Baswell, Carol Pasternack, Carolyn Collette, and David Carpenter. We are also grateful to the graduate students at UCLA, UCSB, Fordham, and York who have discussed *Alban* with us in graduate seminars. In New York, Karen Trimnell (Fordham University) helped us as a Research Assistant to the French of England project. Professor Ian Short has graciously given us permission from the Anglo-Norman Text Society to reproduce passages of the original text as an Appendix. We thank the Modern Humanities Research Association of the UK for funding Dr. Cathy Hume for a year's Research Associateship in the French of England at the University of York, and we are grateful to Dr. Hume herself for all her meticulous and enterprising work on this volume. Kathy Burford Lewis gave us invaluable professional help in preparing the final typescript.

We are much indebted to the press's readers, Glyn Burgess and David Trotter, for many helpful suggestions and improvements and, as always, to Robert Bjork, who saw the merit of the FRETS project and placed his confidence in us; and to Roy Rukkila, Todd Halvorsen, and Leslie MacCoull for their care, efficiency, and hard work in producing FRETS volumes.

Our husbands, Jim Craddock and Howard Robinson, have cheerfully accepted continuing invasions in their domestic lives of work on the French of England: we remain deeply grateful for their patience and support.

Jocelyn Wogan-Browne
Thelma Fenster

ABBREVIATIONS

AA.SS	*Acta sanctorum quotquot toto orbe coluntur. . .*, ed. G. Henskens, D. Papebroch, et al., repr. Paris and Rome: Palmé, 1867
Alban	*The Life of St. Alban* by Mattthew Paris (translated here)
AND	*Anglo-Norman Dictionary*, ed. Louise W. Stone, William Rothwell, et al. London: Modern Humanities Research Association, 1977–1992; 2nd ed., ed. Stewart Gregory, William Rothwell, and David Trotter. Vols. A-C, D-E hardbound currently available. London: Modern Humanities Research Association, 2005; online at: http://www.anglo-norman.net (unless otherwise stated, references are to the online version)
ANS	*Anglo-Norman Studies*
ANTS	Anglo-Norman Text Society
BL	British Library, London
CM	*Matthaei Parisiensis Chronica majora*, ed. H. R. Luard. 7 vols. RS 57. London: Longman and Co., 1872–1891
Crick, *Charters*	Julia Crick, *Charters of St Albans*. Anglo-Saxon Charters 12. Oxford: Oxford University Press for the British Academy, 2007
DEAF	*Dictionnaire étymologique de l'ancien français*, ed. K. Baldinger et al. Tübingen: Niemeyer Verlag, 1972–
Dean	Ruth J. Dean with Maureen B. M. Boulton, *Anglo-Norman Literature: A Guide to Texts and Manuscripts*. ANTS OPS 3. London: ANTS, 1999
EETS	Early English Text Society
EETS o.s.	Early English Text Society original series

EETS s.s.	Early English Text Society supplementary series
FH	*Flores historiarum*, ed. H. R. Luard. 3 vols. RS 95. London: Eyre and Spottiswoode for H. M. Stationery Office, 1890
GA	*Gesta abbatum monasterii sancti Albani a Thoma Walsingham*, ed. H. T. Riley. 3 vols. RS 28. London: Longmans, Green, Reader and Dyer, 1867–1869
HA	*Matthaei Parisiensis Historia Anglorum*, ed. F. Madden. 3 vols. RS 44. London: Longmans, Green, Reader and Dyer, 1866–1869
Harden, *Auban*	*La Vie de Seint Auban: An Anglo-Norman Poem of the Thirteenth Century*, ed. A. R. Harden. ANTS 19. Oxford: Basil Blackwell for ANTS, 1968
HE	Bede, *Ecclesiastical History of the English People*, ed. Bertram Colgrave and R. A. B. Mynors. Oxford: Clarendon Press, 1969
Henig and Lindley, *Alban and St Albans*	*Alban and St Albans: Roman and Medieval Architecture, Art and Archaeology*, ed. Martin Henig and Phillip Lindley. British Archaeological Association Conference Transactions 24. Leeds: British Archaeological Association with W. H. Maney, 2001
James, *Illustrations*	M. R. James, E. F. Jacob, and W. R. Lowe, eds., *Illustrations to the Life of St Alban in Trinity College Dublin MS E. i. 40*. Oxford: Clarendon Press, 1924
Lewis, *Art of Matthew Paris*	Suzanne Lewis, *The Art of Matthew Paris in the Chronica Majora*. Berkeley: University of California Press in collaboration with Corpus Christi College, Cambridge, 1987
McLeod, "Alban and Amphibal"	W. McLeod, "Alban and Amphibal: Some Extant Lives and a Lost Life." *Mediaeval Studies* 42 (1980): 407–30
Morgan, *EGM [I]*	Nigel J. Morgan, *Early Gothic Manuscripts [I] 1190–1250: A Survey of Manuscripts Illuminated in the British Isles*. London: Harvey Miller, 1982
Morgan, *EGM [II]*	Nigel J. Morgan, *Early Gothic Manuscripts [II] 1250–1285: A Survey of Manuscripts Illuminated in the British Isles*. London: Harvey Miller, 1988

OPS	Occasional Publications Series
PSA	William of St. Albans, *Passio sancti Albani*, AA.SS. Jun. IV: 149–59. *Acta Sanctorum Full Text Database*. Cambridge: Chadwyck-Healey, 2001: orig. publ. Antwerp, 1707
R	Rubric
RS	Rolls Series
SATF	Société des Anciens Textes Français
TCD MS. 177	Dublin, Trinity College MS. 177
T.-L.	Adolf Tobler, rev. Erhard Lommatzsch, *Altfranzösisches Wörterbuch*. Berlin: Weidmannsche Buchhandlung, 1925–2002
van der Westhuizen, *John Lydgate*	J. E. van der Westhuizen, *John Lydgate: The Life of Saint Alban and Saint Amphibal*. Leiden: Brill, 1974
Vaughan, *Matthew Paris*	Richard Vaughan, *Matthew Paris*. Cambridge: Cambridge University Press, 1958
VMSA	Ralph of Dunstable, *Vita metrica sancti Albani*. Dublin, Trinity College MS 177 [E. I. 40], fols. 3r–20v
Wallace, *Estoire*	*La Estoire de Seint Aedward le rei, Attributed to Matthew Paris*, ed. Kathryn Young Wallace. ANTS 41. London: ANTS, 1983

Note: Like *CM*, *GA* draws on earlier historiography from St. Albans but its text was composed or accepted by Paris up to the 1250s (Vaughan, *Matthew Paris*, 182–86). The most accessible published edition of *GA* (H. T. Riley's for the Rolls Series) is of Paris's text as continued and sometimes revised by his successor Thomas of Walsingham from c. 1394 on. References are to Riley's edition, checked against Paris's autograph version of *GA* as edited by William Wats, "Viginti trium abbatum," in his *Matthaei Paris monachi Albanensis Angli Historia major . . . duorum Offarum Merciorum Regum et viginti trium Abbatum S. Albani vitae cum libro additamentorum* (London: Hodgkinson, 1640, and Flesher, 1639), 33–145.

Introduction

Matthew Paris and the *Life of Saint Alban*

Matthew Paris, Benedictine monk of St. Albans Abbey from c. 1217 until his death in 1259, is famous as an artist and mapmaker and above all as a Latin chronicler of his monastery, of the court of King Henry III and Eleanor of Provence, and of English and European history and thirteenth-century affairs at large.[1] In addition to producing an important body of historical writing, he composed saints' biographies in vernacular verse, writing an illustrated French life of Edward the Confessor dedicated to Henry III's queen, Eleanor of Provence, and other lives for the noble women and men of the English barony as well as for monastic audiences.[2] French was the language of the court in the thirteenth

---

[1] The principal study remains Vaughan, *Matthew Paris*. For a concise account of Paris's historiography, see Antonia Gransden, *Historical Writing in England c. 550 to c. 1307* (London: Routledge and Kegan Paul, 1974), 1: 356–79. For manuscripts written and illustrated by Paris, see Morgan, *EGM [I]*, nos. 61, 85, 87, 88, 89, 92, 93, at 107–8, 130–45, and *EGM [II]*, nos. 96, 123, at 50–52, 94–98; and for other art historical studies, see Lewis, *Art of Matthew Paris*, 381–88; Paul Binski, *Becket's Crown: Art and Imagination in Gothic England, 1170–1350* (New Haven and London: Published for the Paul Mellon Centre for Studies in British Art by Yale University Press, 2004); idem, *Westminster Abbey and the Plantagenets: Kingship and the Representation of Power, 1200–1400* (New Haven and London: Yale University Press, 1995); and Cynthia Hahn, *Portrayed on the Heart: Narrative Effect in Pictorial Lives of Saints of the Tenth through the Thirteenth Century* (Berkeley and London: University of California Press, 2001), 299–316. On Paris as mapmaker, see P. D. A. Harvey, "Matthew Paris's Maps of Britain," in *Thirteenth Century England IV*, ed. P. R. Coss and S. D. Lloyd (Woodbridge: Boydell Press, 1992), 109–24; Daniel Birkholz, *The King's Two Maps: Cartography and Culture in Thirteenth-Century England* (New York: Routledge, 2004), esp. chap. 2, "Figuring Britain: Matthew Paris and Regnal Maps"; see Dean no. 334 and Daniel K. Connolly, *The Maps of Matthew Paris: Medieval Journeys through Space, Time and Liturgy* (Woodbridge: Boydell Press, 2009).

[2] For the French text of *Alban*, see Harden, *Auban*. An earlier edition is by Robert Atkinson, *La Vie de Seint Auban: A Poem in Norman French* (London: John Murray, 1876). For an excellent study of the life, see Florence McCulloch, "Saints Alban and Amphibalus in the Works of Matthew Paris: Dublin, Trinity College MS. 177,"

century and was also, among its many other functions, a *lingua franca* in the Benedictine monasteries of Britain.[3] Matthew Paris was personally known to Henry III, who visited St. Albans at least ten times, sometimes staying for three or more days.[4] During his Lent visit of 1257, the king had a substantial conversation with Matthew Paris, which Paris recorded in Latin but which must have taken place in French (*CM* 5:618). In 1247 Henry invited Paris to be present at the Holy Blood ceremonies in Westminster (below, 37) and instructed him to make a written record of them (*CM* 4:645).

La Vie de seint Auban (henceforth *Alban*) is presented here for the first time in modern English translation. Composed perhaps as early as 1230 and perhaps as late as 1250,[5] Alban is Paris's life of his monastery's patron saint, a figure proclaimed at St. Albans as the country's first martyr. Paris drew on an earlier Latin life by his fellow monk William of St. Albans but chose the French of England both for his own text and for the rhymed rubrics accompanying its illustrations.

The single manuscript in which *Alban* is extant, Dublin, Trinity College MS. 177 [E. I. 40], was illustrated and, for the most part, written out by Paris himself. Paris is one of the few prominent medieval writers to write out, illustrate, and set up the *mise-en-page* of his own compositions, and his work has a great deal to teach us about the aesthetics and assumptions of medieval manuscript culture. Yet the text of St. Alban's life, integral as it is to the page-by-page design of the *Alban*

Speculum 56 (1981): 761–85. For editions, translations, and studies of the other saints' lives ascribed to Paris (*The History of St Edward the King, Edmund Archbishop of Canterbury, Thomas Becket*), see Suggested Further Reading below, 59. As far as we know, Paris made no French translation of his fragmentary Latin life of Archbishop Stephen Langton (d. 1228): for this *vita*, see F. Liebermann, ed., *Ungedruckte anglo-normannische Geschichtsquellen* (Strassburg: Trübner, 1879), 318–29, and Vaughan, *Matthew Paris*, 159–61; Binski, *Becket's Crown*, 129–30; Brenda Bolton, "*Pastor bonus*: Matthew Paris' Life of Stephen Langton, Archbishop of Canterbury (1207–1228)," *Nederlands Archief voor Kierkgeschiedenis* 84 (2004): 57–70.

[3] A copy of the reformed Benedictine statutes of 1253 placed by Paris in his *Liber additamentorum* states that because in many monasteries the Benedictine Rule is understood by few people when read out, it should be "expounded in the vernacular" (*exponatur in vulgari*) when it is read aloud in chapter: *CM* 6:244, no. 22, and see Michael Richter, *Sprache und Gesellschaft im Mittelalter* (Stuttgart: Anton Hiersemann, 1979), 148–57 (esp. 149–50), also 78–94. For monastic *regulae* in French, see Dean nos. 710–15.

[4] *CM* 4:358, 4:402, 5:233–34, 5:257–58, 5:319, 5:320, 5:489, 5:574, 5:617–18, 5:724, and see the table in Vaughan, *Matthew Paris*, 12–13. The distance between St. Albans and London is not much above twenty miles.

[5] For the dating of the text and illustrations, which continues to be controversial, see 19–20 and Baswell, 171–73 below. The fullest listing of the *Alban* illustrations is Morgan, *EGM [I]*, no. 85, 130–33.

manuscript, has received very little study.[6] The life nevertheless merits attention, not only as a work from so well-known an artist but also as part of the medieval literature of piety, vengeance, and crusade consumed by both religious and lay readers in the high Middle Ages and beyond. The poem can be considered alongside works such as the *Song of Roland*; works from the Old French Crusade Cycle, such as the *Chanson de Jérusalem* and the *Chanson d'Antioche* (a copy of which was provided for Queen Eleanor in 1250 after she and Henry III had vowed to go on crusade);[7] and the *Vengeance of Our Lord*, all of which have rich histories of adaptation and continuation in Latin, English, and French (both insular and continental).[8] Paris's own writings, Latin and vernacular, draw on *chanson de geste* and romance in ways we are only just beginning to appreciate, and his monastery, like others, produced vernacular as well as Latin literature in several genres.[9] Like

---

[6] An exception is Françoise Laurent in her *Plaire et édifier: les récits hagiographiques composés en Angleterre aux XIIe et XIIIe siècles* (Paris: Champion, 1998), who offers rhetorical, stylistic, and narrative analyses of *Alban*, passim, cited below as appropriate.

[7] Margaret Howell, *Eleanor of Provence* (Oxford and Malden, MA: Blackwell, 1998, repr. 2001), 60. On Henry's (unfulfilled) crusade vows, see S. D. Lloyd, *English Society and the Crusade, 1216–1307* (Oxford: Clarendon Press, 1988), 198–232. Henry's sister Eleanor de Montfort accompanied her husband to Brindisi, and his daughter-in-law, Eleanor of Castile, gave birth to her daughter Joan of Acre in the Holy Land (Lloyd, *English Society*, 77).

[8] On *chanson de geste* in England, see Dean nos. 76–82.2 and Ian Short, "Literary Culture at the Court of Henry II," in *Henry II: New Interpretations*, ed. C. Harper-Bill and N. Vincent (Woodbridge: Boydell Press, 2007), 335–61, at 350–54, 355–59. On crusading literature, see D. A. Trotter, *Medieval French Literature and the Crusades 1100–1300* (Geneva: Droz, 1988). *The Old French Crusade Cycle* is edited by Jan A. Nelson and Emanuel J. Mickel, 11 vols. (London and Tuscaloosa: University of Alabama Press, 1977–); the *Chanson d'Antioche* is vol. 4, ed. Jan A. Nelson (2003). See also *La Vengeance de Nostre-Seigneur: The Old and Middle French Prose Versions*, ed. Alvin E. Ford (Toronto: Pontifical Institute of Mediaeval Studies, 1984), and idem, *La Vengeance de Nostre-Seigneur: The Old and Middle French Versions* (Toronto: Pontifical Institute of Mediaeval Studies, 1993). Paris had access to at least seven crusade histories (R. M. Thomson, "The Historical Library of Matthew Paris," paper given at the "Matthew Paris Disbound" colloquium, Parker Library, Corpus Christi College, Cambridge, 3 July 2001, cited with permission). For a continental crusade history with an Anglo-Norman copy, see Marianne Ailes and Malcolm Barber, *The History of the Holy War: Ambroise's "Estoire de la guerre sainte"*, 2 vols. (Woodbridge: Boydell Press, 2003).

[9] It is unlikely that Paris would have subscribed to modern genre divisions among historiography, romance, and hagiography: see further Robert M. Stein, *Reality Fictions* (Notre Dame: University of Notre Dame Press, 2006). On Paris's use of *chanson de geste*, see Heather Blurton, "From *Chanson de geste* to Magna Carta: Genre and the Barons in Matthew Paris's *Chronica majora*," *New Medieval Literatures* 9 (2007): 117–38, and for an argument that the warrior brotherhood of the *chansons de geste* is the imaginative vector through which the sacrificial communities (including monastic communities) of *Alban*

Paris's other saints' lives, *Alban* was not composed solely for internal consumption at St. Albans. It was seen and heard by the lay elite who visited the abbey and frequented Henry and Eleanor's court. Alban is not only the patron saint of Matthew Paris's monastic house and claimed by the abbey as the protomartyr of England: in the vernacular life by Paris, he is the focus of a range of thirteenth-century concerns shared by monastic and lay people alike.

Alban's Story

Alban himself is a figure of shadowy historicity. He is thought to have lived in the Roman-controlled town of Verulamium, just outside medieval (and modern) St. Albans. In the *Chronica majora* (henceforth *CM*), Alban's martyrdom is entered under the culminating year of the Diocletian persecution of Christians,

---

are formed, see Emma Campbell, *Medieval Saints' Lives: The Gift, Kinship and Community in Old French Hagiography*, Gallica 12 (Cambridge: D.S. Brewer, 2008), 140–46. For an example of Paris's use of motifs now considered romance, see *The History of Saint Edward the King*, trans. Thelma Fenster and Jocelyn Wogan-Browne, FRETS 1 (Tempe: Arizona Center for Medieval and Renaissance Studies, 2008), 60 (vv. 506–31). On the vernacular literature of monasteries, see further M. Dominica Legge, *Anglo-Norman and the Cloisters* (Edinburgh: Edinburgh University Press, 1950); Jean-Pascal Pouzet, "Quelques aspects de l'influence des chanoines augustins sur la production et la transmission littéraire vernaculaire en Angleterre (XIIIe–XVe siècles)," *Comptes-rendus de l'Académie des Inscriptions & Belles-lettres* 2004: 169–213; Christopher Cannon, "Monastic Production," in *The Cambridge History of Medieval English Literature*, ed. David Wallace (Cambridge: Cambridge University Press, 1999), 316–48; Andrew Taylor, "Can an Englishman Read a *Chanson de Geste*?" in *Conceptualizing Multilingualism in Medieval England to 1220*, ed. E. M. Tyler (Turnhout: Brepols, forthcoming). St. Albans' vernacular works include the earliest copy of the *Vie de saint Alexis*, produced at the abbey in the second quarter of the twelfth century (Dean no. 505 and see www.abdn.ac.uk.stalbanspsalter). A French verse life of Thomas Becket by Beneit, monk of St. Albans, was composed there c. 1184 (Dean no. 509; and see Ian Short, "The Patronage of Beneit's *Vie de Thomas Becket*," *Medium Aevum* 56 [1987]: 239–56, for lay patrons' use of this text). Some St. Albans' manuscripts included vernacular historiographical writing: for example, the "St. Albans Miscellany" (BL MS. Harley 3775) contains six items in the French of England (Dean nos. 123, 154, 260, 442, 509, 836), and BL MS. Royal 13 E. IX is a verse chronicle of early British history (Dean no. 40). See also James G. Clark, *A Monastic Renaissance at St Albans: Thomas Walsingham and His Circle, c. 1350–1440* (Oxford: Clarendon Press, 2004), 136, 161. Materials concerning Alexander the Great give further evidence of overlapping lay and monastic tastes for epic genres at St. Albans as at other monasteries: St. Albans' library included a richly illustrated verse romance of Alexander the Great, the *Roman de toute chevalerie* (Dean no. 165, Morgan, *EGM [I]*, no. 81: see also Dean no. 166 for a prose *Estorie le roy Alixaundre* possibly at St. Albans). Henry III's palace at Clarendon had an Alexander chamber from at least 1247, and Alexander scenes were made in 1252 in the queen's chamber at Nottingham Castle (Morgan, *EGM [I]*, no. 81, at 129).

304 CE.[10] An early medieval cult of Alban as a Romano-British martyr is attested by an account of his passion, recently redated to the fifth century, and drawn on by Gildas in his early sixth-century *The Ruin of Britain*: this early tradition was also used by Bede in his influential *Ecclesiastical History of the English Church and People*.[11] For Bede, Alban provides a way of linking Romano-British with English sacred history: Alban effectively becomes a Romano-*English* martyr,[12] and this identity is retained in the ninth-century *Old English Martyrology*, in late Anglo-Saxon litanies, and in a late tenth-century vernacular life by

---

[10] *CM* 1:149–54, at 151, but see R71 below and n. An earlier date is also plausible: Martin Henig argues that there is only very late evidence of Christianity in Romano-British Verulamium and that Alban may have been executed for sheltering refugees from Constantius I's reconquest of Britain, rather than for sheltering a Christian priest in the Diocletian persecutions: "Religion and Art in St Alban's City," in Henig and Lindley, *Alban and St Albans*, 13–29, at 24–25. Gildas identifies Alban as a citizen of Verulamium persecuted under Diocletian in his *De excidio Britonum* (also known as *Historia Brittonum*) of c. 530–540 CE: see Gildas, *The Ruin of Britain and Other Works*, ed. and trans. Michael Winterbottom (London and Chichester: Phillimore, 1978), chap. 10.2, 19 (trans.) and 92 (text). Gildas, however, identifies the river that miraculously dries up as Alban goes to execution as the Thames (*Tamesis*, chap. 11.1, 19 [trans.] and 92).

[11] For the dating of the early *Passio sancti Albani* to the fifth century, see Richard Sharpe, "The Late Antique Passion of St Alban," in Henig and Lindley, *Alban and St Albans*, 30–37. Bede's *HE* (finished 731 CE) seems to be the first known text to say explicitly that Alban was martyred outside Verulamium (*HE* 1:7, 34–35). However, archaeological evidence suggests the possibility of continuous Christian occupation of the St. Albans Abbey site from a fourth-century Romano-British cemetery to an Anglo-Saxon monastic burial ground to Abbot Paul of Caen's post-Conquest rebuilding of the abbey slightly to the north of its pre-Conquest site: see Martin Biddle and Birthe Kjølbye-Biddle, "The Origins of St Albans Abbey: Romano-British Cemetery and Anglo-Saxon Monastery," in Henig and Lindley, *Alban and St Albans*, 45–77. For an account of the early texts of Alban's legend, see van der Westhuizen, *John Lydgate*, 26–44.

[12] Lees and Overing argue that "Bede—himself a Deiran—is largely responsible for the formation of the term *English*. . . . From such material as the legend of the Romano-British saint, Bede uses the language of empire, Latin, to forge in Deiran Northumbria an idea of Englishness that will be powerfully influential in the later centuries of Anglo-Saxon England. By the time of Ælfric's vernacular rewriting of the legend in the tenth century, the language of the English and the identification of Alban with St. Albans in the south of the country have combined to make, out of the matter of Britain, a very English saint in a very English place": Clare A. Lees and Gillian R. Overing, *Signifying Gender and Empire*, special issue of *Journal of Medieval and Modern Studies* 34.1 (2004): 1–16, at 7–8. For the useful question as to whether people in high medieval England would have thought themselves to be in any single place called "Engleterre," see Hugh M. Thomas, *The English and the Normans: Ethnic Hostility, Assimilation and Identity 1066-c. 1220* (Oxford: Oxford University Press, 2003), 262–63, 265, 269.

the prominent hagiographer Ælfric of Eynsham.[13] In the late twelfth century, St. Albans Abbey became particularly active in promoting the saint's cult and, at the abbot's request, an expanded and enriched account of the monastery's saint was composed: this was the prose *Passio sancti Albani* (henceforth *PSA*) by William, a monk of St. Albans, whose text, probably written c. 1178, became the basis of most subsequent versions. It was rapidly turned into Latin verse by another St. Albans monk, Ralph of Dunstable, before becoming the main source for Matthew Paris's *Alban*.[14]

The different modes of these three lives—Latin prose, Latin verse, and French verse—produce very different effects, but there is also a shared narrative core.

Alban, a Romano-British patrician of the city of Verulamium, gives hospitality to the wandering Christian cleric and preacher Amphibalus, who converts him. When the Verulamian pagans discover what has happened, Alban exchanges his mantle for Amphibalus's woolly pilgrim cloak and spirits him out of the city. Alban himself is accused, whipped, and imprisoned.

A drought now strikes as the elements protest this treatment of the holy man, but the pagans condemn Alban to death for his continuing denial of their gods and idols. They lead him toward his execution on a hill outside Verulamium. A crowd follows, and some are drowned in crossing the river, but, at Alban's prayer, God dries up the waters and restores the drowned to life. A soldier in the execution party openly converts to Christianity in response to the miracle; the crowd savagely mauls him. At the summit of the hill, Alban's prayers produce a spring to quench the thirst of his suffering enemies. Alban's executioner is blinded when his eyes fall out at the very moment he severs Alban's head.

The soldier who had been converted by the miracle of the river is healed by contact with Alban's body but is then beaten again and beheaded by the pagans. More conversions occur when a beam of heavenly light identifies Alban's burial

---

[13] Alban appears in the Old English version of Bede (*The Old English Version of Bede's Ecclesiastical History of the English People*, ed. Thomas Miller, EETS o.s. 95, 96 [London, New York, Toronto: Oxford University Press for EETS, 1890, repr. 1959; repr. Woodbridge, D. S. Brewer, 1997], Bk. 1, chap. 1, 34–42; in *The Old English Martyrology*, ed. G. Herzfeld, EETS o.s. 116 (London: Kegan Paul, Trench, Trübner and Co. for EETS, 1900), 100; and in *Ælfric's Lives of Saints*, ed. W. W. Skeat, EETS o.s. 76 and 82 (London: Trübner for EETS, 1881), no. XIX, 415–25. For an excellent study of the early cult, see P.A. Hayward, "The Cult of St. Alban, *Anglorum Protomartyr*, in Anglo-Saxon and Anglo-Norman England," in *More than a Memory: The Discourse of Martyrdom and the Construction of Christian Identity in the History of Christianity*, ed. Johan Leemans (Leuven, Paris, Dudley, MA: Peeters, 2005), 169–200.

[14] See O'Donnell and Lamont, 133–65 below. For extracts from Ralph of Dunstable's late twelfth-century *Vita metrica sancti Albani* (*VMSA*) see McLeod, "Alban and Amphibal," 412–16, and for its manuscripts, see Richard Sharpe, *A Handlist of the Latin Writers of Great Britain and Ireland* (Turnhout: Brepols, 1997), 447.

place, and some Verulamians leave the city in quest of Alban's teacher, Amphibalus, eventually to be converted by him in Wales.

An expeditionary force sent to retrieve the Verulamian citizens slaughters them in rage at their conversion and so creates further Christian martyrs. At Amphibalus's prayer, the slain and mutilated bodies become whole and God sends a wolf and an eagle to guard them from carrion eaters. Still more conversions follow when the expedition returns, bringing this news and Amphibalus back to the city.

The remaining Verulamians rush out, seize Amphibalus, and disembowel him before killing him. During a final furious melee, Amphibalus's body is quietly abstracted and buried by the Christians, while the pagans become abruptly crippled and deformed in an act of heavenly vengeance. The narrative of these events is transmitted by a converted pagan, who vows that he will undertake a penitential journey to Rome, bearing with him the story of Alban's martyrdom.

Many elements in Alban's life are standard generic features of martyr passions. These include the holy man's power over the elements as a sign of God's power over creation; heavenly signs such as beams of light and voices from heaven; and conformity between the martyr's passion and Christ's.[15] Disputes between martyrs and their opponents as to the validity of their beliefs and the properties of idols are also common, as are mass conversions and increasing desperation on the part of pagan authorities.[16]

William of St. Albans' own source is unknown. In spite of modern scholarly skepticism, it is conceivable that he may indeed have seen an English life of St. Alban, as he claims.[17] If so, he did not use it: none of the extant Old English lives develops the narrative beyond Bede's version, and they do not account for the rich amplification and narrative development of the *PSA*. William's claim to an English source is more probably testimony to the privileged status of English as a

---

[15] In his execution on Holmhurst hill, Alban lays down his life as a shepherd for sheep (John 10:11) at what *GA* 1:18 calls Verulamium's equivalent to Golgotha, while the reluctant soldier in the execution party recalls the repentant good thief of the Crucifixion (Luke 23:40–43).

[16] See Michael Camille, *The Gothic Idol: Ideology and Image-Making in Medieval Art* (Cambridge: Cambridge University Press, 1989), chap. 2, "Idols of the Pagans," 73–128; chap. 3, "Idols of the Saracens," 129–64, and notes to 18:592–619 and 19:621–25 below.

[17] See *PSA* 1 below. Both the Old English translation of Bede's *History* and Ælfric's life of Alban (composed 993–998 CE) closely follow Bede's narrative. There is nothing inherently improbable in William's having been aware of Old English accounts of Alban. One of the (probably southern) manuscripts of Ælfric's *Life of Alban* (Cambridge University Library, MS. Ii. 1. 33, s. xii²) has thirteenth-century French glosses and marginal quotations from the *Vie de saint Gilles* (fols. 70v, 120r). Another major Ælfric manuscript containing the Alban life (BL MS. Cotton Julius E. VII) has a thirteenth-century *ex libris* from Bury St Edmunds. St. Albans' very large library could easily have included such texts in addition to its Latin holdings for Bede.

contact language with the past. St. Albans' traditions embraced both British and English as early authenticating languages, and William, no less than Geoffrey of Monmouth, whom he also cites, here stakes out a specific position in relation to the past (see further O'Donnell and Lamont, 133–34 below).

The late twelfth- and thirteenth-century lives extend Bede's theme of nature's witness to Alban's holiness by adding the drought that strikes during Alban's period in prison. Bede's tyrant judge insists simply that Alban worship "the mighty gods," but the twelfth- and thirteenth-century lives make the sun god a feature of the pagan-Christian argument.[18] Ideological oppositions between pagan and Christian take on new resonances in Paris's *Alban* in the context of contemporary twelfth- and thirteenth-century anxieties about Islam and the West's persistent hopes for its conversion and the recovery of Jerusalem. For both Bede and for William of St. Albans, the pagans of the narrative are heathens (*pagani*) or pagans (*Gentiles*): one of Paris's most important changes to the life is to make them Saracens (*Sarrazins*, see further 27–28 below).

A major development common to all three lives from St. Albans is Amphibalus's increased prominence. For Bede, this figure had been an unnamed cleric, fleeing persecution (*HE* 1:7, 28), and nothing further is said of him after he and Alban exchange cloaks. But William of St. Albans announces in the Prologue to his *PSA* that, although the name of Alban's teacher had not been available in his "English" source, he had found it in "Geoffrey Arthur's" translation of the history of the kings of Britain from "British" into Latin (*PSA* 1). Geoffrey of Monmouth's creation of Amphibalus's name had in fact been inadvertent: his *History of the Kings of Britain* mistranslates Gildas's *sub sancti abbatis amphibalo* (from Latin *amphimallus*, "woollen cloth shaggy on both sides"; connected with the Greek for "wrapper, something to throw round oneself"), but this "error" is vigorously adopted as new information and Geoffrey of Monmouth is credited for supplying the priest's name (*PSA* 1).[19] This puts the story of Alban into

---

[18] "diis magnis," *HE* 1:7, 30 (where the pagan gods are consistently called "demons" and "images of demons" by Alban and by the narrative); cf. *PSA* 20; *VMSA*, e.g., TCD MS. 177, fol. 13v col. a, 31–32 (with a marginal note by Paris "Paganor*um* preuaricacio"); and *Alban* 19:621–25 and n.

[19] Gildas is writing of a slaying committed "in the habit (*amphibalo*) of a holy abbot": see Winterbottom, *The Ruin of Britain*, chap. 28, 29 (trans.) and 99 (text). Geoffrey of Monmouth understands this as the name of a church in which the sons of Mordret shelter: see *The History of the Kings of Britain*, ed. Michael D. Reeve, trans. Neil Wright (Woodbridge: Boydell Press, 2007), 254–55 (11:180/99). In spite of Geoffrey of Monmouth's mention of Amphibalus it is most unlikely that any cult preceded the St. Albans discovery of Amphibalus's relics in 1178. Geoffrey of Monmouth's *History* continued to feed the cult with more detail in the later Middle Ages: Amphibalus was credited with a chair in theology in Arthur's Caerleon (Jeremy K. Knight, "Britain's Other Martyrs: Julius, Aaron and Alban at Caerleon," in Henig and Lindley, *Alban and St Albans*, 38–44, at 41 and n. 25), while in a later fourteenth-century text from St. Albans he is said to be

conjunction with Geoffrey of Monmouth's influential shaping of British history and also constitutes a claim that the *PSA* narrator has researched his sources and uses them with discrimination.[20] William is specifically praised by his fellow monk Ralph of Dunstable for his account of the martyr and for having added the "glorious triumph" of Amphibalus.[21] Given that there is a missing leaf at the beginning of Paris's French life, it is not possible to know what he did with William of St. Albans' material at the beginning of his own *Alban*, but in *CM* Paris makes the same point as *PSA*: the name of Alban's teacher and companion saint had been found in Geoffrey of Monmouth's work (*CM* 1:149). All three late twelfth- and thirteenth-century lives—William's, Ralph of Dunstable's, and Paris's—develop Alban and Amphibalus's doctrinal discussions and their emotional relationship. Paris alone develops the figure of Alban's own first significant convert and immediate companion in martyrdom: he makes Alban's reluctant executioner not just an anonymous "soldier" (*PSA* 20) but a prominent companion martyr endowed with a name made famous in medieval crusading histories, that of "Heraclius" (*Aracle*).[22]

The lives also elaborate Amphibalus's martyrdom as living disembowelment: he is forced to walk around a stake to which his innards have been attached and so to disembowel himself before he is stoned to death.[23] Paris is close to *PSA* at this point but comments in the rubric to his illustration that Amphibalus's is a new kind of torture (R42:211 below and see Plate 9). The closest parallel seems to be the atrocities reportedly attributed to the Turks by Pope Urban II in preaching the First Crusade in 1095 at the Council of Clermont and vigorously diffused thereafter through accounts of the council in crusading histories.[24] Paris

---

the son of a prince of Wales and a Roman mother and the dedicatee of the Winchester Cathedral built by Constans after the reign of Vortigern (van der Westhuizen, *John Lydgate*, 284).

[20] On the historiographical sophistication of the *PSA*'s narration, see Monika Otter, *Inventiones: Fiction and Referentiality in Twelfth-Century English Historical Writing* (Chapel Hill and London: University of North Carolina Press, 1996), 46–48, 50–51, and O'Donnell and Lamont, 133–35 below.

[21] *VMSA* 11 (TCD MS. 177, fol. 3r col a: McLeod, "Alban and Amphibal," 412, v. 11).

[22] On Heraclius's name and significance, see further n. 72 below.

[23] *PSA* 39; *Alban* 43:1601–10; Ralph of Dunstable, fol. 19r col. a, 30. In Bede, the cleric who converts Alban is not mentioned again once Alban is arrested; instead the reluctant executioner is simply beheaded after Alban's execution and the pagan judge converts (*HE* 1:7, 28–29, 34); Miller, *The Old English Version of Bede*, 40.

[24] A story about Earl Godwin of Wessex told by a number of post-Conquest sources suggests that disembowelment at the stake was also known in England and seen as extraordinary and gratuitous torture when not part of executions for treason: see *PSA* 164, n. 47. The major accounts of Urban's speech are conveniently gathered in the online Medieval Sourcebook (http://www.fordham.edu/halsall/source/urban2-5vers.html). The version of the atrocity story closest to the martyrdom of Amphibalus in *Alban* is

makes Amphibalus's disembowelment continuous with his role as pilgrim and wandering preacher in *Alban*: walking round and round the stake for what Paris explicitly compares to "a day's journey" (*cum a chemin jurnal*, 43:1607), he is like a traveler using the pacing-out of a cathedral labyrinth as a pilgrimage substitute.

Bede's account of Alban in his *History of the English Church and People* (completed by 731) had a continuing career in the later Middle Ages;[25] but, as noted above, William of St. Alban's *PSA* is the source for most of the later medieval lives. Further transformations of William's Amphibalus occurred when the figure of Alban and the shape of his narrative underwent more development in the later Middle Ages.[26] In the fifteenth century, John Lydgate's Middle English *Life of Alban and Amphibal* of c. 1420–40 elaborates a patrician background for Amphibalus, making him Alban's social equal. Lydgate represents them both as knights at the emperor Diocletian's court in Britain, and Alban's armor is left to St. Albans Abbey after King Offa himself has fought in it. Lydgate does not seem to have known Paris's *Alban*, but he did draw on William of St. Alban's *PSA* and on Matthew Paris's account of Offa of Mercia as the founder of St.

---

that of Robert the Monk in the *Historia Iherosolimitana*, a history of the First Crusade composed in the first decade of the twelfth century and based on the purportedly eyewitness account of the Council of Clermont and Urban II's speech given in the *Gesta Francorum*, of 1095–1100 CE: see *Historia Iherosolimitana*, lib. I, cap. I, in *Recueil des Historiens des Croisades: historiens occidentaux*, Académie des Inscriptions et Belles-lettres (Paris: Imprimerie nationale, 1841–1906), 16 vols., vol. 3 (1866), 717–882, at 727–28, and *Robert the Monk's History of the First Crusade*, trans. Carol Sweetenham (Aldershot and Burlington, VA: Ashgate, 2005), 7, 80 and n. 3 (citing a parallel disembowelment from *Njalssaga*). Extant in a hundred manuscripts, Robert's is the most popular of the histories of the First Crusade, widely diffused, reworked, adapted, and translated (Sweetenham, *Robert the Monk's History*, vii). A copy was available to Matthew Paris (Thomson, "The Historical Library of Matthew Paris").

[25] Bede's text, or some version very close to it, is the source of the early *South English Legendary* life of Alban, for instance: see *The South English Legendary*, ed. Charlotte d'Evelyn and Anna J. Mill, EETS o.s. 235 (London: Oxford University Press for EETS, 1956), 238–41.

[26] For the later lives of Alban in England, see Charlotte d'Evelyn, "Legends of Individual Saints," in *A Manual of the Writings in Middle English*, gen. ed. Albert E. Hartung (Greenfield, CT: Connecticut Academy of Arts and Sciences 1970), 2:563, no. 14, and eadem and Mill, eds., *The South English Legendary*, EETS o.s. 235, 238–41; for Lydgate's life of St. Alban and St. Amphibal, see van der Westhuizen, *John Lydgate*, and Karen Winstead, "Lydgate's Lives of Saints Edmund and Alban: Martyrdom and *Prudent Pollicie*," *Mediaevalia* 17 (1994): 221–41. Alban also figures in the Middle English *Gilte Legende* and in William Caxton's *Golden Legend* (see McLeod, "Alban and Amphibal," 418–20) and in John Capgrave's *Nova legenda Anglie* (ed. Carl Horstmann [Oxford: Clarendon Press, 1901]) and hence in Richard Pynson's 1516 *Kalendre: The Kalendre of the Newe Legende of Englonde*, ed. Manfred Görlach, Middle English Texts 27 (Heidelberg: Winter, 1994).

Albans (*CM* 1:356–64). His substantial prelude on Alban's life before his conversion is based on another document produced at St. Albans, the *Tractatus de nobilitate, vita et martirio sanctorum Albani et Amphibali*, extant in a late fourteenth-century compilation by the St. Albans monk and chronicler Thomas of Walsingham (c. 1340–1422).[27] In the later Middle Ages, Paris's *Alban* seems to have been known chiefly to the monks of St. Albans and their secular patrons. But William of St. Alban's *PSA* continued to be copied (see O'Donnell and Lamont, 136 below), and some manuscript copies from outside St. Albans are extant. Lydgate's *Life* of Alban circulated outside its author's monastery at Bury St. Edmunds, and when Alban's relics were claimed by a monastery in Cologne (supposedly brought there by St. Germanus), the St. Albans monks produced and printed a revised version of Lydgate's text in 1534 and dedicated it to Henry VIII and Queen Anne Boleyn.[28]

Inventing St. Albans: Cult, Place, and Book

St. Albans was a long-established and wealthy Benedictine monastery in Hertfordshire just north of London. Like many other great monasteries, St. Albans asserted and maintained its position by a more or less continuous reinvention of itself as a place of the holy. There was a particular necessity in the case of St. Albans: although its saint was a well-established figure in early English and European history, the abbey's own pre-Conquest history is extremely thinly documented.[29] Campaigns were sometimes mounted in response to particular threats: in the *Gesta abbatum* (*Deeds of the Abbots of St. Albans*, henceforth *GA*), for

---

[27] van der Westhuizen transcribes the *Tractatus de nobilitate* from BL MS. Cotton Claudius E. IV art. 9, fols. 334v–336r (*John Lydgate*, Appendix C, 277–85). For a stemma embracing the late lives, see McLeod, "Alban and Amphibal," 429. For the argument that the *Tractatus* may have been composed by Walsingham, rather than John Whethamstede, see James G. Clark, "The St Albans Monks and the Cult of St Alban: The Late Medieval Texts," in Henig and Lindley, *Alban and St Albans*, 218–30, at 225. Walsingham's compilation in this manuscript reproduces William's *PSA* and Ralph's *VMSA* alongside the *Tractatus*. The latter claims to be taken from a French book ("de quodam libro gallico excerpto"), but if so, it was not Paris's *Alban*. For a lost manuscript containing a French verse life of Alban, see n. 48 below.

[28] Clark, "The St Albans Monks and the Cult," 226, 227. The extra stanzas of the 1534 print are edited by van der Westhuizen, *John Lydgate*, Appendix B, 286–95, and the revised version is discussed at 60–63.

[29] For the abbey's history, see William Page, ed. *The Victoria History of the County of Hertford* (London: Constable, 1914), 4:367–416; L. F. R. Williams, *A History of the Abbey of St Alban* (London: Longmans Green, 1917). For a lucid summary of the complex and sometimes spurious medieval historiography of the abbey's origins and its pre- and post-Conquest history, see Crick, *Charters*, 3–13. For the archaeological evidence, see Biddle and Kjølbye-Biddle, "Origins of St Albans Abbey."

example, Paris chronicles the rival claim of the monastery of Ely to have acquired St. Alban's relics during pre-Conquest raids and so to be the place where the country's first martyr should be sought (and where prestige and pilgrimage revenues should accrue).[30] The continuing affirmation of identities and territories focused on saints' relics was a necessary response to political and economic exigencies. But the crafting of institutional identities around saints was neither purely pragmatic nor purely defensive. It was also an ongoing labor of institutional and collective creativity, drawing on many different talents, and accompanied by the production of texts, artefacts, and events, in which artists, scholars, and craftsmen (frequently members of the monastic community itself) played important roles. At St. Albans, several entrepreneurial abbots encouraged this work. From the later twelfth century onward, the saint was promoted as the first martyr with increasing intensity in wall-paintings, new shrine ornaments, sculptures, metal, woodwork, pilgrim badges, liturgy, and narrative.[31] The territory of St. Albans was reinscribed in the communal memories of the monks, their lay patrons, and the neighboring townspeople by attention to old and new shrine sites and by the development of ceremonies focused on them, activities for which

---

[30] The Danes are said to have taken Alban's relics to Denmark under the fourth abbot, Wulnoth (so perhaps in the early tenth century [*GA* 1:14]). For the Ely claim, made during the abbacy of Ælfric, eleventh abbot of St. Albans, in the late tenth and early eleventh centuries, see *GA* 1:34–38 and Vaughan, *Matthew Paris*, 198–201; Mark Hagger, "The *Gesta Abbatum Monasterii Sancti Albani*: Litigation and History at St. Albans," *Historical Research* 81.213 (2008): 373–98 (esp. 382–84). Defending St. Albans against Ely remains a preoccupation of *GA*: see 13 below. Competition for saints' relics and thefts of them are a standard feature of intermonastic rivalry: see Patrick Geary, *Furta sacra: Thefts of Relics in the Central Middle Ages* (Princeton: Princeton University Press, 1978: repr. 1990). Alban's bones are said to have been recovered from Denmark by way of one such holy theft (*furtum sacrum*): Egwin, a monk of St. Albans, works under cover in the monastery at Odense for some years before seizing the chance secretly to ship the relics to England and then to return there himself (*GA* 1:13–18; Vaughan, *Matthew Paris*, 201–4).

[31] *GA* chronicles the commissions of individual abbots: for the material and visual culture and environment of St. Albans, see Henig and Lindley, *Alban and St Albans*, and Rosalind Niblett and Isobel Thompson, *Alban's Buried Towns: An Assessment of St Albans' Archaeology up to AD 1600* (Oxford: Oxbow Books for English Heritage, 2005). On St. Albans' library and its development during this period, see Rodney M. Thomson, *Manuscripts from St Albans Abbey 1066–1235*, 2 vols. (Woodbridge and Totowa: D. S. Brewer for the University of Tasmania, 1982), vol. 1, esp. chaps. 9–11; and for a concise history of the library from the eleventh to the fifteenth centuries, see Richard Sharpe, J. P. Carley, R. M. Thomson, and A. G. Watson, eds., *English Benedictine Libraries: The Shorter Catalogues* (London: British Library in association with the British Academy, 1996), 539–44. For the further development of the cult at St. Albans, see Michelle Still, *The Abbot and the Rule: Religious Life at St Albans, 1290–1349* (Aldershot and Burlington, VT: Ashgate, 2002), chap. 1; Clark, *Monastic Renaissance*, and idem, "The St Albans Monks and the Cult."

the usual medieval terms are *inventio* (the "finding" or "discovery" of a saint's relics), *elevatio* (the ritual display of relics), and *translatio* (the relics' "translation" to a more prominent shrine).

In post-Conquest St. Albans, authenticating traditions were maintained in several ways. In the eleventh and twelfth centuries, forged charters developed St. Albans' claim, already propagated before the Conquest, to have been founded by Offa, king of Mercia.[32] The cult of Alban himself was maintained by Abbot Richard d'Albini (1097–1119) and then received fresh impetus from Abbot Geoffrey de Gorron (1119–1146), best known today for his support of the visionary and holy woman Christina of Markyate.[33] In 1129, Abbot Geoffrey translated Alban's relics to a magnificent new shrine commissioned from the monk-goldsmith Anketil. On this occasion, the bones of the martyr were carefully examined and found to include a gold-lettered silk fillet round the skull, labeled "Sanctus Albanus." Alban subsequently appeared both to doubters and to believers, in a further assertion of the genuineness of his relics *contra* the claims of the monks of Ely (*GA* 1:85–87).

In the twelfth- and thirteenth-century development of the cult, the promotion of Alban's Christian teacher, Amphibalus, as a companion saint and martyr is an important feature. Under Abbot Simon (1163–1183) there was particularly intense activity at St. Albans in the later 1170s, perhaps in response to Becket's martyrdom and the success of his shrine at Canterbury.[34] In a vision vouchsafed in 1178 to Robert, a citizen of the town of St. Albans, Alban himself revealed the presence of Amphibalus's relics at Redbourne, near the abbey.[35] Abbot Simon had recently commissioned a magnificent new shrine for St. Alban, into which the bones earlier enshrined by Abbot Geoffrey de Gorron were placed (*GA* 1:189), and he now ordered the formal excavation—the *inventio*—of Amphibalus and the rehousing of his relics (*GA* 1:192–93). Abbot Simon also commissioned William of St. Albans' new life of the saint, with its increased attention to Amphibalus: we may therefore presume that the *Passio sancti Albani* was com-

---

[32] The most prominent royal pre-Conquest patron of St. Albans was in fact King Æthelred, though three charters of Æthelred represent him as restoring grants previously made by Offa: see Julia Crick, "Offa, Ælfric, and the Refoundation of St Albans," in Henig and Lindley, *Alban and St Albans*, 78–84, at 79–80: also Crick, *Charters*, esp. "The Claims of the Community before and after the Conquest," 56–74.

[33] Abbot Richard gave relics, reliquaries, and a tapestry with Alban's passion on it and dedicated the church of St. Albans before Henry I and Queen Edith-Matilda and many nobles, granting an indulgence to all (*GA* 1:69–71). Abbot Geoffrey gave even more lavish gifts of copes, relics, books, and altar hangings to the monastery (*GA* 1:93–94).

[34] Simon is said to have regretted being unable to suffer martyrdom with Becket in 1170 (*GA* 1:188), and Becket's feast and the invention of St. Amphibalus are noted by *GA* as being celebrated in the same week (*GA* 1:193).

[35] *GA* 1:192–93, *CM* 2:301–4; see also *HA* 1:401–9, and Otter, *Inventiones*, 49–50.

posed for or shortly after the discovery of Amphibalus's relics in 1178,[36] probably in connection with the carefully planned set of ceremonies and processions and new liturgical compositions by which such *inventiones* inscribed the achieved (or hoped-for) expansion of a cult's territories and power.[37] In 1186, Abbot Simon's successor, Abbot Warin (1183–1195), translated Amphibalus's relics to yet another new shrine (*GA* 1:205–6), and Amphibalus appeared in a vision to an inhabitant of Walden, near St. Albans, to require that the place where his relics had been found near Redbourne be regarded as holy ground (*GA* 1:199–200; *CM* 2:301–4). Abbot Warin subsequently built the church and convent hospital of St. Mary des Près at Redbourne, and John de Walden, the son of the visionary, was appointed the hospital's first master (*GA* 1:201).[38] *GA*'s presentation of these events suggests, or at least seeks to represent, a coalition of monastic and civic interests contributing to the monastery's expansion.

Within the monastery itself, the monk Ralph of Dunstable's Latin verse reworking of William of St. Albans' *PSA* was completed in the late twelfth century,[39] and Ralph's text, like the *PSA*, was subsequently copied by Paris into his *Alban* manuscript. As St. Albans' foremost historiographer and one of its most important links with secular royal and noble laypeople, Paris's work was of great importance to the monastery. His *Alban* and its manuscript realization form the capstone of the later twelfth- and thirteenth-century reinventions and developments of St. Albans' patron saint as well as affirming the role of Offa, king of Mercia (757–796 CE), whom the monastery claimed as its founder.[40] The

---

[36] On the dating, see O'Donnell and Lamont, 133, n. 2 below. The title *Passio sancti Albani* is taken from the title as given in Matthew Paris's hand for William of St. Alban's text in TCD MS. 177, fol. 20r col. a.

[37] For the *inventio* of Amphibalus, see *CM* 2:301–8 and, for valuable discussion, Otter, *Inventiones*, 45–57 (see also 23–26 on Alban's own *inventio* by Offa of Mercia and 53–57 on *inventiones* in general).

[38] Paris's own historiography of St. Albans charts continuing institutional attention to Amphibalus, most particularly in his *GA* 1, which includes the *inventio* of Amphibalus's relics (192–93), the building of St. Mary des Près hospital on their site (199–204), the translation of the relics to a new shrine (205–6), the installation of a painting of Amphibalus (233), the further translation of Amphibalus's relics and the creation by Abbot William (1214–1235) of a new altar dedicated to him and to the Holy Cross (282), the dedication of Amphibalus's church at Redbourne (289), and Abbot William's reacquisition of Amphibalus's cross, stained with Alban's blood, and "the first [cross] that was brought to Britain" (292). See also *CM* 1:149–54 (*PSA* excerpts); 2:301–8; *FH* 2:89–90; *HA* 1:401–9, and *Abbreviatio chronicorum Angliae*, printed in *HA* 3:203.

[39] On *VMSA*, see McLeod, "Alban and Amphibal," 412–16.

[40] Paris gives accounts of Offa's invention of Alban and foundation of St. Albans in the *Alban* manuscript (see further R56-R70 below); in *GA* 1:4–8; in *CM* 1:356–61 (also *FH* 1:395–403) and copies of charters by Offa in the *Alban* manuscript (TCD MS. 177, fols. 63r-66r): and in *Liber additamentorum* (*CM* 6:1–8). He composed a biography, *Vitae*

cult and its history continued to expand, with the discovery, shortly before Paris died in 1259, of the "original tomb" at St Albans in which the saint was secretly buried just after his martyrdom (*Alban* 29:979–83: *CM* 5:608).

The Book of St. Albans

Paris took a leading role in the compilation and execution of the *Alban* manuscript, which seems to have functioned as a compendium or dossier of the monastery's saint.[41] In the manuscript, the historiography, ceremonial practices, and legal claims of St. Albans and its cult join the three twelfth-century lives of the saint composed at the abbey, as does Paris's striking series of illustrations (TCD MS. 177, fols. 29v-63r; fifty-four remaining and eight lost). These latter represent the events in Paris's life of Alban and continue on, accompanying the manuscript's Latin liturgical and documentary witnesses, to show the monastery's foundation. Monika Otter points out that Paris represents every stage of an *inventio* and its commemoration: his illustrations move in sequence from the divinely inspired *inventio* of Alban by Offa of Mercia to the *translatio* and *elevatio* of the relics, to Offa's building of the abbey and the appointment of its first abbot, and to the creation of a procession and feast days commemorating the *inventio* and Offa's purported founding endowment.[42] Copies of the abbey's (spurious) charters of donation by Offa are also included.[43]

---

duorum Offarum (perhaps c. 1250; see Vaughan, *Matthew Paris*, 90), in which the eighth-century Mercian Offa's foundation is seen as the fulfillment of an earlier unrealized ambition on the part of the sixth-century Offa of the West Angles (see Vaughan, *Matthew Paris*, 189–94). The text is extant in BL MS. Cotton Nero D. I, fols. 22v-27v, and printed as *Vitae duorum Offarum* in W. Wats, ed., *Historia Matthaei Paris monachi Albanensis angli, Historia major... duorum Offarum Merciorum Regum... viginti trium abbatum Sancti Albani vitae cum libro additamentorum* (London: Hodgkinson, 1640, and Flesher, 1639), 1–32: for Paris's illustrations to it, see Morgan, *EGM [I]*, no. 87, 134–36.

[41] For the making of the manuscript, see Baswell, 169–82 below. The manuscript (now Dublin, Trinity College MS. 177) is described (textual contents only) by Marvin L. Colker (*Trinity College Library Dublin: Descriptive Catalogue of the Medieval and Renaissance Latin Manuscripts* [London: Scolar Press for Trinity College Library Dublin, 1991]), 1:339–43: for the illustrations, see Morgan, *EGM [I]*, no. 85 (130–33). For available reproductions, see Suggested Further Reading below.

[42] Otter, *Inventiones*, 24–26; and on the vivid sensory effects of Paris's illustrations here, see Hahn, *Portrayed on the Heart*, 312–15.

[43] As Crick points out, "the vivid late medieval traditions about Offa belie the fact that not a shred of contemporary evidence connects him with the foundation": she argues that it is not impossible that Offa had an association with St. Albans but that all surviving evidence for this is the product of later generations (Crick, "Offa, Ælfric, and the Refoundation," 78, 79). St. Albans is not the only house to practice "forgery": the twelfth century is a heyday of the practice in monasteries. See also Julia Crick, "St. Albans, Westmin-

Table 1: Contents of Dublin, Trinity College MS. 177

Medieval flyleaves

fols. 1r–2v	medieval flyleaves: on 1v a note [s. xv] that the book was shown to Henry VI.
fol. 2r	Latin verses on the occupations of the months [s. xiii]; an indecipherable note; a note in Paris's hand on the circulation of this and other saints' lives between noblewomen readers.
fol. 2v	incomplete drawing of Virgin and child; prayer to St. Cendonius for restoration of sight; a note on the preparation of saints' images for the countess of "Wint" and French verse captions for the images.

Items in the manuscript

1. fols. 3–20r	Ralph of Dunstable, *Vita metrica sancti Albani*, Latin elegiac verses on the passion of St. Alban (in Matthew Paris's hand).
2. fols. 20r–28v	William of St. Albans, *Passio sancti Albani*, Latin prose (in Matthew Paris's hand).
3. fol. 28v col. b	rubric to a missing tract on "The History of the Discovery of St. Amphibalus and His Companions" (no text after fol. 28v's rubric).
4. fols. 29r–50r	Matthew Paris, *La Vie de seint Auban*, French verse (loss of prologue and one or more *laisses* at beginning of poem): text, illustrations, rubrics, and labels within illustrations in Matthew Paris's hand.
5. fols. 50v–52v	lessons and liturgical responses for the feast of the invention and translation of St. Alban.
6. fols. 52v–62v	treatise on the invention of St. Alban (with cross-reference forward to fol. 66v added by Matthew Paris on fol. 62v).
7. fols. 63r–66r	charters of foundation for the abbey purportedly issued by King Offa and his son Ecgfrid.
	[6b. fols. 66v-68v (continues no. 6 above)]
8. fols. 68v–69v	the invention of St. Amphibalus.

---

ster, and Some Twelfth-Century Views of the Anglo-Saxon Past," *ANS* 25 (2003 for 2002): 65–83; and for later forgery, see Alfred Hiatt, *The Making of Medieval Forgeries: False Documents in Fifteenth-Century England* (London: British Library and University of Toronto Press, 2004). For editions of the charters in the Alban manuscript (also in *CM* 6:1–9), see Crick, *Charters*, nos. 1, 4, 5 (109–11, 132–40) and discussion, 45–48.

9. fols. 69v–70v   the miracles of Amphibalus.
10. fols. 70v–72r   the translation of St. Alban the protomartyr.
                  [fol. 72v blank]
11. fols. 73r–77r   the miracles of Amphibalus (Matthew Paris's hand).

Paris's manuscript, often referred to as the "Book of St. Albans," was kept and used at the abbey. An early fourteenth-century inscription on its opening page reads, "This is the book of the church of Saint Alban, protomartyr of the English, from the small book chest A [*armariolo*]" (TCD MS. 177, fol. 3r). In the later Middle Ages, the manuscript was displayed to visitors in the abbot's study, together with the St. Albans Book of Benefactors (*Liber benefactorum*), and also placed on the high altar for more general veneration.[44] As Table 1 shows, a fifteenth-century note on one of the medieval flyleaves of the manuscript says that it was shown to Henry VI (TCD MS. 177, fol. 1v). The *Alban* manuscript had become an important witness to the cult and was itself an embodiment of the house's identity.

The question of who read the *Book of St. Albans* in the thirteenth and later centuries and how they read it is revealingly complex. The manuscript itself is a multimedia compilation, which would have allowed for a range of uses and literacies. Latin verse captions later inserted below the French text of *Alban* summarize the events of the narrative.[45] French verse captions appear above the illustrations to the French text (TCD MS. 177, fols. 29r–50r) and continue above the manuscript's Latin documents (TCD MS. 177, fols. 50v–63r). Matthew Paris's arresting illustrations themselves offer a further mode of access to Alban's and the monastery's story. They may have been designed with lay audiences in mind: as Paris remarks in his illustrated *History of Saint Edward the King*, "For laypeople who do not know how to read, I have also represented your [i.e., Edward's] story in illustrations in this very same book, for those who want their eyes to

---

[44] Clark, "The St Albans Monks and the Cult," 222, and idem, *A Monastic Renaissance*, 85, 87. Traces of a less august domestic use remain in the apparent personal loan of the manuscript to a monk, William Dolte, between 1420 and 1437 (Sharpe et al., *English Benedictine Monasteries*, 562, no. 50; Dolte was also lent a copy of Ralph of Dunstable's *VMSA*, 561, no. 45). Clark suggests that London, BL MS. Add. 62777, one of the eleven extant manuscripts from the abbot's study, was perhaps a working copy of the Book of St. Albans for the personal use of the abbot: it includes *PSA*, the lives of the two Offas, and *GA*, together with some documents concerning churches owned by St. Albans, but omits the French text (Clark, "The St Albans Monks and the Cult," 222: www.bl.uk/catalogues/manuscripts).

[45] For the texts of these captions, see Atkinson, *Vie de Seint Auban*, 55–60.

see what their ears hear" (vv. 3961–66).[46] While individual silent reading began increasingly to be practiced in the thirteenth century, it was still only one mode among others, and sociable and studious listening to a text read aloud remained an important model of reading. Clerks and chaplains could also be asked to read and gloss *ex tempore*, particularly for shorter written forms such as the French and Latin captions of the *Alban* text. The manuscript's life thus lies as much in its aural and visual as in its textual reception. Given that Paris's illustrations and his French captions for them continue beyond the end of the vernacular text, even the following Latin documents may have been envisaged as a continuous part of what could be exhibited and read aloud to potential patrons. In the later folios of the manuscript, the visual account of King Offa overseeing his masons, carpenters, and builders, and finally placing his charter on his newly built abbey's altar while a triumphant peal of bells rings out from the bell tower (TCD MS. 177, fol. 63r: see Plate 12), offers a vivid model of a patron's achievement. The accompanying Latin script of the documents copied beneath the illustrations would have been in itself an image of monastic historiographic and liturgical authority recognizable as such even by lay patrons who could not read it.

The dimensions of the book and the quality of its materials are noteworthy. The book itself is surprisingly small.[47] Matthew Paris's illustrations, to which we attach value as the original work of the artist, sit on poor-quality pages, many made up of scraps of scarf-jointed vellum. This is perhaps best explained by seeing the text and illustrations as a maquette or prototype, designed to be copied into more lavish forms for lay patrons (as happened with Paris's other saints' lives: both the illustrations and the text of Paris's history of Edward the Confessor, for

---

[46] *Estoire*, vv. 3961–66 and n.; *History of Saint Edward the King*, trans. Fenster and Wogan-Browne, 105; and see further Baswell, 184–87 below. For a study of saints' lives as they reached out in the high Middle Ages to lay audiences and picture cycles moved from liturgical books to books for patrons, see Barbara Abou-el-Haj, *The Medieval Cult of Saints: Formations and Transformations* (Cambridge: Cambridge University Press, 1994), esp. chaps. 1 and 2. See also the St. Albans Psalter (n. 51 below), which includes a French version of Gregory the Great's letter on the value of pictorial representations. An early precedent for lay-monastic exchange at St. Albans may be found in the time of Abbot Paul (1077–1093), when a "learned knight and eager listener to and lover of the Scriptures" (*miles . . . litteratus, diligens auditor et amator Scriptorum*, *GA* 1:57) gave tithes from Hatfield and Redbourne to St. Albans. These were dedicated to the copying of books, and the abbot in turn gave Sir Robert a missal "with other necessary books" for his chapel at Hatfield (*GA* 1:58). On shared lay and clerical reading and studying practices, see Geoffrey Rector, "*En sa chambre sovent le lit*: Otium and the Pedagogical Sociabilities of Early Romanz Literature (ca. 1100–1150)," *Medium Aevum* (forthcoming). Alban and Amphibalus themselves exemplify this in their study together in a *tugurium* or "cabin," *PSA* 9, and in a *maison foreine* or "building outside [the city walls]," 4:75 and see n. to 14:408–10 in the translation below.

[47] Morgan gives the dimensions as 242 × 165 mm (*EGM [I]*, no. 85, 130).

example, were copied into the surviving extant manuscript of that life, which is not in Paris's hand).[48] The distinction we intuitively make between copying out a text and copying illustrations (the illustrations in the original hand being felt to constitute the artist's work, but the text having an existence independent of whose hand copies it) does not always seem to have pertained in manuscript culture. Our attribution of surplus value to the illustrations here may not have been shared by Paris: in an aesthetic where "originals" produced by human craftsmen were not imbued with special authenticity or valued above copies, Paris may not have thought of the pictures as having any greater value as original works than the writing out of the narrative itself (which was a work of considerable labor and varying levels of artistry). It is therefore not impossible that for Paris there was no disjunction between the poor quality of the manuscript vellum and his own artistry and craftsmanship and that the production of better copies for lay patrons was anticipated in the making of the manuscript, even if the book itself was not designed to leave the monastery.

Dating the Book

The dating of the manuscript text and illustrations remains controversial, as does the date when *Alban* was first composed. Some scholars suggest that the text of *Alban* was written out by Paris between 1230 and 1240, but they do not exclude the possibility of earlier composition; some argue that the illustrations

---

[48] *History of Saint Edward the King*, trans. Fenster and Wogan-Browne, 27–28; Baswell, 181–82 below. James notes the former existence of another manuscript of a French life of Alban, BL MS. Cotton Vitellius D. VIII destroyed in the Cottonian fire of 1731 and known only through the older Cottonian scribes' catalogues (M. R. James, *La Estoire de Seint Aedward le Rei . . . Together with Some Pages of the Manuscript of the Life of St Alban at Trinity College, Dublin* [London: Roxburghe Club, 1920], 18). In the catalogue made between 1631 and 1638 (BL MS. Add. 36789), one scribe notes that all the items in Cotton Vitellius D. VIII were in French and that item 12 was a "Vita SS Albani et Amphibali ad eundem modum in metro Gallicano." Also present was a text of "La Vie Seint Edmund le confesseur translaté de latin en romans" (an identically worded rubric appears in the Campsey manuscript's copy of Paris's life of Edmund of Canterbury with the added phrase "par la requeste la cuntasse de aru*n*del," BL MS. Add. 70513, fol. 85vb: Jocelyn Wogan-Browne, *Saints' Lives and Women's Literary Culture: Virginity and Its Authorizations* [Oxford: Oxford University Press, 2001], 171). A second French life of St. Alban, extant in at least six manuscripts of *Mandeville's Travels*, is of "un autre Seint Alban en Almaigne" (another Saint Alban in Germany) because, as Mandeville says, "many people in our country believe there is no other St. Alban than the one from our country" (Josephine W. Bennett, *The Rediscovery of Sir John Mandeville* [New York: MLA, 1954], 269; Dean no. 506.1).

were added by Paris later than the text, c. 1250.[49] Much depends not only on the sequence in which individual elements of the manuscript—illustrations, text, captions, rubrics—were carried out but also on the page-by-page and opening-by-opening makeup of the manuscript.[50] As discussed in greater detail in Christopher Baswell's essay (169–82 below), a great deal of improvisation—of opportunist eliciting of conjunctions and dissonances between various elements—may go on when a single artist is composing text, illustrations, layout, and contents, as well as serving as chief scribe. Moreover, Paris's habitual revision and addition to his texts makes it hard to pronounce *Alban* to be the work of any one particular moment between 1230 and 1250: a long process from composition to copying (and perhaps, in the case of some rubrics, of composition while copying) was involved, and the manuscript's "date" may well embrace several decades.

The Saint and the City

It may be that only the more prominent members of the medieval town saw the *Alban* manuscript itself in the abbot's study, but a wider range of citizens would have been familiar with the wall-paintings, shrine, and furnishings of the monastery church and hence with images in which, as the St. Albans Psalter has it, "those who are unacquainted with letters are able to read [so that] a picture is like

---

[49] A date earlier than 1230–1240 cannot be excluded for the *Alban* text (Harden, *Auban*, xvi-xvii). Paul Binski argues that since the Countess of Cornwall is explicitly mentioned in a note on fol. 2r of the manuscript, and since there was no Countess of Cornwall between 1240 and 1243 (Sanchia, sister of Eleanor of Provence, did not marry Richard of Cornwall, brother of Henry III, until 1243; Richard's previous wife, Isabella Marshal, died in 1240), the illustrated *Alban* must be later than the text and the manuscript itself must be after 1243 ("Abbot Berkyng's Tapestries and Matthew Paris's Life of St Edward the Confessor," *Archaeologia* 109 [1991]: 81–100, at 99 n. 81). Morgan dates the illustrations on stylistic grounds as nearer 1250 than 1240 (*EGM [I]*, no. 85).

[50] Verbal similarities suggest that the captions were usually derived from the main French text: Harden's suggestion that they were later than the text depends on the assumption that the alexandrines of the poem were "old-fashioned" in comparison with the octosyllables (for the most part) of the rubrics, a meter he sees as "normal" for the mid-thirteenth century (Harden, *Auban*, xv). In fact alexandrines were widely used and not necessarily old-fashioned at all: see "Language and Versification," 41–50 below. Latin rubrics (for the texts, see Atkinson, *La Vie de Seint Auban*, 55–60) are subjoined under the two columns of French text on each page: these are probably based on the Anglo-Norman rubrics and on the illustrations rather than directly on the *PSA*: see McLeod, "Alban and Amphibal," 410 and n. 9. Vaughan argues that Paris is responsible for composing as well as copying the Latin verse captions in TCD MS. 177 (Vaughan, *Matthew Paris*, 260).

a lesson for the people."⁵¹ From their attendance at feast days and ceremonies, many St. Albans' citizens must have been familiar with the abbey's representation of its saint and his cult. They must also have experienced the saint's cult as informing both their idea of the town and its day-to-day material fabric, for the monastery was lord of the town of St. Albans, which had been built up by a succession of early abbots from at least the tenth century onward. The monastery had jurisdiction over the town and control of trade.⁵²

The overlordship of a great monastery and the secular lordships of magnates constitute different interest groups, but they are not as opposed in kind as modern accounts have sometimes made them. St. Albans Abbey and the town of St. Albans grew in mutually interdependent fashion in a shared and complex history. After the Roman town of Verulamium was largely destroyed (perhaps in sixth-century Saxon attacks), a royal Anglo-Saxon borough, Kingsbury (Cyngesburh), was established within Verulamium. A second conurbation, the vill of St. Albans, grew up around the walls of the abbey from the ninth century onward and was extended by successive abbots of St. Albans, eventually subsuming the borough. There were thus several sets of potentially conflicting interests and precedents to be called upon: those of the royal town, the abbey's town, and the abbey.⁵³ It was in the abbey's interest to represent its own town as the only successor to Verulamium. In the early eleventh century, Abbot Ælfric II bought and pulled down much of the royal borough of Kingsbury, "which had often been a problem" (*GA* 1:32); and Abbot Robert used King Stephen's visit in the early 1150s to petition for the final destruction of what remained (*GA* 1:121–22). The abbey mostly won in the struggle for power: in its overlordship and role as a cult and pilgrimage center it remained of inescapable economic importance for the town. The twelfth and thirteenth centuries were a period of increasing prosperity; by Henry III's reign, St. Albans was one of the larger boroughs of the kingdom, with extensive trade in Britain and some in France.

---

[51] Gregory the Great, *Epistolae* 9:52, PL 77.982D; for the French version in the twelfth-century St. Albans Psalter, see www.abdn.ac.uk/stalbanspsalter/english/translation/trans068.shtml.

[52] *GA* 1:22 credits Abbot Wulsin with creating a market and building some churches in the town in the mid-tenth century. On church jurisdiction in medieval towns see e.g., Margaret Bonney, *Lordship and the Urban Community: Durham and its Overlords, 1250–1540* (Cambridge: Cambridge University Press, 1990). For further important ideas on the civic functions of urban monastic saints' cults, see Sarah Rees Jones, "Cities and their Saints in England c. 1150–1300: The Cults of St William of York and St Kenelm of Winchcombe," in *Medieval Cities, Texts and Social Networks*, ed. Anne Lester, Caroline Goodson, and Carol Symes (Aldershot: Ashgate, 2010), 193-214.

[53] See Niblett and Thompson, *Alban's Buried Towns*, esp. 190–95 (the Saxon town) and 263–64 and 300–3 (the medieval town).

Town(s) and monastery were also, in quite literal ways, part of each other: Abbot Ealdred (before 979), for instance, blocked up and filled in parts of Verulamium that he believed were being used by criminals and prostitutes. He had undamaged material preserved for use in the abbey (*GA* 1:24–25, 27–28), and some Verulamian stone was later deployed by the first Norman abbot, Paul of Caen (1077–1093), in his rebuilding of the abbey church (*GA* 1:53–54).[54] For their part, the townspeople seem to have enjoyed rights in the abbey church of St. Albans from an early date, and these were maintained by the Norman as well as by the Anglo-Saxon abbots of the monastery.[55] A mutuality of interest, or at least a desire on the abbey's part to inculcate such an idea, is also suggested by the fact that it was a townsman of St. Albans, Robert the Mercer, who was credited with having received the revelation leading to the discovery of St. Amphibalus's body in 1178 (above, 14).[56]

Whatever the townspeople's response to abbey and saint, St. Albans' historians deployed the idea of the city as a witness to the saint's cult. William of St. Albans' prologue in the *PSA* focuses on the ruined walls of the Roman city as chief topographic marker and text of the saint's passion (*PSA* 1). In Paris's *Alban* the city of Verulamium plays a distinctive role in the text and in the manuscript illustrations. Architectural features of the imagined Roman city appear as scene dividers, frames, and backgrounds (e.g., TCD MS. 177, fols. 32r [see Plate 3] 35v, 39r, 43v). The idea of a city ready to accept proper Christian overlordship is implicit in the poem in the development of the community of Verulamium. The pagans are increasingly divided between the unregenerate and the converted, until the entire town has either been punished or become Christian. In his concluding illustration in his *Alban* life proper, a representation of the town's citizens expressing penitence and being baptized, Paris comments that, since the final conversion of the citizens by the martyrs, "Verulamium has been without error and beyond reproach" (TCD MS. 177, fol. 50r and R47, vv. 251–58). In its Romano-British phase as Paris represents it in *GA*, the town's own material fabric becomes a book chest for the saint's life. In the foundations of an old Verulamian palace, Abbot Eadmer's excavations reveal a cache of rolls and books in a hole in a wall, "as if in a small book chest" (*quasi in armariolo*), among them a life

---

[54] Terence Paul Smith, "Early Re-cycling: The Anglo-Saxon and Norman Re-use of Roman Bricks with Special Reference to Hertfordshire," in Henig and Lindley, *Alban and St Albans*, 111–17, at 116; Tim Tatton-Brown, "The Medieval Stones of St Albans Abbey: A Provisional Note," in Henig and Lindley, *Alban and St Albans*, 118–23. On St. Albans' own medieval excavations, see Otter, *Inventiones*, 55–56.

[55] "The City of St Albans: Advowson and Charities," in Page, ed., *The Victoria History of the County of Hertford*, 2:510.

[56] On this vision, see Otter, *Inventiones*, 49–50. For Paris's accounts of Amphibalus's relics, see n. 38 above: his illustrations of them are reproduced and discussed by Lewis, *Art of Matthew Paris*, 114–15.

of Alban (*GA* 1:26–27).⁵⁷ Paris also links the excavation of what were most likely rubbish heaps and oyster middens to Alban's miraculous drying-up of the river and the resurrection of the drowned from the riverbed. He notes that the river Ver had once been able to carry seagoing vessels but had become greatly shrunken since the time of Alban's miracle (*GA* 1:25), and goes on to claim that the very seashells crushed by the feet of the Verulamians as they witnessed Alban's passion were found in Abbot Ealdred's excavations and that the local people gave suitable names to places in the town in the light of these finds, "drawing on what they knew themselves or what they had heard from their elders: Oistrehulle, Selleford, Ancrepol . . . Fishpol" (*GA* 1:25). One catches glimpses of more complicated and conflicted interactions between town and abbey in St. Albans' representations, but the town's role in the monastery's historiography is essentially to be a vessel for the saint and his house and a continuing sign of St. Alban's shaping presence.

Mirrors and Shadows:
Romans, Saracens, and Others in the *Life of St. Alban*

Saints' passions typically assume at least two levels of narrative representation: on the one hand, there are earthly events and figures; on the other, the divine meanings that they signify and in which they participate. God stands behind, and operates through, the saint, and the devil lurks behind, and within, the pagan. This dual structure allows for much mirroring, crossing, and shadowing in key figures and themes. In Paris's vivid narrative, pagans and other oppositional figures speak strongly to Christian preoccupations and anxieties, of which they are often inversions or reflections.

Alban is not strictly an English saint but a Romano-British figure who, by dint of his inclusion in Bede's *Ecclesiastical History of the English People*, becomes the protomartyr of the English. In the late twelfth century, the matter is raised

---

⁵⁷ This life is said to be in "the language of the ancient Britons" (*in idioma antiquorum Britonum*) in "the script used in the time of the Verulamians" (*littera qualis scribi solet tempore quo cives Werlamecestram inhabitabant*), and an elderly, sick priest, Unwona, is called in to decipher it. The priest can understand it in the "old English or rather British language" (*illam antiquo Anglico, vel Britannico, idiomate*); but as soon as Abbot Eadmer has had a Latin translation prepared on the basis of Unwona's dictation, the book crumbles into dust. Another book found in the wall is said to contain the Latin account of Alban as used in contemporary medieval church ritual, its text authorized by Bede, and yet other books and scrolls with accounts of pagan rituals, especially those of Phoebus and of Mercury ("'Woden' in English," as *GA* explains, and said to be the god of merchants, appropriately enough in a trading town like Verulamium with its river access [*GA* 1:26–27]). The latter are burned as being the writings of the devil. For Phoebus in *Alban*, see 19:621–25 below and 115, n. 61.

openly by William of Newburgh, who scoffs at the Britons' charge that the English have exterminated Alban's people and occupied his resting place: "Offended by the sins of his people, which came to his attention even in heaven, he crossed over to the English, and, I say, from a Briton became English, from yours became ours."[58] For his illustration of the first procession in Alban's honor in King Offa's new abbey, Paris gives Alban the title of "first martyr of *Britain*" (fol. 61v: R68, 440), but some of his other usages suggest that "Britain" is the name of ruled territory and "English" the name for the church and state that prevail in it.[59] *Alban*'s account of the Romano-British protomartyr charts, as Bede had done, an ultimately Anglo-Saxon-centered version of British history: Offa, the putative discoverer of Alban's relics and the founder preferred by St. Albans tradition, had crushed the opposition of other groups in establishing the eighth-century Mercian hegemony and is a figure of Anglo-Saxon dominion.[60] Paris had read Geoffrey of Monmouth's *History of the Kings of Britain* closely,[61] and in the closing image of the *Life*, where Alban's blood is said to have "colored . . . the island that Brutus and Corineus conquered" and made it visible in a holy and Rome-centered cartography (48:1837–38), Paris's anglified Romano-British martyr supersedes British history.

---

[58] Quoted from Thomas, *The English and the Normans*, 287: the source is William of Newburgh (attrib.), "Sermo de sancto Albano," in *Guilelmi Neubrigensis Historia sive Chronica rerum Anglicanum libris quinque*, ed. Thomas Hearne (Oxford: Sheldonian Theatre, 1719), 3:819, 874. See also 904 for celebration of Alban as the preeminent saint, gem, and shining pearl of "Britannia."

[59] Paris locates Amphibalus, Alban, and Saints Germanus and Lupus in "Britain" (*Brettainne* 32:1128 and R52:291), the latter as part of the history of "the holy church in England" (*Engletere* R48:259), and makes Offa king of England (*Engleterre* [sic] R56:333) and sole ruler "in Britain" (*Brettaine* [sic], R56:335). The languages actually used by the English church and state are normatively Latin and French for Paris: in *Alban*, Paris quotes English only as the language of the "Saracen" inhabitants of Verulamium who, in the illustration on TCD MS. 177, fol. 36r, jeer at Alban on his way to execution (see R18-R19 below and Plate 7).

[60] Offa reigned 757–796 and consolidated (largely by conquest) a Mercian empire out of the local kingdoms of eighth-century England (Nicholas Brooks, "The Formation of the Mercian Kingdom," in *The Origins of Anglo-Saxon Kingdoms*, ed. Steven Bassett [Leicester: Leicester University Press, 1989], 159–70; Ian W. Walker, *Mercia and the Making of England* [Stroud: Sutton, 2000]). For Offa's marital and dynastic strategies of empire, see Pauline Stafford, "Political Women in Mercia, Eighth to Early Tenth Centuries," in *Mercia: An Anglo-Saxon Kingdom in Europe*, ed. Michelle P. Brown and Carol A. Farr (Leicester: Leicester University Press, 2001; repr. London: Continuum Press, 2005), chap. 3, 35–49, at 35–41.

[61] In the St. Albans' copy, the chapter rubrics of Geoffrey of Monmouth's history and those of the following *Historia Brittonum* (i.e., Gildas's *The Ruin of Britain*) are completed in Paris's hand, as are some of the marginal comments (London BL MS. Royal 13 D. V., no. 35, in Thomson, *Manuscripts from St. Albans Abbey*, 1:98–99).

In his other writings, Paris is frequently ambivalent or openly disgusted about the medieval Roman papacy and its policies; but in *Alban*, Rome is important as the idealized Christian center and reference point for the narrative. Thirteenth-century canonization proceedings involved a journey to the papal court in Rome, in much the same way as the narrator of *Alban* declares his intention of bearing his narrative there on vellum (48:1840). In Paris's illustrations, the chief event represented between the conclusion of the *Alban* text and Offa's subsequent foundation of St. Albans is the mission of the bishops Germanus and Lupus against Pelagianism in Britain (R48–55). They hold their synod at Verulamium, where they visit St. Alban's shrine, thus identifying the site of the future abbey as the central religious complex and *lieu de mémoire* in Britain from the point of view of the early Roman church.[62]

Wales is territory linked with paganism and with Christianity in *Alban*. It is Amphibalus's home country (*Guales mun pais*, 2:34) and also a place in need of conversions: Amphibalus's preaching tour takes place in Wales, and the citizens of Verulamium are both baptized and massacred there (33:1242, 35:1326–48).[63] It seems to be a land at once intimate and other (the root meaning of *Wala* is "foreign, strange"), a place that might know about Christianity but is not felt fully to have absorbed and reproduced it. Paris's attitude to the Welsh seems to have been a typically complex, unresolved, and contingent mixture: he saw them as barbarously disloyal—"the faith of the Welsh is to be without faith" (*CM* 3:385)—but was not unsympathetic to individuals and strongly disapproved of English royal Welsh ventures and policies on the part of both Henry III and his son Edward. Suzanne Lewis characterizes Paris's map of *Wallia* as the representation of "a half mountainous, half marshy land of busy and productive but bellicose men descended from the Trojan Brutus."[64]

---

[62] E. A. Thompson argues that the synod was very unlikely to have taken place in Verulamium, as it would have been disrespectful for the bishops not to visit Alban's shrine first, and that they were more likely to have made a special trip from London after defeating the Pelagians there (*Saint Germanus of Auxerre and the End of Roman Britain* [Woodbridge: Boydell and Brewer, 1984], 49–50).

[63] In *PSA* Amphibalus's homeland is not specified, and he arrives at Verulamium having "crossed over" to Britain (*PSA* 3). In *Alban*, he is returning to Wales from the east (*d'utre mer* and *de l'orient*, "from beyond the sea" and "from the east," 2:27, 33). Some Welsh clergy from the late twelfth century onward attended the schools of England and France and returned to benefices in Wales (Huw Pryce, *Native Law and the Church in Medieval Wales* [Oxford: Clarendon Press, 1993], 76).

[64] Lewis, *Art of Matthew Paris*, 366–72 (with maps); see also 216–20. Wales, to add to its other sins, also probably had a late tradition of copying the works of Pelagius, whose doctrines on grace the French bishops Germanus and Lupus are shown refuting in the rubrics and illustrations of the *Alban* manuscript (David Dumville, "Late Seventh- or Eighth-Century Evidence for the British Transmission of Pelagius," in idem, *Britons and Anglo-Saxons in the Early Middle Ages* [Aldershot and Brookfield, VT: Ashgate, 1993],

No such ambivalence affects the representation of the Jews in *Alban*: they are left in their role as the unredeemable, foundational "other" of Christianity. Amphibalus early explains to Alban that the Jews are "wretched serfs" *(serfs pleintifs*, 6:164), who chose to have their own king killed by the Romans and so were permanently enserfed ("without a king," 6:164 and n.). Augustinian theology saw the Jewish presence in medieval *Christianitas* as a providential form of witness to the Crucifixion and a reminder of evil and of the incompleteness of the Old Law, but gave Jews no political standing. Failing in proper recognition of Christ, their Messiah and king, they had destroyed their own best hope by refusing to embrace their lord's gift (*present e dub*, 11:311) of freedom through the redemption. In England the Jews were owned by the king and called "the King's Jews." Even as he decimated the Jewish community of England by his draconian taxation of them, Henry III remained intent on the conversion of "his" Jews, and he and Eleanor together founded a *domus conversorum* in London for converted Jews to live in, as well as placing such converts in corrodies at English monasteries.[65] But in *Alban* there is no question of Jewish conversion: it is the West's immediate political and military need for "Saracen" conversion that preoccupies the narrative. The native (*naturel*, 38:1415) citizens of Verulamium, although pagan, are seen as recuperable, just as the West had so much hoped the Mus-

---

no. XIII, esp. 52 and n. 53; originally published in *Cambridge Medieval Celtic Studies* 10 [1985]: 39–52). For the appearance of Pelagianism as heresy in *Alban*, see R53:304 and R54:3123–4. *PSA* 37 associates the Welsh and the Picts with "human wildness" (*humana rabies*), but the Picts are omitted in Paris's *Alban*. For William of St. Alban's different treatment of the Welsh, see *PSA* 163, n. 44.

[65] See further Steven Kruger, *The Spectral Jew: Conversion and Embodiment in Medieval Europe* (Minneapolis: University of Minnesota Press, 2006); Jeremy Cohen, *Living Letters of the Law: Ideas of the Jew in Medieval Christianity* (Ithaca and London: Cornell University Press, 1989), and see also idem, *The Friars and the Jews: The Evolution of Medieval Anti-Judaism* (Ithaca and London: Cornell University Press, 1982) for the new thirteenth-century interest in converting Jews (which in England resulted in converts living both in Henry III's *domus conversorum* [*CM* 3:262] and, in arrangements modeled on lay corrodies, at Bury and other monastic houses). For contemporary attitudes and treatment of Jews in Paris's England, see further Robert Stacey, "The English Jews under Henry III," in *The Jews of Medieval Britain, Historical, Literary and Archaeological Perspectives*, ed. Patricia Skinner (Woodbridge: Boydell and Brewer, 2003), 41–54; for Paris, see further Sophia Menache, "Matthew Paris's Attitude toward Anglo-Jewry," *Journal of Medieval History* 23 (1997): 139–62; and, on Paris's own account of Abraham of Berkhamsted and icon desecration (*CM* 5:114–15), see Anthony Bale, "Fictions of Judaism in England before 1290," in *The Jews in Medieval Britain*, ed. Skinner, 129–44, at 136–38. St. Albans, like many English monasteries, had debts to Jewish financiers: Abbot Simon's glorious new shrine (above, 13) put St. Albans into debt with Aaron the Jew, who is said in *CM* to have boasted that he had made "our Saint Alban" a shrine and given him housing out of his own money when he was homeless (*GA* 1:193–94).

lims of the Holy Land might be: the Jews' identity as the defining and doctrinal Christian "other" is maintained intact and untroubled.

As earlier noted (8), Paris turns the "pagans" and "heathens" of William of St. Albans' *PSA* into "Saracens" in *Alban*, a change of some consequence. Diane Speed has argued that Carolingian Saracens are "repositioned as contemporary Islamic enemies" and that Saracens in French literature of the twelfth to thirteenth centuries "are usually oriental or Mediterranean peoples who were, or were regarded as, Islamic: occasionally Saxons; and very occasionally Scandinavians."[66] The living realities represented by the pagan "others" of saints' lives readily embrace both a past to be superseded and the various threats and anxieties of a dangerous present. For Paris, who had interviewed the former physician of Richard Cœur de Lion for an eyewitness account of Saladin, the Saracen past and present must have been vividly intertwined (*CM* 5:221, 2:391, *HA* 2:37). Like the Saracens of the *Chanson de Roland* with their disparate gods Mohammed and Apollo, the Saracens of Paris's Verulamium worship Jove, Phoebus Apollo, Neptune, Pluto, Thetis, and Pallas (Minerva) as well as Mohammed (11:333–37, 31:1103–5). It is specifically Mohammed who is abjured in conversion speeches in *Alban*. This is not carelessness. As Suzanne Lewis has said, in Paris's *Chronica majora* the perception of the Saracens has shifted "from legends of an exotic and distant malignancy to reports of a real and present threat": from the rise of Saladin in the 1180s and the loss of Jerusalem in 1187 through Richard of Cornwall's crusading expedition in 1241–1242 (for which Richard asked St. Albans' prayers, *CM* 4:43) and the Tartar invasions of the same year, the historians of St. Albans view Christendom as "caught in an inexorable vise formed by a resurgent Islam on the one hand and a faithless, morally corrupt papacy on the other."[67]

Paris's most distinctive response to the Saracen threat is to make the poem's narrator a Saracen converted to Christianity. William of St. Albans presents his *PSA* as his own translation of an English narrative by a pagan convert who has seen the story of Alban's martyrdom engraved on the decaying walls of Verulamium, thus distinguishing different eras and Romano-British and Saxon Christianity.[68] Paris's narrator is specifically Saracen and claims, moreover, the status of direct eyewitness to Alban's passion (48:1813). The historical distinctions of the *PSA* are collapsed into a single, culminating figure of conversion in the most startling of *Alban*'s several metamorphoses and variations in its narrating figures. Besides Amphibalus, these include the Verulamian converts, and Amphibalus's converts in Wales, who retell Alban's story (32:1124–201, 41:1519–55). The narrative of Alban's passion is refracted through Alban's companion martyrs and converts until there is, so to speak, no pagan space left in the text. Succession

---

[66] Diane Speed, "The Saracens of *King Horn*," *Speculum* 65 (1990): 564–95, at 572, and see note to 1:13.

[67] Lewis, *Art of Matthew Paris*, 270.

[68] See O'Donnell and Lamont, 134 below.

between narrators is also marked by the progress of cloth and cross.[69] Just as a personal cross of piety and passion is passed along the narrative (especially in its illustrations) from Amphibalus to Alban and back again, so too the narratorial mantle is exchanged by various figures. Initially, Amphibalus in his pilgrim's cloak commands the Christian narrative that changes Alban's life: then Alban self-sacrificingly exchanges his patrician cape for Amphibalus's cloak and pursues his own passion story (see Plate 4). Cloth and cross meet at Alban's execution when a bystander carefully wraps up Alban's bloodied personal cross in what thereby becomes a reliquary fabric (27:900 and illustration with cloth, fol. 38r). The cross returns to Amphibalus when a Verulamian convert narrates the story of Alban's passion to him (32:1124–201).

All these strands are brought together in the final Saracen narrator. He represents the strongest claim made for God's powers of conversion in the text and is also the figure of a writer and maker of a book about a saint. He declares his intention of taking Alban's story to Rome by traveling as a penitent. His feet are to be unprotected by shoes, and he wears a pilgrim's cloak for which he has exchanged his ermine mantle (48.1830: cf. Alban's *estrange atur*—Amphibalus's pilgrim's cloak—at 17:541 and Alban's naked feet at 26:856). This Saracen narrator thus recapitulates the conversion of Alban himself as well as superseding and incorporating all the earlier narrations of the martyrdom. He also explicitly draws together the past, present, and future of the text. He looks back to the island of Britain, once conquered by Brutus and now marked with the blood of Alban the protomartyr (48:1838), and forward (once he has had his story received in Rome) to the translation of his own "barbarian" language into Paris's compositional languages of Latin and French (vv. 1824, 1822–23). The Saracen adumbrates Paris's own narrative work and offers reassurance to the poem's audiences in their own time of the efficacy of the Christian narrative, of its power to convert and effect change in the world.[70]

---

[69] See further McCulloch, "Saints Alban and Amphibalus," 779–85 and Birthe Kjølbye-Biddle, "The Alban Cross," in Henig and Lindley, *Alban and St. Albans*, 85–110 (both with illustrations from the manuscript).

[70] On the *pseudo-narrateur témoin* of *Alban*, see also Laurent, *Plaire et édifier*, 126–30. For other examples of "conversion fantasy," see the *Ordene de chevalerie* texts (composed before 1250 in northern France), in which Saladin asks for instruction and knighthood in Christian chivalry from his knight prisoner, Hue de Tabarie (Dean no. 709: ed. Keith Busby, "Three Anglo-Norman Redactions of *L'Ordene de Chevalerie*," *Mediaeval Studies* 46 [1984]: 31–77). For a discussion, see Margaret Jubb, "The Crusaders' Perceptions of Their Opponents," in *Palgrave Advances in the Crusades*, ed. Helen Nicholson (Basingstoke and New York: Palgrave Macmillan, 2005), 225–44, at 238–39.

Lordship and Conversion

For the lay aristocratic and monastic audiences of his *Alban*, Paris stages a wide-ranging drama of conversion. Not only do the citizens and Saracens, Romano-British, and Welsh (everyone except the Jews) become Christian, but in the person of Alban secular lordship submits to and is enriched by ideal Christian overlordship. Alban's patrician secular status and Amphibalus's role as cleric and teacher are both important in the narrative. In the dual martyrdom of the two saints, the possibility of lay holiness is powerfully represented as Amphibalus converts Alban and guides him to *imitatio Christi*. Alban performs a *translatio* of the holiness lived and taught by Amphibalus when he assumes the cleric's old mantle, gives his own patrician cloak in exchange, and temporarily diverts pagan persecution from the cleric to himself (see Plate 4). The adoption of a pilgrim's cloak, Christ-like in its self-sacrifice (as Paris remarks in *CM* 1:149), becomes a key element in the iconography of the *Alban* narrative and illustrations, the mantle of a new kind of lordship.[71]

In Amphibalus's influence on Alban, Paris's narrative stresses the importance of clerical instruction, but his text is also concerned with the military and affective basis of lordship. In addition to Alban's own high lay status as a patrician magnate of Verulamium, there is also a Roman soldier to whom Paris gives the name Heraclius (*Aracle*) and who is much more prominent than the equivalent (anonymous) character in William of St. Albans' *PSA*. He is presented as the hero of a subsidiary but distinctive "passiun seint Aracle," rubricated and titled as such within *Alban*'s text and illustrations (see e.g. Plates 7, 8), and his name is probably intended to have resonant connotations of crusade and the recovery of the holy cross.[72] Paris's attention to Heraclius is one of many signs that *Alban* is

---

[71] The cloak was also important outside the text and illustrations of *Alban*: as McCulloch points out, Paris notes the use of a piece of woolly cloak by Abbot Ælfric as a guarantee for the Ely monks of "authenticity" for the fake Alban relics sent to Ely in the late tenth century for fear of Danish raiding. According to St Albans sources this was in fact a pious fraud and Ælfric had retained the relics at St Albans (McCulloch, "Saints Alban and Amphibalus," 767, n. 31: *GA* 1:35). On this complicated version of *furtum sacrum* see most recently Hagger, "Litigation and History at St. Albans," at 382–85.

[72] For the treatment of Heraclius in the manuscript, see Baswell, 189 below. The name was particularly associated with legends of the True Cross and crusading through the figure of Heraklios, emperor of Byzantium (575–641 CE). Archbishop William of Tyre's late twelfth-century *Historia in partibus transmarinis gestarum*, a history of Jerusalem to 1184, opens with an account of Heraklios bringing back the relic of the Holy Cross to Jerusalem in 629 at a time when Mohammed's doctrines were beginning to take root in the East. The late twelfth- or early thirteenth-century French translation of the *Historia* uses the form "Eracles" for Heraklios (*L'Estoire de Eracles empereur et la conqueste de la Terre d'Outremer*, in *Recueil des historiens des croisades, Historiens occidentaux*, vol. 1 [Paris: Imprimerie impériale, 1844], 9–10) and was widely transmitted in northern Europe. The

designed to speak directly to, and in part for, a lay world, the baronial and royal courtly world with which Paris was closely involved. In *Alban*, Christ addresses the newly martyred Verulamians as "my knights" (*mi chevaler*, 41:1535), and Alban's own relationship with Christ is seen as a relation of freely chosen affinity within the bonds of lordship and retainer. As Amphibalus urges Alban, "Give allegiance and homage to him, as you ought to do; allegiance is as sacred and binding as baptism and marriage. Do not be fickle or flighty of heart . . . be a true friend and liegeman: for he has chosen you freely and you him" (10.297–301 and n.; 12.346 and n.). So too, the Saracen converts of *Alban* find Christ impressive because he gives good juridical and feudal warranty for his lieges, protecting their bodies after death and healing them when alive (42:1556–62). As the Saracens are made to observe, "What great lordship is exercised by the Christians' God" (39:1463): this lord has complete and free choice as to those with whom he makes and dissolves allegiances.

St. Alban the Romano-British patrician accepts and internalizes a suffering, devotional Christ as his lord. But Alban also knows seigneurial anger: he exhibits it in his initial outrage at the irrationality of the Trinity and, after his conversion, ruefully acknowledges the anger and tension of his class. "I know your cruelty, your customs, and your ways," he says to his fellow Verulamian patricians, as they debate whether they can legally crucify him or bury him alive before they finally accept the argument that a man of lineage must be beheaded: "you would no more have listened to him [Amphibalus] than the ass to the harp . . . you have always been inclined to sin and filth: a foal does not easily forget what he has learned during his breaking-in" (18:614–19). After his conversion Alban rejects anger in his own life, but it remains as a norm in the seigneurial anger constantly displayed by the pagan prince of Verulamium and also in God's own represented acts, most notably in the crippling of the pagans in revenge for Amphibalus's torture (47:1770–80: Plate 10). Anger is both that which is to be

---

death of Heraklios "Augustus" is noted in *CM* under 641 CE (*CM* 1:281): Paris also notes that St. Albans kept a copy of William of Tyre's *Historia* (*HA* 1:163) and cites the emperor Heraclius's bringing of the True Cross as a precedent for Louis IX's exhibition of his newly acquired True Cross and crown of thorns relics (*CM* 4:91). No doubt the resemblance between the names Heraclius and Heracles, this latter the classical hero (who also figures in the twelfth-century *romans d'antiquité*), added further resonance; but Paris seems carefully to have selected for the soldier a name that would evoke the conflict between cross and crescent. Hahn argues that, by means of the chivalric passion of Heraclius, *Alban* directs its audiences to "more correct forms of chivalric practice," that is, a more ascetic and penitential chivalry (*Portrayed on the Heart*, 302–6). The Benedictine Alban life might in this respect be compared with the thirteenth-century Cistercian reimagining of chivalry in the *Quest del Sangreal*. Heraclius is not mentioned in *GA*, although events involving the other new figure in Alban's life, Amphibalus, are detailed there (see n. 38 above). This further suggests that Heraclius was developed as a chivalric figure of outreach to lay patrons.

abjured in Christian love and that which repeatedly returns, indissociable from normative governance and its anxieties.

If hagiographic passion characteristically places Christianity and its others in opposition in its narrative structure and themes, it is also the case that the "others" of a given hagiographic text have their own narrative. Saracens suggest that God's miracles for Alban are the work of the sun and hence of their own god, Phoebus (25:832–34), and that the heavenly voice addressing their converts is produced by Amphibalus's necromantic sorcery (35:1336–37). In three parallel moments in *Alban*, the prince of Verulamium, the leader of the poem's Saracens, offers oppositional interpretations of Alban's conversion, of his executioner Heraclius's witness, and of the figure of Alban's teacher, Amphibalus. For the prince, Alban's is primarily a class betrayal: Alban has abandoned the faith of his noble ancestors, temporarily bamboozled by an unlicensed foreign vagrant working in secrecy. "Doesn't the stink [of Amphibalus's pilgrim cloak] annoy you?" the prince asks, trying to persuade Alban back to his ancestral seigneurial role (17:569). So too, the prince mocks Heraclius's new service in Alban's and Christ's lordship (29:947–60), and the healing of the converted soldier's wounds is interpreted by the Saracens as necromancy (29:998).[73] Finally, in the prince's view, Amphibalus, the traveling preacher of the true word, is a mere jongleur and religious quack (*clergastre*), and the prince eloquently denounces Alban's master as "barefoot and tattered, clad in an old tunic" (34:1248–9), peddling fraudulent doctrine (*trufle*) and fabrication (*cuntruvure*), and offering a fable fit to be sung to "rote or viol" (34:1259).[74] For the prince, Amphibalus is clownish but nonetheless dangerous, spreading stories likely to arouse unrest. The seigneurial viewpoint and the anger and "rational" control abandoned by Alban at his conversion are maintained by the prince to the end but revealed as self-destructive in the continuing slaughter of one another by the

---

[73] Necromancy is aligned with fiction and potential falsity in some other thirteenth-century saints' lives: see n. to 29:998. On wandering preachers (especially associated with the crusades, and much distrusted in the thirteenth and fourteenth centuries in comparison with the First and Second Crusades of the twelfth), see Sophia Menache, *Vox Dei: Communication in the Middle Ages* (Oxford: Oxford University Press, 1990), 108–10.

[74] The prince here plays on long-standing medieval Christian traditions that both conflated and opposed clerics and jongleurs. Clerics might properly be joyous minstrels of God (as the friars were sometimes called), but they might also be more like goliards and scurrilous entertainers. See Jean Leclercq, "'Ioculator et saltator': S. Bernard et l'image du jongleur dans les manuscrits," in *Translatio Studii*, ed. Julian G. Plante (Collegeville, MN: St. John's University Press, 1973), 124–48 (129–31 for thirteenth-century sources); John Baldwin, "At the Periphery of the Court: Entertainers," in idem, *Masters, Princes, and Merchants: The Social Views of Peter the Chanter and His Circle* (Princeton: Princeton University Press, 1970), 2:130–44. (We thank Professor Andrew Taylor for information on minstrels.) King David is presented as a jongleur, with Psalm 44 as his song at "la joie de la court" (Christ's nuptials with the church) in the French poem known from the first word of that psalm as *Eructavit* (Dean no. 705).

Saracens. In his attention to the prince's viewpoint, Paris carefully imagines and addresses lay culture, considering and preparing refutation for objections and questions that might be addressed to his monastic saint by contemporary Christians.

Unsurprisingly, the obverse of seigneurial anger is also important in *Alban*'s models of lordship, whose bonds, conceived as those of free allegiance and love, are strongly desired. The community of heaven under Christ's overlordship is characterized by amicability and voluntary adherence: Alban is to be prominent in the celestial baronage there (10:301) and Christ's knights, Heraclius and the converted and martyred Verulamians are welcomed into its ranks as to some immensely courtly Valhalla, joining one another and the angelic hosts in indissoluble affective union (27:911–12, 29:1019–22, 35:1331–33, 41:1535–38). Like much else in the life, this is a conventional trope, but one realized with particular intensity and thematic point in *Alban*.[75]

Women Readers

Apart from the Virgin Mary, St. Genevieve of Paris,[76] and the scene of Alban's burial, women are seldom seen in the *Alban* manuscript: they normally do not appear in crowd scenes and are shown only at the burial of Alban (fol. 39r) and among the lamenting Verulamians (fols. 45v). But women readers formed an important section of Paris's audience. On its second flyleaf, the *Alban* manuscript has well-known notes in Paris's handwriting that give information about the circulation of his works among contemporary noblewomen. One says that a message is to go to "the lady Countess of Arundel, Isabel, that she is to send you the book about St. Thomas the Martyr and St. Edward, which I translated [or copied] and designed [*transtuli et protraxi*], and which the lady Countess of Cornwall may keep until Whitsuntide."[77] Paris dedicated his French life of Edmund of Canterbury to Isabella of Arundel (widowed 1243, d. 1279): the Countess of Cornwall must be Sanchia of Provence, sister of Henry's III's queen and wife of his brother Richard of Cornwall (they married in 1243 and Sanchia died in 1262).[78] Another note on the manuscript's flyleaf consists of instructions by Paris for a set of paired illustrations of saints with French captions to go into the book

---

[75] See Laurent, *Plaire et édifier*, 459–60.

[76] The Virgin features in references to Christian doctrine (5:102, 5:128, 47:1802) and in invocations to Christ as her son (33:1231, 39:1443). The most vivid account of her is given by the pagan prince (34:1252–54, 34:1261). For St. Genevieve, see R49-R51.

[77] Fol. 2r. See James, *La Estoire de Seint Aedward*, 20. (The note may be addressed to an unknown "G," but "G" is probably a paraph mark.) It is generally agreed that the note refers either to Paris's own illustrated lives of these saints or to copies of them.

[78] Noel Denholm-Young, *Richard of Cornwall* (Oxford: Blackwell, 1957; New York: William Salloch, 1947), 112–13: T. W. E. Roche, *The King of Almayne* (London: John Murray, 1966), 167–68. Cf. above, 20 n. 49.

of the Countess of Winchester (*in libro comitisse Wint*). The fourth pair in this set is formed by Alban, with the caption "I was the first to undergo martyrdom in Britain for Jesus," and Amphibalus, with the caption "Through me, Alban abandoned the faith that poisons and maims the soul."[79] The Countess of Winchester may have been Matilda, daughter of Humphrey de Bohun IV, Earl of Hereford and Essex (d. 1275), and second wife of Roger de Quincy, Earl of Winchester (d. 1262), or Eleanor de Ferrers (d. 1274), married in 1252 to Roger de Quincy as his third wife. Eleanor may also be the patron of the Lambeth Apocalypse, which includes several full-page images of saints.[80] Thus at least one noblewoman of the magnate class expected to have images of Alban and Amphibalus, probably, like the Lambeth Apocalypse *memoriae* of saints, included at the end of her psalter or apocalypse as part of its customizing to her particular devotional requirements. The earliest known manuscript representation of the martyrdom outside St. Albans is also in a woman's book, in the Huntingfield Psalter (New York: Pierpont Morgan Library, MS. 43, fol. 24v) thought to have been made for Lucie, child bride of Sir Roger de Huntingfield, at Lesnes Abbey in Kent, 1210–1220.[81]

Noblewomen, then, were audiences for Paris's saints' lives and integral to the dissemination and practice of St. Alban's cult. Their presence in the monastery's life and connections was inescapable. Eleanor of Provence, Henry III's queen, may herself have read a life of Alban: she certainly vowed to make a pilgrimage to St. Albans when ill in 1257, a vow that she fulfilled in company with Eleanor of Castile and others in what Margaret Howell suggests was a "community of

---

[79] "Albanus Li primers fu ki pur ihesu mort sufri en brettainne
Amphibalus Auban par moi guerpit la loy kalme entusche e mahainne"
(fol. 2v): for the remaining images and captions (now almost illegible in the manuscript itself), see James, *La Estoire de Seint Aedward*, 20–24.

[80] For Eleanor de Quincy, see Loveday Lewes Gee, *Women, Art and Patronage from Henry III to Edward III* (Woodbridge and Rochester: Boydell Press, 2002), 147; Nigel J. Morgan, ed., *The Lambeth Apocalypse* (London: Harvey Miller for Lambeth Palace, 1990), 2:75–79, 254. On fols. 52r and 52v of the Lambeth Apocalypse are a pair of archbishop saints, while Saints Lawrence, Margaret, and Catherine form a three-page grouping at fols. 49v-50v. The previous Countess of Winchester, Roger's mother, Margaret (wife of Saher de Quincy, d. 1219), died in 1235, a date generally agreed to be earlier than the note on the manuscript flyleaf, and the line of the Earls of Winchester died out with Roger himself, so one of his two wives is the likely intended recipient of the saints' images envisaged by Paris.

[81] The manuscript's illustrations are on-line at http://corsair.morganlibrary.org/msdesc/BBM0043.htm. For a hard-copy reproduction of fol. 24v, see Eileen Roberts, *Images of Alban: St Alban in Art from the Earliest Times to the Present* (St. Albans: Fraternity of the Friends of St. Albans Abbey, 1999), pl. 4. For the manuscript see Morgan, *EGM [I]*, no. 30.

devotion" among aristocratic women.[82] Even a record as preoccupied with monastic rights and their defense as Paris's *GA* notes that Abbot Geoffrey's unfinished shrine to Alban was not permitted to have fixed into it an antique cameo given to the monastery by King Æthelred, father of Edward the Confessor, because of its value to women in childbirth (implying that it was taken to women in labor and was not just an object of *vertu* in the abbey church).[83] Reworking in French his own Latin life of Edmund, archbishop of Canterbury (d. 1240), for Isabella, Countess of Arundel, Matthew Paris specifically addresses her as the patroness of St. Albans' daughter house of Wymondham.[84] The St. Albans *Book of Donors* (*Liber benefactorum*, compiled from 1380 onward) includes throughout the abbey's history women from a surprisingly large class range (Queen Matilda and the Countess of St. Pol figure, but so does Margareta, wife of Willelmus Noreys, *villanus sancti Albani*, and Johanna, wife of Willelmus Hosiere), and of varying family status (*uxor, soror, vidua, filia*); women of independent means (*Godoleva, quaedam matrona Londoniae*, 446) were also the abbey's benefactors. Some, such as Domina Petronilla de Banstede, giver of precious altar and shrine vessels (452–53), are accorded portraits accompanying the commemoration of their gifts.[85] As James Clark notes, this book presents the story of the monastery as the story of the cult and the story of the cult as a collaborative endeavor by the monks and their lay benefactors.[86]

---

[82] Howell, *Eleanor of Provence*, 91–92; *CM* 5:653–54.

[83] *GA* 1:83–84. On the cameo, see Martin Henig and T. A. Heslop, "The Great Cameo of St Albans," *Journal of the British Archaeological Association* 139 (1986): 148–53. Paris's copy of the reformed Benedictine statutes of 1253 (see n. 3 above) states that no woman is to be permitted to enter when offices are being sung except for consecrations, indulgences, and principal feasts (*CM* 6:242, 244), which itself suggests more contact than might at first seem likely. For the connections of a St. Albans psalter of the mid- to late twelfth century with Matilda, Abbess of Wherwell, or her mother, Euphemia de Balliol, see Thomson, *Manuscripts from St Albans Abbey*, 1:59–60. On relations between St. Albans and women, see further Stephanie Hollis and Jocelyn Wogan-Browne, "St Albans and Women's Monasticism: Lives and Their Foundations in Christina's World," in *Christina of Markyate*, ed. Samuel Fanous and Henrietta Leyser (London and New York: Routledge, 2004), 25–52.

[84] A. T. Baker, ed., "La Vie de seint Edmond, archevêque de Cantorbéry," *Romania* 55 (1929): 332–81, at 343, v. 48.

[85] For Petronilla de Banstede, see Cambridge, Corpus Christi College MS. 7, fol. 101r, and *Liber benefactorum*, in *Johannis de Trokelowe... chronica et annales*, ed. H. T. Riley, RS 28c (London: Longmans, Green, Reader, and Dyer, 1866), 427–64, at 435–36, 463.

[86] Clark, "The St Albans Monks and the Cult," 223. In addition to the display of the *Liber benefactorum* at the "Matthew Paris Disbound" Colloquium in the Parker Library, Corpus Christi College, Cambridge, July 2001, we are grateful to sub-librarian Gill Cannelle, for affording us a further look at the *Liber benefactorum* in 2003 and other help.

St. Albans Abbey knew the value of female patrons. But even without the monastery's specific connections and histories, *Alban* is the kind of text frequently found in women's books, especially in women's devotional reading. Concerned with conversion and holy violence, *Alban* and other saints' passions, like *chansons de geste*, crusading narratives, and the "Vengeance of Our Lord" cycles, did not exclude female audiences and were indeed often dedicated or directed to women patrons and readers.[87] Paris himself seems to have been aware of *chansons de geste* in several ways. His life of Edmund of Canterbury claims that Edmund "did not value vernacular stories of Ogier or Charlemagne at the worth of a chestnut."[88] This topos is common to a number of late twelfth- and thirteenth-century writers and indicates not that *chansons de geste* were despised but that they were heard and read.[89] One function of such literature may well have been to solicit the support of the wives and mothers of thirteenth-century crusaders and to attempt to reconcile them to the mutilation or slaughter of kinsmen and friends.[90] In *CM*, Paris ascribes to Countess Ela of Salisbury a premonitory vision of her son William Longespee's death and reception into heaven during the battle of Mansourah in 1250, thereby suggesting that noblewomen can understand the battlefield deaths of their relatives as martyrdom.[91]

---

[87] For an informative account of the chivalric-religious culture of Eleanor of Provence and her circle of noblewomen as expressed in their books and reading, see Howell, *Eleanor of Provence*, 82–92. An important example of such reading is *Rossignos*, a poem of some 5,000 lines composed for the queen, which combines lyrical meditation on the Passion with the celebration of chivalric and crusading heroes from Judas Maccabaeus to Lancelot to Eleanor's own son Prince Edward: see *Rossignos*, ed. Glyn Hesketh, ANTS 63 (London: ANTS, 2006), vv. 3969–4048, and cf. n. 8 above. Continental and Anglo-Norman versions of the *Pseudo-Turpin Chronicle* (related to the *Chanson de Roland*) circulated in England and France, and some were dedicated to and owned by noblewomen, including the Countess of St. Pol (to whom Nicholas de Senlis dedicated his French version) and Alice de Curcy (d. 1229, wife of Warin Fitzgerold and with him the dedicatee of the Anglo-Norman *Pseudo-Turpin* by William de Briane: Dean no. 79). For a *Vengeance* text in a nunnery manuscript, see Ford, *Vengeance de Nostre-Seigneur* (1993), 52–64.

[88] "Romanz d'Oger u de Charlemeine / Ne preisa il une chasteine": Baker, "La Vie de seint Edmond," 349, vv. 331–32.

[89] As noted earlier, *chansons de geste* featured in monastic libraries and were sometimes copied for lay patrons by religious houses, while Paris's own writings, in both Latin and French, show signs of *chanson de geste* influence: see further nn. 8 and 9 above.

[90] Natasha R. Hodgson, *Women, Crusading and the Holy Land in Historical Narrative* (Woodbridge and Rochester: Boydell and Brewer, 2007), 116–18 (wives), 203–12 (widows), and discussion of women as "inhibitors" of crusade, passim.

[91] *CM* 5:53–54, 173. For an Anglo-Norman poem on this death, see Simon Lloyd, "The Making of an English Crusading Hero," *Nottingham Medieval Studies* 35 (1991): 41–69, and idem and Tony Hunt, "William Longespee II: The Making of an English Crusading Hero: Part II," *Nottingham Medieval Studies* 36 (1992): 79–125.

Blood Matters

The blood of martyrdom plays a role in many saints' lives but is seldom as explicitly and vividly present as in Paris's text.[92] The reader or hearer of *Alban* is repeatedly invited to visualize encrusted blood, spouting blood, flowing blood, blood spattered like dewdrops. Specifically noted effusions of blood accompany the violence done to Alban and his companions (20:653, 25:839, 25:843, 29:936 and R29:128, 41:1532, 41:1545, 43:1611); at Alban's execution, his head flies "bleeding from his shoulders" (27:897) and "the cross that Alban carried and the hill itself flowered with the glorious holy blood that gushed from his body" (27:897–98). Paris's illustration of the execution shows a Christian convert collecting the bloodied cross reverently into a cloth, while the rubric points out the cross "stained with red blood" (R24:104, fol. 38r: see cover image). At the conclusion of *Alban*, the martyr is said to have been the first to have "colored" (*teinte*, 48:1838) the island of Britain with his blood, just as it is seen at his execution that he "stained" (*teinst*, 32:1187) the personal cross he carried with the blood flowing from his body (32:1186–87). *Alban*'s heightened focus on the blood of martyrdom had many contemporary resonances. For audiences and patrons, whether aristocratic or aspiring, blood was a key aspect of lineage and class identity: the blood and lineage of Christ feature in insular genealogical rolls as well as in Arthurian Grail quest narratives, while the desired purity and the inevitable hybridity of bloodlines are a constant source of cultural turbulence and invention.[93] The pierced and bleeding body of the highest-ranking lord, Christ, was repeatedly imaged as a focus for affective meditation in poems on the Passion, as well as in book illustrations, private and public altars, and wall paintings,[94] and Christ's

---

[92] Most martyrs' passions revolve around the willingness of saints to shed their own blood in witness to Christian truth, but the narrative detail and focus with which bloodshed is represented can vary greatly from one *passio* to another. In thirteenth-century lives of St. Catherine, for instance, the saint's blood is barely seen: Catherine is beaten and imprisoned, but blood is mentioned principally to note that her beheaded trunk bleeds milk ("Passio sancte Katerine," in *Seinte Katerine*, ed. S. R. T. O. D'Ardenne and E. J. Dobson, EETS s.s. 7 [Oxford: Oxford University Press for EETS, 1981], 202, line 1136).

[93] See Dean nos. 6–10; Olivier de Laborderie, "Les généalogies des rois d'Angleterre sur rouleaux manuscrits (milieu du XIIIe siècle-début du XV siècle): conception, diffusion et fonctions," in *La généalogie entre science et passion*, ed. T. Barthélemy and M.-C. Pingaud (Paris: Editions du CTHS, 1997), 181–99; John Spence, "Genealogies of Noble Families in Anglo Norman," in *Broken Lines: Genealogical Literature in Medieval Britain and France*, ed. Raluca L. Radulescu and Edward D. Kennedy, Medieval Texts and Cultures of Northern Europe 16 (Turnhout: Brepols, 2008), 63–77.

[94] See *'Cher alme': Religious Practice and Devotion in Anglo-Norman Piety*, ed. and trans. T. Hunt, H. Leyser, and J. Bliss (FRETS OPS 1, 2010). Prayers and meditations on Christ's Passion, five wounds, and name and on the Eucharist and the canonical hours to be said "before the crucifix in the minster or over a crucifix painted in a book" abound

suffering is also frequently troped as chivalric.⁹⁵ The presence of Christ's own blood on earth, in the Eucharist or in holy blood relics, was the subject of intense debates and the focus of ritual practices and miracles.⁹⁶ Whether contemplated in a devotional image, revered in a relic, consumed in the Eucharist, or shed in the sands of Syria (the medieval name for Palestine), blood was a concern of religious and lay men and women alike at home and abroad in the thirteenth century.

The high status of blood relics is reflected in Henry and Eleanor's thaumaturgical and devotional fashions. The queen eventually acquired her own relic of Becket's blood, sent to her from Pontigny by Edmund of Canterbury,⁹⁷ and in 1247 Henry III announced his acquisition of a relic of Christ's blood and ordered a procession in which he himself, barefoot, carried it to Westminster. The dating of *Alban* is not sufficiently fixed to link the work to these events, but it is continuous with the sensibilities and values involved. Paris himself was certainly, by Henry's command, a direct witness and reporter of the procession and related ceremonies. His account includes the *determinatio* of Robert Grosseteste, bishop of Lincoln, on the Holy Blood, especially on the question of how Christ could be resurrected in perfection yet leave bodily fluids on earth. This was given publicly before the court (surely in French, though recorded by Paris in Latin).⁹⁸ There

---

("devant le crucifix del muster u sur crucifix peint en livre," BL MS. Arundel 288, fol. 4v, Dean no. 492); see also *The Anglo-Norman Lyric*, ed. David L. Jeffrey and Brian J. Levy (Toronto: Pontifical Institute of Mediaeval Studies, 1990), nos. 10–15. On Edmund of Canterbury's devotion to the five wounds, to the body of Christ, and to the Eucharist, see Mother Mary M. Philomena, SHCJ, "St Edmund of Canterbury's Meditations before the Canonical Hours," *Ephemerides Liturgicae* 78 (1964): 35–57.

⁹⁵ On the pervasiveness of this iconography in insular culture, see Michael Evans, "An Illustrated Fragment of Peraldus' *Summa* of Vice: Harleian MS. 3244," *Journal of the Warburg and Courtauld Institutes* 14 (1982):14–68; and on "chevaliers de la foi" in saints' lives, see Laurent, *Plaire et édifier*, 453–58.

⁹⁶ On twelfth- and thirteenth-century debates over the Eucharist and blood relics, see Caroline Walker Bynum, *Wonderful Blood* (University Park, PA: Penn State Press, 2007), chap. 4, 85–108. The fullest treatment of the Holy Blood in England is Nicholas Vincent, *The Holy Blood: King Henry III and the Westminster Blood Relic* (Cambridge: Cambridge University Press, 2001): see chap. 5 for scholastic debate (at 82–117) and chap. 4 (at 31–81) for an account of Holy Blood relics in Europe from the ninth century onward.

⁹⁷ Howell suggests that the queen acquired her Edmund relic at the translation of the saint to his new shrine on 16 June 1276 (*Eleanor of Provence*, 136).

⁹⁸ Paris gives an account of the day's proceedings at *CM* 4:641–45 and includes a version of Grosseteste's argument in his *Liber additamentorum* collection of supporting documents (*CM* 6:138–44): see Bynum, *Wonderful Blood*, 85–90; Vincent, *Holy Blood*, 87–88. Grosseteste distinguishes the inmost blood of the heart that is the true core of human nature and that is consubstantial with God. This sort of blood is not physically available on earth, unlike the superfluous blood generated from nutrients and shed in nosebleeds, etc. Of the second, superfluous kind of blood, by far the most valuable is that

may well have been a dimension of rivalry in Henry III's attempts to establish a Westminster cult of the Holy Blood: Louis IX had acquired True Cross and crown-of-thorns relics in 1239 and built his exquisite Sainte Chapelle in Paris to house them (*CM* 4, 90–92).[99] But, as Nicholas Vincent has shown, Henry's fostering of the cult of the Holy Blood also belongs in several further contexts, including Henry's relations with the Holy Land, to which he and Eleanor made an (unfulfilled) vow to go on crusade: "the relic of the Holy Blood itself was clearly intended as a means of focussing men's minds upon the sufferings of Christ and hence upon the need for a crusade to deliver the land of Christ's birth and crucifixion."[100] The issues surrounding the Holy Blood remained inextricably devotional and theological, military and political.

Alban's own chief signifier of how much blood matters is the cross exchanged between Amphibalus and the newly converted Alban. As Florence McCulloch has shown, this bloodied personal cross is the object of special attention in the text and the illustrations.[101] The cross is first seen as Amphibalus enters Verulamium, when it is described as ornamented not with precious gems or ivory but with a crucified figure, with "blood from the heart" flowing down one of its sides

---

shed from Christ's heart and right side, and it was of this blood, according to the Latin patriarch of Jerusalem's authenticating letter, that Henry's relic consisted (Vincent, *Holy Blood*, 98). As Vincent points out, Grosseteste focuses on the role of Joseph of Arimathea and hence of English associations in the relic's transmission, perhaps reflecting the currency of the *Estoire del Saint Graal*, composed 1220–1230 (Vincent, *Holy Blood*, 89–90). Like Paris himself, Grosseteste wrote in French as well as Latin (for texts and attributions, see Dean nos. 392, 563, 622, 645, 660, 662, 670, 686, 859, 937). Paris also records the bishop of Norwich's argument in his sermon that, holy as the cross of Christ may be, it is the still holier blood on it that confers holiness in the first place. England therefore has even more cause to rejoice in the possession of the Holy Blood than the king of France does in his acquisition of a True Cross relic (*CM* 4:642–43). Paris makes the same claim in French in his life of Edmund of Canterbury dedicated to the Countess of Arundel: see Baker, "La Vie de seint Edmond," 380, vv. 1997–2000.

[99] Louis IX of France purchased the crown of thorns in 1239 from Baldwin, Latin emperor of Constantinople, and in 1241 also bought portions of the True Cross and other relics: see Vincent, *Holy Blood*, 8, and Richard Vaughan, *The Illustrated Chronicles of Matthew Paris: Observations of Thirteenth-Century Life* (Stroud: Alan Sutton in association with Corpus Christi College Cambridge, 1993), 51, for Paris's *CM* illustration of Louis displaying the relics (Cambridge, Corpus Christi College MS. 16, fol. 141r), and M. E. Roberts, "The Relic of the Holy Blood and the Iconography of the Thirteenth-Century North Transept Portal of Westminster Abbey," in *England in the Thirteenth Century: Proceedings of the 1984 Harlaxton Symposium*, ed. W. M. Ormrod (Woodbridge and Dover, NH: Boydell Press, 1986), 129–42, at 137.

[100] Vincent, *Holy Blood*, 16, and, for other contexts (Henry's rebuilding of Westminster; his many gifts of relics to it; his knighting of his half-brother, William de Valence, at the Holy Blood ceremonies), 11–14, 17–19.

[101] McCulloch, "Saints Alban and Amphibalus," 779–85, and see n. to 1:2–7 below.

(1:7). Alban subsequently sees this blood with his "own eyes" in the Crucifixion vision that converts him from seigneurial impatience with an irrational God (born of a mortal woman in the service of a doctrine as perverse as that of the Trinity) and into affective service to his new lord, Christ (9:257–59 and R22:90). Like the crucifixes of contemporary thirteenth-century Passion meditation, this cross is used in Amphibalus's and in Alban's own devotions; but it is also, like the relics so much desired at Henry and Eleanor's court, a Holy Blood relic, the more so as Alban's own blood, "hardened and sticking" (31.1114), joins the represented "blood from [Christ's] heart" painted on it (1:7). The bloody cross is also an emblem in the politics of conversion: Alban holds steadfastly to it (illustration above 18:580–19:617, fol. 34v); his converts go under its sign to Amphibalus and further fuel his mission in Wales (32:1186–87, 33:1202–3: see also R32:143–44, fol. 39r). Conversion itself is accompanied by bloodshed in many saints' lives, but Alban's reiterated and cumulative conversions are especially marked by slaughter and violence.[102]

Although Henry III's assertion of royal and Christian authority in the cult of the Holy Blood ultimately failed, this icon of holy violence, crusading vengeance, and intense piety seems an appropriate choice for his era. In Henry's reign, the conjunction of Christ's blood as the devotional center of a fervid piety with the blood so copiously shed in the East by Christians and "Saracens" alike is perhaps nowhere as vividly represented as in Paris's *Alban*: "a faithful knight has to suffer much for his lord's sake," says the narrative of Alban's passion (21:686): "Whoever sheds his blood for God in this world is healed; whoever holds back in fear of death is no true loving friend," say the converting Saracens (32:1200–1).

The Burial of the Dead

Blood and violence go together with *Alban*'s focus on slaughtered bodies. Appropriate treatment and burial of bodies was a matter of great concern and perhaps had special though not exclusive meaning for noblewomen in England, who, even if they did not go on crusade themselves as some did, must often have had to arrange for burial or shipment back of remains for husbands and kinsmen who had died in Palestine or elsewhere on crusade.[103] According to Paris, Richard of

---

[102] So, for instance, Heraclius is not just converted (as in some lives' treatment of the "reluctant executioner" figure) but savagely and bloodily beaten, with some degree of narrative detail (25:837–49, 29:1010–14); in Wales, the converted Verulamians are cut to pieces by their relatives (35:1340–48, 41:1499–500); the Saracens' final dispute is exceptionally brutal (46:1747–49, 47: 1767–68).

[103] On dismemberment and burial, see Elizabeth A. R. Brown, "Death and the Human Body in the Later Middle Ages: The Legislation of Boniface VIII on the Division of the Corpse," *Viator* 12 (1981): 221–70. The separate burial of particular body parts was a custom manifested earlier at the English than at the French court, where it seems to

Cornwall, Henry III's brother, became celebrated among the French not so much for his relatively successful crusade as for his burial of the bones of their dead at Ascalon, on the Palestine coast between Gaza and Jaffa (*CM* 4:144–45). In *Alban*, it is difficult not to see the pagans' fury against Amphibalus—"[Your preaching has] delivered over to death many a worthy baron . . . who gave themselves over to the crucified god . . . and were lost beyond recall" (44:1649–56)—as at some level expressive of the horrors and longings of the disastrous thirteenth-century crusades. In a society whose sons, brothers, and husbands were vanishing on a series of frequently ill-judged and ruinous expeditions, many at home might echo Paris's Verulamian pagans, and say of their crusader kin, "How unfortunate that you professed the God hanged on the cross!" (*Tant mar reclamas le Deu k'en croiz pendi!* 41:1509).

As the Verulamians lament the slaughter of their relatives, their great anxiety is that their kinsmen's bodies lie "in the wasteland [of Wales] as abandoned carrion," unshrouded and without tombs, to be devoured by birds and beasts (41:1506–8). The bleakness of this Welsh scene—the bodies lie "despoiled and abandoned in those fields, where a man could not have known his own from strangers" (41:1541–42)—would have made equally eloquent reporting from the Holy Land. By way of consolation it is stressed in *Alban* that the Verulamian bodies are all accounted for: "We counted them all, in a verified and sure count, and we had it recorded in black ink" (41:1546–47). The miracle that restores the beheaded and disemboweled bodies to wholeness, with "the blood that had stained them earlier blanched whiter than milk" (41:1545) and with a wolf and eagle sent to mount guard over them, is seen in *Alban* as a powerful instrument of conversion. Moreover, as knights of Jesus (35:1331–32, 41:1535), the converts go as securely to paradise as William Longespee in the vision attributed to his mother (35 above) or as Roland himself in his *chanson de geste*.

It seems telling that the decorous handling of the dead is an important consolation here: no more powerful action can be imagined, except for the vengeful crippling and disfigurement of the remaining Saracens in *Alban*'s final massacre: "Whoever had once been a brave and celebrated knight / was now crippled or demon-infested" (47:1776–77). The narrative underlines this punishment in what seems a sign less of Christian triumphalism than of Christian longing: "God took vengeance on them [the Saracens] for having waged so much war. . . . They learned that there is no point in any man born of a mother making war on earth against the king of majesty" (47:1769, 47:1782–83).

---

have arrived through the cult of Edmund of Canterbury (Brown, "Death and the Human Body," 231), who himself had an influential heart burial (*CM* 4:72–74). On the custom, as adopted by Henry III and Eleanor of Provence for themselves and their relatives, see Brown, "Death and the Human Body," 229–30. For an account of the entrail burial and the embalming of Abbot William of St. Albans (d. 1235), see *GA* 1:301–2.

Language and Versification

Speaking and Writing French

At the very end of *Alban*, a linguistic supersession is invoked by the poem's Saracen narrator as he deplores his own "barbarian" language and predicts that it will be replaced with the purportedly better, more suitable languages of French and Latin (48:1822–24). In Paris's main source text, William of St. Albans' narrator figure is said to have composed in English a narrative of events from Romano-British Verulamium, which William is commissioned to translate into Latin and which he is able to supplement from the book by Geoffrey of Monmouth translated from the British (*de Britannico in Latinum*, *PSA* 1). Paris's decision to represent his *Alban* text as a translation from the "Saracen language" into French is a pragmatic choice but also an imaginative continuation of these linguistic and ethnographic politics. The French spoken by King Henry III and the secular nobility set them apart from speakers of English. Latin was the province of a clerical elite, which included Matthew Paris and his fellow religious at St. Albans Abbey. In his conclusion to *Alban*, as also in an earlier prophecy by Amphibalus (3:68–70), Paris elevates French, making it equal to Latin as a vehicle for Christian history. As against the Saracen narrator's tongue, French becomes a communal language for the linked purposes of sacred and secular Christian elites. So too, Paris's *Alban* manuscript readily intermingles French and Latin on many of its pages, addressing monastic audiences and lay patrons alike.

Although the use of French among English nobles gave it a status relative to Latin in England that it did not yet enjoy in France itself, the French of England did not have the prestige of Parisian French (i.e., the language of the Ile de France called "francien" by nineteenth-century scholars).[104] Matthew Paris must have been familiar with the charges by some intellectuals in England that insular French was barbarous and false; and by pronouncing the French of England fit to transmit the life of an English martyr, he may have intended a refutation of such views.[105] It is notable that, among writers of the French of England,

---

[104] Ian Short, *Manual of Anglo-Norman*, ANTS OPS 7 (London: ANTS, 2007), 11; R. A. Lodge, "Language Attitudes and Linguistic Norms in France and England in the Thirteenth Century," in *Thirteenth Century England IV*, ed. Coss and Lloyd, 73–83 (77–78 for examples); Ian Short, "On Bilingualism in Anglo-Norman England," *Romanische Philologie* 33 (1979–1980): 467–79; R. M. Wilson, "English and French in England 1100–1300," *History* 28 (1943): 37–60. For an argument against overliteral reading of the topoi of linguistic depreciation, see Thomas O'Donnell, "Anglo-Norman Multiculturalism and Continental Standards in Guernes de Pont-Sainte-Maxence's *Vie de Saint Thomas*," in Tyler, ed., *Conceptualizing Multilingualism*, forthcoming.

[105] If Paris had spent time at Parisian schools, as his name has suggested to Michael Clanchy (*England and Its Rulers, 1066–1272*, 2nd ed. [Malden, MA, and Oxford: Blackwell, 1998], 129), he may have been capable of speaking and writing the language of

Paris nowhere qualifies or apologizes for his French. In his *History of St. Edward the King*, he argues that insular French is an inappropriate target of attack (vv. 93–96), and in his life of St. Edmund of Canterbury he presents French to the Countess of Arundel as a *langue apert*, a more open language (in the sense of "open to more people" as well as "plain," "intelligible").[106] In any event, the fact that Paris's audiences included members of the aristocracy as well as the king and queen would have provided incentive enough to write in their language, regardless of the prestige of "francien."[107]

Verse Form

Alban's long verse line of (usually) twelve syllables is the meter of the *chansons de geste* and a number of other narrative genres, mainly historiographical and para-biblical, in twelfth- to fourteenth-century England.[108] Paris's choice of

---

Paris. There is nothing in *Alban*, however, to suggest that Paris wanted to write in anything but "the king's French." Henry's queen Eleanor, like her sister Marguerite, queen of Louis IX of France, presumably would have had some regional form of Occitan as her mother tongue and may also have acquired some form of continental French as a second language while she was still a child; later, as queen of England, she would have acquired a command of English court French (Howell, *Eleanor of Provence*, 6). Louis IX was at different times perceived to be Henry's political and cultural rival, and Paris distrusted the foreigners from both northern and southern France who served and influenced Henry III, so his own use of the French of England may have had various agreeable political implications for him.

[106] Wallace, *Estoire*, vv. 93–96 (*History of Saint Edward the King*, trans. Fenster and Wogan-Browne, 54); Baker, "La Vie de Seint Edmond," 343, vv. 42–43.

[107] Paris's *History of Saint Edward the King*, as earlier noted, is dedicated to Queen Eleanor. See further Lodge, "Language Attitudes," 80–81.

[108] In his edition of *Le Chant des Chanz*, Tony Hunt makes the point that monorhymed stanzas of alexandrines in French of England texts are used mostly in historical and pseudo-historical works, though also in a "few religious texts." To Hunt's list of religious texts in monorhymed alexandrine *laisses* (see *Le Chant des Chanz*, ANTS 61–62 [London: ANTS, 2003–2004], 31–2) can be added a twelfth-century life of St. Eustache, by "Beneoiz" (Dean no. 543), Herman de Valenciennes's widely copied vernacular fourteenth-century "Bible," the *Roman de Dieu et de sa mere* (Dean no. 485), the brief homiletic poem known as "God's Mercy" (Dean no. 616), and an "Exhortation to Love God" (Dean no. 618). Other religious works composed in alexandrines but not necessarily in monorhymed *laisses* include the remaining fragment of a life of St. John the Baptist (Dean no. 531.1), a collection of stories of Mary and Jesus (Dean no. 482), a life of Christ in alexandrine couplets (and monorhymed *laisses*) (Dean no. 485), the so-called Charter of St. Patrick (Dean no. 552), *Le Char d'orgueil* by Nicholas Bozon (Dean no. 687) and Bozon's *Tretys de la passion* (Dean no. 688), a salutation to the Virgin (Dean no. 740e), the *Three Joys of the Virgin* (Dean no. 741), a prayer to the Virgin (Dean no. 752), a prologue to a prayer on the Virgin's five Joys (Dean no. 753), and various prayers (Dean nos. 888,

verse-form therefore creates a heroic nexus where *chanson de geste* and romance are joined with a story of martyrdom.[109] Verse lines are organized into monorhymed *laisses* (also known as *tirades*) of uneven length, whose function is analogous to that of a stanza or a verse paragraph. As in other poems using this meter, *laisse* length may vary from only a few lines to a hundred or more. The shortest *laisse* in *Alban*, for example, is a prayer to Heraclius and a reflection on his martyrdom that is only thirteen lines long (30:1040–52).[110] *Alban's* longest *laisse* occupies ninety-nine lines (35:1270–368), consisting of a vivid sequence of pursuit into Wales, massacre, and burials there. The *laisse's* significance is further emphasized by the four pictures across fols. 40v-42r (only three survive) and five rubrics (R34-R38).[111]

Paris gives careful attention to the rhythm of his narrative, varying the tone and pacing between individual *laisses*, each of which is structured as a distinct entity that begins on a new thought or speaker or takes a new direction. *Laisse* 33, for example, in which Amphibalus baptizes a group of Verulamians, is brought to closure with *Lors les ad baptizé pur la loi acumplir* ("Then he baptized them in fulfillment of the faith," 33:1242); *laisse* 34 then begins with a brisk resumption of the narration, accompanied by a change in scene: *Tost est a Verolame venue la nuvele* ("This news came quickly to Verulamium," 34:1243). Later, *laisse* 37 ends with the memorializing of nearly a thousand new Christian martyrs: "and

---

889). St. Albans may have owned a late thirteenth- or early fourteenth-century verse paraphrase of Genesis and commentaries thereon in rhymed "irregular alexandrines" (BL MS. Harley 3775: see Dean no. 442). On the similarity of manuscript layout as between biblical and historiographical French narrative verse, see Michael Camille, "Seeing and Reading: Some Visual Implications of Medieval Literacy and Illiteracy," *Art History* 8 (1985): 26–49.

[109] As was recognized by McCulloch, "Saints Alban and Amphibalus," 777–78.

[110] In the manuscript, the *laisse* is further set off in the text-column by a rubricated explicit (*Ci finist la passiun seint Aracle*, fol. 46r, col. a, line 3), and it is accompanied by an illustration and rubricated caption on Heraclius's martyrdom (R30). On the prayers of *Alban* (28:923–35 [to Alban], 30:1044–52 [to Heraclius], 46:1762–66 [to Amphibalus and possibly also to his converts]), see Laurent, *Plaire et édifier*, 224–26.

[111] After the first illustration (missing), the Saracen troops are shown arriving on horseback at the scene of Amphibalus's baptism of their relatives (fol. 41r). They are then seen slaughtering their kinsmen in a densely depicted, furious melee (fol. 41v), the ground sprinkled with blood and covered with body parts. In the third illustration, a different tonality is at work as the bodies of the converts are presented once more, now lying peacefully under the guardianship of the wolf and eagle (fol. 42r). In contrast to the scene of slaughter on the verso of the opening, this illustration is full of smoothly reiterated visual rhythms as the roundness and wholeness of the bodies on the ground is repeated across the scene. Thus the devastation of the Saracen fratricide is visually already framed within God's larger purposes before the narrative sums up the miracle of the bodies in the brief following *laisse* 36 (16 lines, 1369–84); see James, *Illustrations*, nos. 23–5.

they recorded and preserved how many had died in a document so that it would long remain noted and read in remembrance" (37:1402–3). Contrasting with the solemnity of these final lines, which reach briefly outside the poem toward a past-in-the-future, the opening verse of *laisse* 38 steps up the pace and moves toward a new subject: *Mut en sunt curucez li Sarrazin cruel* ("The cruel Saracens were furious at this," 38:1405). Within *laisses*, thematic blocks of material are often structured and deployed to vivid effect: for an example in the original, see Appendix, Passage 3 (*laisses* 24–25).

Syllable Count

Syllable count, the basis of the metrical line in continental French prosody, is flexible in much narrative poetry written in the French of England, and *Alban* is no exception.[112] (In the following discussion samples are taken, wherever possible, from the passages reproduced in the Appendix.) The continental French alexandrine consisted of two hemistichs of six syllables each, with a caesura, or pause, after the sixth syllable. In *Alban*, the twelve-syllable line is preponderant but often depends for its realization on the general instability of weak –*e* in insular French, allowing the vowel to be counted or not, as needed.[113] This option appears to be systematically exploited particularly at the caesura in the French of England, whereas final weak –*e* was most often not counted in continental prosody, yielding an "epic" caesura. In the first example from *Alban* here, the final –*e* of *visage* is not counted and the caesura is therefore "epic":

           1   2   3   4   5 6   7   8   9   10 11 12
24:778   Le / quor / e / le / vi/sa/ge   vers / le / ciel / ad/dres/cé

But, in the case of the "lyric" caesura, –*e* at the caesura *could* be counted in order to make six syllables. Although only occasional in continental French poetry, the lyric caesura seems to have been regarded as an acceptable option in insular poetry and used accordingly. In the following line, for example, the syllable –*ne* on *guverne* must be counted if the first hemistich is to be considered six syllables:

           1   2   3   4   5 6   7   8   9   10 11 12
24:784   Deu / ki / tut / gu/ver/ne   reg/nant / en / ma/jes/té[114]

---

[112] For a concise introduction, see Jeffrey and Levy, *Anglo-Norman Lyric*, 17–27.

[113] Such fluctuation in –*e*, also part of the history of continental French, is not usually systematically exploited in its poetry. On the flexible Anglo-Norman alexandrine and "super-alexandrine" in lyric verse, see Jeffrey and Levy, *Anglo-Norman Lyric*, 20.

[114] There are also verses in which a pause does not fall after the sixth syllable:
30:1320 K'en / cest / mund / prin/ces cu/ru/nez / re/gner (3 + 7)
30:1325 Ba/tesme / of / nus / pur / voz / maus / es/pur/ger (7 + 3? or 4 + 3 +3?)

In other positions, weak *–e* is treated variably. Internally in each hemistich it may follow the rule for continental poetry by being elided before another vowel, as at the end of the word *riche* in this second hemistich:

                  7   8   9 10 11 12
12:357   tant / ri/che e / tant / fef/fé

But it may also be that *–e* before a vowel is to be counted, as in *requeste* in this example:

              1 2 3 4 5 6   7 8   9 10 11 12
24:787   La / re/ques/te /Au/ban   du/ce/ment /ad /gran/té

These variable quantitative reckonings of syllables allow otherwise irregular lines to be taken as alexandrines. Yet, given the fact that there remain many verses in *Alban* that, for various reasons, do not lend themselves to being made "regular" in the continental sense, we may question whether regularity according to continental standards is a useful approach to the prosody of the French of England. For example, "uncorrectable" hemistichs of five syllables are frequent (in lines of 6 + 5 or 5 + 6 syllables):

              1 2 3   4   5   6 7   8   9   10   11
25:835   Ki /au/tre/ment / le / dit / fa/bleur / est / men/tant (6 + 5)

              1 2 3   4   5   6   7   8 9 10   11
25:836   E / a / ço / pru/ver / sui / prest / ploi/er / le / gant (5 + 6)

Hemistichs may also contain four or fewer syllables, or seven or, occasionally, more than seven syllables (which means that the lines in which they occur may contain fewer or more than twelve syllables). The following is probably to be seen as a line of 7 + 4 syllables:

              1   2   3   4 5 6   7   8   9 10 11
25:825   Es / le / vus / sei/si / e / pris / de / mein/te/nant

The following is a line of 4 + 6:

                 1   2 3   4   5   6   7   8 9 10
12:340   Seint / Es/pe/ritz / ad / tun / quor / es/lu/mé

As for French rubrics in *Alban*, they are composed in the approximate octosyllables of the French of England. That is, they are generally of seven or eight syllables, sometimes nine, since variation seems to have been regularly permitted in insular verse (whereas continental French called for adherence to an eight-syllable line). Of the eight lines of *Alban's* R24, for instance, all built on the same rhyme, five are octosyllabic and three are heptasyllabic, a variation exemplified in the very first two lines of the rubric:

       1 2 3   4   5   6 7 8
97   Ci /de/co/le un / gluz / de/pu/lin (the final –e of *decole* is elided)

       1   2   3   4   5 6 7
98   Au/ban / du / brant / a/ce/rin

Of the eight lines of R65, four are of eight syllables, three of seven, and one of seven or eight, depending on how final –e (on *peine*) before a vowel is counted:

         1   2   3   4   5   6   7
405   Mut / met / li / reis / pei/ne e / cure[115]

or

     5   6   7   8
     pei/ne / e / cure

R68 contains eight lines, of which six can be thought octosyllabic. A seventh can be made so with the retention of final –e in *arceweske*, even though it precedes *e*, "and":

       1   2   3   4   5   6   7 8
435   Ar/ce/wes/ke / e /suf/fra/gan

Similarly, in R67, only the nonelision of final –e before a following vowel permits line 425 to be thought strictly octosyllabic:

       1 2 3 4 5 6   7   8
425   U/ne /e/gli/set/te /fun/dee

In his edition of *Alban*, Harden suggests that variation in line length is often expressive, with fourteen-syllable lines used for doctrinal and non-narrative exposition (for instance, in *laisse* 18, Alban's measured disquisition on the worship of inanimate idols and his rejection of pagan gods), and shorter lines of ten syllables for argument and dissension (as in *laisses* 7 and 8).[116] Explanations based on rhetoric have their force, but they remain ad hoc. If syllable count is

---

[115] In both continental and insular French, unaccented –*e* at the end of a line (called a feminine rhyme) was never counted.

[116] Harden, *Auban*, xviii. The versification of *Alban* was intensely studied in the late nineteenth century by scholars such as G. Gröber, W. Foerster, Paul Meyer, H. Suchier, and E. Uhlemann; for a complete bibliography, see *Auban*, ix, n. 4.

indeed the basis of poetry in the French of England, then a pattern of sustained meter (for example, one *laisse* whose verses are all in the same meter) ought to be demonstrable.

Several scholars have argued for an analysis of French of England meter based on accent or stress rather than strict syllable count.[117] In his edition of Jordan Fantosme's *Chronicle*, R. C. Johnston argues that the fundamental structure of the Anglo-Norman alexandrine is not the line but the hemistich. He offers the basic, minimal "rule" that the alexandrine in England "differs from the regular 6/6 of continental French in allowing either or both hemistichs to be shorter or longer than the norm"; as we have seen, this is also the case in *Alban*. Johnston nonetheless believes that the basic requirement for the alexandrine line written in England is still the twelve-syllable line.[118] An awareness of syllable count seems also to weigh with Paris, in spite of a few lines that range from nine to sixteen syllables.

More recently Roger Pensom has analyzed Jordan Fantosme's *Chronicle* and argued that the principle followed in this text is that of alternating stress.[119] Observing that it has been known for some time that the stress pattern in words of two or more syllables in medieval French was one of naturally alternating weak and strong stresses,[120] Pensom examines monosyllables in the *Chronicle* to see whether, when two or more occur in succession, they behave accentually like

---

[117] Robert Atkinson, in his early edition of the *Vie de seint Auban*, argued that the "general principle of three beats in each half is unmistakeable," although he admitted that it was not always easy to determine which of two or three "smaller words" should receive stress (*Vie de Seint Auban: A Poem in Norman French, Ascribed to Matthew Paris* [London: John Murray, 1876], 61). The early editor of the poems of "Chardri" reaches the same conclusion (John Koch, *Chardri's* Josaphaz, Set dormanz *und* Petit Plet: *Dichtungen in der anglo-normannischen Mundart des XIII Jahrhunderts*, Altfranzösische Bibliothek 1 [Heilbronn: Henninger, 1879], xliv). Iain Macdonald sees in the twelve-syllable lines of Jordan Fantosme's *Chronicle* a two-beat hemistich in 99.6 percent of cases ("The Chronicle of Jordan Fantosme: Manuscripts, Author and Versification," in *Studies in Medieval French Literature Presented to Alfred Ewert* [Oxford: Clarendon Press, 1961], 242–58, at 257–58).

[118] Johnston explains that because of the numerous 6/6 lines that he finds in the *Chronicle* he concludes that numerically scanned lines are primary but that "two strong beats in each half-line," or "variations of it," may also be present as a "subordinate" system: *Jordan Fantosme's Chronicle* (Oxford: Clarendon Press, 1981), xxx–xxxi and n.2.

[119] Roger Pensom, "Pour la versification anglo-normande," *Romania* 124 (2006): 51–65. He discusses continental prosody in *Accent and Metre in French: 1100–1900* (Berne: Peter Lang, 1998, repr. 2000), but a summary of the rules that underlie his views may be found in "Pour la versification," 52, n. 12.

[120] That is, a word of two syllables is stressed on the final syllable; when there are three syllables, stress falls on the final syllable, with a secondary stress on the first syllable; in a word of four syllables, stress falls on the fourth and second syllables.

words of two or more syllables. He finds that groups of more than two *atonic* (unstressed) syllables and groups of two *tonic* (stressed) syllables are consistently (but not absolutely) avoided. In *Alban* too, this distribution often appears to be the case; but there are enough exceptions to cast doubt on whether this latest analysis, applied to Jordan Fantosme alone, will also work for *Alban*.[121]

There is a great deal of useful information in editions of Anglo-Norman texts so far completed showing that the stereotypical view of insular verse as always syllabically irregular is exaggerated, even without allowing for the regularly variable syllable count, so to speak, that is apparently permitted. For example, the editor of *Corset*, an octosyllabic poem of c. 1240–1250, states that syllable count "is consistently met by the poet," except in a very small number of cases.[122] The extent and principles of variation among authors in the French of England have yet to be thoroughly studied and understood. As Martin Duffell has argued, the "norm of versifying changed over time"; while twelfth-century Anglo-Norman poets tended to observe continental rules for meter, later poets did not, and a more nuanced appreciation of Middle English influence than has hitherto been offered is required.[123]

---

[121] As an example, in the following verses the "iambic" rhythm provides three evenly spaced beats per hemistich, or six in the complete verse:

                1   2   3   1   2   3
35:1307   Res/punt / pur / Am/phi/bal / sanz ve/ri/té ce/ler

              1   2   3   1   2   3
35:1344   Tant / cum / li / pe/re / au / fiz / la / plai/e / va / ben/der

But the following six-syllable hemistich presents four beats (rather than three) and three juxtaposed tonic syllables (assuming that final *–e* of *vespre* is elided):

              1   2   3   4
30:1311   de/vant / ves/pre es/pru/ver

and a number of first hemistichs offer juxtaposed tonic syllables:

              1 2
30:1347   Ne / fail/li run/de/ment

               1   2
30:1333   Ço / ou/ent / Sar/ra/zins

                 1   2
30:1345   Li / fre/re / li / curt / su/re

[122] *Corset, by Rober le Chapelain: A Rhymed Commentary on the Seven Sacraments*, ed. K. V. Sinclair, ANTS 52 (London: ANTS, 1995).

[123] Martin Duffell, "Some Phonological Features of Insular French: A Reconstruction," in *Studies on Ibero-Romance Linguistics Dedicated to Ralph Penny*, ed. Roger Wright and Peter Ricketts (Newark, DE: Juan de la Cuesta, 2005), 103–25, esp. 112, 118–20.

Enjambement

Because of its length, the twelve-syllable line offers greater latitude than the octosyllabic couplet for making the end of a sentence or syntactic unit coincide with the end of a line of verse. So, for example,

>9:222 La nuit estoit peisible, li tens beus e seri. (The night was peaceful, the weather fair and calm)

>9:223 En mun lit fu chuchez e ferm fu endormi. (I had gone to rest in my bed and was fast asleep.)

Nonetheless, Paris freely uses enjambement, which suggests that it was a desired effect and that a well-placed *rejet* or syntactic overflow from one line to the next was sought after for semantic and poetic reasons.

The term enjambement covers various types and degrees of overflow. Adjectives can be separated from the noun they modify, as in the following:

>9:224 Avis m'ert ke **li cels** se desclot e uvri

>9:225 **Beus** e **delitables** e **purs** e **esclarci**...

>(lit.: It seemed to me that **the skies** were revealed and that they opened / **Fine** and **delightful** and **pure** and **bright**...)

More striking are instances where the verb is separated from the noun clause:

>9:229 **Un poples** cuntre lui e cruel e hardi

>9:230 **Vint**, ki sa doctrine despit e eschivi

>(lit.: **A group of people** against him both cruel and bold / **Came**, who despised and rejected his teaching)

In this example the verb *vint* is carried over to the second line, where it completes the thought. As a monosyllable occurring abruptly in first position in the line, *vint* also receives stress and creates a brief pause in the narrative flow.

These examples combine enjambement with other rhetorical devices to poetic effect. The frequency of enjambement in Matthew Paris's narrative poetry in *Alban* and elsewhere speaks to his awareness of its expressive possibilities.[124]

---

[124] See further *History of Saint Edward the King*, trans. Fenster and Wogan-Browne, 34.

Rhyme

Among *Alban*'s monorhymed *laisses*, those built on *-er* verbs, whether infinitives or past participles in *-é* (many used as adjectives), are the most numerous: five of forty-eight *laisses* end on *-er*, and four end on *-é* (for *-é*, see Appendix, Passages 1 and 3). Although the selections here offer only a limited sample of pronunciation, some features of French of England phonology appear.[125] For example, although the distinction between /a/ + nasal consonant as in *avant* and /ɛ/ + nasal consonant as in *vent* became blurred in continental French, it is a notable feature of the French of England to have kept them separate, as *laisse* 25 shows (Passage 3), with one exception: *sergant* (< Lat. *serviens*, vv. 812, 846, but written as an eye rhyme in *-ant*).[126] *Laisse* 17 (Passage 2) is the only one of the poem to rhyme in *-ur*:[127] the spelling in *-ur* masks the falling together in England of sounds that remained distinct from each other in continental French. For instance, the retention of nonpalatal /u/ in the French of England (where the continental equivalent develops into /y/)[128] yields *maur* (*mûr*, v. 550) and *seur* (*sûr*, 573), rhyming with *amur* and *jur* (from Latin close /o/ free and checked, respectively) and with other words that in continental French yielded *-eur*, such as *flur* (*fleur*, v. 588); the spelling *-eur* (as in *empereur*, v. 567) should not mislead. Feminine rhymes in *-ure* behave similarly: *cure:labure* (Passage 6, R65, vv. 405–6).

The rubrics are built on rhyming couplets but, as in the *Estoire de seint Aedward le rei* and the *Vie de seint Thomas*, Paris often extends the rhyme over four, six, and sometimes even eight verses (see Passage 4, R24, for eight lines on *-in*, and Passage 6, R65, for four verses rhyming in *-un*). The leveling of the diphthong *ui* to *u*, a French of England trait, is shown in *nuire: defigure* (vv. 237–38), and the leveling of the diphthong *ei* to a single vowel, probably /ɛ/, is attested at the rhyme in *terre: creire* (continental Fr. *croire*; R17, vv. 71–72); in England *ei* never became *oi*, as it did in continental French in words such as *rei > roi*.

---

[125] A complete tally of rhyme types in *Alban* may be found in Harden's introduction (xviii–xix). Readers may also consult Short, *Manual*, for an accessible summary of features characterizing French of England phonology.

[126] Harden finds no exceptions to this rule (*Auban*, xx): see Short, *Manual*, 40, with a discussion of exceptions, 42–43.

[127] *Laisse* 18, which rhymes in *-ure*, shows many of the same developments as rhymes in *laisse* 17.

[128] See Short, *Manual*, 40 and 60–62. Paris follows the conventions of French of England orthography: most conspicuously, the raising of *o* to *u*, as in *vus, tun, sunt, humme, cum*, etc. (for continental French *vous, ton, sont, homme, comme* or *com*), and the maintenance in writing of the diphthong *-ei*, as in *lei* (*loi*; Passage 3, v. 741) and *seit* (*soit*; Passage 3, vv. 743, 744); *dreiture* (*droiture*, Passage 3, v. 744).

Style and Treatment of the Source

Paris closely follows William of St. Albans' *PSA*, his main source, in that he includes all its narrative events. He nevertheless produces a work of completely different tonality and effect. Much of this is due to his choice of working in French and in verse, of course, but Paris brings a further range of stylistic choices to bear in *Alban*. His chief strategy is to amplify and develop his source material, most frequently through represented speech. Nearly all the speeches already in *PSA* are retained and elaborated, and their range is transformed or widened by the addition of proverbs and similes, invective, or asseveration; and where *PSA* narrates, Paris frequently turns narrative into direct speech.[129] The largest such expansion occurs when the Verulamian converts seek out Amphibalus in Wales: in the *PSA* they are said merely to explain why they have come (*PSA* 27), while in *Alban* they relate the martyr's passion in full to Amphibalus (32:1124–201) and a further *laisse* (without equivalent in *PSA*) is devoted to Amphibalus's speech in response to them (33:1206–33). Such repetition and reinforcement is characteristic of Paris's narrative in *Alban* (where every participant except the prince successively becomes a teller in his own person of the Christian conversion story) and in combination with the structuring and marking out of each martyr's passion as a separate, though related, subsection may suggest that the poem was designed for reading aloud in episodes.

As elsewhere in Paris's writings, speech or its absence is used with great flair and thematic point in *Alban*.[130] Verulamium's pagan prince is one of the best orators of the text, but his speeches are also the most suspect, the opposite of Christian silence and simplicity.[131] The prince's attempt to persuade Alban back from Christianity modulates through a wide rhetorical range, slipping between reconciliation, appeals to "reason" and self-interest, flattery, and fury as his anger and frustration with Alban mount. Here, as in other speeches designed to inflame the Verulamians with his own rage and contempt, the prince's speech makes for intensely dramatic audition (see further Appendix, Passage 2). Alban answers the prince *simplement* (19:633), a word that for Paris's audiences would no doubt have called up the Christian ideal of *simplicitas*, a way of life made per-

---

[129] So, for example, Alban and Amphibalus's early encounter is represented by dialogue from its first moment (compare *PSA* 3 and *Alban* 2); where the *PSA* narrates the heathen informer's approach to the judge (*PSA* 10), *Alban* gives the Saracen spy vivid illustration (TCD MS. 177, fol. 32r col. a) and an equally vivid insinuating speech to the prince (fol. 32r, col. B, *Alban* 14:417–44), together with an extra speech from a weeping Alban, who tells Amphibalus of their danger (*Alban* 15:456–77); the Verulamian discussion of Alban's death sentence becomes an argumentative counsel and debate (*PSA* 17, *Alban* 23); etc.

[130] *History of Saint Edward the King*, trans. Fenster and Wogan-Browne, 36–39.

[131] On the visual contrasts between the prince and King Offa (who, unlike the prince, is given no speeches), see Baswell, 187–8 below.

fect in truthfulness, lack of dissembling, guile, or ulterior motive—the capacity to "go straight ahead, without any detours and with complete rectitude of intention."[132] As applied to style in public speaking or in writing, *simplicitas* denoted a welcome absence of rhetorical purpose or effect; occasionally it would have prescribed silence. (Medieval scholars, while embracing the writing techniques of literature in Latin, were, in principle, sometimes ambivalent about the eloquence recommended in an increasing number of treatises [*artes*] on rhetoric, suspicious that it called for sleight-of-hand inappropriate to a Christian.) The link in *Alban* between pagans and verbal excess appears in the questions and arguments that the prince puts to Alban. The prince's aggressive manner contrasts with the future saint's demeanor: Alban is unmoved, controls his heart and spirit through wise moderation, and replies as one who has no interest in flattery (18:589–91), and the prince's speech becomes pagan bombast as it is thrown into relief by Alban's Christian modesty. The Saracens' own invocation of *simplicitas* to refer to "simple people" (*simple gent*, 35:1296) who cannot protect themselves against Christian spells and who are easily tricked by words (44:1652) opens up the dangerous possibility that simplicity can be credulity. No doubt medieval audiences would have been alive to the irony—as against the prince's attempts to persuade Alban—of accusing Amphibalus, the very model of simple faith, of deploying verbal trickery and playing on simple gullibility (18:589–91, 19:633). The Saracen concern for the *simple gent* is designed, like much else, to show pagan enemies as perverters of a purportedly stable system of Christian truth.

If the prince's rhetoric is excessive, so is the noise with which the Saracens are more generally represented. Cries, shouts, and screams are heard throughout *Alban* as the general tenor of Saracen response: "with violent threats and a great noise and cry" (*A haut manaces e grant bruit e criee*, 16:505), "a great hubbub arose" (*si unt grant noise cumencee*, 16:518), etc.[133] Then there is the pounding insistence of the many verbs of violence and mishandling, the repeated striking, beating, battering, crushing, trampling, stoning, breaking, crushing, dragging, pulling, and jostling in the text.[134] These are matched by lists of the weapons used in affray and by the many occasions on which people are seized and inflamed by anger or tremble and quiver with fury.[135] There are also extended

---

[132] C. Spicq, "La Vertu de simplicité dans l'ancien et le nouveau testament," *Revue des Sciences Philosophiques et Théologiques* 22 (1933): 5–26, at 7–9. *Simplicitas* is a quality associated with Jesus Christ himself in Matt. 10:16, John 1:47, and 1 Pet. 2:22. See further Erich Auerbach, "Sermo humilis," in idem, *Literary Language and Its Public in Late Latin Antiquity*, trans. Ralph Manheim (New York: Bollingen, 1965), 27–66.

[133] See also 19:620, 26:866, 27:885, 41:1501, 46:1734.

[134] See further 6:156–57, 9:233, 19:631, 20:652, 24:757, 25:840–41, 29:1011–12, 32:1164, 35:1340–42, 43:1608–9, 44:1626, 45:1701–3, 45:1730–31, 46:1748–49, 47:1768, 47:1775. See also Laurent's analysis of vv. 837–46, *Plaire et édifier*, 386.

[135] For example, 42:1598; 44:1640, 45:1698–99, etc.

descriptions of juridical and mob violence: to Alban (dragged and tousled by the mob, 16:531–34, 19:630–32, and scourged, 20:649–53); to Heraclius (two mob beatings, 25:837–47, 29:1010–14); to Amphibalus (45:1700–3). The cacophony of the mob greets the Christian figures throughout the narrative.[136]

As with rhetorical elaboration versus *simplicitas*, so too, the noise, heat, and mob violence of the sun-god-worshipping Saracens is opposed by Christian solitude, darkness, and quiet. When Christian sounds are heard, they are in another and more harmonious tonality: Saracen shouting on earth contrasts with heaven's angels "singing in clear voices" (*a clere voiz chantant*, 32:1183, 35:1354, etc.). In its extant form in the manuscript, *Alban's* narrative opens tranquilly at evening as Amphibalus seeks hospitality for the night: he and Alban speak together, going away to a little secret house for their study (4:74–75 and see further Appendix, Passage 1).[137] The scenes of intimate conversation between Alban and Amphibalus in this secluded location create a sense of interiority that parallels the material closed spaces in which their relationship flourishes, and it contrasts with the noise-filled panoramas of open, public roads and squares. Alban's vision of the Crucifixion occurs during the peace of the night, and it is in the night that the heavens open (twice illustrated in the manuscript), releasing a little of their eternal light in a great beam to show Alban's tomb to his immediate followers (32:1181–82, TCD MS. 177, fol. 46v) and later to King Offa in his dream-vision of the martyr's burial place (TCD MS. 177, fol. 57r). This Christian night, with its glowing beams of light and heavenly glory signaling a future eschatological dawn, is the very opposite of the dreadful permanence of hell's fiery darkness, the *grant tenebrur* of *nuit sanz enjurner* (44:1678 and elsewhere), where no hope of revelation exists.[138]

---

[136] This textual noise embraces not only onomatopoeia but also the broader sense of noise as pollution: "Noise . . . does not exist in itself, but only in relation to the system within which it is inscribed . . . . [Noise is] experienced as destruction, disorder, dirt, pollution, an aggression against code-structuring messages. In all cultures, it is associated with the idea of the weapon, blasphemy, plague": Jacques Attali, *Noise: The Political Economy of Music*, trans. Brian Massumi (Minneapolis: University of Minnesota Press, 1985), 26–27, quoted in Jeffrey J. Cohen, "*Kyte out yugilment*: An Introduction to Medieval Noise," *Exemplaria* 16 (2004): 267–76, at 269.

[137] For analysis of the opening dialogue between Alban and Amphibalus, see Laurent, *Plaire et édifier*, 339–43.

[138] These two economies, sound and light, darkness and peace, are sharply opposed at the moment of Alban's execution, which takes place amid the poem's typically Saracen mob noise and imprecation (27:885–89), while Alban steadily prays (27:895 and TCD MS. 177, fol. 38r). Heavenly light breaks upon the earthly scene and the singing of the heavenly legions is heard as angels carry Alban's crystalline soul to heaven (27:902–7). The day of a saint's martyrdom is often said to be a birthday into eternal life, and here, at the midpoint of the text, Paris deploys a common trope of martyrdom to great effect: Alban goes into the light as his executioner's eyes fall out: "For Alban, day had begun

In spite of the suspicions of rhetoric encoded in Christian simplicity, Paris will have been trained in the Latin rhetoric that was a traditional part of clerical and monastic schooling.[139] His bravura description in *Alban* of the drought-stricken land and people during the saint's imprisonment (21:690–712) recalls Geoffrey of Vinsauf's directions in his Latin *Poetria nova* (composed 1215 CE) for elaborating seasons and elements.[140] Alban's brief invocation of the *mundus inversus* topos (*Gravele semmez . . . ruisseu cure vers munt*, "You plant stones . . . brooks [will] run uphill," 19:635–36) and Amphibalus's apostrophe to Alban's blood-stained cross (*Croiz gloriuse! Croiz ki tant desir*! "Glorious cross! Cross that I so much desire!" 33:1206–19) are other examples of figures found in Latin handbooks. The *ubi sunt* topos of worldly transience is used by Amphibalus:

> Trespassable est li mundz e tute sa beuté . . .
> U est Alexandres li princes alosé . . .
> N'unt ore plus de tere fors saet pez mesuré (12:348–59)

> (The world and all its beauty are transient. . .
> Where is Alexander the renowned prince? . . .
> Now they have no more than a seven-foot portion of earth)

It is also found in narratorial comment on Alban's lost splendors as he lies in the Verulamian dungeon:

> Ne beit mais des bons vins . . .
> Pur lit ad roche bise si dure cum acier (21:676–84: no equivalent in *PSA*)

> (No longer did [lit. does] he drink the fine wines . . .
> His bed is a grey rock as hard as steel)

The full power of such well-established figures can be brought to bear by the briefest invocation, as when the converted Verulamians lament "their ancestors who had passed on already" (*lur ancesurs ki sunt ja devié*, 47:1795–97). For them, as for the contemporary audiences of the poem, the always haunting "where are

---

and for this man it was finished" (*le jur Auban cumence e li suens est finiz*, 27:917): for the executioner, all is "darkened" (*enobscuretez*, 27:916). For illustrations of this scene, see cover and Suggested Further Reading below.

[139] On Paris's particular interest in and collection of Latin poetry, see Vaughan, *Matthew Paris*, 259–60, and David Townsend and A.G. Rigg, "Medieval Latin Poetic Anthologies (V); Matthew Paris' Anthology of Henry of Avranches (Cambridge, University Library MS. Dd.ll.78)," *Mediaeval Studies* 49 (1987): 352–90.

[140] Ernest Gallo, *The* Poetria Nova *and Its Sources in Early Rhetorical Doctrine* (The Hague and Paris: Mouton, 1971), 54–57, vv. 770–817.

they now?" question of *ubi sunt* laments here has the dreadful answer: "they are damned forever to hell" (*ore sunt en enfer a tutdis damné*, 47:1797).

Since such figures of speech were thoroughly integrated in vernacular narrative rhetoric by the thirteenth century, it is not always possible or profitable to distinguish whether Paris is hearing such forms via his Latin training or his experience in French.[141] Certainly, at a more local level, the liturgical and scriptural resonances of William of St. Albans' prose are frequently exchanged for or supplemented by elaborations from a wider range of registers common in many cases to vernacular and Latin writing. So, for example, *Alban*'s animal similes (much more frequent than in *PSA*) are sometimes closer to epic, sometimes more biblical or proverbial. The animals who are themselves actors in the narrative, the wolf and the eagle, are Christianized forms of Germanic pagan beasts of battle and carrion (37:1386–87, 41:1549–51); but the beasts who appear in similes are often from the scriptural-didactic repertoire.[142] Some are proverbial, like the wolf or fox "spotted by the shepherd" (17: 555: see also 18:615, 18:619). Others, such as the pagan gods who hate Jesus "as a sparrowhawk does the lark" (2:50), are reminiscent of Latin figures and topoi.[143] Most of the similes associated with the Saracens emphasize bestiality and ferocity: there is none of the military respect sometimes accorded by Christian knights to Saracen warriors in the *chansons de geste*.[144]

---

[141] See, e.g., Douglas Kelly, "Bridge Works in and between the Medieval Latin and Vernacular Traditions," in idem, *The Conspiracy of Allusion: Description, Rewriting, and Authorship from Macrobius to Medieval Romance* (Leiden: Brill, 1999), chap. 3, 79–120 (summary of models of interrelationship at 113).

[142] God transforms a savage lion into a lamb in Alban's conversion (10:281); the voice of the lion revives its cub (11:317: a medieval bestiary); Satan the old dragon (11:320: a biblical animal from Revelation 12:9, 20:2).

[143] On Paris's innovation in placing proverbs in the mouths of pagans (in addition to their more frequent uses in the narrative voice of saints' lives), see Laurent, *Plaire et édifier*, 205–6.

[144] So, for example, the Saracens will no more listen to reason than would a wild tiger (15:470); are more outraged at the sight of Alban worshipping the cross than a serpent or wounded lioness (16:521–22); quiver like lions at the sight of prey when Heraclius is converted (25:827); are angrier than a bear or boar and more bloodstained than a lion devouring its prey in pursuit of Amphibalus (35:1357–58); are more furious than a lioness who has lost her cub in seizing him (38:1405–6); and resemble a lion who desires the flesh of a beast's body in their killing of him (43:1603). These implications of bestiality and ferocious consumption would go on to have a vigorous career in Middle English romance: see Nicola McDonald, "Eating People and the Alimentary Logic of *Richard Coeur de Lion*," in *Pulp Fictions of Medieval England: Essays in Popular Romance*, ed. eadem (Manchester: Manchester University Press, 2004), 124–50. For the perception of some Saracens as good warriors whose only failure is to be of the wrong faith, see, for example, the Emir Baligant in the *Chanson de Roland*, of whom it is said *Deus! Quel baron, s'oüst*

Paris's transformation of the *PSA* is founded chiefly in his handling of speech and in the widened range of rhetorical coloring with which he amplifies his chief source. His few additions of new incidents are made outside the text of *Alban* and within the continuing French and Latin manuscript presentation of the saint and his abbey: they are primarily concerned with the origins and prestige of the abbey (see Baswell, 182–86). The material for most of these would have been readily to hand in Paris's historiographic work.[145] Within the narrative of *Alban*, the chief effect of Paris's stylistic choices is to heighten the represented opposition of Christian and Saracen,[146] and to transpose his monastic source into the shared keys of vernacular and Latin crusade and *chanson de geste* narrative.

---

chrestïentet! ("God! What a brave knight, if only he were Christian": *The Song of Roland: An Analytical Edition*, ed. and trans. G. J. Brault [University Park, PA: Penn State Press, 1978], vol. 2, *laisse* 228, v. 3164). So too, the thirteenth-century historian Gervase of Canterbury speaks of Saladin as "a pagan, but an excellent soldier" (*vir paganus sed miles egregius*: *The Historical Works of Gervase of Canterbury*, ed. William Stubbs, RS 73a–b [London: Longman and Co., 1879–1880], 1:373).

[145] St. Albans' library (of which no full medieval catalogue is extant) is likely to have provided all that Paris required: "it would not surprise me if St. Albans had upwards of 1,000 volumes by c. 1200; in any statements about its twelfth-century books we have to take . . . huge losses into account" (R. Thomson, pers. comm. and paper given at the St. Albans Psalter Conference, St. Albans' School, July 2002). Information on St. Germanus's mission to Britain was available in Bede, who (in *HE* 1:17, 54–59; 1:18, 58–61) interpolates material from Constantius's life of St. Germanus of Auxerre with an account of St. Germanus's visit to St. Albans probably taken from the mid-fifth century *Passio s. Albani*: see Richard Sharpe, "The Late Antique Passion of St. Alban," in Henig and Lindley, *Alban and St. Albans*, 30–37, at 36. However, Paris does not follow Bede in having devils try to prevent the passage of Germanus's ship to England (see n. to R51:289). Material on Offa's *inventio* and *translatio* of Alban and foundation of the abbey was part of Paris's work as a historiographer of the abbey and its founder (one of his most vivid combinations of romance, hagiography, and historiography is his *Vitae duorum Offarum*, taken, Vaughan argues, largely from his predecessor Roger of Wendover's *Flores historiarum*: Vaughan, *Matthew Paris*, 191–93: see also 197–98 for the *inventio* narrative). On the most surprising addition, that of St. Genevieve, foundress virgin saint of Paris, see R49:270 and n.

[146] Paris heightens and expands the Christian doctrine and practice as much as he does the Saracen. In addition to the visual and narrative emphasis on the cross first pointed out by McCulloch, "Saints Alban and Amphibalus," 779–85. Paris narrates and illustrates Amphibalus's baptism of new converts, a matter more rarely referred to in William's *PSA*. *PSA* 27 deals with Alban's baptism as the seal of Christ, but Paris describes and illustrates baptisms at *Alban* 12:368–70, 33:1241 (fol. 42r col. b); 35:1293, and R47:251–54 (fol. 50r col. b), this last being the baptism of Verulamian citizens, the final image of the French narrative. Amphibalus's initial exposition of redemptive theory to Alban is given at much greater length than in *PSA* (though nowhere near the lengthy expansion of Ralph of Dunstable, TCD MS. 177, fols. 5r-9r). At 5:105–41 to 6:143–74,

Paris was by no means an unquestioning proponent of crusade: he was critical of many aspects of crusading and opposed certain crusades outright.[147] But for the sake of propagating his abbey's saint as protomartyr to audiences outside as well as within his monastery, he was prepared to use the conventions of crusade writing. In this way, he undertakes a form of writing much practiced by other clerical and monastic writers after the First Crusade: making historiography a form of chivalric and *chanson de geste* narrative. As Matthew Bennett has noted, it is hard to distinguish the overlapping ways in which vernacular and Latin writings fed this kind of narrative, and the influences are in any case diachronically layered as First Crusade stereotypes and expectations become supplemented by the closer knowledge of Islam gained from successive crusades.[148] Paris draws on motifs common to various periods of crusade and *chanson de geste* writing. His Saracens invoke Tervagant and Mohammed as in the First Crusade histories and in earlier *chansons de geste* such as *Roland*, but he also makes use of the Eastern emperor Heraklios's close association with the recovery of the Holy Cross (n. 72 above), a theme of crusade writing after the loss of Jerusalem in 1187 and one that perhaps also underpinned thirteenth-century development of the vernacular Grail legend. Not only did crusading require much preaching, such as Amphibalus's preaching in *Alban*, but crusade preachers were actively encouraged to cite the older heroes from the *chansons de geste*.[149] Crusade was also conceived as a form of pilgrimage,[150] and this is another image inhabited in turn by Amphibalus, Alban, and the converted Saracen narrator of Paris's text as Amphibalus's pilgrim cloak passes between them. As medieval Europe learned more about the difficulties of occupying foreign territory, salvation rather than military success became a characteristic emphasis of crusade writing: this is also underscored in *Alban*.[151]

Alban greatly expands *PSA*'s brief account of the incarnation (*PSA* 4) by placing the story of the fall (seen in terms of subject and overlord relations appropriate to the conversion of a Verulamian aristocrat) before it (5:105–21) and by adding after it an expanded account of Christ's ministry of healing, the Passion, and anti-Jewish material (6:143–74).

[147] Paris was critical of much of the financing of the Third and Fourth Crusades for instance: see Elizabeth Siberry, *Criticism of Crusading 1095–1274* (Oxford: Clarendon Press, 1985), 132–38 (Paris against papal crusade taxation); 150–53 (Paris against the use of vow-redemption as a source of papal revenues and against the friars' collection of it for the papacy); 179–82 (Paris against papal crusades within Europe).

[148] Matthew Bennett, "First Crusaders' Images of Muslims: The Influence of Vernacular Poetry?" *Forum for Modern Language Studies* 22 (1986): 101–22.

[149] Lloyd, *English Society*, 97.

[150] Trotter, *Medieval French Literature*, 45–49.

[151] Trotter locates the watershed between the traditional epic presentation of holy war and the newer, more historically accurate depiction of offensive strategy underlying the crusades in the late twelfth-century *Jeu de saint Nicolas*, where an initial defeat leads to victory via divine intervention (*Medieval French Literature*, 240–41).

Paris's *Alban* seems never to have had the export value of the vernacularizations of Latin writings by Robert the Monk, Archbishop William of Tyre, and the other crusade historians known at St. Albans (as throughout much of Europe); Paris's French text remained primarily important within elite insular culture (in spite of some attempts, such as that of the monks of Cologne, to capture the value and prestige of Alban's relics).[152] Crusade literature has been well described as creating a "fictional world with a historical role".[153] One could say of Paris that his *Alban* re-creates a historical world so as to endow it with the power of fiction and to capture the engagement of audiences beyond his monastery: that, like the world of the *Cycle de la Croisade*, the world of his text "endlessly claims historicity but is largely legendary, operating within a register inherited from fictional works."[154] Certainly, *Alban*'s combination of experimental French verse, Latin historiography, and manuscript art is as original as any of Paris's highly individual and uncategorizable works.

---

[152] There is, for example, a lack of development and quantity in later medieval pilgrimage badges of St. Alban, which suggests a relatively restricted cult (Geoff Egan, "Pilgrims' Souvenir Badges of St. Alban," in Henig and Lindley, *Alban and St. Albans*, 213–17, at 215, illustrations 214). On the monks of Cologne's claim to Alban, see 11 and n. 28 above; Thomson, "The Historical Library of Matthew Paris," shows that Paris had access to the *Historia Hierosolimitana* by Baudri of Bourgueil, as well as to those by Fulcher of Chartres and Robert the Monk; to the *Gesta Francorum*, Guibert of Nogent's *Gesta Dei per Francos*, Jacques de Vitry's *Historia Orientalis*, and William of Tyre's *Historia in partibus transmarinis gestarum* and one of its continuators.

[153] Trotter, *Medieval French Literature*, 104–5.

[154] Trotter, *Medieval French Literature*, 116–17.

Suggested Further Reading

1. Matthew Paris's French Works: Editions and English Translations

(i) Life of St. Alban

Atkinson, Robert, ed. *La Vie de seint Auban: A Poem in Norman-French, Ascribed to Matthew Paris*. London: J. Murray, 1876.
Harden, A. R., ed. *La Vie de seint Auban*. ANTS 19. Oxford: Blackwells for ANTS, 1968.

(ii) Life of St. Edward the Confessor

www.lib.cam.ac.uk/MSS/Ee.3.59 (manuscript text and illustrations).
Fenster, Thelma, and Jocelyn Wogan-Browne, trans. *The History of Saint Edward the King*. FRETS 1. Tempe: Arizona Center for Medieval and Renaissance Studies, 2008.
Wallace, Kathryn Young, ed. *La Estoire de seint Aedward le rei*. ANTS 41. London: ANTS, 1983.

(iii) Life of St. Edmund of Canterbury

Baker, E. T., ed. "La Vie de seint Edmond, archevêque de Cantorbéry." *Romania* 55 (1929): 332–81.
Lawrence, C. H., ed. *Vita sancti Edmundi auctore Matthaeo Parisiensi*. In C. H. Lawrence, trans. *St Edmund of Abingdon: A Study in Hagiography and History*, 222–89. Oxford: Clarendon Press, 1960.
———, trans. *The Life of St Edmund by Matthew Paris*. Stroud: Alan Sutton in association with St. Edmund Hall, Oxford, 1996. (Paris's own Latin *vita* of the saint, source of his *Vie de seint Edmond*.)

(iv) Life of St. Thomas Becket

Backhouse, Janet, and Christopher de Hamel. *The Becket Leaves*. London: British Library, 1988.
Bilous, Katharine. "Reading the Becket Leaves: A New Edition and Translation." M.A. thesis, Centre for Medieval Studies, University of York, 2008.
Meyer, Paul, ed. *Fragments d'une Vie de saint Thomas de Cantorbéry en vers accouplés*. SATF 22. Paris: F. Didot, 1885.

2. Matthew Paris

Connolly, Daniel K. *The Maps of Matthew Paris: Medieval Journeys through Space, Time and Liturgy*. Woodbridge: Boydell, 2009.
Giles, J. G. trans. *Matthew Paris's English History from the Year 1235 to 1273*. 3 vols. London: Henry G. Bohn, 1852–1854.
Huillard-Bréholles, A., trans. *Grande Chronique de Matthieu Paris*. 9 vols. Paris: Paulin, 1840–1841.
Lewis, Suzanne. *The Art of Matthew Paris in the* Chronica Majora. Berkeley: University of California Press, in collaboration with Corpus Christi College, Cambridge, 1987.
Luard, H. R., ed. Matthew Paris. *Chronica majora*. 7 vols. RS 57a-g. London: Longman and Co., 1872–1891.
Vaughan, Richard. "The Handwriting of Matthew Paris." *Transactions of the Cambridge Bibliographical Society* 1 (1953): 376–94.
———. *The Illustrated Chronicles of Matthew Paris: Observations of Thirteenth-Century Life*. Stroud: Alan Sutton in association with Corpus Christi College, Cambridge, 1993. Color illustrations include Henry III carrying the holy blood to Westminster, 38; Louis IX with cross and crown of thorns, 51; martyrdom of St. Alban (from *CM*), 56; Offa's *inventio* of Alban (from *CM*), 99; Saladin and Saracens in the Holy Land and Mohammed, 161.
———. *Matthew Paris*. Cambridge Studies in Medieval Life and Thought, n.s. 6. Cambridge: Cambridge University Press, 1958.
Weiler, Björn. "Matthew Paris on the Writing of History." *Journal of Medieval History* 330 (2009): 1–25.

3. St. Alban and His Abbey

Clark, James G. *A Monastic Renaissance at St Albans: Thomas Walsingham and His Circle, c. 1350–1440*. Oxford: Clarendon Press, 2004.
Crick, Julia. *Charters of St Albans*. Anglo-Saxon Charters 12. Oxford: Oxford University Press for the British Academy, 2007.
Gesta abbatum monasterii sancti Albani a Thoma Walsingham. H.T. Riley, ed. 3 vols. RS 28a-c. London: Longmans, Green, Reader and Dyer, 1867–1869. (The St. Albans' house history carried on by Paris, his predecessors, and successors.)
Hayward, P. A. "The Cult of St. Alban, *Anglorum Protomartyr*, in Anglo-Saxon and Anglo-Norman England." In *More than a Memory: The Discourse of Martyrdom and the Construction of Christian Identity in the History of Christianity*, ed. Johan Leemans. Leuven, Paris, Dudley, MA: Peeters, 2005, 169–200.
Henig, Martin, and Phillip Lindley, eds. *Alban and St Albans: Roman and Medieval Architecture, Art and Archaeology*. British Archaeological Association

Conference Transactions 24. Leeds: British Archaeological Association with W. H. Maney, 2001.

McLeod, W. "Alban and Amphibal: Some Extant Lives and a Lost Life." *Mediaeval Studies* 42 (1980): 407–30.

Niblett, Rosalind, and Isobel Thompson. *Alban's Buried Towns: An Assessment of St Albans' Archaeology up to AD 1600*. Oxford: Oxbow Books for English Heritage, 2005.

Still, Michelle. *The Abbot and the Rule: Religious Life at St Albans, 1290–1349*. Aldershot and Burlington, VT: Ashgate, 2002.

Thomson, Rodney M. *Manuscripts from St Albans Abbey 1066–1235*. 2 vols. Woodbridge and Totowa, NJ: D. S. Brewer for the University of Tasmania, 1982.

The Victoria History of the County of Hertford. Ed. William Page. Vol. 4: 367–416. London: Constable, 1914.

van der Westhuizen, J. E. *John Lydgate: The Life of Saint Alban and Saint Amphibal*. Leiden: Brill, 1974.

4. The Alban Manuscript

James, M. R. *La Estoire de Seint Aedward le Rei . . . Together with Some Pages of the Manuscript of the Life of St Alban at Trinity College, Dublin*. London: Roxburghe Club, 1920.

———, E. F. Jacob, and W. R. Lowe, eds. *Illustrations to the Life of St Alban in Trinity College Dublin MS. E. i. 40*. Oxford: Clarendon Press, 1924.

Kjølbye-Biddle, Birthe. "The Alban Cross." In Henig and Lindley, *Alban and St Albans*, 45–77. Figs. 3a-8 are color details of the Alban manuscript.

McCulloch, Florence. "Saints Alban and Amphibalus in the Works of Matthew Paris: Dublin, Trinity College MS. 177." *Speculum* 56 (1981): 761–85. Includes black and white reproductions of the Alban manuscript illustrations.

Morgan, Nigel J. *Early Gothic Manuscripts [I] 1190–1250: A Survey of Manuscripts Illuminated in the British Isles*. London: Harvey Miller, 1982. For illustrations from TCD MS. 177, see pls. 282, 283–285; for other illustrations by Paris, see pls. 292–294 and color pl. 1.

———. *Early Gothic Manuscripts [II] 1250–1285: A Survey of Manuscripts Illuminated in the British Isles*. London: Harvey Miller, 1988.

———, and Richard Marks. *The Golden Age of English Manuscript Painting*. London: Chatto and Windus, 1981. For color reproductions of Alban's and Amphibalus's martyrdoms, see pls. 6 (50), 7 (53).

Roberts, Eileen. *Images of Alban: St Alban in Art from the Earliest Times to the Present*. St. Albans: Fraternity of the Friends of St. Albans Abbey, 1999. 85 color and black and white images from the twelfth century to the twentieth: for images from TCD MS. 177, see 28–32, pls. 8–19.

5. History and Culture: General

Binski, Paul. *Becket's Crown: Art and Imagination in Gothic England, 1170–1350*. New Haven and London: Published for the Paul Mellon Centre for Studies in British Art by Yale University Press, 2004.

Birkholz, Daniel. *The King's Two Maps: Cartography and Culture in Thirteenth-Century England*. New York: Routledge, 2004.

Carpenter, David. *The Struggle for Mastery: The Penguin History of Britain 1066–1284*. Oxford: Oxford University Press, 2003; repr. London: Penguin, 2004.

Clanchy, M. T. *From Memory to Written Record: England 1066–1307*. Cambridge, MA: Harvard University Press, 1979. 2nd ed. Oxford and Cambridge, MA: Blackwell, 1993.

Clark, James G., ed. *The Culture of Medieval English Monasticism*. Woodbridge: Boydell Press, 2007.

Crick, Julia. "St. Albans, Westminster, and Some Twelfth-Century Views of the Anglo-Saxon Past." *ANS* 25 (2003 for 2002): 65–83.

Geary, Patrick J. *Furta sacra: Thefts of Relics in the Central Middle Ages*. Princeton: Princeton University Press, 1978; repr. 1990.

Gransden, Antonia. *Historical Writing in England c. 550 to c. 1307*. Vol. 1. London: Routledge and Kegan Paul, 1974.

Hahn, Cynthia. *Portrayed on the Heart: Narrative Effect in Pictorial Lives of Saints of the Tenth through the Thirteenth Century*. Berkeley and London: University of California Press, 2001. Includes black and white reproductions of some *Alban* manuscript illustrations.

Hiatt, Alfred. *The Making of Medieval Forgeries: False Documents in Fifteenth-Century England*. London: British Library and University of Toronto Press, 2004.

Otter, Monika. *Inventiones: Fiction and Referentiality in Twelfth-Century English Historical Writing*. Chapel Hill: University of North Carolina Press, 1996; repr. 2002.

Remensnyder, Amy. *Remembering Kings Past: Monastic Foundation Legends in Medieval Southern France*. Ithaca: Cornell University Press, 1995.

Short, Ian. "Literary Culture at the Court of Henry II." In *Henry II: New Interpretations*, ed. C. Harper-Bill and N. Vincent, 335–61. Woodbridge: Boydell Press, 2007.

Stacey, Robert C. *Politics, Policy, and Finance under Henry III, 1216–1245*. Oxford: Clarendon Press, 1987.

Stein, Robert M. *Reality Fictions: Romance, History, and Governmental Authority, 1025–1180*. Notre Dame: University of Notre Dame Press, 2006.

Strickland, Debra Higgs. *Saracens, Demons and Jews: Making Monsters in Medieval Art*. Princeton: Princeton University Press, 2003.

Thomas, Hugh M. *The English and the Normans: Ethnic Hostility, Assimilation and Identity 1066–c. 1220*. Oxford: Oxford University Press, 2003.
Trotter, D. A. *Medieval French Literature and the Crusades 1100–1300*. Geneva: Droz, 1988.
Vincent, Nicholas. *The Holy Blood: King Henry III and the Westminster Blood Relic*. Cambridge: Cambridge University Press, 2001.

6. Saints and Sainthood

Ashley, Kathleen, and Pamela Sheingorn. *Writing Faith: Text, Sign and Miracle*. Chicago and London: University of Chicago Press, 1999.
Campbell, Emma. *Medieval Saints' Lives: The Gift, Kinship and Community in Old French Hagiography*. Gallica 12. Cambridge: D.S. Brewer, 2008.
Head, Thomas, ed. *Medieval Hagiography: An Anthology*, New York: Garland, 2000; repr. New York: Routledge, 2001.
Heffernan, Thomas. "The Liturgy and Literature of Saints' Lives." In *The Liturgy of the Medieval Church*, ed. E. Ann Matter and idem, 73–105. Kalamazoo: Medieval Institute Publications, 2001.
Laurent, Françoise. *Plaire et édifier: les récits hagiographiques composés en Angleterre aux XIIe et XIIIe siècles*. Nouvelle bibliothèque du Moyen Age 45. Paris: Honoré Champion, 1998.
Rees Jones, Sarah. "Cities and their Saints in England c. 1150–1300: The Cults of St William of York and St Kenelm of Winchcombe." In *Medieval Cities, Texts, and Social Networks*, ed. Anne Lester, Caroline Goodson, and Carol Symes. Aldershot: Ashgate, 2010, 193–214.
Ward, Benedicta. *Miracles and the Medieval Mind: Theory, Record, and Event, 1000–1215*. Philadelphia: University of Pennsylvania Press; London: Scolar Press, 1982.
Wogan-Browne, Jocelyn. *Saints' Lives and Women's Literary Culture: Virginity and Its Authorizations*. Oxford: Oxford University Press, 2001.
Yarrow, Simon. *Saints and Their Communities: Miracle Stories in Twelfth-Century England*. Oxford: Clarendon Press, 2006.

7. The French of England: Language and Literature

Calin, William. *The French Tradition and the Literature of Medieval England*. Toronto and Buffalo: University of Toronto Press, 1994.
Crane, Susan. "Anglo-Norman Cultures in England 1066–1460." In *The Cambridge History of Medieval English Literature*, ed. David Wallace, 35–60. Cambridge: Cambridge University Press, 1999.
Dean, Ruth J., ed., with the collaboration of Maureen B. M. Boulton. *Anglo-Norman Literature: A Guide to Texts and Manuscripts*. ANTS OPS 3. London: ANTS, 1999.

Ingham, Richard, ed. *The Anglo-Norman Language and Its Contexts.* York: York Medieval Press, 2010.
Jeffrey, David L., and Brian J. Levy, eds. and trans. *The Anglo-Norman Lyric.* Toronto: Pontifical Institute of Mediaeval Studies, 1990.
Legge, Mary Dominica. *Anglo-Norman in the Cloisters: The Influence of the Orders upon Anglo-Norman Literature.* Edinburgh: Edinburgh University Press, 1950.
———. *Anglo-Norman Literature and Its Background.* Oxford: Clarendon Press, 1963; repr. Westport, CT: Greenwood Press, 1978.
Lusignan, Serge. *La Langue des rois au Moyen Age: Le français en France et en Angleterre.* Paris: Presses Universitaires de France, 2004.
Pensom, Roger. "Pour la versification anglo-normande." *Romania* 124 (2006): 50–65.
Rothwell, William. "The 'Faus franceis d'Angleterre': Later Anglo-Norman." In *Anglo-Norman Anniversary Essays,* ed. Ian Short, 309–26. ANTS OPS 2. London: ANTS, 1993.
———. "The Role of French in Thirteenth-Century England." *Bulletin of the John Rylands Library* 58 (1975): 445–66.
———. "The Tri-lingual England of Geoffrey Chaucer." *Studies in the Age of Chaucer* 16 (1994): 45–67.
Short, Ian. *Manual of Anglo-Norman.* ANTS OPS 7. London: ANTS, 2007.
———. "Patrons and Polyglots: French Literature in Twelfth-Century England." *ANS* 14 (1992): 229–49.
———. "*Tam Angli Quam Franci*: Self-Definition in Anglo-Norman England." *ANS* 18 (1995): 153–75.
Trotter, David. "L'Anglo-Normand: variété insulaire, ou variété isolée?" *Médiévales* 45 (2003): 43–54.
———. "Language Contact and Lexicography: The Case of Anglo-Norman." In *The Origins and Development of Emigrant Languages: Proceedings from the Second Rasmus Rask Colloquium, Odense University, November 1994,* ed. Hans R. Nielsen and Lene Schøsler, 21–39. Odense: Odense University Press, 1996.
———, ed. *Multilingualism in Later Medieval Britain.* Cambridge: D. S. Brewer, 2000.
———. "Not as Eccentric as It Looks: Anglo-French and French French." *Forum for Modern Language Studies* 39 (2003): 427–38.
Tyler, Elizabeth M., ed. *Conceptualizing Multilingualism in Medieval Britain to 1220.* Studies in Early Medieval Europe. Turnhout: Brepols, forthcoming.
Wogan-Browne, Jocelyn, ed., with Carolyn Collette, Maryanne Kowaleski, Linne Mooney, Ad Putter, and David Trotter. *Language and Culture in Medieval Britain: The French of England c. 1100–c. 1500.* York: York Medieval Press, 2009.

Note on the Treatment of the Text and Rubrics

Our aim has been to produce an English translation that captures the flair of Paris's verse. We have chosen to do so in prose not only because it is impossible adequately to reproduce many of the effects of Paris's verse in modern English but also because prose is as expected a medium today as poetry was in the thirteenth century. We have aimed at clear and fluent modern English while seeking to reproduce the tonal and stylistic range of Paris's text. French medieval narrative shifts tense as a matter of style, and we have consistently used the past tenses as the standard English narrative form. We have sometimes rearranged lines or word-order in pursuit of readable modern prose narrative. Where semantic differences between Old French doublets have no modern English equivalents, we have resolved paired words into a single term. In cases where the medieval French convention of using pronouns or no explicit subject at all creates ambiguity, we disambiguate pronouns by replacing them with proper names. Full line numbers, keyed to Harden's edition for ease of reference, are given at the end of each *laisse* and wherever we have deemed it helpful within a *laisse*. References to folios are by recto and verso except in the case of the Appendix of passages from the original, where reference is by text column (a,b,c,d) for consistency with Harden's edition.

Forty-seven French rubrics accompany the thirty-six illustrations in Paris's autograph text of *Alban* in Dublin, Trinity College MS. 177, and a further twenty-four French rubrics are found with the illustrations that continue beyond the text of *Alban* to show St. Germanus's visit to the saint's shrine, King Offa's discovery of Alban's relics, and the foundation of St. Albans Abbey. Translations of the French rubrics here are geared to Harden's line numbering in his *Auban* edition for ease of reference and are given their own Arabic R number and folio reference; since the *Alban* manuscript (henceforth TCD MS. 177) is not yet digitized, a brief identification of the surviving illustrations that the rubrics accompany is included in the translation. Two folios of the manuscript were misbound at some point in its career, but were corrected in the course of conservation at Trinity College Dublin (see further the essay by Quinn in this volume). We follow the sequence of the corrected folios adopted by Harden and by Morgan, *EGM [I]*, no. 85: fols. 38, 47, 46, 39, 40, 41, 42, 43, 44, 45, 48, 49.

Matthew Paris
The Life of Saint Alban

1. . . . which is so intensely feared by the devil of hell.¹ But it was not adorned with gold or any other metal, with precious stones, with ivory or walrus bone; nor did it have a setting of gems or crystal. On it there was a mortal man's body formed from wood, hanged and nailed according to the law regarding traitors; blood from his heart flowed down one of his sides.² (1–7)

Amphibalus honored this cross morning and evening, as one who was the special friend of Jesus.³ He came to Verulamium, an imperial town,⁴ a noble city almost without equal were it not stained by a despicable faith.⁵ But Saracens held it,⁶ the cause of great sorrow and evil, for they believed in Apollo, Satan, and Belial.⁷ The cleric arrived and entered at one of the main gates. He came upon a palace of stone, that seemed no mean shelter, with upper rooms, stories, and great cellars below, and the lord, sitting at the entrance to his house, a noble citizen in magnificent attire, in a robe of beaten gold with enamel clasps. His name was Alban, a high official of the city.⁸ No one was better known or more sociable: his ancestors were Roman in origin. The cleric greeted him and his greeting was this: (8–24)

2. "May God who governs all the world bless you and keep you, who seem so noble a man! I am a passing stranger who has come from beyond the sea, exhausted and lacking a palfrey to ride. I seek hospitality in the name of God who deigned to create us."

The nobleman granted it to him with a good will, welcomed him, and bade him enter. He took him aside and asked him:

"Who are you and where do you come from? Where do you intend to go?"
The other man replied:

"I have come from the east without stopping on the way. I intend to make for my own country, Wales,⁹ to preach and proclaim the joyous news of the Son of God, Jesus Christ, who deigned to redeem us: to be born, to die on the cross, and to rise again from the dead, to rescue us from hell and then to ascend to heaven, who will come afterward to judge us all at the Last Judgment, and without whom this world is not worth a penny." (25–40)

When Alban heard him speak of the Son of God, he was amazed at his words.

"How dare you," he said, "name him by whom our gods have been harmed and threatened? And how dare you preach before me in my own house that Jesus has the whole world in governance? And how did you manage to get here without death or hindrance, since our gods, who hate this Jesus as a sparrowhawk does the lark,[10] maintain their power and their law here?" (41–50)

3. "Alban, gentle host," replied the pilgrim. "You have sheltered me in your marble palace—do not turn a hardened or iron heart to my words! I profess Jesus Christ and am subject to him who reigns and will reign without beginning or end. He marks out and ordains my journey and my route: he is a greater shield and protection to me than a stone castle. I pray to him and honor him morning and night, he who keeps and comforts the poor and the wretched; who feeds the hungry and sustains the orphaned; who was born in Bethlehem; who made wine out of water when he ate at the wedding of the lord[11] Architriclin.[12] I have come into this foreign and barbarian country for you and for many other misguided Saracens.[13] For Jesus' sake, you will leave the faith of Apollo, who lies in hell stinking like a goat or hound next to Satan, the evil one, his companion and neighbor. To you I say and prophesy that you will die a martyr for God. There is no place from here to the river Rhine where the story will not be told, both in French and in Latin." (51–70)

4. When the noble Alban heard his guest, who had entered his house and been received there,[i] he was wonderfully moved by what he said. He took him aside and went with him to a building outside the city walls where they would not be seen or heard by neighbors or guards.[14]

"I marvel greatly," he said, "at what you tell me, bringing me news of an unknown God called Jesus, the son of a virgin, and who, according to what you say, was God and the Son of God. Such a thing, in my opinion, cannot be grasped or understood even by the most careful reasoning. Nor have I been taught, seen for myself, or read anywhere that God, who is of such great power and strength—who made the elements, the earth, the ocean, air, and fire, and by whom the world was created and is sustained—might have deigned to be born of a woman and to be hanged on a cross, nailed to a shaft of wood, struck to the heart with a spear, tormented and mocked and given gall to drink, and, when dead, removed from the cross and placed in a small and humble tomb like one of us mortals.[15] You are too greatly beguiled by this, too much deceived.[ii] Should

---

[i] **R1, fol. 29v col. a** *As a learned cleric, Amphibalus tells Alban how God was born, was put on the cross, then rose again: at the end, he will judge us all.* (1–4) The rubric is over the left-hand chamber of the illustration, showing Amphibalus seated and expounding doctrine.

[ii] **R2, fol. 29v col. b** *Alban hears him but does not believe him. Alban angrily leaves him and night falls.* (5–8) The rubric is over the right-hand chamber of the illustration, showing Alban, seated and listening, his hand raised in protest.

the citizens find out about you, you could not be ransomed by gold, nor could a mortal man prevent your beheading by the sharpened edge of a blade." (71–95)

Amphibalus replied: "Don't be angry, for it is because of God, who brings me here for your salvation, that I have passed through this country and stayed here. God does not wish you, who have devoted your time in generosity and almsgiving, to be damned or lost. You will reign with him as his friend and beloved." (96–101)

5. In the name of the son of Mary, who has everything under his governance, Amphibalus began to lay out his lesson. Alban heard and listened carefully and earnestly.

"When God made Adam and Eve, his companion, he forbade them to eat the fruit of a particular tree. They disobeyed him without asking his leave. God, who is just, did not spare them: he commanded them both to be exiled from paradise. Thereafter they had to live their lives in labor and sorrow, illness and death, and enter hell's prison and stay there, with all their lineage, in the enemy's snare. No one could go warranty for them,[16] nor was it in anyone's jurisdiction to prevent them from having to go down to Satan, whose counsel they had been pleased to heed and with whom they had to dwell for a very long time, until it pleased him who deigned to create us to deliver us from there. And it was necessary that the devil who brought trouble to humanity should be undone and overcome by a man.[17] The High Father of heaven who made land and sea would trust none other than his Son to undertake and complete such a great task. He made the angel Gabriel his messenger, who came to announce the news on earth and greeted a virgin in this way: 'Mary, may God save you, blessed woman filled with grace, and so greatly to be loved! You will give birth to the one who comes to save the world: you have heard about him from books and prophecies, the Messiah who will redeem all the world.'[18] She was astounded: she marveled at this, for she did not wish to have intercourse with a man. He comforted her by explaining: 'The Holy Spirit, who wishes you to be a mother, will come to dwell in you.[19] It is right that he who has lordship and power over the world be born, and that you should give birth to him, without the loss of your virginity or any harm to it, and without your knowing a man, or experiencing disgrace.'

"At that, she granted it without objection or fear. (102–42)

6. "Exactly as I am telling you, the king of paradise was born for the sake of us all and on the eighth day was circumcised in the temple. His relatives and friends called him Jesus. A very short time after he had been placed among us, he performed great feats: he cured paralytics, those with fevers, the blind, the insane and epileptics, lepers and crippled people, and those possessed by demons; he resurrected the dead and cured those with dropsy. But when he had reached adulthood and was thirty years old, and his renown and fame had grown, his enemies became jealous. He was sought by the Jews and by Judas the traitor,

betrayed for money, laid in wait for, found, captured, wrongly accused, tortured, and put on the cross and pierced through the heart by the knight Longinus. He died: then the earth trembled in all regions and countries, the moon changed color, and the sun became dark. Then the Jews, who well knew that they had failed to understand and had done wrong, became troubled and downcast; and they went from bad to worse after that, bereft, sorrowful, wretched serfs without a king.[20] But Jesus arose on the third day, a powerful lord, and rescued all hell's wretched captives; he ascended to heaven, where he is seated at the right hand of his Father. From there the Holy Spirit was sent to the apostles, whose chosen number was twelve. And from there Jesus will come to judge the dead and the living, when he will say: 'Come, my loyal and gentle friends! Receive the joy I have promised you, thanks to which there will be[21] no death, disquiet, sorrow, or strife. As for you sinners, be damned[22] to the fire that burns forever!'" (143–74)

7. Alban listened carefully and earnestly and responded in simple fashion:[23]
"I do not know your faith or your way of life, nor what Jesus teaches by way of religious observance; but if by chance I were moved by your teaching to become a Christian, tell me what I would do first, what next, and what is involved."

Then the cleric replied very humbly:
"If God so illumines and kindles your heart that you desire steadfastly to believe in the Trinity, the Father and the Son, and likewise the Holy Spirit, three persons and one God in truth, you will make of yourself a gift and sacrifice to him. For anyone who does not believe this, the eternal torment of hell awaits after death." (175–90)

Alban said angrily to him:
"This does not admit of any sense or reasoning: it cannot be proven by argument that one is three, and three only one. From now on, I renounce your sorcery, since it does not conform to what is right or reasonable."[24]

Thereupon Alban left in anger and displeasure. He went to bed, for night had come on. Amphibalus remained alone and waited: he spent the night in prayer before his cross. (191–200)

8. Alban went off to bed; he fell asleep in his bed in an upper room. But God, who would reveal his mystery to him and soften his heart through a vision, did not wish to abandon or forget him. For Alban came to believe without doubt or error that God deigned to descend from heaven and come down into the world to live and mingle with mortals and, after that, to end his life on the cross. God showed him everything a Christian ought to believe, without concealing anything. In the morning he arose with the dawn and went quickly to speak with his guest, so as to reveal his vision to him openly. (201–14)

"Fair guest," he said, "I have slept a great deal since yesterday, but my heart took no rest, nor my thoughts, for I dreamed a dream whose like you have never heard.[iii] If you can explain what it signifies to me, you will be my master and I your pupil. Whether we are parted in death or life I will always want to live by your teaching. (215–21)

9. "The night was peaceful, the weather fair and calm. I had gone to rest in my bed and was fast asleep. It seemed to me that the heavens parted and opened, beautiful, joyous, pure, and bright: God's glory appeared and shone resplendently. A man came down from above to earth: he lived on earth and was brought up there. A people both fierce and cruel, who hated and despised his teaching, arose against him and accused him unjustly; they seized him and subjected him to various torments. They bound and mocked him, injured and scorned him,[iv] beat him with scourges until the blood flowed. They slapped his face viciously. They fastened him with nails to a beam of wood they had erected, with another across it in the middle; they crucified him and crowned him with thorns and gave him gall to drink. They knelt before him in mockery and said:

"'Ha! King of the Jews, mighty and powerful, now it's clear that you are despised and abandoned. You saved others: you are that much more shamed. You rescued those condemned people and now you are being killed by them. Save yourself as you saved others! Come down now from the cross in front of all the people here and we will all worship you and beg for your mercy!' (222–46)

"He never made a sound or answered one word, but suffered whatever they did and said. He died, and in dying cried aloud:

"'Into your hands, my Father Almighty,[v] I commend my spirit, for now it is finished.'

"The whole world trembled, the sun was hidden; a great veil in the temple was torn and rent apart, stones cracked and the moon paled, the sun shed no ray of light.[25] One of them opened up his heart with a spear: as the lance was withdrawn, blood and water flowed from his body, clear to see. I saw this with my own eyes. Then the cruel tyrants were appeased, that cowardly and wretched people who had previously hated him. He was taken from the cross and buried. The

---

[iii] R3, fol. 30v col. b *Here Alban sees in his sleep what Amphibalus had told him before. His body sleeps, but his soul keeps watch, so that he sees the great marvel in heaven.* (9–12) The rubric is directly above the sleeping Alban in the middle of the illustration: above the rubric is the Crucifixion scene of Alban's dream vision: see Plate 1.

[iv] R4, fol. 31r col. a *Here Alban sees through the window what Amphibalus is doing. [Alban] wants to show him in good faith all the mystery of his dream.* (13–16) Alban is shown observing Amphibalus through a small hatch positioned between the two chambers of the illustration: see Figure 6.1

[v] R5, fol. 31r col. b *On his knees, Amphibalus honors the cross, and he sighs and weeps: neither forgetting, nor sleeping, nor dozing keeps him from performing his customary devotions.* (17–20) In the right-hand illustration, Amphibalus kneels before an altar on which stands his cross: see Figure 3B.1

sepulcher was well sealed and well fortified, but he who had been dead rose on the third day and ascended to heaven. A great crowd followed him, as glory and brightness surrounded and adorned them. Troops of angels clad in white came to meet him, rejoicing and celebrating, all of them strengthened and buoyed up in joy. They sang, and I understood[26] and remembered their song:[vi] "'Blessed is the Father who saved us all and his Son who is his equal and one with him!'

"The heart cannot conceive of the rejoicing that I heard there, nor can I fully express it to you. God revealed to me more of the heavenly mystery that I cannot reveal to you; for I do not dare to reveal it, you may be sure of that. But I beg you, fair guest and friend, tell me, without deception or error, what this vision means." (247–79)

10. When Amphibalus understood the man's heart and mind, and that God had transformed the wild lion into a lamb, he first of all, as a wise and learned person, thanked God, who created the earth and the sea, the birds, and the fish in the sea.[27] He showed Alban the cross, which comforted and sustained him.

"Alban," he said, "citizen of noble lineage, behold here the cross of Jesus who saved humankind from the devil and from servitude in hell. He was fully grown and thirty years of age[vii] when the whorish Jews put him on the cross.[28] He suffered much pain and shame, as you see represented in this crucifix. He offered no gold or silver for our ransom or pledge, but made his own flesh a hostage and sacrifice. You can accept your dream without illusion or folly on your part.[29] God has changed your heart not through the arguments of others, through teaching or words, but through revelation. Give allegiance and homage to him, as you ought to do: allegiance is as sacred and binding as baptism and marriage.[30] Do not be fickle or flighty of heart, for you will die a martyr in vassalage to him and you will reign with him forever among the celestial baronage.[31] (280–301)

11. "He whom you saw served and honored by the angelic legions in your revelation was the very Son of God, who made salvation possible for all us mortals through his incarnation. The wicked and cruel people you saw[viii] are the Jews,

---

[vi] R6, fol. 31v col. a *Here Alban recounts his dream. The cross's power allows him to see: it is no lie. Amphibalus does not conceal from him what the vision signifies.* (21–24) In the illustration Alban kneels before the cross as Amphibalus holds it: see Plate 2.

[vii] R7, fol. 31v col. b *Alban is baptized in the name of the Trinity. Amphibalus teaches him everything pertaining to salvation.* (25–28) The illustration shows Amphibalus baptizing Alban in a font: see Plate 2.

[viii] R8, fol. 32r cols. a and b *A Saracen who becomes aware of this hears all they say and sees what they do. He is eager to reveal to a prince everything they are doing and that Alban has abandoned the pagan faith for the Christian. [Alban] is accused and betrayed by this wretched Saracen.* (29–36) A double illustration shows the Saracen, first as he listens and looks to the left (i.e., back to the illustration of Alban and Amphibalus on the previous page) and then as he speaks his message into the prince's ear: see Plate 3.

who in their envy and great error condemned Jesus to death and damnation.[32] They were formerly the slaves of the tyrant Pharaoh, but God released them from servitude and captivity, gave them the gift of faith, and led them into the Promised Land. He sent his Son to them and delivered him into their power, but they never did anything except evil in return for his good, and they subjected him to suffering and death. In your vision, you saw him arise as the lion cub does at the voice of the lion,[33] and he ascended into heaven, and with him his companions whom he had already delivered from hell; and he firmly bound Satan, the bloodthirsty old dragon, in hell, where his dwelling will be forever."[34] (302–21)

Alban listened as earnestly as a clerk attends to his reading. When he saw the cross and the crucified man raised upon it, he understood what its carving and fashioning signified. With intense devotion, he knelt down and made a true confession of his errors. He prayed with tears and sighs, and, lamenting and with joined hands, he said:

"I ask pardon for my sins, fair Lord God. Ah, Jesus, fountain of forgiveness, whom I saw in heaven when I lay sleeping in my house, I become your servant from now on, subject to you. I openly renounce the sorcery of Mohammed; I do not value Apollo one jot; I disavow Jove and his brother Neptune, as well as Thetis, Pallas, subterranean Pluto, and all the pagan faith that so treacherously sends humankind to great ruin and perdition."[35] (322–38)

12. "Friend," said Amphibalus, "it will not be hidden from you: the Holy Spirit has illumined your heart. Others are taught and instructed through human agency, but you have been visited by God himself and have come to know him through his revelation. Now I beg and adjure you for the sake of God, tortured on the cross, to be a true friend and liegeman: for he has chosen you freely and you him.[36] Do not abandon him for some hollow trifle. The world and all its beauty are transient, like the flower of the field and the grass of the meadow. But whoever serves God, carries out his will, and dies in his service is fortunate: he will reign, crowned, in heaven forever. But the miserable sinners who have forgotten God, the sorrowful wretches—ah, how unfortunate they are! Where is Alexander the renowned prince? The mighty and much-feared Caesar? And the other princes who were so powerful and had so many fiefs, who had so much wealth and status?[37] Now they have no more than a seven-foot portion of earth.[38] But the soul is immortal, living forever, and will find its true home according to what the body did when it was on earth. The reward prepared for the good is great. Do not be dismayed by any adversity that evil men may do to your body or heart, for in the end you will be a martyr, tested by God; you will have the kingdom of heaven that is stored up for you." (339–67)

He asked for water, and it was brought to him. He baptized Alban with great humility in the name of the true and high Trinity. By his words, he confirmed him in the love of God and he taught and showed him the essence of belief in

God. And when Amphibalus had completed all that, he sought permission to leave, saying to him:

"Friend, do not be dismayed. I am going to my country as I had intended.[39] May you, fair host, be commended to Jesus. I believe I can be very certain and sure of you, as God himself has set his seal on your heart.[40] I have stayed long enough and I am returning to my country to convert Saracens, of whom there are so many." (368–81)

13. Sighing, Alban said to him:

"For God's sake, wait; don't leave me yet. I would be very sad and disconsolate. It would be too cruel of you to leave me alone. Stay just one week with me and teach me more of the faith I have adopted. Please, good master, grant this to me, for the sake of God!"

Amphibalus replied:

"You will not be refused this. You may be sure that I will do all that you wish." (382–90)

He stayed, as Alban had begged him to do. Because of the brutality of the wicked Saracens who were watching them, they held their meetings in the secret dwelling, where they had been before. They had their secret discussions and hidden counsels there in the afternoons and when the evenings were drawing on. It was then that Amphibalus showed Alban ancient writings about Adam and how Adam lost the right to paradise; about Abel, and how Cain his elder brother killed him; how the world was purged by the flood and then restored by Noah and his sons; about Abraham and Moses, the praiseworthy elders, and how they were both close in God's counsel; about the sacraments of the church and how they were established; and about the great Judgment that is so feared.[41] Thus Alban was well taught and instructed in many points of doctrine through which a man may be saved. (391–407)

14. Now, there was a Saracen who peered through a window and saw them, but they did not see him spying on them.[42] He heard their discussion and saw what they did. He saw how Alban knelt before the cross, how he abandoned Mohammed and professed Jesus. The Saracen hastened to a wicked prince who at that time governed the city of Verulamium, and he revealed the news about Alban and told all.[43]

"Ah, noble prince," he said, "listen to this. You have lost Alban, who has abandoned our gods and been baptized, from which great evil will result. For he is a Christian; if we doubt it, it will be our misfortune. I saw and heard how he prostrated himself before one Jesus, Son of God, whom he worshipped. A passing pilgrim, who has completely deceived him and who comes directly from overseas (he knows more about sorcery than anyone can say), goes around here preaching about a strange God whom the Jews in Syria[44] tortured on a cross. If something is not done about it, the result will be great sorrow. Before anything more happens, the person who believes me will do what a shepherd does the moment he sees a sick sheep: he will distance it from the others, for if he does not, the sickness spreads through the rest. Now you should do what I'm telling you, if you agree, and before anyone notices what's happening: have your men, who won't be half-hearted about it, search Alban's palace and chambers and take him and his teacher by surprise. Have them come here, for then the court will openly hear what Alban says to you, and everything I've told you will be shown as the truth. Take what vengeance is necessary so that everyone who finds out about it will learn from it and they will all say, 'It will be disastrous for the rest of us if we start doing such things, when Alban dies for it!'" (408–44)

15. When the cruel tyrant heard these words, he quivered and shook with rage. He swore by the great powers of his friend Mohammed that if what he had heard there about Alban was true, and if Alban had abandoned the Saracen gods, he would have Alban's head fly from his body at the edge of a burnished blade:[45] [ix] never would Alban be spared because of his lineage. Warned about all this by someone at court to whom he was dear, Alban came, dismayed, to his master when dark night was falling. Weeping, he said:

"Friend, listen to what I tell you. What we have been doing here has been revealed to that scoundrel of a tyrant and enemy of God who is lord and ruler of this country and more wicked than an old wolf. If we are both captured and led before him, he will shame you, by which you will be badly harmed and will receive foul and undeserved treatment. What does it matter about me, an aging sinner? But there would be great sorrow over you, if you were to perish in your youth, you who are God's chosen beloved: many a man can still be saved through you. Dear master, leave here, I beseech and beg you; do not be shamed by these wicked pagans, for they will no more listen to reason than would a wild tiger.[x] I'm staying, and will take with a glad heart whatever God has ordained and arranged for me, and you shall have my mantle shining with burnished gold. Neither the cowardly nor the brave would dare to harm you when they see you

---

[ix] R9, fol. 33r col. b *Alban returns to his palace before dawn, downcast, weeping, and sorrowful. Amphibalus, as a pilgrim, makes his way directly toward Wales.* (37–40) R10, fol. 33r col. b *Amphibalus, forewarned, has left the city. Weeping, Alban accompanies him; he keeps Amphibalus's cross and surrenders his own mantle.* (41–44) Two separate rubrics sit above a single illustration in which Alban offers his mantle on his left arm while receiving the cross from Amphibalus's outstretched hand. Amphibalus is dressed as a pilgrim with hat and stave, and Alban wears the cloak previously worn by Amphibalus in the illustrations to the manuscript: see Plate 4.

[x] R11, fol. 33v col. a *The Saracens find Alban barefoot and bowed before the cross. They have captured him: there is no one in the crowd who does not drag, strike, or beat him.* (45–48) The illustration shows Saracens crowding in on Alban, who is yanked backward by the hair and threatened with various weapons as he kneels before the altar. One Saracen holds the door of the chamber, ripped off its hinges: see Plate 5.

clothed in it and in possession of it, and I will take your pilgrim's cloak, which I have seen you wear here: I like it better than white ermine fur."[46] (445–77)

Amphibalus agreed to obey his counsel. They both left their secret place and Alban accompanied Amphibalus out of his city, escorting him a distance along the way.[47] What great sorrow you would have seen when they parted from one another! Alban, out of affection, groaned, wept, and grew pale. He said:

"Fair master, for the sake of God who was born in Bethlehem, pray to him that I do not yield."

Amphibalus replied:

"Have no fear of that! For Jesus is with you, who descended from heaven. I commend you to him, give you over to him, and bind you to him, so that no one may separate you from him who founded and built his church on a rock. I give you my cross so that you may never forget about Jesus."

Alban thanked Amphibalus for it and never afterward relinquished it. Then the cleric departed and Alban turned back. (478–93)

16. The next day, when the morning had passed and the risen sun shone brightly, the evil tyrant commanded all his retinue to have Alban's house thoroughly searched and to make him and his guest come before the assembled court, whether they liked it or not, and especially the man who was preaching in this country about a new God, Jesus of Galilee, who had died in Syria fixed high on a cross. They went racing through the paved streets, carrying clubs, bludgeons, axes, or swords. With violent threats and a great noise and cry, like people preparing for mortal combat, they went instantly to Alban's house. They went searching through the chambers, not overlooking any; they broke down entries and doors if they found them locked. Like people in a frenzy, they went searching for Alban, seeking the Christian who had reviled their faith, until they found a private chamber and saw Alban, who had set up his cross there, alone inside. Barefoot and on his knees, he repeatedly venerated it. His face was wet with the tears he shed, and he called on the faith of Jesus again and again for its strength to be transmitted to him. They went in, and a great hubbub arose about the pilgrim's mantle that they saw Alban wearing and the new cross that he so intensely revered. They were more furious than a serpent or a hunted lioness when she feels herself wounded.[48] They shouted aloud with cruel taunts:

"Where is this false vagabond of vile purpose who goes around here preaching a concocted faith?"

In plain and temperate speech, Alban said that Amphibalus had gone away well before dawn:

"May He who created the earth and the salt sea preserve him. I will vouch for him all the days of my life, wherever truth and justice exist."

Then they seized him and dragged him through street and roadway, one by the hair, violently and pitilessly, the other by his mantle, which they quickly tore.[49] Alban's mantle was bloodied from their dragging and shoving. Alban hung onto his cross, which he had not forgotten, and that made these wicked people still angrier. The city was in complete turmoil and confusion, and the situation quickly became known everywhere. They soon arrived at court, where a crowd had gathered, waiting to hear what the end would be. (494–540)

17. When the prince saw Alban in the strange attire that he had retained out of love for his teacher, anger and ill will made his color change. Then in a furious rage he said to Alban:
"Who are you who have so dishonored us that you have abandoned what your noble ancestors believed? Were you not a citizen of high lineage you would already have been delivered over to a painful death. Both great and small are wondering at you, wisely taught and now of mature age, who ought to be an example and a mirror for others. You believe what a foreign vagrant preaches,[50] a wretch who wanders forlornly from region to region without stopping, and who has now stolen away in secret before daybreak, like a wolf or a fox spotted by the shepherd. Understand that what he teaches is folly and error; indeed it seems that he was afraid his teaching would be proven false. He ought to have come boldly before us here like a master, an advocate, and a recognized and reliable preacher, to be both warrant and aid for his disciple.[51] But now he's proved that he is a deceiver. 'Falsity besmirches itself in the end,' they say.[52] [xi] (541–62)

"Think of your ancestors, born great conquerors in Rome and commanders of the world, noble Saracen lords of great territories who believed completely in our worthy gods. Kings, dukes, and emperors follow their ways. Repent of your error: you'll not be the worse for it. Throw away these clothes! Doesn't the stink annoy you? And that cross you are holding there, why are you so afraid of it? This sorcerer who's made off with your mantle can really boast about it. Ha, what a bargainer! But there's no one so wise, so strong, or so secure as to resist being seduced by folly at some time or another. Many a count and many a vavasour[53] has perished through treason, along with merchants in their fairs, and knights in battle.[54] You're neither the first nor the last to have this done to you. Everybody is caught unaware at some time;[55] you can retrace your steps and repent of this great folly. There is great nobility and gentleness in our gods,[xii] who are

---

[xi] R12, fol. 34r col. b *Alban, the new Christian, is dragged barefoot along the road by these pagan scoundrels to the temple where the people were assembled.* (49–52) Alban is shown being violently hustled and prodded along by a group of pagans.

[xii] R13, fol. 34v col. a *By common agreement, Alban is dragged into the temple of the sun god to worship their deity, but Alban has no interest in that.* (53–56) R14, fol. 34v col. b *Neither by threats nor by flattery can the prince make Alban yield and stop calling aloud to Jesus, who died on the cross.* (57–60) On the left side of an illustration two columns wide, Saracens attempt to push and drag Alban toward a sacrificial animal and an idol of the sun god (labeled Phebus), but he remains turned away from them and toward his cross, as the prince and his advisors look on from the right: see Plate 6.

quick to have mercy on a repentant sinner. They will not continue to be angry or annoyed with you. Deny Jesus, whom you call the Son of God, the Savior, and from now on honor our powerful gods! You will be able to garner honors and reward for this, lands and cities, grants, fiefs, castles and keeps. For the regret would be great—none greater—if you, the flower of the city, were to die for this." (563–88)

18. Alban was not moved by any of this, nor did he groan, moan, or weep. He controlled his spirit and his heart through wise moderation. Then he replied as one not susceptible to blandishments and said:

"Friend, if God happens to give you good fortune, is he higher, as creator, or are you, his creation?[56] Do you believe that I should acknowledge as a god metal or hard stone that by nature does not speak, hear, feel, or see and is the handiwork of a mortal craftsman?[57] It is ingeniously transformed by carving and painting; it is a semblance, a counterfeit—dreamed up and invented.[58] It contains demons who lie in the dark prison of hell. The cleric whom you have slandered and vilified beyond measure is not untrustworthy: rather, his teaching is true and sure, his life spiritual, holy, clean, and pure; and night and day he honors God, who made the whole world. I have this cloak of mine through his friendship, as well as this cross where the figure of Jesus is carved. I will never abandon what he has taught me for as long as I live, nor will I yield on account of any death, however cruel or violent. I renounce Mohammed, who leads anyone who serves or honors him into hell: I believe in Jesus, I invoke Jesus; may Jesus help and succor me. Whoever wishes to call me away labors in vain. If you were a people of intelligence, reason, and moderation, and if you wished to hear the truth, to act well and justly, this cleric would have come to you and not have remained in hiding or fled; but I know your cruelty, your customs, and your ways: you would no more have listened to him than the ass to the harp.[59] I warned him of all this and rightly told him about it: I told him about your evil, your contentiousness and your upbringing, and that you have always been inclined to sin and filth:[xiii] a foal does not easily forget what he has learned during his breaking-in."[60] (589–619)

19. When the crowd had heard him they protested loudly. By chance, it was the day when they celebrated Phoebus the sun god, whom they were to worship as he stood in a chariot, holding a round ruby: an image of burnished gold around which they all assembled to discharge their annual service and vow.[61] They said they would go to the temple straight away and make their enemy Alban come there, so that, willingly or not, he would see their sacrifice. The temple-goers seized him and dragged him there pitilessly. One pulled, another shoved,

---

[xiii] **R15, fol. 35r col. b** *Here Alban suffers shame, pain, and scorn for God, as he is beaten with clubs and sticks by these wicked scoundrels.* (61–64) The illustration shows Alban being beaten with clubs by three pagans.

another tore his clothes, and they struck and injured his face, nose, and brow.[62] Alban did not waver, but responded simply:

"All those I see here will have labored for nothing. You plant stones and make a bridge from ice. The sea will dry up and the brooks run uphill before I forget Jesus, who made all the world. Not for a galley's worth of refined gold or for all mortal men now alive; no neighbor, relative, or friend, either brown-haired or blond, can do anything to make me ever again honor devils deep in hell. A curse upon gods who are made of stone or wood or metal! Stone breaks up and perishes, wood burns, and metal melts."[63] (620–44)

20. When the prince, who sat as judge, saw that Alban despised their belief and their faith so intensely (he truly hated and insulted them by his speech), and that none of their exertions availed, he commanded that Alban should thenceforth be beaten without respite. They rushed up, not one disobeying, and struck or beat him with stakes and cudgels. His bones shattered, his flesh swelled, and his skin paled, and blood spurted and spread from many places on his body. As he suffered all of this, he prayed to Jesus and said:

"God who made Adam and who so greatly loved him that he made him in his own likeness, Adam who sinned through the treason of the serpent, and for whose sake and that of his lineage God sent his Son from heaven, who took flesh of a maiden on earth: may he, the powerful one who created me and put my soul in my body, give me strength and steadfastness. In you I place my hope, my love, and my delight, and I give myself to you in sacrifice, Jesus Christ!" (645–63)

21. When in spite of everything the evildoers could not prevail, they commanded him to be thrown into a dark prison and bound in chains, and to stay there until his will weakened and changed, for time does a person more damage than quickly passing pain. He was placed in chains and narrowly confined under the guard of an evil jailer to make it worse for him; he could receive no help or rescue. In the dungeon Alban did not cease to pray to God: this was his unwearying task, day and night. He endured his penance there as a means of purging his sins. No longer did he drink the fine wines lying in his cellar,[xiv] served in rich vessels by wine-bearers; no longer did he have delicious food to eat. For his hall and his chamber he had a dark prison; he had chains and shackles instead of bright golden arm bracelets. No longer did he have silk, down, or cotton from beyond the sea: no longer did he have silk counterpanes for his bed. He was hungry and

---

[xiv] **R16, fol. 35v col. a** *Alban has been put in prison: he stays there six months and more. As long as he is in prison, no rain falls in the region.* (65–68) **R17, fol. 35v col. b** *The people are dying through the misery that comes from the drought; the leaves wither and the grass in the earth: the people do not know which advice to trust.* (69–72) **R16** and **R17** are positioned over a tripartite illustration showing, from left to right: Alban being shoved into a dungeon, the palace roof, and people suffering extreme thirst.

thirsty and cold in the evening and at dinner time, and his bed was a grey rock, as hard as steel. (664–84)

Alban suffered this loyally: a faithful knight has to suffer much for his lord's sake.[64] God who beholds everything did not forget him: he commanded the elements to avenge the wrong done him in the way you will hear me relate.

A heat that knew no tempering flared from the sun. It made everything hot and bright: the wheat withered in the ground and the orchards died, as did the woods and the gardens, the meadows and herb-gardens; nor did any wind blow that could aerate them. You could have seen the leaves blanching, the young shoots burning, the great marshes drying up, and the earth cracking; you could have heard birds and dumb beasts panting, open-mouthed. People threw off their clothes, their skin sweating and darkening; to see flowers dying on their stems was a sorrowful sight. The heat did not abate at night; no clouds appeared that could shade the earth, nor could morning or evening help; there was no rain or dew in the evening or at dawn. Various sicknesses and troubles arose, fevers that made people go yellow and shaky: those with dropsy swelled up from drink and heat. No one was protected from flies and vermin. Cruel and ferocious, these great evils continued from the time that the base and wicked tyrant had had Alban held and bound in iron chains, injured, beaten, and shut up in the dungeon. An entire half-year went by. (685–712)

22. Now all the citizens were assembled, the princes of the land, the bailiffs and wardens, summoned and sent for from distant regions [*there is a gap in the manuscript: in the* PSA *the narrative continues, showing how the people's civic feeling leads them to accept the afflictions of Verulamium as the work of Alban's god, so that it is decided to review Alban's case. An elite faction campaigns for his release: he is at least to be sent before the judge (*PSA's *equivalent of the prince) unshackled. Alban is alarmed at this turn of events: ready for martyrdom, he prays for the devil not to be allowed to prevent it and at the hearing confirms himself to be an enemy of the pagan gods. There is then unanimous agreement that he should be executed at the place known as Holmhurst and a debate as to the manner of his death, for which crucifixion in imitation of Christ is first proposed*: PSA 15–17].[65] (713–15)

23. ". . . who was crucified in the country of Syria:[xv] Alban is his disciple and believes and trusts in him. The servant shall not die differently from his master, so it is right that Alban should be crucified on a cross."

[xv] R18, fol. 36r col. a *There is a great pressing forward in this crowd; each person pushes to get past the other. They fall off the bridge and drown in the extremely deep and strong current.* (73–76) **R19, fol. 36r col. b** *Alban sees this and weeps for pity; he prays to God on behalf of his enemies. Jesus hears his prayer, the dead arise, the flood dries up.* (77–80) R18 and R19 sit over a single illustration showing the pagans clustered on the bridge and drowning beneath it while Alban is led onward by Heraclius: see Plate 7. The foremost pagan in the crowd on

Many of the Saracens agreed strongly with him, but one of them replied that he could not consent, saying:

"What's right is that the arrogant Alban, who in pride and envy slanders and repudiates our celestial gods, be buried alive. That is an appropriate death for a man who abjures his god." (716–25)

Most of the court who heard him were swayed and agreed. One pagan of exceptional wickedness said:

"Now hear what sentence reason requires and demands and urges, one that causes far more harm and torment than death, debility, or disease. I wouldn't want Alban to lose his life just yet. Let his eyes be gouged out and his sight taken away: that will show and signify that his eye and his heart are both blind. He should see no one; but others should see him and be frightened and say, 'He who learns from others mends his ways well.'[66] Let him be driven away so that nothing is ever heard of him again; let him follow the man whose teaching he so intensely prizes and emulates."[67] (726–36)

24. The prince and his community of barons did not agree to that, nor did Alban's kinsmen gathered there, nor the townspeople or the town elders, for Alban was of gentle birth and good family.[68] According to Roman law, a high-born man of lineage who is condemned to death, and who is an enemy of the people but not a proven thief, should by custom and right be decapitated.[69] Alban was condemned and delivered over to such a death. Young and old alike affirmed the sentence. Everyone both great and small was satisfied with that, and they retracted the other judgments and declared them false. Straightaway they bound Alban in chains once more and dragged him out of the city. So many people followed him that the temple and the city where they had been before were nearly emptied. People kicked and pulled at him and bared their teeth and said:

"Get out of the city, go, enemy of our gods![70] What you've deserved is now ready for you. You'll die without delay: you'll die, ill-fated man!"

They grabbed at him and pulled him along, they beat and vilified him, and he said nothing but just bowed down.[71] He prayed to Jesus, who suffered on the cross for us. (737–59)

There was a great press of people jostling one another to see the judgment carried out. On foot and on horseback they pounded along. Some outstripped others, pulled along unwillingly or by their own volition. The field and the paved road were both too narrow for them. They came to a river that was wide and deep and without a ford. They found no boat or ferry to take them across, but they did find a bridge, which some got across. No one held back then: rather, everyone pressed forward to get across. The bridge was narrow and the people were many:

---

the bridge cries out in Middle English: *Ga. Ga ure castrisse foa* ("Get out, get out, enemy of our city") to Alban, whom Heraclius (labeled "Aracle" in the illustration) leads by a chain. Both inscriptions are in Paris's hand.

they struggled across with great difficulty, pushed along against their will. The young and eager swam energetically and powerfully across the wide, deep river; but some perished there, to great sorrow. Some tripped and fell off the bridge into the water, and some who swam were drowned. Alban was distressed and saddened as he looked on. He knelt down, groaning in pity. He turned his face and his heart to the heavens and said:

"Fair lord God, who formed the world, whom in a vision I saw placed upon the cross: out of your nobility and goodness, make the river subside that is troubling these people, for they desire to see what has been prepared for me."

God reigning in majesty, who governs all, who looks after all that he has created,[72] who gives high rewards[73] to his elect, graciously granted Alban's request. (760–87)

25. The prayers and soulful tears that Alban offered to God in deep devotion were of such efficacy that the river, which was deep and rapid with a noisy current, grew narrow in its channel and so shallow that nothing could float, neither boat or barge.[74] Whereas a man who swam could not have made it across before, now even the small children walked through the dry plants. The drowned sat up, returned to life, and stood up, rejoicing, light, whole, and healthy as if they had merely been asleep. The unbelieving pagans were astonished. A noble knight named Heraclius was pulling Alban up the slope toward his martyrdom, as he had received the order from the tyrant to decapitate him.[75] When he saw the miracle that testified to Jesus, and saw those who had been resuscitated praising God there in the sandy river bottom where no man had walked before, he fell at Alban's feet, threw his sword away, and said in a loud voice, within hearing of the Saracens:[76]

"This is Almighty God about whom Alban has preached. There is none other; he is the all-powerful! My entire life has been lost and wasted because I did not serve that God, but from now on, although it's late for me, I become his man and his servant.[77] Ha! Noble Jesus whom Alban prizes so much, I ask forgiveness, Lord, for all my sins. I give and commend my body and soul to you. The water shows your power by obeying you, and what men deny, perversely fighting against it, is borne out by the water in its attendance on you.[78] Man, to whom God gives reason, in his own image, and to whom God constantly calls, why do you delay?[79] Abandon Mohammed! Give up Tervagant! Profess Jesus, the true living God!" He looked at Alban with a sorrowful countenance and said:

"Pray to Jesus reigning in heaven on my behalf!"[xvi]

[xvi] **R20, fol. 37r col. b** *When the knight Heraclius sees God's great powers and miracles, he throws away his sword and falls to the ground to seek pardon at Alban's feet.* (81–84) **R21, fol. 37r col. a** *Heraclius is taken and trampled, beaten and stoned. He lies bleeding, overcome and exhausted, his heart hardly beating in his body.* (85–88) **R20** and **R21** caption a single illustration of two scenes: to the left Heraclius kneels at Alban's feet under a tree that

And there he was instantly seized. (788–825)

If they were angry before, now they were doubly so: they quivered like lions stalking their prey. Hefting a club, a pagan cried aloud:

"It's clear that you're lying, you stupid, stinking fellow! Unlucky for you that you said that! How unlucky that you went around making things up! But I know the reason and I'll tell the truth about it: the warm and radiant sun that we worship sees the disgrace[80] of the man on whom we are about to take vengeance. It is the sun that completely dried up the flood that was hindering us; anyone who says differently is a liar and spinner of tales, and to prove this I am ready to throw down the gauntlet."

At once he struck Heraclius with his fist and with his heavy club, making his front teeth fly from his gums: the blood spurted and ran from his nose and mouth. They smashed and mauled the rest of his body. These criminals broke his arms and legs; his sinews were torn and all his body was in pain, his flesh black and swollen and his face bloody. Nothing remained sound or unbroken in his body: his heart was barely warm and beating in his breast. Knights and soldiers trampled him with their feet and left him lying on the sand for dead. They took him for a corpse growing cold, without a soul, left to the wolves and dogs and to the birds. (826–49)

26. Those who were leading Alban along had now come to the hill designated for his martyrdom. They were all clad in robes or in hauberks with a double layer of mail and shields with bosses and carried broadswords and great sharply ground knives. Only Alban was unarmed and barefoot, walking on the thorns and small flints, on nettles and thistles that were sharp and stinging. There they found a great crowd awaiting them: not having drunk during the day, which is long in that season,[xvii] they were extremely hot and thirsty. They wailed and screamed and lay on the earth, and the sun, hotter than fire, tormented them. They could find no spring, river, or marsh. Some were dead, some ill, others exhausted: they trembled and cried out in angry suffering, cursing Alban and howling like wolves:

"Through your sorcery we are all lost!"

Alban looked at them and felt pity. He was moved to sorrow by the sufferings of his enemies, and he said, weeping:

---

divides the illustration. To the right side the pagans are shown violently beating the prone Heraclius: see Plate 8.

[xvii] **R22, fol. 37v col. a** *"God," says Alban, "from whose side I saw blood flowing mingled with water, command that a spring gush out of this mountain."* (89–92) **R23, fol. 37v col. b** *A fountain of living water emerges: each scrambles to drink the water, but the perverse sons of the devil are not grateful to God for it.* (93–96) A single illustration shows Alban to the left, raising his cross as he prays: to the right the thirsty pagans are refreshed from the miraculous spring.

"Fair sweet lord Jesus, whose reign is, has been, and ever will be powerful, who gave water to Moses, your beloved, when your people were overcome by thirst in the desert,[81] now I appeal to your nobleness; show your power, do not allow your people to be lost on account of me! They are your creation, though they may not have recognized you as God."

At that you could see the hill cracking and fissuring. A stream brighter than smelted and refined silver came flowing out of a beautiful spring and ran down the slope. The unbelievers drank from it, taking it in their cupped hands, and they were refreshed and sustained by the water. They did not recognize who was sending them this salvation, and they gave thanks to the sun god. (850–84)

27. Now clamor, noise, and shouting arose among them. One of the pagans cursed by God cried out:

"Through Alban's sorcery and his charms and spells, our faith and our people are in a sorry plight. What are you waiting for, you fools, you cowards, you wretches?"

He drew his sword and leapt forward. He seized Alban as the wolf does a sheep and tied the curly locks of Alban's hair to the low, short branches of a tree there. Alban did not groan or grumble or flinch in any way: he called upon the Holy Spirit and the Father and the Son. The pagan struck him with his burnished blade,[xviii] and the blow made his head fly bleeding from his shoulders. The cross that Alban carried and the hill itself flowered with the glorious holy blood that gushed from his body. A noble Christian, who secretly believed in the holy name of Jesus Christ, took the cross and hid it. Alban's spirit was carried by angels to heaven, pure and gleaming[82] as polished crystal, shining like the sun that blazes forth at midday. He was crowned with a crown of shining refined gold, set with choice jasper, emeralds, and sapphires.[83] The song of the angelic legions was heard. Alban was forever secure, joyful, and blissful. He no longer feared wicked and hardened mortal tyrants: he had arrived in a safe port[84] and been given his reward. God welcomed him honorably among his chosen to receive the realm he had well merited. But the man who had beheaded him, the miserable, damned wretch, was not happy for long about what he had done, for, as he struck the blow, his eyes leapt out of his head and down they fell; all was darkened.[85] For Alban, day had begun and for this man it was finished. The pagans were terrified and also amazed. Willingly or reluctantly, they praised

---

[xviii] **R24, fol. 38r cols. a and b** *Here a vile wretch beheads Alban with a steel blade. For the Saracen, night begins: for the martyr, brightness without end. One rises to heaven, the other descends; one is at vespers, the other at matins. A nearby Christian takes the cross, stained with red blood.* (97–104) The illustration shows Alban's head being struck off while the executioner's eyes fall out: the head remains tied by its hair to the tree, while blood gushes down from Alban's trunk to the earth and the cross is caught from his hand into a cloth. In the center of the illustration Alban's soul goes to heaven in the form of a dove.

the power of Jesus: some were joyful about it, some unhappy. They said quietly among themselves:

"It's not right that he should be despised, this God of Alban's for whom Alban has suffered mockery and death." (885–922)

28. Ah, noble martyr, who has conquered the devil! You renounced the world's glory, did not spare your flesh, and gave your body over to martyrdom for the religion of God. In heaven you now reign and will reign forever, you who prayed earnestly to God for your enemies when you dried up the water for them and then restored it. May pity seize you for all us wretched sinners, and may Satan have no part of those who worship you. You who first honored England by your martyrdom,[xix] pray to him for us; for he is the true Messiah, who, betrayed by Judas, suffered death on the cross that he might not lose us, his creation, but rather save us: let all say "Amen!" to this, both high and low. (923–35)

Here begins the passion of Saint Heraclius[86]

29. When he heard about the miracles that Jesus had performed through the beheaded martyr Alban, the knight Heraclius, bleeding and shattered, turned his face with considerable effort toward heaven and humbly thanked God. He crawled up the hill on his knees and elbows, for he wanted at least to see Alban's body. The pagan prince had mounted on his war-horse to see the marvels God had performed there, and when he arrived and saw Heraclius, who had been so badly mauled, he scorned and mocked him wickedly:

"Aha!" he said. "Heraclius, famous knight! To your misfortune you acknowledged Jesus, the crucified God, and Alban, whose head has now been severed from his trunk. Go seek your lord, your teacher and protector! You can find his head tied to a tree, where it hangs by the hair, knotted to a branch. His bloody body lies on the springtime grass. Tell him to heal your shattered body, your torn sinews, and your dislocated bones. He ought not to fail you, as you've acknowledged him as lord. Guard his body well so it's not stolen by eagles or vultures or devoured by wolves. Do as you should to see him buried, his body placed in a marble tomb."

And Heraclius replied with great humility:

"I haven't the will or taste to hear mockery and gibes. If you were wise, you wouldn't rejoice at having given Alban over to martyrdom, for I faithfully believe

---

[xix] **R25, fol. 38v col. a** *The prince who found Heraclius mocks him viciously, saying: "Now call on your master Alban! Tell him to heal your body!"* (105–8) **R26, fol. 38v col. b** *Heraclius groans and sighs and says, "You have nothing to mock here. He who has helped others today can, if he chooses, restore my health."* (109–12) On the left side of the illustration, the prince is shown on horseback as Heraclius is pointed out to him: on the right, Heraclius takes down Alban's head from the tree to which it had been tied for his execution.

and am assured that he is a crowned martyr in heaven's kingdom.[xx] He can heal me if he wants to: he has worked greater marvels than that over the course of this day." (936–68)

The prince passed on with his retinue, but the noble knight Heraclius stayed there. He removed Alban's head from the tree where it hung and placed and positioned it with the body, which lay on the ground. Behold the great miracle that God showed there! When Heraclius touched the holy body of the honored martyr, he felt himself completely relieved of his pains: his wounds were healed and his body restored. He had never felt freer since the day he was born. Then he had the sepulcher prepared for the martyr. Alban's kinsmen, his close friends, and many covert and secret Christians helped the noble knight Heraclius. They put the head to the body and wrapped it in cloth; they placed it in a marble sarcophagus and closed it up. Alban's kinsmen grieved greatly. Then they went away. (969–85)

The pagans became aware of what was happening. They were furious when they saw that God had looked after Heraclius, whom they had abandoned and left for dead and cold, lying on the hillside, trampled by horses. Now they saw him completely healthy, his body renewed, light and free as a bird on the wing ever since he had touched the body of the martyr. Because of this Jesus's renown shone and grew. They were seized with hatred and poisonous anger. In their envy the unfortunate wretches said:

"The pilgrim cleric who passed through here[87] was very well taught in necromancy:[88] he has sown his deceit very widely throughout this country. The Christians have been taught and poisoned by it. They make the rivers dry up and the grass in the meadow wither, they make the dead seem alive and the living dead, they turn aside the mace's blow or the sword's, and what is false they cause to appear as true. And this one, whom we had grown tired of beating, considering him carrion for the wolves and dogs, is now as whole and quick as a molted goshawk, so much has he been enchanted by spells and rites.[89] But by the faith that we owe the fearsome Mohammed, all this won't be worth a rusty spur to him." (986–1009)

Then they tormented Heraclius again, and much more than before. They beat him with bludgeons, trampled him underfoot, stoned him with rocks, injured and wounded him. When they had done whatever they felt like doing, one of them severed Heraclius's head from his body with a sword. His soul departed, his body fell back on the ground, and his kinsmen and friends hid it in the earth. His deathless spirit reigns in the starry heaven, possessed of the reward he so much desired. God

---

[xx] R27, fol. 47r col. a *With care and concern, Heraclius puts the body of Alban in a sepulcher. When he touches the martyr's body, he feels himself eased, healthy, and sound.* (113–16) R28, fol. 47r col. b *Alban's relatives and kinsmen, as well as the free Christians who had not previously revealed themselves, help the knight.* (117–20) A single illustration across both text columns shows Heraclius arranging Alban's body in a sarcophagus, while Alban's head is reverently passed over to him and male and female mourners look on. To the right a mourner gestures toward Alban's cross, held by another onlooker.

in his majesty welcomed him among the glorious and crowned holy martyrs, his chosen ones, and he was enrolled in Alban's retinue to receive a kingdom which will never end. The miserable wretches who martyred him are held and damned in the evil one's prison forever, without ransom or rescue. (1010–25)

Now they all departed and went back into their city. They thought they had worked their will, enough to have destroyed Christianity.[90] But they scarcely knew what God had planned. An overflowing river is hard to control, a mountain dwelling cannot be hidden.[91] Among the worthiest, wealthiest, and most propertied of their citizens, there were a good thousand or more who had sincerely given themselves to God.[xxi] They said and swore that they would not weaken, however much they were attacked or tormented for it, because they were sure about the great miracles that God had deigned to show to his special martyrs, Alban and his companion Heraclius. (1026–39)

30. Heraclius lives in eternal and everlasting glory and no longer fears any tyrant, prince, or commander. His name has been made memorable in story and writing, but there is no song or story about the one who killed him. Ah, blessed martyr, now help those who are well disposed and loving toward you! You who already possess the longed-for reward and who will reign forever in everlasting joy, pray for us sinners to the heavenly king so that he may keep us from the devil's perdition! May he who is so powerful and so merciful[xxii] grant us the joy that is truly blissful at our departure from this transient world. (1040–52)

Here ends the passion of St. Heraclius

Here begins the passion of St. Amphibalus

31. Alban's martyrdom was finished and over. The people who were there had left the place. The sun was already setting and the day turning to evening, the air growing dark with the night's advance. The pagans took their rest, asleep in their beds. Jesus, who had by no means forgotten Alban, revealed Alban's glory in the following way. The air was clear and calm, without a cloud, and a beam came down from the heavens, shining with a flame brighter than the midday sun, and fixed itself at Alban's tomb.[92] The heavens opened and fair angels descended and rose

---

[xxi] **R29, fol. 47v col. b** *Out of jealousy the pagans say that it is entirely through necromancy that Heraclius's body has been healed. They resume tormenting him.* (121–24) The illustration shows Heraclius (again labeled "Aracle") being attacked by pagans, who use various weapons.

[xxii] **R30, fol. 46r col. a and col. b** *They wound and trample, beat and stone Heraclius, the noble knight, who is baptized in his own blood. At the end of all this, one of them beheads him: Heraclius's soul departs and flies to heaven. The martyrs live in glory: their memory will never die.* (126–32) The illustration shows the beheading of Heraclius (again labeled "Aracle" in Paris's hand) by the pagans while his soul flies to heaven in the form of a dove.

again, singing and rejoicing.[93] [xxiii] Watchmen and pagan shepherds, alerted by this, marveled and were amazed.[94] Young and old alike clearly saw Alban's tomb, which was completely illuminated. The pagans saw the angels: they were more beautiful than a rose or a flowering lily, and this is what they were heard to sing: "Alban, who suffered death on earth for Jesus, is crowned as a glorious and shining martyr." (1053–74)

A Saracen who was wiser and bolder than the rest spoke straightaway to the others around him and said to them:

"Citizens, neighbors, kinsmen, friends! All of you, listen to me and to what I say to you and advise you to do. For a long time we have followed the Saracen gods, as did our ancestors, who are now dead, their bodies rotted away, and who have all gone the same way, to the prison of hell (unless God had mercy on them), where they are buried. If we don't take care, we will be too. I beg and entreat you, let us do penance, each for himself, for as long as we are alive here in this world, so that we are not lost. Let us seek that Christian who converted Alban, and who as a wanderer sought housing and shelter here: now we know that he was neither a vagabond nor a fraud. We can be confident that his disciple Alban, who is saved and healed, witnesses to his goodness. The master's wisdom is demonstrated in the disciple, whom the air obeyed during the great drought; by the earth that yielded neither fruit nor grass for half a year; by the water he took away from us that then sprang from the hillside; and by the flame that shone and blazed at his tomb. The four elements have all served him well, as have the gladdened and rejoicing angels of heaven. He is nobly invested with the reward that he well merited through his earthly martyrdom. I henceforth renounce the gods I have served, for they are treasonous enemies to the lineage of humankind. I openly renounce Jove and lord Phoebus, watery Neptune, and dark Pluto. From now on I acknowledge Jesus and entrust myself to him."[95] (1075–105)

The others all responded in concert with a single cry:

"And we say the same: let us be brothers united! We will never allow ourselves to be weakened or turned away from the love of him for fear of the burnished blade!"

They swore oaths to each other and pledged their faith that they would not abandon their undertaking for anyone.[96] At once they made their way directly toward Wales[xxiv] and carried with them the cross of the crucified, Alban's blood

---

[xxiii] **R31, fol. 46v cols. a and b** *That night a beam from heaven brighter than any light appears in the sky, and a resplendent brightness comes down over Alban's tomb. Shepherds, watchmen, and pagans are alerted by this and marvel greatly.* (133-38) In the illustration an inscription around the light as it strikes the tomb reads "Auba*n est* martir glorius en ciel curunez ca sus" (James, *Illustrations*, 25, reads "desvs"): "Alban is a glorious martyr crowned in heaven above."

[xxiv] **R32, fol. 39r cols. a and b** *A thousand citizens have assembled. They say, "Let us seek this Christian who converted Alban." At once they set off toward Wales looking for him. As a sign*

visible on it, hardened and sticking. There were a thousand of them, except for one who stayed behind. He had become sick and was pale with the illness that befell him. A mortal illness attacked his heart, and he remained by the roadside, waiting and languishing there until Amphibalus returned.[97] (1106–19)

32. These citizens went searching through the country until they found Amphibalus preaching in Wales, performing great wonders and baptizing pagans. The man who carried the cross greeted him first:

"Friend!" he said. "May Jesus the omnipotent keep you! For his sake, I beg, give us a hearing. We were all rich and powerful citizens in Verulamium, where you lodged with Alban when you passed through Britain coming from the east. I shall tell you the truth about what happened then. You caused Alban to abandon the faith of Tervagant and you baptized him, if you remember. You were both betrayed to a cruel tyrant. Alban, who was warned by one of his well-wishers, led you out of there before dawn. He gave you his robe embroidered with shining gold, and you gave him your cross to keep. Alban was immediately arrested the next day. He openly acknowledged what he had done and concealed nothing. Then he was imprisoned for six months on end; for half a year, there was no rain at all on the earth, because of which we incurred great loss, more than at any time before. The peasant farmers lost corn and fruit, and all green things withered and perished. We saw that it was because of Alban that these evils continued. He was taken from the prison in the sight of all the court, barefoot, thin, and pale, like a penitent. We believed that he would already be regretting what he had done, but he was as firm and stable as iron or a diamond. No living man could conquer him or make him flinch. We offered him enough jewels, silver, and gold coins, but he did not value the whole of it at a spur.[98] He was condemned to death and led outside the city toward the rising sun. (1120–53)

"In crossing over a bridge where the water was raging underneath, knights and soldiers fell and perished. When Alban saw this, he said, sighing:

"'God, who deigned to create man in your image, now make good this misfortune.'

"And there they were, coming up again, the water all dried up! On account of that they went about praising God. Heraclius, a brave and venturesome knight, who was leading Alban, bound in chains, threw away his sword and gave himself to Jesus from that moment on. He did not value our gods at a glove.[99] We left him for dead, lying at the foot of the hill, beaten and battered, trampled and bleeding. Following that, we saw many people suffering from thirst. Through Alban's prayer there arose from the slope a cold and clear spring with a strong current. Now some said—but

---

they carry with them Alban's bloodied cross. One of them, overtaken by illness on the road, does not go with them. (139–46) A single rubric runs across the top of the illustration, which covers two columns and shows the Verulamians leaving their city on the left and their progress through Wales with Alban's cross on the right.

they were falsely inventing it—that it was the power of the sun's rays, bringing us this comfort for taking vengeance against the enemies who were opposed to him. Under a tree growing on the hill Alban was beheaded, praying to God on his knees. But the man who struck him did not go around boasting about it, for both his eyes fell straight out of his head. Meanwhile I seized Alban's cross on which his blood was visible, for many of us understood and had no doubt that Jesus governs heaven and earth, and Alban with him as his faithful servant. The next night after that, a gleaming ray from heaven shone down on Alban's tomb. Angels appeared there, singing in clear voices:

"'Alban is a glorious martyr reigning in heaven.'

"We all saw what I'm telling you. (1154–85)

"You see here Alban's cross that, as he died, he stained with the blood that flowed down his body. Because of this, we have all come together with one mind. We are a thousand in number (lacking only one, who was sick and stayed behind), seeking only you, for the love of Jesus about whom you preach and for whom we have left wife, home, and child. As all these others did, we ask for baptism; you are a cleric and you have learned about it by reading your books. Tell us what is necessary for salvation: we are ready to do everything with cheerful and joyful hearts. Not for flattery, the threat of death, or the promise of transient riches will we fail to carry out your command with zeal. Whoever sheds his blood for God in this world is healed; whoever holds back in fear of death is no true loving friend."[100] (1186–201)

33. When Amphibalus saw them holding the cross stained with the blood of Alban, he knew they had told their tale without lying. He heaved a deep sigh and could not restrain himself from moaning and weeping. He said:

"Glorious cross! Cross that I so much desire! Cross more desirable than emeralds or sapphires![101] Most glorious cross, when I gaze upon you, I certainly ought to remember noble Alban, who deigned to welcome me when I was passing through.[xxv] He looked after me in his palace with great honor, so courteously loving and caring for me that he graced and clothed me with his embroidered robe to keep me safe from my mortal enemies. Not only did he understand my teaching, but he obeyed

---

[xxv] **R33, fol. 40r cols. a and b** *The citizens of Verulamium seek Amphibalus by following the news of him. They find him preaching and baptizing Saracens in Wales. They tell him the story of Alban: they show him the cross on which the blood is visible as a memorial sign, and he readily recognizes the cross.* (149–54) On the left the Verulamians hold up Alban's cross; on the right new converts cluster under a heavenly maniple, waiting to take off their Saracen hats and join their naked relatives in baptismal tubs. In the center, Amphibalus reaches out to the cross with his right hand while his left blesses the head of a convert in the tub. **R33:152 sign and commemoration** *enseingnes . . . memoire* Harden emends MS *e memoire to e[n] memoire*: but given the quasi-technical use of *memoire* in connection with the memory of the martyrs, it seems appropriate to leave the line as a double description of the cross.

my commands so faithfully that he wanted never to break or infringe them, or to falter or yield because of long imprisonment, or to deliver his body from torment and death. Now I beg and pray to you, ah! glorious martyr! Grant me, through your help, to come to the martyrdom through which I may reach the great reward that God was pleased to give to you. Pray to him, who wished to disclose his mysteries to you and to convert you to himself through a vision, that he may allow me by his grace to end this life in torment and insult and to suffer death for him; and, through your example, to merit the glory of heaven. May God grant that I come forever into your company that I have so greatly desired. And you, noble citizens, whom it has pleased to choose Jesus the son of Mary and to relinquish Mohammed, does it please you then to love without treason or betrayal and to acknowledge God and faithfully serve him?"[102]

And they all replied, "Yes! without a moment's doubt! We won't stop even as our heads are given to the sword's blade, or on account of deceits, gifts, or blandishments."

When Amphibalus had confessed them thoroughly, he preached a sermon, which they were extremely pleased to hear, on the Trinity, in which a Christian must believe without fail if he does not wish to perish.[103] They responded:

"Lord, just as you will."

Then he baptized them in fulfillment of the faith. (1202–42)[xxvi]

34. This news came quickly to Verulamium, and the prince burned and blazed, aflame with anger. He summoned his vassals, his allies, and his closest advisors.

"Lords," he said, "this evil, by which the honor of the sovereign gods is already unsteady and teetering, is being greatly increased and renewed through a wretched vagabond of a cleric who hops around the land barefoot and tattered, clad in an old tunic. But he knows more about sorcery, magic, and sly stories than a hammering blacksmith knows about tongs. He goes around preaching about Mary, a simple handmaiden,[104] who gave birth to Jesus and fed him from her breast and who remained a virgin mother after the birth.[105] He says that it's the true faith that her son is God and man, and that this God who made humanity male and female in paradise afterward became man and suffered a hard and cruel death on the cross. The prophecy of the ancients confirms and seals this, but it's a fiction, a fabrication, a fable fit to be sung to rote or viol, no more to be believed than the wind that blows in the air, for both Jesus and Mary were like other mortals. Wherefore, by the faith I owe Pallas and Diana the beautiful, I'll have the heart cut out of anyone, his head and brain crushed as well, who henceforth preaches about this new faith. And I shall have this vagrant, who must be sought from here to Bordeaux,[106] captured,

---

[xxvi] **R34, fol. 40v cols. a and b** *When the prince sees this, he sends his men to Wales. He commands that Amphibalus be brought back in heavy bonds with all his Christians or all of them killed painfully and with suffering. And they depart, furnished with arms and mounted like a fully summoned army.* (155–62) Illustration removed.

and his bowels dragged out of his belly. For as long as I live, and can use a stirrup to mount a horse, I will not worship Jesus, for whom I don't give a haw. I require agreement from you on this matter, my loyal people."[107] (1243–69)

35. The Saracens replied:
"We won't conceal from you our determination to avenge our gods' dishonor. The messengers say that a thousand citizens who have allied themselves with the cleric from overseas are lost to us, our neighbors and friends and kinsmen whom we held dear. The loss will be irreparably great if we can't bring them back home. We will go there, if it pleases you to command it, to call their hearts back by promise or threat,[xxvii] or by giving away treasure on a generous scale. And if none of that avails, we will put them all to the sword without sparing any of them."

And the prince replied:
"This intention pleases me very much."

He commanded them all to go to Wales without waiting so as to conclude this great mission without delay. They went as a fully summoned army,[108] with a raised pennon portraying the sun and the moon, which they worshipped.[109] They brought saddle-bags filled with gold and silver to give away should they not succeed in any other way. For days they rode without stopping, in closed ranks, until by dint of asking they found the cleric preaching and baptizing, as was his profession. Their leader spoke first, and said to him angrily:

"You wretched scoundrel, what are you doing, deceiving simple people who don't know how to protect themselves against your spells? But if you want to escape death and condemnation, deny what you've said and give up these absurdities, so that we may return with our people here, without more trouble and upset from you. We'll make you a gift of a large sum of money. Failing that, all these people must die. No one will escape being beheaded with a steel blade. You should know that this decree has been pronounced and cannot be revoked."[110] (1270–305)

The firmest and most loyal of the Christians answered openly for Amphibalus. Without concealing the truth, he said:

"Little do you know this worthy man with whom you have begun to quarrel so vehemently. He is the friend of the true God who was pleased to create us all. You may, I hope, see the truth of this before the day is out, by seeing a sick person cured and restored to health. You know nothing of this man's strength and

---

[xxvii] **R35, fol. 41r cols. a and b** *They have found Amphibalus and found their neighbors already baptized. They take them aside and exhort them vigorously to listen no longer to the enchanter who has led them into such error. But they cannot make any headway by promising or threatening.* (163–70) The rubric runs continuously above a scene two columns wide, in which the pagans on the left encounter Amphibalus baptizing his converts on the right.

power or of his great abilities, judgment, and knowledge.[xxviii] The proverb says 'He wounds himself who does not see.'[111] May Jesus, who rules over everything, not allow you to separate us from his teaching by bribes, torture, or the threat of death. It is right to desire to die for Jesus more than to reign as crowned princes in this world. This is our decree that can never be annulled. But if you wish to share with us in heavenly joy such as the heart cannot conceive, you must abandon Mohammed and receive baptism with us to cleanse you of your sins." (1306–25)

When the Saracens heard this, their only response was fury. Without further delay or mercy for neighbor or kinsman, they seized their swords and cut down and slaughtered son, brother, and nephew, all of whom heard a voice comforting them:

"Come, my friends, who are my soldiers: you will be enlisted as faithful knights." The Saracens, foul enemies, heard that. They became all the more savage and cruel, saying that it was the preacher's sorcery: he had learned so much necromancy as a student that he could make the air reverberate and resound at will.[112]

The others died gladly, certain of praise: whoever was last wanted to be first. Over here you could have seen people being decapitated, over there, people being disemboweled, killed, and dismembered, struck down and cut to pieces, trampled by horses. There was no man who did not feel great pity. As the father went to bind up the son's wound, the brother rushed at the father to cut off his arm.[113] In this praiseworthy company,[xxix] only one was lacking for there to be a round thousand, for one had been left sick by the wayside. (1326–48)

Amphibalus watched all this, weeping and groaning sincerely: he could not look at the martyrs' suffering without himself suffering (they were martyrs of the body, but he was a martyr of the heart).[114] He brought them before God, who deigned to call them to himself, and they went to dwell eternally in heaven. Angels escorted them, singing "Glory and praise" loudly and clearly to express

---

[xxviii] **R36, fol. 41v col. a** *They do not spare those who have turned to Jesus, painfully killing even their relatives, kin, and neighbors by the lance, causing pain and suffering.* (171–74) **R37, fol. 41v col. b** *The members of this company do not worry about being killed. Even before they are completely dead, Jesus is there comforting them.* (175–78) R37:177–78 **completely dead** *ocise e morte*: we follow Harden, 73, n. to 177–8r, in translating as "it [the company] was not completely killed and dead before Jesus was comforting them." The two rubrics run above columns a and b, respectively, over a single vigorous scene of slaughter; in the top right-hand corner St. Peter with his keys leans out of heaven.

[xxix] **R38, fol. 42r cols. a and b** *Those who had previously been all cut to pieces, all bloody and trampled, are now recognizable: no blow or wound appears on them. A wolf and an eagle have come there who protect the bodies, the wolf from the beasts, the eagle from the birds. This miracle was a new thing.* (179–86) The illustration shows the bodies in orderly display under their watchful animal guardians. R38:75 **this company** *ceste cumpainnie*: according to Paris, these martyrs are traditionally the thousand martyrs from whom Lichfield was said to have derived its name: see *PSA*, n. 39.

their joy. When the pagans had killed everyone without missing a single one, they—crueler and angrier than a bear or wild boar, bloodstained as a lion tearing his prey to pieces—seized Amphibalus violently. All of them blamed him for this deadly conflict. They bound his arms as tightly and painfully as possible. They swore to their peerless and highest god Jove that they would fast, not taking even one meal, until they had brought the cleric back to Verulamium, to sacrifice him in the temple before their altar, thus greatly pleasing their gods. "We will have him killed with the cruelest death that can be devised by men as a warning to others."[115] (1349–68)

36. May God, who never forgets his own people but honors them always, cherish and cause to prosper those who love him and have their love and hope in him. The bodies, which were completely unrecognizable, without heads, disemboweled by sword or lance, became beautiful and whole at once. Their limbs, feet, and arms were all restored to them: the blood that had previously stained their bodies now looked like milk, their bodies themselves whiter than the pleat or bend of a shirt sleeve, so that they could be recognized without doubt or error,[xxx] some young, some old, some of high birth, some short, some average, and some tall. Not since their day of birth had they been more beautiful. Jesus' enemies were jealous and downcast at this; his friends, who had seen it, and who believed in Jesus as the true faith, had no doubt about it. (1369–84)

37. God performed another great deed and miracle for his martyrs. By his command a great wolf came from the wasteland, and an eagle with him, who flew down to the ground.[116] They watched over and protected the bodies of the noble martyrs so not even a hair was damaged and lost; the eagle chased away the birds and the wolf the beasts. Such a marvel had never been seen before in this world: the wolf of the forest, unfed and unsated, and the ravening eagle became guardians of the dead through Jesus' power. When the people of the region saw this marvel, they honored, revered, and feared the bodies that they had previously despised. They gave thanks and gratitude to God that such a miracle had been shown them in their land. They prepared sepulchers and a coffin for each one; they put them in shrouds and sewed them up; and they recorded and preserved how many had died in a document so that it would long remain noted and read in remembrance. The total came to nine hundred and ninety-nine. (1385–404)

[xxx] R39, fol. 42v *When the people of the region see the miracle of the slain, they learn from dumb beasts how to serve the king of paradise. They seek out a great quantity of coffins and lay the bodies in them with honor, for they have no doubt that they will reign forever in heaven.* (187–94) The illustration has been removed (some bleed-through from the image on fol. 42r is visible), but the rubric remains.

38. The cruel Saracens were furious at this, more than a lioness who loses her cub. For this trouble, so great that they had never had any like it, they all blamed Amphibalus, the cleric from the east. They seized him as the wolf does the lamb; they tied his hands with deliberate cruelty and pain.[xxxi] They swore to Mohammed and their great gods of heaven that they would not remove the saddle or saddle-cloth from a horse, nor would they sleep in a bed under a linen sheet or eat at a table, in a tent or in a hostelry, until they had brought their mortal enemy, alive or dead, to their native city of Verulamium.[117] They would give him to Phoebus as a more pleasing sacrifice than an ox or dove and make an annual festival of it. The pagans were a formidable force when commanded into battle to assail a king's army, a city, or a castle. Every one of them was mounted on a fine palfrey, a hunter, a strong rouncy, or a swift war-horse. Only the preacher Amphibalus was on foot, without shoes and entirely naked except for a cloak. They made the noble youth run before them: they cried and whooped more loudly than a pup, and they ordered him forward with lance and knife. The rocky, rough, uneven road wearied him and bloodied the skin on the soles of his feet. His blood ran and spread like the water of a brook; he ached in every sinew and his head felt weak; but whatever he suffered for God was sweeter to him than honey. Since he was drawing near to Alban, the new holy martyr with whom he desired to be, he sought nothing else. (1405–34)

39. That ailing man who had remained behind because, overcome by illness, he had not been able to follow his companions, called out aloud when he saw Amphibalus coming:

"Amphibalus, friend of Jesus who rules heaven and earth, have pity on me, I who am dying without help!"

The troop of Saracens warned him against crying out, but for all that he did not cease calling still more loudly and urgently.

"I am from Verulamium, the rich city," he said. "I have given myself completely to Jesus the son of Mary,[xxxii] since the moment when Alban, for whom

---

[xxxi] **R40, fol. 43r cols. a and b** *The pagans lead Amphibalus back, fiercely tormenting and injuring him, for he runs barefoot in front of them, while they are mounted on war-horses. None of them fails to prod him to run, to prick him on with spear and knife. The sick man sees him coming and receives the good health for which he begs.* (195–202) The illustration on fol. 43a has been removed (with extensive bleed-through from fol. 43v visible), but the rubric is in place. **R40:198 war-horses** *destriers*: horse names are too significant to be represented by a single modern term. The young pagans of Verulamium also have "*destrers*" (40:1485). For other types of horse, see 38:1421–22.

[xxxii] **R41, fol. 43v cols. a and b** *The pagans stop three leagues outside the city. The martyr does not sleep or slumber in spreading abroad the word of God. Some people come to the city to report what has happened. The citizens certainly grieve unrestrainedly at this situation.* (203–10) **R41:209–210 the citizens ... grieve** *li citoien ... funt duel:* James (*Illustrations*, 27 n. 29) reads the scene as the people bewailing the departure of Amphibalus, suggesting that

God deigned to work miracles in this life and to glorify his soul after his pure body's death, was beheaded with a burnished sword. Because of that we all came together as a group: it was our opinion that there is no other God than the God who died on the cross in Syria to free us from the infernal dungeon, and for whose sake Alban is a great martyr, whatever the envious may say. We were a thousand, leaving Verulamium in a troop, carrying the cross stained and adorned with Alban's blood, to be baptized by you, who bless people.[118] Overtaken by illness, I have remained by this hedgerow: my body is weakened and wasted away, my flesh pale and withered. I believe that if you pray for me your prayer will be heard." (1435–56)

Amphibalus took pity on him. He bent down before him and very humbly prayed and beseeched Jesus on his behalf. And there the man's malady left him: he was whole and completely healed, for which he thanked Amphibalus fervently, and praised and glorified the great power of Jesus. In response, every one of the Saracens said, willingly or not:

"What great lordship is exercised by the Christians' God, who binds to himself those who freely come to him, and who unbinds as he pleases!"[119] (1457–64)

40. They were near Verulamium and could already see the walls, turrets, and battlements of their temples and palaces. They stopped on a flat, green plain, where the cruel Saracens rested, unlacing their visors, helmets, and caps. Amphibalus alone among them took no rest. His body was weary, but his good heart was completely fresh and ready to do the work of Jesus as his loyal follower. He said:

"Gentle knights, why do you acknowledge your hellish devils instead of the God who made all us mortals in his own image? How very unfortunate that you were born in this material world, for you are very cruel, hard, and unnatural. But God is sweet and courteous and just. He calls all of you to him as a shepherd does his lambs. Repentant sinners are his particular objects of affection: the heavenly angels rejoice over such people."[120]

At that the majority gave themselves over to God to be beheaded for Jesus, and now they reign in heaven. Thereupon some of the young men who had the strongest and swiftest war-horses mounted and arrived at their homes in Verulamium to say that the eastern traitor who betrayed so many people by his false preaching had arrived. (1465–88)

41. When the Verulamians heard the news about Amphibalus, through whom they had lost their good friend Alban and by whom their kinsmen had been attracted and besotted, they were comforted and made bold by their great joy, for, as they loudly proclaimed, they would be avenged on him. One of them related what had happened: how those on whose account they had all been summoned

---

the city depicted here is in Wales. But fol. 43v more probably refers to the second and later scene of grief at Verulamium.

and assembled had gone so deeply and stubbornly into error, and were so given over to Jesus who suffered death on the cross, that they could not be redeemed for all the gold of Damascus:[121]

"We were angered, sorrowful, and distressed about it, and we cut them all down with our burnished swords."

When the others heard this there was a great tumult and outcry: their joy had been turned into tears and great sorrow. Each one said, weeping:

"Alas! Why was I born? Son, brother, nephew! What misery that I ever saw you! We are miserable wretches, alone and orphaned. You lie in the wasteland as abandoned carrion; you have not been put in a tomb or buried: birds and wild wolves will devour you. How unfortunate that you professed the God hanged on the cross! This necromancer who passed through here caused us these great evils through his enchantments. Dear heavenly gods, whom we have so long served, take vengeance on this useless vagrant!" (1489–513)

Young and old wept and lamented, tore their hair, and shredded their clothing: they cursed Amphibalus the preacher, through whom so many of their relatives had been destroyed and ruined. But when the returning pagans heard their keen lament they said:

"Restrain yourselves, for it is not as you believe it to be, dearly beloved friends. For you should know that they are not lost or destroyed: they are honored and welcomed into the glory of heaven. From the time we found them and took them aside with us, they were insistently threatened, entreated, and flattered. But we could not get even one of them to yield for a valley filled with gold, and so we killed them without pity or mercy. But each one of them offered to die first, and it weighed on the last of them that he was spared so long. You would have seen the father of the son struck in the heart as the brother reached out his hand to bind his wounds.[122] The blood flowed like a brook on the ground. Then the glory of Jesus shone out; we heard a voice, everyone understood it well: 'Come, my knights, who have served me well, from now on you will be with me in radiant paradise. In exchange for the bodily torments that are already past and over, you will have the eternal realm of heaven.' We were glad and we rejoiced that God had not consigned our people to oblivion. They lay despoiled and abandoned in those fields, where a man could not have known his own from strangers. You may be completely certain that Jesus restored them as if they lay quite alive, whole, healthy and healed, the blood that had stained them earlier blanched whiter than milk. We counted them all, in a verified and sure count, and we had it recorded in black ink: we found a thousand bodies there except for one that was missing. So that none was harmed by dogs or by other animals, a great gray wolf came to guard the bodies, and an eagle, to protect the bodies from birds. Those who previously hated them and held them in contempt have already gathered them into tombs with honor. All of us should be joyful that God has taken so many of our people for his own purposes."[123] (1514–55)

42. The pagans replied, saying truthfully:

"This Jesus who protects those who believe in him from shame or disgrace is a great teacher.[124] The cleric who preached about him, who came from the east, is not to be despised as many think and believe. If he were a trickster we don't think he would have worked such healing on the dismembered bodies. By this we may know clearly that his preaching is true without doubt."

When the prince, who was present, heard this, he was inflamed with anger and bitterness. He was so enraged that he nearly burst. Then, like a liar defending his false belief, he said:

"This fraudulent trickster knows so much enchantment that no one can say how much. I believe it's nothing more than wind. By the faith I owe Phoebus, resplendent throughout the whole world, whoever speaks well of this false rascal who openly lies to us, or attends to his words, will be sentenced to lose his head. Whoever hears these people and agrees with them is wilder than a beast. But by Jove who rules the earth and the firmament, this deception and these troubles have gone on for too long! He has done us too much damage and taken too many people from us: he will do more if he lives for long. This clerical son of a whore—it's a shame he's not hanged, but he'll never sink his teeth into food again without paying dearly for what he's done. I will straightaway take the supreme vengeance that's fitting for such a vicious traitor." (1556–84)

Then he had a royal command cried round the city and wherever his power extended that everyone, as they loved their lives and their holdings, should follow him fully armed to his destination. At this summons no one remained behind or tarried. There were so many people the roads could not hold them; nevertheless, they tried hard to go very fast, for the last man, and anyone who went slowly, would be in trouble. Some of them went by a short cut and spurred on swiftly so as to arrive early. They found Amphibalus intent on preaching, with more than a hundred new Christians around him who had just given themselves to Jesus. When the crowd saw him, their anger was ignited: they violently seized, stripped, and tormented him as the devil instructed them to do. (1585–600)

43. The despicable pagans fixed a stake in the earth and, like a lion who desires the flesh of a beast's body, drew out Amphibalus's bowels from his belly.[125] They fixed him to the stake through his navel, causing him great pain; they tied his hands to a horse's rein. They did not let him rest or halt anywhere and drove him around the stake for the length of a day's journey. They struck, beat, and pierced the suffering man with lances, knives, and large pointed sticks so that all his entrails fell out of his body. They beat him with rods until the blood ran down like a flowing stream from a fountain. It stained the breast, back, and sides of the martyr, who fixed his thoughts on the heavenly king who became a mortal man to save his servants and who allowed himself to be bound like a faithless thief to

a pillar, and his blessed royal body beaten: the faithless Jews[126] hung him on the cross with a crown of thorns as a chaplet for his head.[xxxiii]

"Ah," said Amphibalus, "this is not torture such as God suffered for me, it is far from being its equal!"

Then he rejoiced as if he had no pain at all, which made the pagans furious, those sons of Belial: they did not see what a marvel this was in this finite world. (1601–24)

44. As a result, they became more eager to torment him, to beat him again and again and to wound him with knives. They did not want to kill him outright, but to prolong his torture — such was their anger and their desire to double his agonies, to make him die over and over and suffer in pain for a long time. He did not stop praying and thanking Jesus for considering him worthy of enduring such torments. At this, several of them whom God was pleased to save gave themselves to Jesus with a good and true heart. They had no desire to hide and said aloud:

"We profess Jesus, who made earth and sea, and we renounce Mohammed and shall never undo this. Amphibalus! friend of God who rules all, now we see the glory God wishes to give you; entreat Jesus that we may share in it!"

When the prince heard this, he could only fly into a rage. He commanded that all those people should lose their heads instantly. The pagans beheaded them with steel blades in front of Amphibalus, who began to preach and confirm them in the faith of Jesus.

"Martyrs," he said, "go! Go, faithful knights, to the high king of glory and receive his kingdom!" (1625–46)

"Ha!" said a Saracen. "Cruel, base creature, it is a great misfortune that you have given us this mortal distress today. You have delivered over to death many a worthy baron who didn't know how to guard against your snares. You never get enough of chattering on about Jesus, deceiving simple people and tricking them with words. You alone are the cause of this great trouble. We've already lost a thousand today who have not been spared and who gave themselves to the crucified God because of your preaching and were lost beyond recall. You are condemned and in a sorry plight, and you'll not escape. All those whom you see here are your enemies. Now do what I tell you and you'll be acting very wisely. Deny what you have said to deceive people, renounce Jesus whom the Jews dared to crucify, and profess our gods who have such power. You have angered them by your great ignorance: but you'll gain great benefits and honors, lands, and

---

[xxxiii] **R42, fol. 45r cols. a and b** *A novel torment is devised by the man who attaches the martyr's bowels to a stake fixed in the earth and draws them out. They make him circle the stake and so draw out his entrails. Even suffering such torment, he does not cease converting pagans by preaching.* (211–18) The illustration shows Amphibalus being disemboweled and attacked with knives and spears: see Plate 9.

treasure of silver and bright gold for this, and you'll be pardoned if you agree to pray to them. They can heal you of these mortal wounds and revive those who have died here because of you." (1647–68)

After he heard him speak, Amphibalus replied:

"Listen to me, pagan enemy!" he said. "You are flagrantly sinning and telling lies when I hear you praise your gods, for their power is not worth the bud of a wild rose. Only God can call the dead to life and, if it pleases him, heal and restore my body. The devils whom you serve and whom you are pleased to worship suffer death in the pit of hell, without finally dying. That is their dwelling forever and endlessly, where there is great darkness, night without dawn, fire that cannot be extinguished, the worm that cannot be killed.[127] All those who obey their evil will in this world will have to dwell there: perjurers and evildoers who refuse to love God, adulterers and murderers, devilish warmongers: it's fitting for all of them to dwell with their gods in hell. You will have to go there with the damned if you don't abandon your gods straightaway and profess Jesus, who is ready to save everybody. Since it pleases him to grant you the opportunity, you ought to retreat from your position and start anew at once, for none can tell in full the generosity of God.[xxxiv] He welcomes repentant sinners without blaming them, and his arms are always outstretched, ready to embrace.[128] He allows you to cleanse your sins through baptism: that is the gate through which you must enter heaven and that is what gives a man rebirth and renewal. You'd be wise to look out for yourselves soon lest you perish utterly through delaying too long." (1669–97)

45. The nearby Saracens heard this. They shook and blazed like dragons or serpents, then they all rushed at him with a common will. They knocked him down with rocks, logs, and blocks of stone. They beat and shattered his body with rods and maces, so that it was completely split from forehead to heel. And he, as he was suffering death, looked toward heaven and made his prayer. He saw Jesus standing to the right of his Father, a great troop of angels surrounding him. He looked further and saw Alban, his companion, among them.

"Help!" he said. "Help, martyr, noble lord, look upon me, in such a mortal plight! I have no hope except in God and yourself. Beseech God that through his redemption he may allow me to share with you on high in that land where there is life without death, peace without strife, and send me consolation from the angels. May these wicked criminals not overcome me, and may these sons of hell,

---

[xxxiv] **R43, fol. 48r cols. a and b** *It cannot be hidden in the shadows that the number of Christians is growing, so that after a skirmish a deadly battle arises between the Christians and the pagan enemies. In the meantime, the trampled body of the martyr is secretly taken away from them.* (219–26) The illustration shows a furious melee, amidst which a Christian is speared to death and his soul flies to heaven as a dove. To the right Amphibalus's body is quietly drawn away from the battle.

who are trying so hard to defeat me by giving me over to the infernal Mohammed, not get any part of me."[129]

At that, there they were: two angels came down from their heavenly dwelling, and they were whiter than linen or cotton, or a lily opening in season.[130] God sent them to his loyal champion, to comfort him in his tribulation. Amphibalus heard a voice that greatly strengthened his resolve:

"Today you will receive the reward for your labor. Together with Alban, your disciple, you will be placed in possession of a gift immune to fire, worms, or thieves."[131] [xxxv]

The evil Saracens were terrified at this voice and they stoned him without restraint; they wounded him and had him speedily trampled by horses. His soul thereupon left its fleshly dwelling: angels carried it to heaven in a great procession. (1698–733)

46. At once there arose a noise and a great struggle as the evil pagans began fighting each other. This was because those who had sought Amphibalus, who had found him preaching and had brought him back from Wales, had sworn by their gods Phoebus, Mohammed, and Tervagant that they would all bring back the cleric, dead or alive, to their city of Verulamium and would torture and kill him there before the people; such was their compact. But the wicked prince, who did not want to wait so long, came to meet them, so eager was he. God Almighty saw to it that all the bloody traitors perjured themselves and the savage tyrants did not have their way.

Then there was an uproar followed by a huge, intense battle: they struck, wounded, and slashed with maces and knives, lances and blades. Because the press of battle was so great and so deadly, a Christian was able to draw away the body of the valiant martyr without the Saracens noticing. He buried the body in the earth, in a suitable sarcophagus, along with Amphibalus's fellow martyrs who had been obedient to the Christian faith he preached. The Christian buried the bodies under the green turf so that animals or birds would not devour them. May God who made the sun shine give him honor! The martyrs are in glory in the everlasting kingdom and the evil pagans in the stinking fires of hell, for they did not repent in this world.

Glorious martyr! I beseech and ask of you that for those in this world who honor you—your servants, friends, and well-wishers—you should be our[132]

[xxxv] R44, fol. 48v cols. a and b *The Christians bury the body that they have discreetly removed. The number of Christians who help with the burying multiplies. They do not stop until they have buried the martyr and his company. He did not come to Verulamium at the appointed time: the pagans are perjurers.* (227–34) The rubric runs across a two-column frame: the illustration has been removed, and bleed-through from fol. 45r is visible.

shield and warrant against the devil,[xxxvi] so that we may be saved: let the old people and the children say, "Amen!" to this. (1734–66)

47. The battle was intense, with many injured there, many dead and trampled, wounded, and finished off. God took vengeance on them for having waged so much war. God worked one of the greatest marvels ever told for his renowned martyr Amphibalus: no one who had ever reviled or harmed him escaped becoming deformed, disfigured in face or arm, hand or foot, driven insane, blinded, injured, or killed. Whoever had once been a brave and celebrated knight was now crippled or demon-infested. Their limbs were twisted, disjointed, and dislocated; their mouths turned sideways, their eyes turned inward, their tongues burned, and their fingers bent back.[133] The prince of the city flew into a rage at this. They learned that there is no point in any man born of a mother making war on earth against the king of majesty. No one present there could boast that he had dishonored God or his noble martyrs, whom they had put to death, without there being great vengeance for it. (1767–86)

The news quickly spread throughout the kingdom: Jesus' power could no longer be concealed. Those who heard about it went to see it with their own eyes, and they all thanked God with one voice; all the city-dwellers gave themselves to Jesus. Placing their temples and altars at his disposal, they broke their gods—or rather, devils—to pieces with hammers; they much regretted having loved them so intensely.[134] They mourned their ancestors who had passed on already and who had served their gods so thoroughly: ah, how unlucky they were, for they are damned forever to hell![135] They worshipped the cross of Jesus with great humility and they all honored him, who died tormented on the cross and whose death redeemed us from the power of hell.[xxxvii] Well did they recognize his high godhead and that he took humanity from the Virgin on earth! He is lord of earth and of the starry heavens; they confessed that he worked with righteousness. They all had themselves baptized in the name of the Trinity, abandoned their errors, their evils and vanities; they confessed their folly and sin, performed their penance,

---

[xxxvi] **R45, fol. 49r cols. a and b** *God cripples and disfigures the murderers and perjurers who have gone out of their way to torment Amphibalus and to blaspheme and damage Jesus. There is not one who does not labor under injury, madness, or blindness. The prince becomes enraged with good reason: no god aids or succors him.* (235–42) The rubric runs across a single illustration over columns a and b. Demonic figures atop the pagan riders' shoulders vigorously twist and yank their features and limbs: see Plate 10.

[xxxvii] **R46, fol. 49v cols. a and b** *When they arrive at Verulamium, Jesus's honor and renown increase. No one in the crowd has failed to experience beyond doubt the pointlessness of any mortal making war on the King of Heaven. They have struck down their idols and worshipped the cross of Jesus.* (243–50) The rubric runs across the entire two-column frame; the illustration has been removed.

The Life of St. Alban

and went to Rome to be taught the Christian faith and tell the pope the whole truth about how God in his strength gave them comfort.[136] (1787–811)

Here the converted Saracen speaks who was present at all these events and put everything into writing; and it was then translated into Latin and afterwards from Latin into the vernacular.

48. I, who was at that time a Saracen of false belief, saw the beginning and end of this story, from the time that Alban received his guest Amphibalus in his stone palace, the pilgrim who was passing through, until the two of them were laid in a marble sarcophagus.[137] Along with the other pagans, I was of the faith of Apollo, Pallas, Diana, Phoebus, and Jove,[138] who are devils damned in hell below. But the honor of Jesus is growing and theirs is declining. I have recorded these events on parchment as I saw them. The day will yet come, I say and indeed predict, when the story will be translated into French and Latin.[139] I know no other language than my own barbarian one, but by the faith that I owe to him who made wine from water, may I not have uttered a falsehood for all the gold of Constantine.[140] I have given myself to Jesus just as my neighbors have.[xxxviii] From now on, let me become a penitent and take up my ashen staff. Barefoot and without shoes of Cordovan leather,[141] I will exchange my ermine mantle for a pilgrim's cloak. Until I take ship at the nearest seaport I will not sleep in the evening where I arise in the morning.[142] I will cross Mount St. Bernard,[143] the steep alpine mountain, and will keep steadily on the road to the city of Rome, to announce to the Romans, people of Caesar, everything that I, a wretched sinner, have seen and heard on the island that Brutus and Corineus conquered.[144] For the sake of Alban, who first colored the island with his red blood and who was beheaded for God by a steel blade, I'll display my book written there on vellum. I will have many an old man and youth with me as witnesses. As a pagan of foul lineage, I do not dare name myself except as a culpable sinner, sorrowful, poor, and wretched. In Rome I will seek baptism with a true and sincere heart. I surrender myself entirely to Jesus as his loyal and faithful servant, and here I end the story of Alban. (1812–46)

Here ends the vernacular version of the history[145] *of St. Alban, the first martyr of England, and of St. Amphibalus, and of his companions.*

[xxxviii] **R47, fol. 50r cols. a and b** *Belief and preaching, baptism and confession, prayer and penance are the remedy for their sins. They give themselves to Jesus and all condemn their previous error. Since then Verulamium has been without error and beyond reproach.* (251-58) The rubric runs across a scene of penitential scourging in cols. a and b. This is the final illustration for *Alban*: the text finishes part-way down col. b, with the rest of the column blank.

Rubrics 48–71

After the text of *Alban* finishes on fol. 50r col. b, the French rubrics continue above the illustrations for the narratives of St. Germanus and of the foundation of St. Albans by King Offa of Mercia. The Latin rubrics that frequently appear at the bottom of the text-columns throughout the Anglo-Norman text are discontinued. On fol. 50v, exceptionally, there is neither illustration nor rubric: they were probably present on a paste-in (inserted to deal with the copious bleed-through from the illustration on fol. 50r) that was subsequently removed.

 R48, fol. 51r cols. a and b *A new war has arisen against the holy church in England.*[146] *Lupus of Troyes and Germanus of Auxerre have been sent on this business.*[147] *It is decreed in the synod that they will set out on a journey there to teach the people who have gone astray to love God and believe truly in him.* (259–66)[148]

 R49, fol. 52r cols. a and b *They immediately arrive in Paris, where they are honorably received. There they find a maiden, Genevieve, born in Paris.*[149] *She has heard talk about these holy men who intend to cross the sea. She has come to St. Germanus: she vows chastity before him.*[150] (267–74)

 R50, fol. 52v cols. a and b *He takes her gently by the hand: he approves her intention. He hangs a brightly shining metal penny around her neck.*[151] *"Take care that you do not become pregnant or make any vow that you break. So as to remain steady of purpose, carry this sign from me."* (275–82)

 R51, fol. 53r cols. a and b *When St. Germanus parts from her, he prays fervently to God to watch over her. He asks for the direction of the port and goes toward it: he is eager to be off. A short time afterward, the bishops put to sea. They run with a full sail before a good wind and come to port without mishap.*[152] (283–90)

 R52, fol. 53v cols. a and b *They arrive in Britain.*[153] *They go to London, where they hold a council, at which a great assembly of bishops was summoned to meet them. There by common assent it is decided that their great debate will be held at Verulamium.*[154] *Report of this is announced throughout the land.* (291–98)

 R53, fol. 54r cols. a and b *The bishops Germanus and Lupus come to Verulamium. They ask to know the story of Alban, about whose deeds and glory they have been hearing so much. Germanus exclaims: "Alban the martyr, confound the Pelagians! I commend my whole cause to you: I will honor you all my life."* (299–306)

 R54, fol. 54v cols. a and b *Peace and silence are enjoined upon the gathering: let no one grumble or argue. Bishop Germanus invokes the authority behind his judgment.*[155] *The company of Pelagians is confounded and overcome, for the Gospel and prophecy surpass their thinking.*[156] *They do not have a creator who goes guarantor for their fabrications and foolishness.* (307-16)

 R55, fol. 55r cols. a and b *The bishops have now returned holy church to good order so that no one believes strange doctrine, whatever anyone may sing or read to them.*[157] *They return to their own regions and give glory to God for their victory. They will everywhere preach the story of the martyr whom they commemorate.*[158] (317–24)

R56, fol. 55v cols. a and b *Through war and its destruction, strife and persecution, through trespass and sin that stained the world, the honor of holy church was consigned to oblivion; for many a long year St. Alban was forgotten. King Offa of England, a lamb in peace, a lion in war, reigns alone in Britain, which no one has done before him.*[159] *He brings down the pride of his enemies and maintains the kingdom in good order, like a man of good life and the flower of chivalry.*[160] (325–40 and see Plate 11)

R57, fol. 56r cols. a and b *Jesus gives victory to King Offa and his people. Bastard claimants leave, discomfited, driven off the land by the king,*[161] *who remains as king in his inheritance with his native baronage, and he maintains justice and freedom for his barons and for holy church.*[162] (341–48)

R58, fol. 56v cols. a and b *The king I am telling you about as God wishes, thanks be to him, lies sleeping one night in his bed. He sees the firmament illuminated: a beam from heaven, shining more brightly than the sun at midday, is shown him by an angel who descends, then leaves.*[163] (349–56)

R59, fol. 57r cols. a and b *The place where the martyr was beheaded was formerly called Holmhurst because it was so thickly overgrown with holly.*[164] *There the light descends that makes night seem like day.*[165] *King Offa clearly sees where it comes from and where it falls.* (357–64)

R60, fol. 57v cols. a and b *Upon awakening in the morning as dawn breaks, the king gets up. Now he draws closer to the heavenly falls of light until they find the place with the treasure that surpasses silver and gold. They surely resemble the men who once came from the East to offer their gifts.*[166] (365–72)

R61, fol. 58r cols. a and b *The beam from heaven*[167] *that shines clearly day and night is their guide. A city set upon on a hill cannot be hidden in shadow.*[168] (373–76)

R62, fol. 58v cols. a and b *The king commands his people to come; he sends for archbishops and earls.*[169] *Clerks, knights, and noblemen come when they are summoned. The king tells them the reason for his course of action and they are very joyful. Without delay, the king sets out to do what God commanded him.* (377–84)

R63, fol. 59r cols. a and b *They dig with spades and picks, clear scrub and wood, dig out stumps and roots, carry off turf and remove thorns; they carry away stones and earth in baskets. They do not cease searching and seeking, high and low. The king, who is present, has exhorted them to find the treasure and the relics of the holy body,*[170] *wrapped as they were in a silken cloth that always keeps its color and shape.*[171] (385–96)

R64, fol. 59v cols. a and b *The king has a church founded that is positioned in this very place where the holy martyr Alban suffered scorn and death for God.*[172] *He summons masons and engineers, who build*[173] *the foundations of the walls, the arches and paved stone floors, the pillars, the bases, and the entablatures.* (397–404)[174]

R65, fol. 60r cols. a and b *The king takes a great deal of trouble to choose all the people for his works: carpenters, masons, glaziers, each according to his trade. One lays stone, another chisels it: one man cuts, one man splits, and one man hammers; one with an axe, one with a hammer, and one with mallet and chisel.* (405–12)[175]

R66, fol. 60v cols. a and b *Offa, the noble king of virtuous life, completes his abbey. He sees that it has the approval of God, who furthers what he has begun.*

Following the counsel of his familiars, wise and well-educated prelates, he installs in his fine house a community of monks with an abbot named Willegod and people of high religion. (413–22)[176]

R67, fol. 61r cols. a and b *Outside the city of Verulamium a little church of great antiquity had been founded, named St. Syon. Pagan converts built it in the year St. Alban was beheaded.*[177] *They had it constructed in honor of him as the first martyr of England. The martyr's reliquary was placed there until they completed the great church.* (423–32)

R68, fol. 61v cols. a and b *The feast of St. Alban is celebrated on the third day before the feast of St. John.*[178] *Archbishops, suffragan bishops, clerks, and nobles, summoned by proclamation, celebrate the feast of his invention on the fourth day before the nones of August.*[179] *His title is true and unique to him: "The first martyr of Britain."* (433–40)

R69, fol. 62r cols. a and b[180] *The king, arriving in his land, is not slow to make good his intention. Barons and earls come to meet him: he summons his horse and mounts. He is tired and weary from traversing seas and mountains, but he does not let that hinder him in the service of Alban the martyr.* (441–48)

R70, fol. 62v cols. a and b *A feast is held at St. Albans for the arrival of the king, who, in the sight of his people, makes a gift of his property on the high altar.*[181] *This is the end of the story of Offa. It is fitting that he, so noble a king and such a Christian, should be commemorated: may God save his soul. Amen!* (449–56)

R71, fol. 63r cols. a and b *Alban suffered his passion two hundred and eighty-six years after God took flesh of a virgin. After another hundred and sixty-three years, Germanus came to put down false belief.*[182] *After three hundred and forty-four more years, Offa, who reigned for thirty-nine years, raised Alban from the earth:* see Plate 12.

Notes

[1] The manuscript is damaged at the start of *Alban* (which now begins on TCD MS 177, fol. 29r): the previous folio remains as a very narrow stub of Latin text, and the extant French text opens in the middle of a description of the cross that Amphibalus brought to Verulamium. In Paris's source text, the *Passio sancti Albani* by William of St. Albans (henceforth *PSA*), the first narrative event is Amphibalus's arrival at Alban's house, so it is likely that little of Paris's narrative is missing. As in *PSA* and in saints' lives composed by Paris himself, *Alban* presumably opened with a prologue and some account of the provenance and purposes of the work, but this is completely lost. Since Paris alters the *PSA* narrator's status to that of direct eyewitness in the conclusion to *Alban* (see below, n. to 48:1812), it is not clear that Paris would have followed William of St. Albans in the prologue at all closely. In his own copying of *PSA* into the *Alban* manuscript, Paris omitted the preface with which William precedes his *PSA* prologue and text (TCD MS 177, fol. 20r and see *PSA*, 139–40 below).

[2] 1:2–7 **But it was not adorned with gold ... one of his sides** *Mes ne ert d'or adubbee ... l'un des costez*: Amphibalus's cross is not mentioned at this point in *PSA*, being first shown to Alban by Amphibalus only after Alban's dream in *PSA* 7 (corresponding to Paris's 10:284). In his illustrations to *Alban*, Paris both highlights Amphibalus's cross and represents it, unusually, as round-headed: elsewhere he draws a standard four-armed cross. On the cross's design and its thematic importance in *Alban*, see McCulloch, "Saints Alban and Amphibalus in the Works of Matthew Paris." Birthe Kjølbye-Biddle argues that ornaments acquired by St. Albans not long before Paris was writing (described at *GA* 1:292 and itemized in a later St. Albans relic list, *GA* 3:539–45) included a Coptic cross and that this, not the Roman *signum* fragment proposed by McCulloch, influenced Paris's representation of the cross and perhaps prompted the writing of *Alban* ("The Alban Cross," in Henig and Lindley, *Alban and St Albans*, 85–110).

[3] 1:8–9 **Amphibalus honored this cross** *ceste croiz aure*: Amphibalus is named in the rubric to *PSA* and at the beginning of his conversation with Alban, *PSA* 3, but not in what survives of this *laisse*. In the current state of the *Alban* manuscript, the first mention of Amphibalus by name is not until 4:96, and we cannot know how Paris may have presented Amphibalus's name in the opening of the poem. For the origin of Amphibalus's name, see Introduction, 8.

[4] 1:10 **Verulamium ... an imperial town** *Varlam, un liu emperial*: Verulamium was a self-governing *municipium* until the third century and deserted by the fifth (R. G. Collingwood and J. N. L. Myres, *Roman Britain and the English Settlements* [Oxford: Clarendon Press, 1936; 2nd ed. 1937, repr. 1963], 86, 206, 317: see further Rosalind Niblett, *Verulamium: The Roman City of St Albans* [Stroud: Tempus, 2001]). Paris seems to envisage the prince of Verulamium as having a jurisdiction over a *provincia* corresponding to the Angevin empire (see below 34:1265 and note). The medieval town of St. Albans (on the opposite bank of the river Ver from the Roman Verulamium) was not founded until c. 950 by Abbot Wulsin: see Maurice Beresford, *New Towns of the Middle Ages: Town Plantation in England, Wales and Gascony* (Gloucester and Wolfeboro, NH: Alan Sutton, 1988), 326. The Abbey had control of the town throughout the Middle Ages, though this was often tested and contested by the town (see further Introduction, 21–22).

⁵ 1:12 **a despicable faith** *lei criminel*: *criminel* has the senses of "wicked, corrupt, deadly" and "mortal," as well as a legal sense (*AND*). At this date criminal and civil offenses were not distinguished in medieval law: see Paul R. Hyams, "Law, Literature and the Discourse of Dispute," in *Cambridge Companion to Medieval English Culture*, ed. Andrew Galloway (Cambridge: Cambridge University Press, 2011).

⁶ 1:13 **But Saracens held it** *Mes Sarrazins la tindrent*: Paris's use of the term "Saracen" here does not designate a particular ethnic group but rather people who are "not Christian" or "pagan." Although the term is usually pejorative in *Alban*, it can also be neutral; cf. 17:565, where Alban is reminded that his is a family of "noble Saracen lords of great territories" (*Sarrazins nobiles de grantz terres seingnur*). In this, Paris repeats a usage considered a hallmark of the *chanson de geste* or epic, in which Saxons, Danes, Wallachians, Hungarians, Slavs, and even other Christians (for example, the Greeks and the Armenians) are variously called "Saracens"): see Jean-Pierre Martin, "La construction de l'espace sarrasin dans les chansons de geste," in *Plaisir de l'épopée*, ed. Gisèle Mathieu-Castellani (Saint-Denis: Presses Universitaires de Vincennes, 2000), 71–84, at 73–74, 78. Pierre Nobel points out that in the *Poème anglo-normand sur l'Ancien Testament* all those in open conflict with the Hebrews are called *sarazin*, *gent sarazine*, or *pople sarazin*, and he notes further that biblical translators used the term "Saracen" to render the Latin *gentes*, "gentiles" or "pagans": see "Les Hébreux au péril des Cananéens et d'eux-mêmes dans *Le Poème anglo-normand sur l'Ancien Testament*," in *La Chrétienté au péril sarrasin: actes du colloque de la section française de la société internationale Rencesvals (Aix-en-Provence, 30ème septembre-1ᵉʳ octobre 1999)*, Sénéfiance 46 (Aix-en-Provence: Université de Provence, 2000), 183–202, at 194–95. See also Introduction, 27–28.

⁷ 1:14 **Apollo, Satan, and Belial** *Apolin . . ., Sathan e Belial*: a pagan Trinity is frequently alluded to in *chansons de geste* and other writings, such as narratives of the First Crusade (Matthew Bennett, "First Crusaders' Images of Muslims: The Influence of Vernacular Poetry?" *Forum for Modern Language Studies* 22 [1986]: 101–22, at 114–15). Paris focuses particularly on Phoebus/Apollo (see n. to 19:621–25 below) and Mohammed (see n. to 11:333 below).

⁸ 1:21 **a high official** *un haut mareschal*: *PSA* makes Alban a prominent citizen of high lineage and honor but gives no specific office to him. The level of rank implied by Paris's term *mareschal* depended on the rank of the person served: for an account of the marshals and other officers at a thirteenth-century court in England, see *The Court and Household of Eleanor of Castile in 1290: An Edition of British Library Additional Manuscript 35294 with Introduction and Notes*, ed. John Carmi Parsons (Toronto: Pontifical Institute of Mediaeval Studies, 1977), 28–40.

⁹ 2:34 **my own country, Wales** *Guales mun pais*: in *PSA* Amphibalus is given no specific country of origin, and his destination emerges only on his departure by the road that goes toward "Aquilonis" and his arrival in Wales ("Walliam," *PSA* 10). Paris, however, stresses the role of Wales (see also n. to 12:376 below and Introduction, 25).

¹⁰ 2:50 **as a sparrowhawk . . . the lark** *cum aloue esperver*: while this could also be translated "as the lark hates the sparrowhawk," it makes better sense for the unconverted Alban to regard his gods as the more powerful element of the pair.

¹¹ 3:62 **the lord** *lu ber*: Paris frequently uses the archaic masculine singular oblique *lu* in possessive constructions: for further examples, see Harden, *Auban*, xxv, and Wallace, *Estoire*, xxxix.

¹² 3:62 **at the wedding of the lord Architriclin** *as nosces lu ber Architriclin*: Architriclin is a name given to the bridegroom at the wedding of Cana (John 2:8–9) in the Middle Ages, arising from misinterpretation of *architriclinus*, "wine steward." An alternative medieval tradition (disputed by, among others, Rupert of Deutz) suggests that the bridegroom is John the Evangelist. The wedding at Cana is not referred to in *PSA*, but "Archedeclinus" had wide currency as the Cana bridegroom's name, especially following Herman de Valenciennes's use of it in his late twelfth-century vernacular bible, *Le Roman de Dieu et de sa mere*. See further D. A. Trotter, "The Influence of Bible Commentaries on Old French Bible Translations," *Medium Aevum* 56 (1987): 257–75.

¹³ 3:64 **misguided Saracens** *mescreant Sarrazin*: on the use of the term "Saracens," see n. to 1:13 and Introduction, 27–28 above. *Mescreant* is usually translated as "faithless," but in context it is clear that the Saracens have the wrong faith rather than no faith at all.

¹⁴ 4:74–76 **He took him aside ... seen or heard** *une part l'acoilt ... ne aperceu*: the withdrawal to a secret place is brought forward by Paris. In *PSA* (both in the full text and in the abbreviated version copied by Paris in his *CM* 1:149–54), master and pupil retire to a secluded house only after Alban's conversion. *AND* gives *foreine* in *maison foreine* 4:75 as "remote, out of the way," but the sense "outside the jurisdiction of the town" is equally important here.

¹⁵ 4:81–91 **one of us mortals** *nus morteus*: Alban shows here not the contumacy but the rational despair of the virtuous pagan. By the thirteenth century, Western theologians were in general agreement that virtuous pagans might be saved by divine revelation to those who had used their powers well or by arriving through natural understanding at a basic belief in a just and providential God (the Thomist doctrine of *fides implicita*). Alban qualifies on both counts. See further Gordon Whatley, "The Uses of Hagiography: The Legend of Pope Gregory and the Emperor Trajan in the Middle Ages," *Viator* 15 (1984): 25–63.

¹⁶ 5:114 **warranty** *guarantz* [Latin *warrantus*]: i.e., no one could stand as pledge for Adam and Eve; humanity lacked the resources for any juridical solution and had no other lord to whom it could legitimately appeal to stand warranty for it: see further Paul R. Hyams, "Warranty and Good Lordship in Twelfth Century England," *Law and History Review* 5 (1987): 437–503. In his *Chasteau d'amour*, Robert Grosseteste argues that Adam is no longer a free man after his disobedience to his lord and hence cannot plead in court but requires someone free from sin to do so (C. W. Marx, *The Devil's Rights and the Redemption in the Literature of Medieval England* [Cambridge: D. S. Brewer, 1995], 68, quoting *Chasteau*, vv. 183–90). Paris elaborates this explanation of the need for redemption (5:105–24) and transfers it here from its later position in *PSA*, where it is given by Amphibalus not in *PSA* 4 but in *PSA* 7.

¹⁷ 5:121 **should be undone and overcome by a man** *par humme cuvint descumfire e mater*: on the theology of the incarnation and redemption, especially on Anselm and his influence, see further Marx, *Devil's Rights*, esp. 17–27.

¹⁸ 5:125–42 **the angel Gabriel ... without objection or fear** *l'angle Gabriel ... sanz nier u duter*: Paris follows *PSA* 4 in selecting from and elaborating on Luke 1:24–42. Paris's Amphibalus continues here with the story of the Crucifixion and the Ascension (6:143–74), a narrative later repeated with increased vividness as Alban retells his dream (9:222–79). *PSA* retells the Crucifixion and Ascension only in Alban and Amphibalus's exchange over Alban's dream (*PSA* 6).

[19] 5:137 **who wishes you to be a mother** *Ki toi cumme mere vudra enumbrer* ("virtus Altissimi obumbrabit tibi," *PSA* 4, taken verbatim from the Vulgate text of Luke 1:35): *enumbrer* is literally "overshadow, cast a shadow over," a word especially redolent in Song of Songs exegesis (cf. Song 2:3) but also with a sense of "be conceived": see, e.g., *Le Chant des chanz*, ed. Tony Hunt, ANTS 61–62 (London: ANTS, 2004), vv. 31, 235, 247.

[20] 6:155–64 **Then the Jews . . . wretched serfs** *Par Jueus . . . serfs pleintifs*: church teaching underpinned this subjection in various ways. Paris makes explicit reference to the doctrine that Jews had voluntarily chosen to have their own king killed by the Romans and so were permanently enserfed ("without a king," *sanz rei*, 6:164; see also notes to 10:289 and 11:306–15 as well as 43:1619, where the Jews are called *desloial*, "faithless"); Augustinian theology saw the Jewish presence in medieval *Christianitas* as a providential form of witness to the Crucifixion for Christians and a reminder of the incompleteness of the Old Law. See further Introduction, 26–27.

[21] 6:173 **there will be no** *n'afra*: as Harden notes (*Auban*, 67, n. to 173), this is more likely to be the future of *aver* impersonal than Atkinson's *nafra*, preterite of *navrer*.

[22] 6:174 **damned** *dampnez*: it is not possible to know whether this should be translated as "be damned" or "you are damned," as this verse contains no auxiliary verb. The passage alludes to Matt. 25:34, 41.

[23] 7:176 **in simple fashion** *simplement*: on the Christian rhetorical ethos evoked by this mode of speech, see Introduction, 51–52.

[24] 7:196 **since it does not conform to what is right or reasonable** *ke droitz ne raisuns n'i assent*: for Alban's theological situation as a virtuous pagan, whose own reasoning requires the supplement of divine inspiration, see n. to 4:81–91 above. For Paris, the doctrine of the Trinity marks an important distinction between Christianity and Islam (see his account of Mohammed's life and teachings, *CM* 3:344–61, at 352–53, and see also n. to 33:1238–39 below). As a virtuous pagan, Alban's anger is recuperable, unlike that of the prince of Verulamium, who here fills the *passio* role of pagan tyrant (on legitimate and illegitimate forms of medieval anger, see Barbara H. Rosenwein, "Controlling Paradigms," in eadem, *Anger's Past: The Social Uses of an Emotion in the Middle Ages* [Ithaca and London: Cornell University Press, 1998], 233–47).

[25] 9:252–53 **The whole world trembled . . . a great veil in the temple was torn** *Trembla tretuz li mundz . . . un grantz veilz du temple desira e rumpi*: cf. Matt. 27:45, 51–52; Mark 15:38; Luke 23:44–45 (from which accounts the crucifixion narrative is summarized in *PSA* 6).

[26] 9:269 **I understood** *entendi*: the senses of *entendre*, "understand, hear, pay attention to," are not easily distinguished from each other, and *entendi* could here be translated as either "understood" or "heard." The question of whether angelic song can be understood by humans is raised elsewhere in medieval literature: for example, in the thirteenth-century *Holkham Bible Picture Book*, in whose Anglo-Norman narrative the shepherds are initially fearful about the angel's "Gloria in excelsis" but eventually sing it themselves at the Nativity (color facsimile in *The Holkham Bible Picture Book*, ed. Michelle Brown [London: British Library, 2007], fol. 13r: for a transcription, see F. P. Pickering, ed., *The Holkham Bible Picture Book*, ANTS 23 [Oxford: Blackwell for ANTS, 1971], 22). For comparable scenes in the English cycle drama, see Richard Rastall, *The Heaven Singing: Music in Early English Religious Drama* (Woodbridge and Rochester: D. S. Brewer, 1996), 1: 344–64 (summary at 347). For a Middle English example, see William Langland, *Piers Plowman* B text, Prol. 128–45 (ed. A.V. C. Schmidt, *The Vision of Piers Plowman* [London: Dent, 1995]).

²⁷ 10:281–83 **the wild lion into a lamb . . . who created the earth and the sea** *aignel d'un leun sauvage . . . Ki fist e terre e mer*: Paris elaborates *PSA* with biblical phrases from Genesis and the Psalms (cf. Gen. 1:26, 28; Ps. 8:9). For the Oxford psalter text, see Francisque Michel, ed., *Libri psalmorum versio antiqua gallica* (Oxford: Clarendon Press, 1860), 8, and for the Cambridge text, idem, *Le Livre des psaumes: ancienne traduction française* (Paris: Imprimerie nationale, 1876), 10.

²⁸ 10:289 **the whorish Jews** *li Giue[u] de putage*: medieval Christian doctrine saw the Jews as a people who had abandoned their king and maintained that, as a consequence, all Jews since the Crucifixion were born unfree, as serfs (see n. to 6:155–64 above).

²⁹ 10:294–96 **without illusion or folly . . . but through revelation** *sanz fentosme u folage . . . mes par avisiun:* medieval dream theory allows for many grades of meaning in dreams, from the revelatory to the trivial (see Steven F. Kruger, *Dreaming in the Middle Ages* [Cambridge: Cambridge University Press, 1992; repr. 1996], e.g., 23, 29–31, 39). Much like a confessor determining the value of a visionary's dream, Amphibalus is assuring Alban that his dream has a divine, not a demonic, source and that it is neither deceptive nor meaningless (a *fantasma* or *visum*) but an authentic vision (*avisiun*, 10:296, i.e., a *visio* or *revelacio*).

³⁰ 10:297–98 **Give allegiance and homage to him . . . baptism and marriage** *Fai lui . . . lingance e humage . . . batesme e primer mariage*: the role of marriage in this passage is puzzling. Baptism makes sense as an entry ritual: in contrast to the enserfed Jews of his vision, Alban is welcomed into full allegiance to his heavenly lord and king by Amphibalus, who urges him to baptism as the formal pledge of fealty and homage ("lingance e humage," 10:297: see T.-L., s.v. *lijance*), a relation that has a strong affective as well as a social and legal content (see, e.g., H. B. Teunis, "Benoit of St. Maure and William the Conqueror's *amor*," *ANS* 12 [1990]: 199–210). For the various uses of homage ritual in the high Middle Ages, see Paul R. Hyams, "Homage and Feudalism: A Judicious Separation," in *Die Gegenwart des Feudalismus*, ed. Natalie Fryde, Pierre Monnet, and Otto Gerhard Oexle (Göttingen: Vandenhoeck and Ruprecht, 2002), 13–49: especially "[homage's] essence lay in making manifest an act of submission, the conveyance of self into some state of dependence" (49). Baptism seems here to function as a commendation ritual, as Alban enters a new affinity where he can expect to be among the most elevated courtiers at the celestial court (see also J. H. Baker, *A Manual of Law French*, 2nd ed. [Aldershot: Scolar Press, 1990], s.v. *baptismer, -izer*). In the parallel with marriage in 10:298, Paris may be thinking of degrees of sacramentality for laypeople. At 10:333 (a moment also described at 31:1101) Alban ends his relations with pagan gods and authorities with a formal repudiation similar to the dismantling of *fides* or *fidelitas* by which homage could be ended (see Hyams, "Homage and Feudalism," 34–35; *AND*, s.v. *defier*).

³¹ 10:300–1 **martyr in vassalage . . . celestial baronage** *martir par vasselage . . . celestien barnage*: *barnage* is the standard term for the thirteenth-century English barony (see also R57:346). *Vassalage*, often translated as "courage" (see T.-L., s.v. *aliance*), has as its root meaning the idea of a deed that shows one to be worthy of one's overlord. It embraces the notion of suffering for one's overlord in what is conceived of as an affective relationship: the final pair of lines in the *laisse* emphasizes martyrdom not as an alternative to but as part of *vassalage*.

³² 11:306–15 **people that you saw . . . suffering and death** *Le peuple ke veistes . . . serfs au tirant Pharaun . . . mort e passiun*. This evocation of the Jews' life in Egypt, found in the

Hebrew Bible, is Paris's addition to his source (see *PSA*, 7). For the theory of the Jews as willfully faithless to an overlord, see n. to 6:155–64 above.

³³ 11:317 **the lion cub** *li liunceus*: in medieval bestiaries, lion cubs are purportedly born dead and revived three days later by the breath or voice of their parent lion; see, e.g., Philippe de Thaon's early twelfth-century bestiary (*Le Bestiaire de Philippe de Thaün*, ed. Emanuel Walberg [Lund: Möller, and Paris: Welter, 1900], 14), vv. 363–70: the whole item on *Leün* in this bestiary (2–15, vv. 25–388) is a concise account of redemptive theology, in which Jewish culpability, kinglessness, and vengeance on the Jews are part of the explication of the relations between the lion and the ass: see also Guillaume le Clerc's late twelfth-century *Bestiaire divin*, *Le Bestiaire: Das Thierbuch des Normannischen Dichters Guillaume le Clerc*, ed. R. Rentsch (Leipzig: Reisland, 1890), 226–29, vv. 162–222.

³⁴ 11:320 **the . . . old dragon** *le viel . . . dragun*: cf. Revelation 12:9, 20:2; also Ps. 90:13. On Christ's harrowing of hell see further *The Medieval Gospel of Nicodemus*, ed. Z. Izydorczyk, MRTS 158 (Tempe: ACMRS, 1997).

³⁵ 11:333 **the sorcery of Mohammed . . . perdition** *l'enchantement Mahun . . . perdiciun*: these lines are Paris's expansion of *PSA* 9. *PSA* does not name Mohammed or the pagan gods: Mohammed is regularly invoked in *Alban* in scenes of allegiance or conversion.

³⁶ 12:346 **for he has chosen you freely and you him** *Kar eschoisi vus a e vus lui de bon gré*: cf. "Homage binds two persons by their mutual consent; and by their mutual consent it may be released and undone, but not by the assent of one of them only" ("Homage lie deus hommes par lour commun assent, et par commun assent purra homage estre delié et defet, et ne mie par le assent de un de eus soulement": *Britton*, ed. and trans. F. M. Nichols [Oxford: Clarendon Press, 1865], vol. 2, bk. 3:4, 27, *De Homage*). Paris expands *PSA* 9.

³⁷ 12:355–58 **Where is Alexander . . . so much wealth and status** *U est Alexandres . . . tresor e tant nobilité*: this *ubi sunt* topos is not present in *PSA* 9; nor is the following promise of martyrdom (12:364–67). Alexander and Caesar are used as types of *potestas* and *libertas* by Honorius in his twelfth-century *Elucidarium* and drawn on together with other figures by many subsequent writers: see Geoffrey Shepherd, "'All the wealth of Croesus': A Topic in the *Ancren Riwle*," *Modern Language Review* 51 (1956): 161–67.

³⁸ 12:359 **a seven-foot portion** *saet paez mesuré*: in the saga of Harald Sigurdsson, the king of Norway known as Harold Hardrathi or "Ruthless" who was killed at the battle of Stamford Bridge, 25 September 1066, King Harold Godwinson of England offers the invader "seven feet of ground or as much more as he is taller than other men" (from Snorri Sturlusson, *Heimskringla*, trans. as *King Harald's Saga* by Magnus Magnusson and Hermann Palsson [Harmondsworth: Penguin, 1966, repr. 1976] chap. 91, 150). In Alexander literature the *Ubi sunt* topos usually includes some form of this topos: cf. e.g. *The Anglo-Norman Alexander: The Roman de toute chevalerie*, ed. Brian Foster and Ian Short, ANTS 29–31 (London: ANTS, 1976), 1: w.8013–14.

³⁹ 12:376, 380 **my country** *mun pais*: in *PSA*, Amphibalus expresses a general intention to continue traveling and converting people (*PSA* 9). Paris here continues his association of Amphibalus with Wales (see n. to 2:34 above).

⁴⁰ 12:379 **has set his seal on your heart** *ad tun quor saelé* (Song of Songs 8:6): following the baptism of v. 369, Alban is now Christ's (see also *PSA* 27 and n. 36). Baptism itself was termed a 'seal' (*sphragis*). For the role of the seal in medieval conceptions of personal identity, see Caroline W. Bynum, *Docere verbo et exemplo: An Aspect of Twelfth-Century Spirituality*, Harvard Theological Studies 31 (Missoula, MT: Scholars Press,

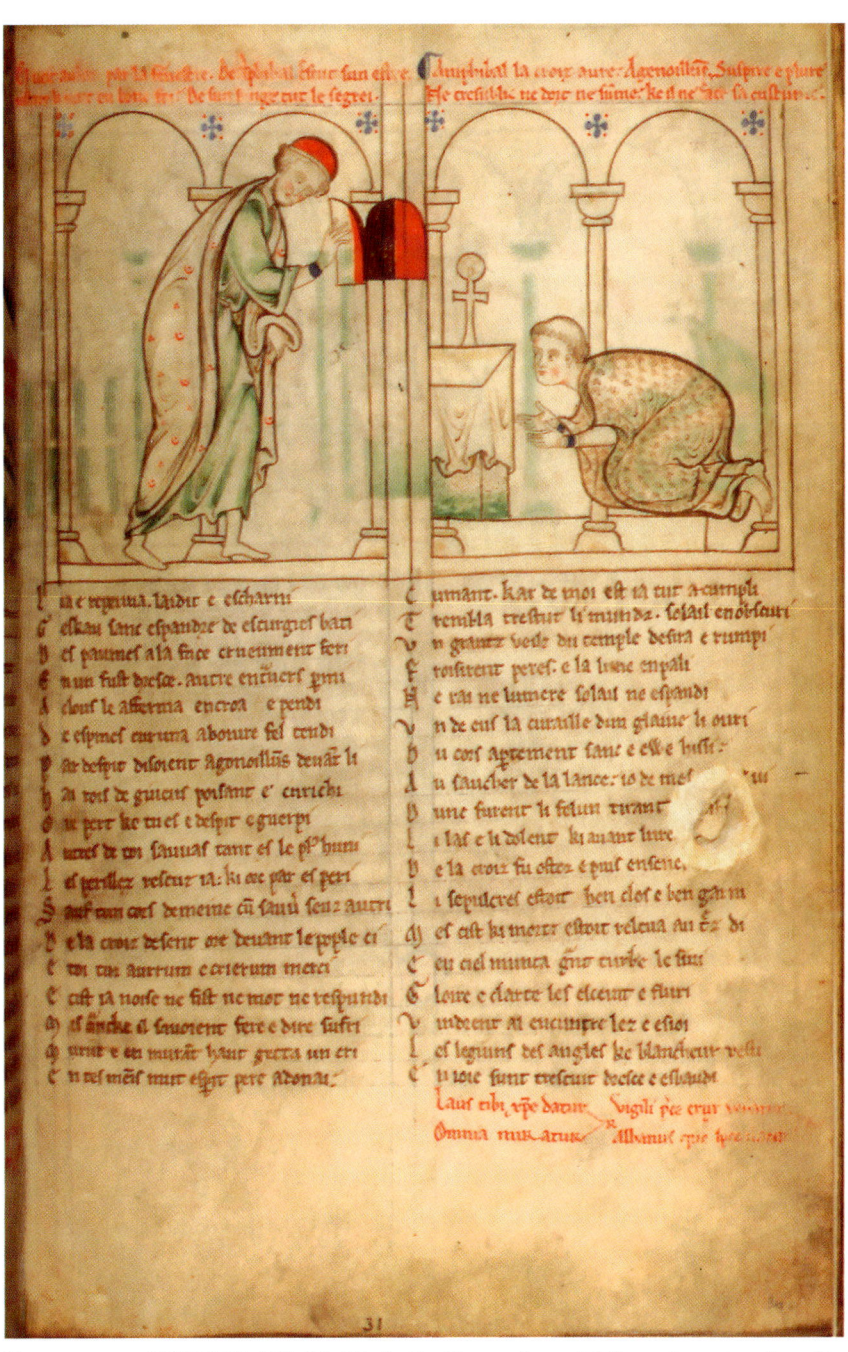

FIGURE 3B.1. TCD MS 177, fol. 31r (with illustration of Alban observing Amphibalus praying before his cross): an example of an area of vellum with natural lacunae covered by a patch which is no longer extant.
The Board of Trinity College Dublin. Reproduced by permission.

FIGURE 3B.2. TCD MS 177, fol. 13r (detail): traces of the temporary pinning and subsequent readherence of the corner fragment of the leaf.
The Board of Trinity College Dublin. Reproduced by permission.

FIGURE 3B.3. TCD MS 177, fol. 49r (detail): surface modelling of vellum creating a relief effect on the necks and haunches of horses. See also Plate 10.
The Board of Trinity College Dublin. Reproduced by permission.

Figure 3B.4. TCD MS 177, fol. 60r (detail): surface modelling of the vellum creating a relief effect on the brickwork of King Offa's new abbey church.
The Board of Trinity College Dublin. Reproduced by permission.

PLATE 1. Alban's dream, TCD MS 177, fol. 30v. The writing has most probably been entered before the illustration was made.

The Board of Trinity College Dublin. Reproduced by permission.

PLATE 2. Alban and Amphibalus spied on by a Saracen, TCD MS 177, fols. 31v–32r. The organization of the images encourages rightward reading with a sense of narrative movement.

The Board of Trinity College Dublin. Reproduced by permission.

PLATE 3. Alban and Amphibalus spied on by a Saracen, TCD MS 177, fols. 31v–32r. The Board of Trinity College Dublin. Reproduced by permission.

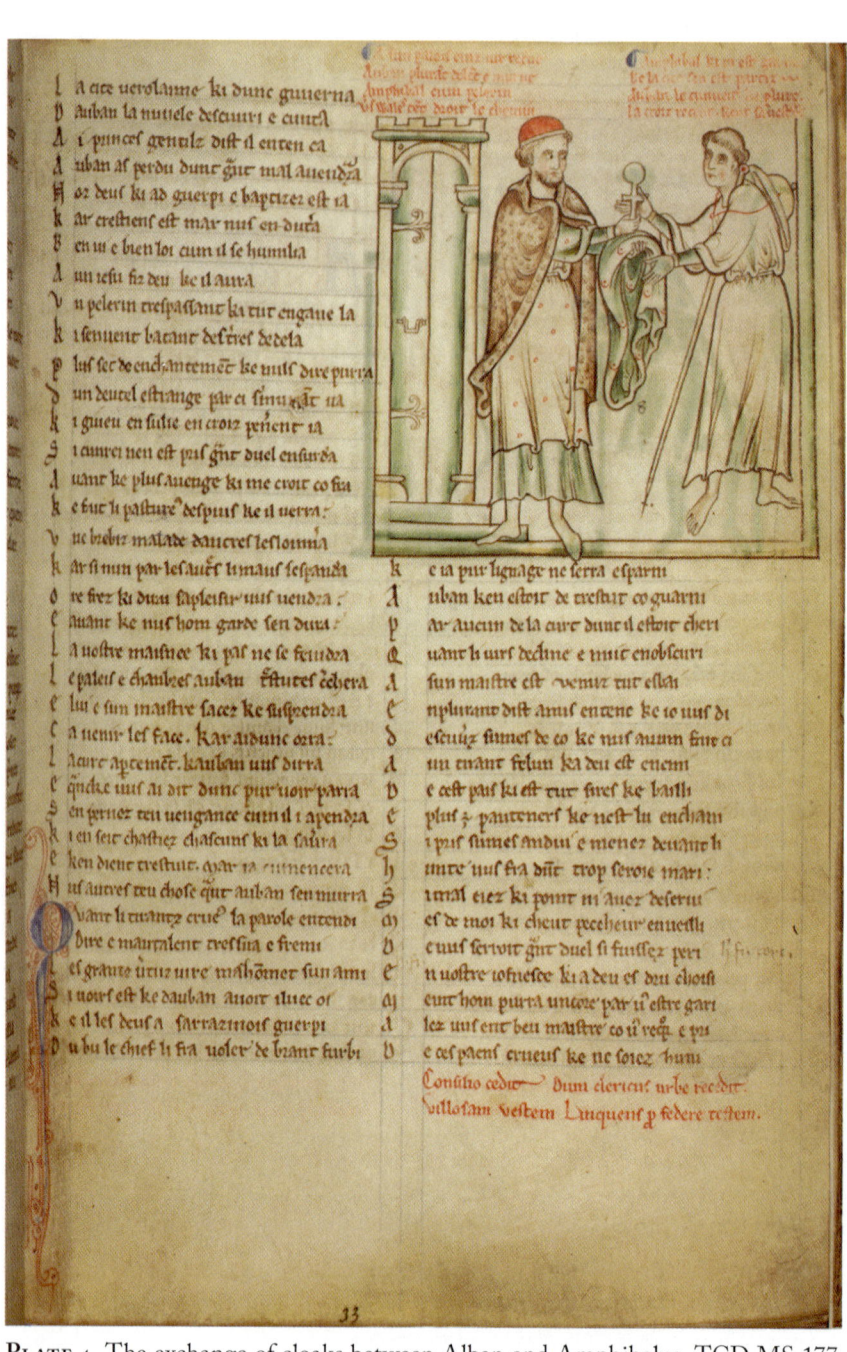

PLATE 4. The exchange of cloaks between Alban and Amphibalus, TCD MS 177, fol. 33r.

The Board of Trinity College Dublin. Reproduced by permission.

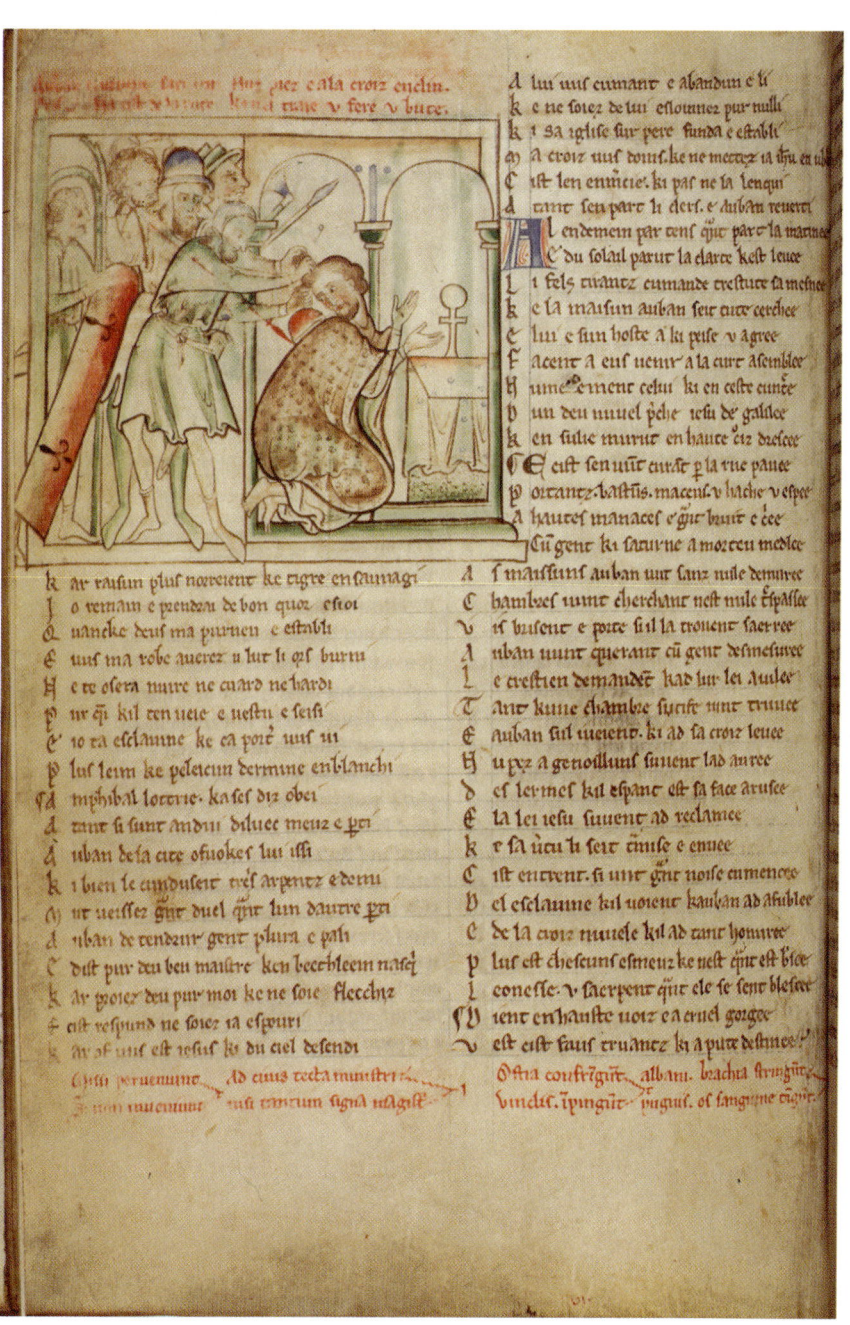

PLATE 5. Alban worships Amphibalus's cross as the pagans burst in on him, TCD MS 177, fol. 33v. The illustration has been entered before the text.
The Board of Trinity College Dublin. Reproduced by permission.

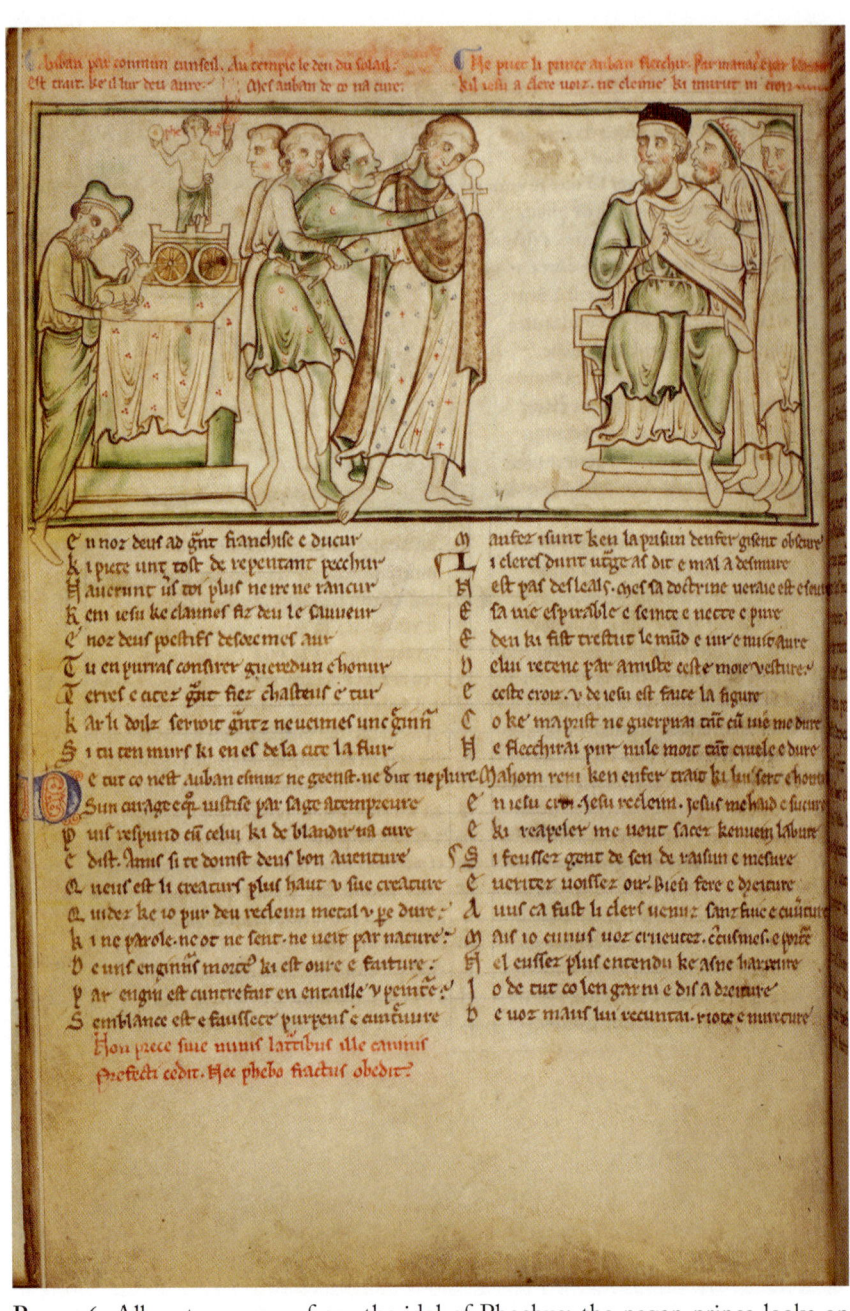

Plate 6. Alban turns away from the idol of Phoebus: the pagan prince looks on across a blank white column of space in the illustration, TCD MS 177, fol. 34v. The Board of Trinity College Dublin. Reproduced by permission.

PLATE 7. Alban's banishment from Verulamium. Heraclius, identified in Matthew Paris's hand as "Aracle," leads Alban toward execution, TCD MS 177, fol. 36r. The illustration was entered before flourishes were added to the capital in the text.
The Board of Trinity College Dublin. Reproduced by permission.

Plate 8. Heraclius's conversion: he is left for dead after being beaten, TCD MS 177, fol. 37r.
The Board of Trinity College Dublin. Reproduced by permission.

Plate 9. Amphibalus's martyrdom, TCD MS 177, fol. 45r.
The Board of Trinity College Dublin. Reproduced by permission.

Plate 10. God makes the pagans twisted and deformed in punishment, TCD MS 177, fol 49r.

The Board of Trinity College Dublin. Reproduced by permission.

t ianua paradisi. + sursum atque deorsum cū
sacres sunt. + comates nr̄i. Inter descen
dunt + adre ascendunt cuies angeli
a. + sursum atque deorsum cōsores sunt
+ comates nr̄i. P nomen xp̄i nomen ubi
q: beati congnoscat nisi albani cuies
sub q: uictor occubuit nesciat uocabu
lum intoto orbe tiranni. Sed adeū
calamū iam uertamus articulum. Hau
dis cuis titulos. honor cōtrepet sim
phoniā. O maris tipro nobilis ostro.
Virtutum radios tempore nr̄o. Sparg
ut runtē luna fante. Ortum o dissimili
sole repente. O ih̄u domini ogenite

uestis. Quī certe rose impura
uestis. Oum lictor gladiis tangē
titat. Oum de mente sac̄ passio
dicat. Te candore detet clara diap
sis. Quā mordet uiridans sibī
la iaspis. Hanc saphir̄ l̄r glia
regis. Per quos stat celebris sa
ncio legum Angeloru regia co
mūus edes. In nob parte sit
tua sedes. Hic xp̄o statuas sig
nifer atam. Ost satirem repmā
mortis amaram. Huic discepto
sat sit detet equis lilia queque. Qui non tuo

PLATE 11. The first image of Offa in the manuscript: King Etheldred's head rolls at the feet of Offa's horse, TCD MS 177, fol. 55v.
The Board of Trinity College Dublin. Reproduced by permission.

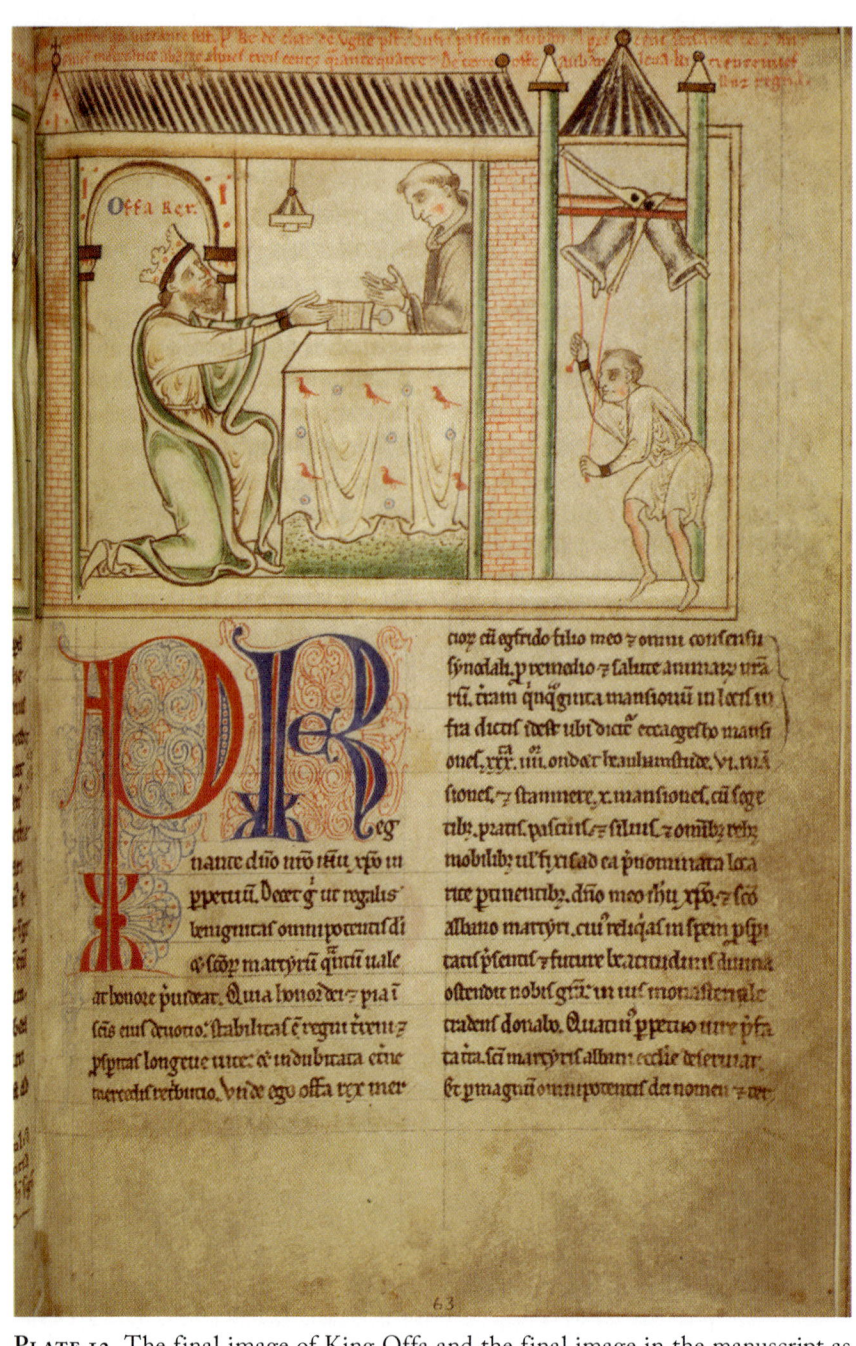

Plate 12. The final image of King Offa and the final image in the manuscript as a whole. Offa lays his charter on the altar to the ringing of the bells in celebration, TCD MS 177, fol. 63r.

The Board of Trinity College Dublin. Reproduced by permission.

1979), 82–83, and Binski, *Becket's Crown*, 133–34; for God's seal, see M. T. Clanchy, *From Memory to Written Record: England 1066–1307*, 2nd ed. (Oxford: Blackwell, 1993), 213–14.

⁴¹ 13:397–405 **It was then that Amphibalus showed Alban . . . so feared** *Lors li ad desclos. . . tant est redutez*: this account of Amphibalus's further teaching of Alban in Old Testament and salvation history is not present in *PSA* 9 (Ralph of Dunstable creates a similar but still longer elaboration in his verse version of *PSA*, TCD MS 177, fols. 5r-9r). The late twelfth and early thirteenth centuries, especially after Lateran IV and the Council of Oxford in 1222, saw intense production of *pastoralia* in England, in Latin and to a large extent in French. Thus Paris's attention here to the issue of what a layperson needs to know and should be taught is very much of its time, as well as providing (in Paris's version) the legal and feudal underpinning of the redemption, by way of appropriate explanation to Alban.

⁴² 14:408–10 **Now, there was a Saracen . . . spying on them** *Es vus un Sarrazin . . . les espia*: the Saracen soldier has not come to Alban and Amphibalus's secret schoolroom because he suspects that a foreign and subversive religion is being practiced. His attention is caught at first by the attempt at seclusion and privacy, which in the Middle Ages was frowned upon, unless formally structured in the various forms of solitary religious life. See Diana Webb, *Privacy and Solitude in the Middle Ages* (London and New York: Continuum, 2007), Introduction, vii–xvii, and, on the later medieval development of separate spaces for intellectual work for monastic and laypeople, chap. 10, "Studies," 157–72. Both *PSA* and *Alban* are significantly vague about exactly where Amphibalus and Alban go to study together: a separate place on the estate, a secret house? (see "une maison foreine," 3:75; *PSA* 9: *domum remotiorum, quae tugurium* [cabin] *vulgo solet appellari*). The first separate studies for scholar monks at St. Albans were built in the mid-fourteenth century (Webb, *Privacy*, 163).

⁴³ 14:414 **a wicked prince** *un prince felun*: Paris changes the pagan judge of *PSA* into "the prince" of St. Albans. The prince is unsurprisingly unnamed (there is no clear evidence of the identity of the contemporary ruler in St. Albans in the early hagiographical tradition: see Richard Sharpe, "The Late Antique Passion of St. Alban," in Henig and Lindley, *Alban and St Albans*, 30–37, at 33–35).

⁴⁴ 14:427 **Syria** *Sulie*: the term by which Saracens refer to the Holy Land throughout *Alban* (see further 16:502, 23:716, 39:1448); it is the standard medieval French name. Palestine was a province within *Sulie*.

⁴⁵ 15:450 **burnished blade** *brant furbi*: *AND* gives "furbished"; for the sense of "polished, scoured, rubbed-up," see T.-L., s.v. *forbir*. See also 27:896, 31:1108.

⁴⁶ 15:477 **white ermine fur** *peleiçun d'ermine enblanchi*: ermine (an expensive white fur with small black markings from the animals' tail-tips) was used as a trimming around the edges of fur cloaks. It often figures in images of worldly status and wealth. The term for Alban's mantle in *PSA* and *CM* is *chlamydem auro texto* (*PSA* 10; *CM* 1:150): a military cloak, woven with gold (thread), though also used in representations of Christ and Mary (J. F. Niermeyer et al., eds., *Mediae latinitatis lexicon minus* [Leiden: Brill, 2002], s.v. *chlamyda*). Amphibalus's cloak is a more ecclesiastical *caracalla* (*PSA* 10): see *Dictionary of Medieval Latin from British Sources*, ed. R. E. Latham and D. R. Howlett, vol. 1 (Oxford: Oxford University Press for the British Academy, 1975–1979), s.v. *caracalla*. On cloaks in *Alban*, see further Introduction, 29.

⁴⁷ 15:481 **a distance along the way** *treis arpentz e demi* (lit. "three and a half *arpents*"): *arpent* is defined by *AND* as "a measure of length" and as "an acre": the general idea of a good distance seems meant here.

⁴⁸ 16:521–22 **a serpent or a hunted lioness . . . wounded** *bersee / Leonesse, u saerpent . . . blescee*: the lioness is standardly associated with cruelty and ferocity (T.-L., s.v. *lionesse*; see also 38:1406 below). The pairing (usually as opponents) of lion and dragon (cf. Psalm 90:13) or serpent is common in bestiaries (Debra Hassig, *Medieval Bestiaries: Text, Image, Ideology* [Cambridge: Cambridge University Press, 1995], 50–51 and n. 64, 135): for an example in romance, see *Yvain*, ed. T. B. W. Reid (Manchester: Manchester University Press, 1942, repr. with corr. 1974), vv. 3348–81.

⁴⁹ 16:533 **his mantle, which they quickly tore** *la robe k'il unt tost desiree*: the focus on the mantle here is perhaps another parallel with Christ's passion: see Matt. 27:35, Mark 15:24, Luke 23:34, and John 19:23–24.

⁵⁰ 17:552 **vagrant** *tafur* (see also 34:1265): the name of a Saracen people and also by extension "a wretch, scoundrel" (T-L., s.v. *tafur* s. m. and adj.: *AND* gives "necromancer"). Thought by Guibert de Nogent to designate a Norman leader, the word was in fact principally associated with the Flemings who followed Peter the Hermit on the First Crusade (1095–1099) and with the *chansons de geste* about the siege of Antioch: see Lewis A. M. Sumberg, "The Tafurs and the First Crusade," *Mediaeval Studies* 21 (1959): 224–46. There may also be an implied parallel with the apostle Paul.

⁵¹ 17:559–60 **a master, an advocate . . . warrant and aid** *cum maistre e avoué . . . e a sun desciple e guarant e sucur*: *avoué/advocatus* and *guarant/warantus* are terms that usually denote protective lordship in legal contexts in thirteenth-century England. Both words continued to hold non-technical meanings, so the prince's point here may be that he would expect Alban to have brought with him a proper sponsor, perhaps to guarantee the correctness of his doctrine, perhaps to guarantee that he will do no harm and/or that he, the guarantor, will see that the harm is made good if it happens. Alban is defending his (i.e., Christ's) cause in the absence of the principal, whose business and right this really is. Alban should therefore vouch his *garant* (warrantor/guarantor) but, having chosen not to do so, must die in his stead. *Sucur* probably echoes a lord's duty to offer his vassal "counsel and aid" (*consilium et auxilium*), in the same way that the vassal owes these to him. We are indebted to Paul Hyams for generous help on these points.

⁵² 17:562 **in the end** *au chef de tur*: perhaps with a pun on "the end of the tower" (i.e., the garderobe). For the phrase, see *AND*, s.v. *chef* (*a, au el chef de tur*). In T.-L., "fausseté" is said, *inter alia*, to be Renart's "cousin germain."

⁵³ 17:575 **vavasour** *vavasur*: a lower or sub-infeudated vassal, a minor noble (*AND*, s.v. *vavasur*).

⁵⁴ 17:572–76 **bargainer . . . knights in battle** *changeur . . . chevalur en estur*: "bargainer" could apply either to Amphibalus for getting a good deal, as the prince sees it, or to Alban for making a bad one. In either case, the prince's thought continues, a knight may be seduced into betraying his class and values as easily as a merchant.

⁵⁵ 17:578 **Everybody is caught unaware at some time** *ki ne prent sum*: this topos, derived from Horace's saying that even Homer "nods" and that a "drowsy mood" may overtake a long work (*Ars poetica*, in *Horace: Satires, Epistles and Ars poetica*, trans. H. Rushton Fairclough, Loeb Classical Library [Cambridge, MA: Harvard University Press, London: William Heinemann, and New York: G. P. Putnam, 1926; repr. 1978],

ll. 359–360, 480–481), is also used by Paris in *Estoire*, v. 92, and *GA* 1:215 (of Abbot Warin): see *The History of Saint Edward the King*, trans. Fenster and Wogan-Browne, 118, n. to v. 92.

⁵⁶ 18:592–619 "Friend... breaking-in" *'Amis... en sa adanture'* Paris adds the opening topos of idols as the product of human manufacture (18:592–99), as he does Alban's speech on their inanimate status and their frangibility at 19:634–44. This is a frequent topos (derived from Ps. 115 [113]:4–6 and Ps. 135 [134]:15–17) in Anglo-Norman saints' lives and elsewhere: see, e.g., Camille, *The Gothic Idol*, 119–28. See also the Verulamians' worship of Phoebus 19:621–25 below and n.

⁵⁷ 18:594 **Do you believe** *Quidez*: after his first sentence, with its second person singular pronoun, Alban uses the more formal plural. For alternation of singular and plural, see also 25:820 below.

⁵⁸ 18:598 **a counterfeit—dreamed up and invented** *fausseté, purpens e cuntrevure*: i.e., an image created by humans, not God, and so, in this context, idolatry.

⁵⁹ 18:615 **the ass ... to the harp** *ke asne harpeure*: James W. Hassell, Jr., *Middle French Proverbs, Sentences, and Proverbial Phrases* (Toronto: Pontifical Institute of Mediaeval Studies, 1982), A137, "l'âne à la harpe."

⁶⁰ 18:619 **a foal... his breaking-in** *pulein... sa adanture*: cf. Thomas's *Tristan*: "Que puleins prent en danteüre / U voille u nun, lunges li dure," in Thomas of Britain, *Tristan*, ed. and trans. Stewart Gregory (London and New York: Garland, 1991), 78, vv. 1516–17, and Joseph Morawski, *Proverbes français antérieurs au XVe siècle* (Paris: Champion, 1925), no. 1765.

⁶¹ 19:621–25 **the day when they celebrated Phoebus... vow** *au jur quant feste funt / A Febum... servise e wu anvel*: in *PSA* 14, Alban is to be compelled to a "sacrificia daemonum"; Paris adds a vivid description and an illustration of the sun god idol (TCD MS. 177, fol. 34v: see Plate 6). Paris discusses the medieval excavations at St. Albans as producing traces of a Verulamian cult of Phoebus as sun god in *GA* 1:27 (see also Introduction, 23 n. 57). Camille reproduces the illustration on TCD MS. 177, fol. 34v and suggests that Paris may have seen an astrological depiction of Sol Apollo (Camille, *Gothic Idol*, 106–7). Paris's terms for the pagans' relations with Phoebus are (like his terms for Christians' relations with their God) taken from the lexis of feudal service. Homage *de fide et servicio* is one of three categories of homage classified in the Norman *Summa de legibus* of c. 1236 (see Hyams, "Homage and Feudalism," 30).

⁶² 19:630–32 **dragged him there... face, nose, and brow** *Auban i trainent... face e nes e frunt*: a parallel with Christ's Passion is probably to be seen here: cf., e.g., the Passion reenactments carried out on her own body by Elizabeth of Spalbeek (d. 1270), which included the dragging and buffeting of Christ (the text of her thirteenth-century *vita* is in *Catalogus codicum hagiographicorum Bibliothecae regiae Bruxellensis* [Brussels: Polleunis, Ceuterick et Lefébure, 1886], pt. I, vol. 1, *Codices Latini Membranei*, 362–78, at 364/30–38, 365/38–41).

⁶³ 19:634–44 **"All those I see here... and metal melts"** *'Tuit cist ke ci vei... et metal funt'*: Alban's speech in the temple after his scourging is Paris's addition: *PSA* moves directly from the injunction to sacrifice to the scourging (*PSA* 14).

⁶⁴ 21:676–86 **No longer does he drink... a faithful knight** *Ne beit mais... leal chevaler*: Alban's use of his imprisonment as both a penance and a demonstration of chivalric loyalty to God is Paris's addition. *PSA* moves directly to the effects of Alban's

imprisonment on the surrounding countryside (*PSA* 15). On *ubi sunt* topoi, see n. to 12:355–58 and Introduction, 54–55.

⁶⁵ 22:715: The lacuna covers about three paragraphs of *PSA* 16–17, but Paris's rate of expansion in relation to his source varies, and it is not clear how long *laisses* 22 and 23 were. Some of Paris's reworking of *PSA* 17's debate over Alban's execution survives in the remains of *laisse* 23 in the Alban manuscript (TCD MS. 177, fol. 35v): characteristically, it is turned into direct speech, not simply reported.

⁶⁶ 23:734 "**He who learns from others mends his ways**" "*Ki par autres est garniz, cist beu se chastie*": cf. Morawski, *Proverbes français*, 314: for variations, see Guernes de Pont-Ste-Maxence, *Vie de saint Thomas le martyr*, ed. E. Walberg (Lund: Gleerup, 1922), 101, v. 2976 ("süef se chastie qui d'autrui se chastie"), and *Le Roman de la Rose*, ed. E. Langlois, SATF (Paris: Firmin Didot, 1921), vol. 3, vv. 8003–4 ("Mout a beneüree vie / On qui par autri se chastie") and n. to 8003–4, at 283–84.

⁶⁷ 23:735–36 "**Let him be driven away ... emulates**" "*Enchacez seit ... maistrie!*": in 23:736 (*Celui sive ki doctrine tant prise e maistrie*), Harden takes *maistrie* as a noun: we take it as a verb (see *AND*, s.v. *mestrier*).

⁶⁸ 24:737–39 **The prince and his community of barons ... town elders** *Li prince e la comune*: *commune* here probably indicates the prince's council (or *communitas regni*, as suggested by the prince's comment in 34:1265 below; and see note), or the town governance of Verulamium, rather than any more inclusive range of the city's inhabitants; see Bryce Lyon, "Commune," in *Dictionary of the Middle Ages*, ed. Joseph Strayer (New York: Scribner, 1982–1989), 3:493–503. Paris seems to envisage an older combination of hereditary or royally appointed town governor and burgesses.

⁶⁹ 24:741–44 **Roman law ... by custom and right** *la lei de Rumme custumme ... e dreiture*: the term "Roman" and references to Rome itself vary in implication according to their context. Sometimes a more honorable strain of pagans is meant; sometimes, as at 48:1834, the Christian Rome of the popes. Here "Roman law" means the law-codes still current in Paris's day as the foundations of civil law; it is not a pejorative reference to the customs of the pagans. Roman law itself had not always made distinctions of civil rank when administering punishments, but different capital punishments for *honestiores* (people of high status, as opposed to the *humiliores*) had been established by the reign of the emperor Severus Alexander (222–235 CE; thus presumably in time to be applied to Alban's case). *Humiliores* could be sent to the mines, crucified, thrown to the beasts, or burned alive (see Richard A. Bauman, *Crime and Punishment in Ancient Rome* [London and New York: Routledge, 1996], 129–40). On Roman law in medieval England (for which St. Albans may have been one of several schools), see Francis de Zulueta and Peter Stein, *The Teaching of Roman Law in England around 1200*, Selden Society, SS8 (London: Selden Society, 1990); R. V. Turner, "Roman Law in England before the Time of Bracton," *Journal of British Studies* 15 (1975): 1–25, at 6, 11; see also Eleanor Rathbone, "Roman Law in the Anglo-Norman Realm," *Studia Gratiana* 11 (1967): 254–71.

⁷⁰ 24:754 "**Get out of the city**" "*Va t'en ... de la cité*": in Paris's illustration of this scene (TCD MS. 177, fol. 36r), the Verulamian who shouts this at Alban speaks early Middle English, or perhaps late Anglo-Saxon: see R18 and Plate 7. This would be a logical choice for the pagans of *PSA*, whose narrator says he is translating an English book (*PSA* 1), but Paris's Verulamians probably ought to speak British. On the other hand, Paris's comments sometimes suggest that he thought the two languages were interchangeable (e.g., a book is said to be in English "or rather, British" *GA* 1:27).

⁷¹ 24:758 **just bowed down**: *les ad encliné*: the French presents a questionable syntax: *les* is probably the adverb *les, lez*, meaning "alongside." The idea here is that Alban offers no resistance to his persecutors and instead turns to prayer (in this as in most other details, the narrative parallels his passion with Christ's). On *simplicitas* and Alban, see Introduction, 51–52.

⁷² 24:785 **who looks after all that he has created** *Ki de tut prent cure quancke il ad crié*: *crié* is the past participle of *créer*, "to create."

⁷³ 24:786 **rewards** *soudee*: in a secular context, the verb refers in particular to a soldier's pay.

⁷⁴ 25:790 **the river, which was deep** *l'ewe ki ert parfunde*: the Ver, a river running between Verulamium and St. Albans Abbey, is normally said to be fordable almost everywhere. For Bede, the miracle is a function of Alban's impatience for martyrdom: the bridge is choked with spectators, Alban looks to heaven, and the river dries up to provide a path for him to continue to his execution (*HE* 1:7, 32–33). In *PSA* 19, the miracle embraces the crowd of spectators, its value as a sign of God's powers underlined by the echoes of the miraculous crossing of the Red Sea, typologically a sign of salvation (cf. Exod. 13:18; also Exod. 14:27).

⁷⁵ 25:799–801 **A noble knight named Heraclius** *Uns chevalers gentilz . . . Aracle*. In *PSA*, this figure is an anonymous soldier and reluctant executioner as he is in Bede (*HE* 1:7, 32–35). See further Introduction, 29–30, and Baswell, 189–90 below.

⁷⁶ 25:807 **Saracens** *Sarrazins*: see n. to 1:13 above.

⁷⁷ 25:812 **his man and his servant** *sis hom e sis sergant*: Old French *sergant, serjant*, is both "servant" and "man-at-arms."

⁷⁸ 25:817 **perversely fighting against it** *purvers recumbatant*: as argued by Harden (70, nn. 816–18), *purvers* can be accepted as an Anglo-Norman form of *pervers*.

⁷⁹ 25:819–20 **man . . . to whom God constantly calls, why do you delay** *Hem . . . E tei tuz jurs apele, k'alez vuz demurant*: see also loose concord at 18:594 above and R64:401–2. Collective nouns freely take singular and plural in Old French and in Anglo-Norman.

⁸⁰ 25:833 **the disgrace** *la huntage*: as Harden notes (70, n. to 833) the feminine is surprising here, but his suggestion that the word could be read as *l'ahuntage* is not confirmed by *DEAF* (see Fascicule H4-H5, col. 575, *ahontage).

⁸¹ 26:871–72 **Moses . . . overcome by thirst** *Moyseus . . . de sei fu cunfundu*: cf. Exodus 17:1–6, and see also Numbers 20:1–11. Paris adds the parallel here: it is not used in *PSA*.

⁸² 27:903 **gleaming** *esmirables*: the form is not recorded in T.-L. or F. E. Godefroy, *Dictionnaire de l'ancien français et de tous ses dialectes du IXe au XVe siècle*, 10 vols. (Paris: Vieweg, 1880–1902; repr. Paris: Librairie des Sciences et des Arts, 1938), who give the noun and verb only: *AND* gives the adjective.

⁸³ 27:906 **set with choice jasper . . . sapphires** *De jaspes . . . safirs eschoisiz*: for the curative and protective powers ascribed to these gems in medieval belief, see Paul Studer and Joan Evans, eds., *Anglo-Norman Lapidaries* (Paris: Champion, 1924), 33–34, 81–82, 98, 122, 161, 242–43. Cf. also Revelation 21:19 (the heavenly Jerusalem).

⁸⁴ 27:910 **arrived in a safe port** *a bon port arivez*: not in the standard collections of Old French proverbs cited in nn. to 18:615, 18:619, and 35:1315 but with a figurative sense of "happily arrived" (see *Oxford English Dictionary Online* [2008], s.v. port, *n.*¹,

sense 3b: earliest citation from Chaucer, but under "Etymology" *OED* notes thirteenth-century circulation of the phrase "a bon port").

⁸⁵ 27:915 **his eyes leapt out of his head** *li sunt li oil du chief sailliz*: this scene is detailed both in the narrative (twice: see also 32:1176) and in Paris's famous illustration of the martyrdom: see, e.g., Nigel J. Morgan and Richard Marks, *The Golden Age of English Manuscript Painting* (London: Chatto and Windus, 1981): see pl. 6 (50) and see cover illustration here. Paris also illustrates it in a bas-de-page washed drawing in *CM* (Cambridge, Corpus Christi College, MS. 26, fol. 58v, c. 1244–45?, reproduced in Eileen Roberts, *Images of Alban: St. Alban in Art from the Earliest Times to the Present* [St. Albans: Fraternity of the Friends of St. Albans Abbey, 1999], 25, pl. 6) and in the margin of his copy of Offa's Charter (Cotton Nero D. I, fol. 149r); it was also represented on the counterseal of Abbot John of Hertford (1235–1263), extant on BM Charter L. F. C. VII, 6. It is unclear whether Alban's shrine in the monastery showed the loss of the executioner's eyes: the scene is referred to simply as Alban's *decollatio* in *GA*'s account of the shrine commissioned from John the Goldsmith by Abbot Simon (*GA* 1:189). For illustrations of the martyrdom, see Roberts, *Images of Alban*, which includes two early representations of Alban's execution: the psalter of Christina of Markyate (Roberts, *Images*, 19, pl. 2, see also www.abdn.ac.uk/stalbanspsalter, 416), which shows the loss of the executioner's eyes, and the Huntingfield Psalter (1210–1220: New York, Pierpont Morgan MS. 43, fol. 24v), where the scene is just before the decollation and the executioner's eyes and Alban's neck are still intact (Roberts, *Images*, 23, pl. 4). Paris's scene is imitated in the Psalter of Johannes de Dalling (1246–60: BL MS. Royal 2. B. VI fol. 10v; Roberts, *Images*, 33, pl. 20), made at St. Albans, and echoed in the Exeter Psalter of c. 1330 (Cambridge, Sidney Sussex College, MS. 76, fol. 34r; Roberts, *Images*, 36, pl. 23) and a fourteenth-century shrine carving in St. Albans (Roberts, *Images*, 34, pl. 21), in late medieval pilgrim badges (Roberts, *Images*, 38, pl. 24), and in the woodcut for John Lydgate's *Life of Alban and Amphibalus*, printed at St. Albans in 1534 (Roberts, *Images*, 57, pl. 40).

⁸⁶ Rubric: **Here begins . . . Saint Heraclius** *Ci cumence . . . Seint Aracle*: Heraclius remains unnamed throughout *PSA*: Paris, who has already named him in 25: 801 above, now gives him a separate passion with its own rubric.

⁸⁷ 29:997 **The pilgrim cleric** *cist pelerim lettré*: literally "the literate pilgrim" (i.e., Latinate).

⁸⁸ 29:998 **necromancy** *nigromancie*: a term used by the pagans is once again expressive of Christian concerns; as the art of obtaining knowledge through conjuring spirits, necromancy, the magical art of the literate, was regarded as spiritually dangerous (see Lynn Thorndike, *A History of Magic and Experimental Science* [New York: Columbia University Press, 1923–1958, repr. 1975], vol. 2). In the thirteenth-century Anglo-Norman life of St. Clement of Rome, for example, the saint is warned that necromancy is a presumption against God and faith (*La Vie de seint Clement Pape*, ed. Daron Burrows, ANTS 64–65 [London: ANTS, 2007], 1:23, vv. 808–15). When Amphibalus's lettered status is specifically mentioned in this sentence in *Auban*, it is to prepare for the accusation of necromancy: (29:997: see n. 87). Yet the line between heretical necromancy and orthodox Christian invocation could be thin: conjuring spirits could sometimes be in effect a "Christian magical replacement for necromancy," as Flint says of Christian distinctions between resurrection and resuscitation of the dead (V. I. J. Flint, *The Rise of Magic in Early Medieval Europe* [Princeton: Princeton University Press, 1991], 271–73, with an example of St. Martin calling up and interrogating a dead robber). See also Claire

Fanger, ed., *Conjuring Spirits: Texts and Traditions of Medieval Ritual Magic* (Stroud: Sutton, 1998). Paris himself wrote and illustrated an astrolabe manual and other scientific and fortune-telling texts (Morgan, *EGM [I]*, no. 89, 140).

[89] 29:1007 **by spells and rites** *par caractes e par sortz enchanté*: in *PSA* 24, the pagans claim that it is sorcery on the part of the anonymous soldier convert that keeps him alive and makes him impervious to the iron of swords. Paris has his Saracens impute the sorcery instead to Amphibalus, thus leaving this Christian cleric as the sole figure associated with arcane knowledge (however understood) and Heraclius as purely chivalric.

[90] 29:1027 **They thought they had worked their will** *bien quident tut eient lur voler achevé*: at this point *PSA*'s pagans begin to mutter against their unjust judge (*PSA* 24), but this is omitted by Paris, who concentrates instead on the martyrdoms of Alban and Heraclius. *Laisse* 30 (no equivalent in *PSA*) is one of Paris's many elaborations of Heraclius's role.

[91] 29:1031 **a mountain dwelling** *Herberge en muntainne*: see Matt. 5:14 and n. to R61:375.

[92] 31:1062 **a beam** *Un rais*: this is a well-established hagiographic convention, favored among others by Bede in *HE*. The beam indicating Alban's tomb is given three illustrations in the manuscript, one in *Alban* (TCD MS. 177, fol. 46v, now bound as 40r, and R31) and two in the following story of King Offa of Mercia's discovery of Alban's relics (fols. 57r and 58r; see R59 and R61 below).

[93] 31:1065 **the heavens opened** *du cel ki desclot e uveri*: the construction suggests the pervasiveness of heaven's light; this is not so much a beam out of heaven as an opening allowing heaven's glory to be perceived from earth, a perception usually closed to living humans but revealed here through the martyr.

[94] 31:1066 **Watchmen and pagan shepherds** *aguetes e pasturs paens*: Paris nuances *PSA* 25's *concursus hominum* in line with the details added in 31:1053–57, specifying watchmen and shepherds (the only pagans who would not be in their beds, as in 31:1057).

[95] 31:1077–105 **Citizens, neighbors . . . entrust myself to him** *Citoiens, vesin . . . en lui me fi*: Paris changes the tenor of this speech in his source (*PSA* 26). The speaker is identified as a Saracen; abstract reclassification of the pagan's gods is replaced with fear of mortality registered through lineage, injunctions to penance, and the exemplary renunciation of specific deities; commentary on the beam of light is shortened and partially replaced by a recapitulation of Alban's powers over the elements; and a play on the darkness of the world and the revelation of Alban's merits is not translated. *PSA*'s declaration that the converting pagan said "haec *et alia*" (*PSA* 27) may have acted as a cue for Paris.

[96] 31:1110–11 **They swore oaths to each other . . . for anyone** *Entrejurez se sunt . . . pur nulli*: this scene of communal oath-taking is Paris's addition to the source (in *PSA*, the pagans simply leave in pursuit of Amphibalus after their conversions, *PSA* 27). Because they are converts, their oath is plain and straightforward, unlike the oaths of unregenerate Saracens in *Alban* (see n. to 38:1411–14).

[97] 31:1115 **one who stayed behind . . . become sick** *li uns remist, enmaladi*: the expedition to Wales is not included in Bede (*HE* 1:7, 28–35) and not mentioned in *PSA* at this point (*PSA* 27) but appears in *PSA* 30. Paris is again rearranging source material for repetition and emphasis.

⁹⁸ 32:1151 **value . . . at a spur** *un esperun vaillant*: a phrase also found in chivalric romance and mock-epic; see T.-L., s.v. *esperon*; see also 32:1163 below.

⁹⁹ 32:1163 **value . . . at a glove** *a valur d'un gant*: see T.-L., s.v. *gant* (cf. 32:1151 above).

¹⁰⁰ 32:1124–201 **"Friend!" he said. " . . . true loving friend"** *'Amis' dist il . . . verai amant'*: the Saracen convert's recapitulatory narrative is Paris's addition (cf. *PSA* 27).

¹⁰¹ 33:1206 **"Glorious cross! Cross that I so much desire!"** *Croiz gloriuse! Croiz ki tant desir!* Paris adds this direct speech, for which there is no equivalent in *PSA* 27. Cf. the response "O crux gloriosa! Crux adoranda" (PL 78.803B) and Bede: "O gloriosa fulgidis / crux emicas virtutibus" (PL 94.633B).

¹⁰² 33:1224 **through a vision** *par avisiun*: see n. to 10:294–96 above.

¹⁰³ 33:1238–39 **a sermon . . . on the Trinity** *un sermun . . . de la trinité*: that the sermon is on the Trinity is Paris's addition to *PSA* 27, thus making the converts' instruction echo Alban's own. The Trinity is stressed as a crucial aspect of doctrinal adherence by Paris: cf. Alban's anger at its irrationality before his conversion (7:191–96 above), and Paris's illustration of a Trinitarian crucifix in the vision God sends to Alban (*laisses* 8–9 above and illustration, TCD MS. 177, fol. 30v col. b). The final phrase perhaps also alludes to the so-called 'Athanasian Creed': "quam nisi quisque integram inviolatamque servaverit, absque dubio in aeternum peribit."

¹⁰⁴ 34:1252 **simple handmaiden** *simple ancele*: frequently imputed to women, *simplicitas* was a "virginity of the soul"; see P. Antin, "'Simple' et 'simplicité' chez saint Jérôme," *Revue bénédictine* 71 (1961): 371–81, at 372; and see n. to 7:176 above and Introduction, 51–52. There is also an allusion to Luke 1:38 (*ancilla*).

¹⁰⁵ 34:1254 **who remained a virgin mother after the birth** *après l'enfantement remist mere e pucele*: the pagan prince's grasp of Christian doctrine reflects a concern of special intensity in the thirteenth century as "the notion of pollution became increasingly part of scientific discourse": Peggy McCracken, *The Curse of Eve, The Wound of the Hero: Blood, Gender and Medieval Literature* (Philadelphia: University of Pennsylvania Press, 2003), 63 (also 2–6, 61–65). See also Charles T. Wood, "The Doctors' Dilemma: Sin, Salvation, and the Menstrual Cycle in Medieval Thought," *Speculum* 56 (1981): 710–27, at 721–23; Dyan Elliott, *Fallen Bodies: Pollution, Sexuality and Demonology in the Middle Ages* (Philadelphia: University of Pennsylvania Press, 1999), 107–26. Paris had a copy of Grosseteste's *De probatione uirginitatis beatae Mariae* (from Grosseteste himself): see *English Benedictine Libraries: The Shorter Catalogues*, ed. Richard Sharpe, J. P. Carley, R. M. Thomson, and A. G. Watson (London: British Library in association with the British Academy, 1996), 539–44, at 541. On the perpetual virginity of Mary, a doctrine established both by the early church fathers and the Koran and newly important in thirteenth-century discussion of the doctrine of the Immaculate Conception, see Hilda Graef, *Mary: A History of Doctrine and Devotion* (London: Sheed and Ward, 1963, repr. 1965, 1990), 28–81, 94–96, 159–60, 264–302.

¹⁰⁶ 34:1265 **And . . . this vagrant . . . here to Bordeaux** *E ceu tafur . . . de ci k'a Burdele*: on the term *tafur* for a vagrant (also used of Amphibalus at 41:1513), see n. to 17:552 above. Bordeaux is one limit of the contemporary Angevin empire. On the torture planned for Amphibalus here see Introduction, 9–10, *PSA* 39, and n. to 43:1602 below.

¹⁰⁷ 34:1246–69 **"Lords," he said, ". . . my loyal people"** *'Seignurs,' dist il, . . . 'ma gent k'estes loiele'*: Paris replaces the source's account of gathering rumors and a census of who is missing in Verulamium (*PSA* 27) with direct speech by the prince of Verulamium as he takes

counsel with his people. In **I require agreement from you** (*A vus cunsel... demant*: 34:1269), *cunseil* can mean both "counsel" (in the sense of "advice" or of "a deliberative body, a council") and "agreement": see *AND*, s.v. *cunseil*. Acting with the formally secured consent of their nobles was a strategic necessity for medieval rulers; conversely, vassals had a duty to give counsel: see e.g. Geraldine Barnes, *Counsel and Strategy in Middle English Romance* (Cambridge: D.S. Brewer, 1993), chap. 1, "Working by Counsel in Plantagenet England," 1–28. This scene between the prince and the Verulamians is Paris's addition: in *PSA* 27 the furious citizens set out in pursuit of their friends and relatives once it is known who is missing.

[108] 35:1286: **as a fully summoned army** *ost bani e plener*: an army gathered by proclamation and called out to military duty (not a standing army, which was very rarely kept by medieval English kings). The same phrase is used in R34:162.

[109] 35:1288 **which they worshipped** *k'[l] lur plut aurer*: on the pagans' worship of the sun god, see n. to 19:621–25 above.

[110] 35:1305 **this decree ... cannot be revoked** *Dunee est la sentence... sanz returner*; 35:1321 **our decree ... never be annulled** *nostre sentence...ja fauser*: Paris follows *PSA* 28 and 29, where the same formula, *Stat sententia*, is used by a pagan to threaten Amphibalus and by the Christian converts to declare their new allegiance.

[111] 35:1315 " 'He wounds himself who does not see'" ' "*Cist se fert ki ne veit*'": cf. Morawski, *Proverbes français*, nos. 2259, 1942, and Elisabeth Schulze-Busacker, *Proverbes et expressions proverbiales dans la littérature narrative du Moyen Age français: recueil et analyse* (Paris: Champion, 1985), 287, no. 1942 ("Qui fiert ferir se vuet: Se tu fiers mi, jou ferrai ti").

[112] 35:1336 **necromancy** *nigromant*: a precise use of the term (as opposed to the more usual *enchantement* or *sorcerie*) in the context of miraculous healing of the dead or near dead, since the particular art of the necromancer was to interrogate spirits conjured from the dead (see n. to 29:998 above). Paris adds the pagan explanation for the heavenly voice: the incident is not in *PSA* 30's narrative account of the slaughter, though it is narrated by the returning converts in *PSA* 35 without rebuttal or alternative interpretation.

[113] 35:1345 **cut off his arm** *esmanker*: Harden and *AND* give "to injure, to maim," but see T.-L., s. v., *esmanchier* for the sense "to deprive someone of their hand" (*der Hand berauben*), citing this instance. *AND* allows the past participle (but only the past participle) as "one-armed." *PSA*'s *manum ... amputavit* at a later stage of its narrative (*PSA* 35) supports a reading of the French here as "cutting off an arm." In *PSA*, however, it is the son who attempts to bind the father's wounds and is prevented from doing so by his own brother cutting off his hand: in *Alban*, it is the father whose attempt to help one son is thwarted by the other. In *PSA* the image occurs only in the returning Verulamians' narration of the massacre (*PSA* 35): in the narrative of the event as it happens (*PSA* 30) there is an unelaborated statement of fratricide, patricide, and filicide. Paris repeats the image with variation, using it both here in the narration and again in the Verulamians' report to their fellow citizens (41:1530–32). Both passages partly echo Matt. 10:21, 35.

[114] 35:1350 **He could not look at the martyrs' suffering without himself suffering** *Ne puet sanz martire les martirs regarder*: Paris puns on martyrdom and suffering in the double meaning of *martire*. The notion of substituted martyrdom is common: so, for example, the martyrdom of ascesis is often credited to saintly figures who do not undergo a martyrdom by *passio*.

[115] 35:1362–68 **They swore to their . . . god Jove . . . "as a warning to others"** *Jurent Jovin lur deu . . . "pur autres chastier"*: Paris fleshes out the Latin (*PSA* 31), in which there is no mention of Jove, with a mixture of reported and direct speech.

[116] 37:1386–87 **a great wolf . . . an eagle** *un grant lu . . . un aigles*: the wolf and eagle are traditional beasts of battle and disposers of carrion. God causes them to act *contra naturam*, in the miracle here. Although their guardianship is claimed as an unprecedented miracle in 37:1391 (*Tel merveille en tere ne fu unc mais veu*), the saintly patron of the rival great house of Benedictine monks at Bury St. Edmunds King Edmund of East Anglia famously had his severed head guarded by a wolf until it was recovered for burial. *Laisses* 36 and 37 have no equivalent at this point in *PSA*: there the care of the martyrs' bodies does not feature until the report of the Verulamians (*PSA* 35–37: *laisses* 41–42 in *Alban*).

[117] 38:1411–14 **They swore to Mohammed . . . in a hostelry** *Juré unt Mahomet . . . n'en ostel*: Paris elaborates the swearing of the Saracen oath (cf. *PSA* 31). This elaboration by Paris may be to underline his Saracens' inevitable perjury as pagan oath-swearers (cf. 46:1744–46).

[118] 39:1453 **to be baptized by you, who bless people** *Pur aver de vus batesme ki la gent seintifie*: the antecedent of *ki* here is probably Amphibalus but could also be *batesme*.

[119] 39:1464 **who binds to himself those who freely come to him, and who unbinds as he pleases** *ki lie k'a pleisir li vent e ki li plest, deslie*: clearly *vent* not *veut* in the manuscript (fol. 43v col. b). While *PSA* 32 mentions only the great power of God, Paris's French terms have further implications, with their play on bonds between lord and vassal (*lie* and *deslie*: see Baker, *Manual of Law French*, s.vv. *lier* [1] and *delier*). In the reciprocities of power lords could not always afford their obligations to all the vassals they might wish to retain. As often in *Alban*, the perceptions accorded the Saracens express Christian social and cultural structures.

[120] 40:1473–81 **"Gentle knights . . . the heavenly angels"** *"Gentilz chevalers . . . li angre espiriteus"*: Amphibalus's direct speech is Paris's addition to *PSA*'s brief narrative of the journey back to Verulamium (*PSA* 31) with an allusion to Luke 15:4–7 in vv. 1479–81.

[121] 41:1498 **all the gold of Damascus** *tut l'or de Damas*: silver was more common coinage of medieval Europe, but the Christian kingdoms of the crusader states in the Holy Land struck gold coins imitating Islamic Fatimid dinars of the eleventh and early twelfth centuries: see Catherine Eagleton and Jonathan Williams, *Money: A History*, 2nd ed. (London: British Museum, 2007), 98.

[122] 41:1530 **You would have seen the father of the son struck** *Veisez ke le pere le fiz . . . feri*: see n. to 35:1345 above.

[123] 41:1519–55 **"restrain yourselves . . . for his own purposes"** *"Esmesurez vus . . . a sun uoes tant seisi"*: unusually, Paris shortens direct speech: this is cut down from a long lament for the absence of future hope in *PSA* 33.

[124] 42:1558 **who protects . . . from shame** *de huntage defent*: Saracen perceptions again illuminate the poem's Christian conception of God's lordship. A lord's ability to protect or, if necessary, avenge the honor of his liege people was crucial.

[125] 43:1602: **drew out Amphibalus's bowels from his belly** *la buele en sachent du ventre*: on this torture (first envisaged by the prince of Vendamium at 34:1266), see Introduction, 9–10, and *PSA* 39 and n. 47.

¹²⁶ 43:1619 **the faithless Jews** *li Giu desloial*: for the Christian sense in which Jews are "faithless" or *desloial*, see n. to 6:155–64 above.

¹²⁷ 44:1679 **fire . . . the worm** *Feu . . . verm*: cf. Mark 9:43–48.

¹²⁸ 44:1692 **his arms are always outstretched, ready to embrace** *les braz ad estenduz tuz tens pur embracer*: in thirteenth-century affective piety of the kind marking Alban's dream (*laisse* 9 above), Christ is sometimes portrayed as leaning down from the cross and embracing his followers: see, e. g., Adelaide Bennett, "A Book Designed for a Noblewoman: An Illustrated *Manuel des Péchés* of the Thirteenth Century," in *Medieval Book Production: Assessing the Evidence: Proceedings of the Second Conference of the Seminar in the History of the Book to 1500: Oxford, July 1988*, ed. Linda L. Brownrigg (Los Altos Hills, CA: Anderson-Lovelace, 1990), 163–81 (at 170, fig. 10): illustration also repr. in Binski, *Becket's Crown*, 187. See also *Ancrene Wisse* in *Anchoritic Spirituality: Ancrene Wisse and Associated Works*, trans. Anne Savage and Nicholas Watson, Part VII (New York: Paulist Press, 1991), 401, n. 32, for analogues in Anselmian piety.

¹²⁹ 45:1714–19 **life without death . . . the infernal Mohammed** *vie sanz mort . . . l'enfernal Mahun*: Paris amplifies *PSA* 43 with a brief evocation of the "qualities of heaven" list (a standard mode of describing heaven often matched by equivalent lists for hell: see, for instance, the influential work often attributed to Anselm, "De custodia interioris hominis," in *Memorials of St Anselm*, ed. R. W. Southern and F. S. Schmitt, Auctores Britannici Medii Aevi I [London: Oxford University Press for the British Academy, 1969], 354–60, and cf. Amphibalus's description of hell in 44:1678–79). At this point, *PSA* has Amphibalus pray to Alban to send him a good angel lest his soul be attacked by devils en route to heaven (*PSA* 43): as usual in *PSA*, there is no specific naming of pagan deities, as in Paris's *Mahun* in 45:1719.

¹³⁰ 45:1721–22 **whiter than linen . . . lily . . . in season** *plus blancs ke cheinsil . . . lis en sa saison*: Paris adds the two similes to *PSA* 43's "caelesti fulgore radiantes." Cf. also Luke 24:4.

¹³¹ 45:1728 **fire, worms, or thieves** *de fu, de verm, ne de larrun*: cf. Matt. 6:19–20, Mark 9:43–48 and see 44:1679.

¹³² 46:1765 **our** *lur*: Paris's syntactic concord is looser here than is usual in Modern English, but accepted in Old French and Anglo-Norman.

¹³³ 47:1772–80 **no one who . . . their fingers bent back** *N'i out ki . . . li doi sunt replié*: Hahn cites a parallel with Rev. 16:10 (*et commanducaverunt linguas suas prae dolore* "and they gnawed their tongues for pain"); see Hahn, *Portrayed on the Heart*, 301, and *PSA* 45, 159 below.

¹³⁴ 47:1793 **they broke their gods** *lur deus . . . unt depecé*: *PSA* has no equivalent scene of idol-smashing at this point (*PSA* 46), but these occur in *chansons de geste*: cf., e.g., the smashing of the idols Apollo, Mohammed, and Tervagant by the pagans of Saragossa in the *Chanson de Roland*: see *The Song of Roland: An Analytical Edition*, ed. and trans. G. Brault (University Park, PA: Penn State Press, 1978), vol. 2, *laisse* 187:2580–91.

¹³⁵ 47:1797 **damned forever** *a tutdis damné*: Christian orthodoxy was not in fact conclusive on this point; see Whatley, "Uses of Hagiography" (n. to 4:81–91 above), and Nicholas Watson, "Visions of Inclusion: Universal Salvation and Vernacular Theology in Pre-Reformation England," *Journal of Medieval and Early Modern Studies* 27 (1997): 145–87.

¹³⁶ 47:1811 **gave them comfort** *les a revisité*: the verb is particularly characteristic of God's manifestations and of shrine visiting by humans: nearly all citations in T.-L. are

from Anglo-Norman saints' lives. The iterative form perhaps has a sense here that God has always already "visited" people with creation and revelation and now offers a repeated revelation. The usage goes back to an echo of Luke 1:68.

[137] 48:1812 **I . . . a Saracen of false belief** *Jo . . . mescreant Sarrazin*: on the meaning of *mescreant*, see n. to 3:64 above. On the narrator figure, see Introduction, 28, and *PSA* 47.

[138] 48:1817–18 **the faith of Apollo . . . Jove** *de la loi Apolin . . . Jovin:* on the treatment of the classical gods, see n. to 19:621–25 above. For Paris's *CM* drawing of Brutus sacrificing to an idol of Diana, see Lewis, *Art of Matthew Paris*, 159, fig. 89. In the *chansons de geste*, Saracens are often said to worship the trio of Apollo, Tervagant, and Mohammed. See also n. to 1:14 and 47:1793 above.

[139] 48:1823 **translated into French and Latin** *translatee en franceis e latin*: cf. 3:70 above; both Amphibalus and the Saracen envisage French and Latin as normative languages. On the representation of ethnicity and language, see Introduction, 28, 41.

[140] 48:1826 **all the gold of Constantine** *tut l'or Costentin*: perhaps a reference to the so-called donation of Constantine, a forgery of the eighth century in which the emperor was purported to have given the city of Rome and the palaces and provinces of Italy to Pope Sylvester I, or possibly a reference to Constantinople itself. Knowledge of the city's riches was confirmed for Westerners by the Fourth Crusade which captured Constantinople in 1204. The form 'Costentin', however, is not usual in Old French for the city as opposed to the emperor.

[141] 48:1829 **shoes of Cordovan leather** *chauceure de cordewon caprin*: in *GA*, Paris notes approvingly that Abbot William of Trumpington (1214–35) had the monks' sheepskin shoes replaced by superior ones of "cordevan," tawed goat or ox leather (*de vili corio quod vulgariter* bazan, *in alutam, id est* cordewan, *civiliter commutavit, GA* 1:293).

[142] 48:1831 **I will not sleep . . .** *Ne dormirai . . .*: this form of oath, seen as the cause of perjury in the pagan Saracens (46:1745), is not used by the *PSA* narrator of his own penitential journey to Rome (*PSA* 47), but cf. Ps. 132 (131), where David vows not to rest till he finds a dwelling place for the Lord.

[143] 48:1833. **Mount St. Bernard** *Mungiu*: Mount St. Bernard: the pass over the mountain lies along the old Via Flaminia, apparently a pilgrimage route; see Wace's *Roman de Brut: A History of the British*, ed. and trans. Judith Weiss, Exeter Medieval English Texts and Studies (Exeter: University of Exeter Press, 1999), 73, n. 2.

[144] 48:1837 **Corineus** *Cornelin*: in Geoffrey of Monmouth's *History of the Kings of Britain*, Corineus accompanies Brutus to England, where he fights and defeats Gogmagog, leader of the giants of Totnes (the victory helped to rid Albion of its giants). The *History* explains that just as Brutus named Britain after himself, Corineus called his part of the land Corinea, which later became Cornwall (Geoffrey of Monmouth, *The History of the Kings of Britain*, ed. Michael D. Reeve, trans. Neil Wright [Woodbridge: Boydell Press, 2007], 28–29 [1:21, lines 462–89]). Paris quotes the *History* extensively in *CM* 1:21–22 and n. 1, including Corineus's naming of Cornwall as *Corineiam vel Cornubiam*.

[145] Explicit: **the vernacular version of the history** *li rumantz de l'estoire*: for *estoire* and other historiographical terms, see Peter Damian-Grint, *The New Historians of the Twelfth-Century Renaissance: Inventing Vernacular Authority* (Woodbridge: Boydell Press, 1999). On the insular development of the term *romance*, see Jane Zatta, "The 'Romance' of the Castle of Love," *Chaucer Yearbook* 5 (1998): 163–85.

146 R48:259–66, fol. 51r **new war . . . against holy church in England** *Vers seinte iglise en Engletere . . . nuvele guere*: the couplet rhymes of the preceding rubrics here become monorhyme, signaling the change of theme. A possible source for this story is Bede, who (in *HE* 1:17, 54–59; 1:18, 58–61) interpolates material from Constantius's life of St. Germanus of Auxerre with an account of St. Germanus's visit to St. Albans probably taken from the mid-fifth century *Passio sancti Albani*: see Sharpe, "The Late Antique Passion of St. Alban," in Henig and Lindley, *Alban and St Albans*, 30–37, at 36. However, Paris does not follow Bede in having devils try to prevent the passage of Germanus's ship to England (see n. to R51:289 below). The illustration on TCD MS 177, fol. 51r labels a single episcopal figure to the left "Sinodus," while on the right "Germanus Autissiodorensis episcopus" and "Lupus trecasinus episcopus" are identified (all in Paris's hand).

147 R48:262. **Lupus of Troyes and Germanus of Auxerre** *Lous de Trois, Germain de Aucere*: St. Germanus of Auxerre (d. 448) campaigned against the views and followers of the British-born theologian Pelagius (fl. 408 and condemned 431). For Constantius's life of Germanus, composed 475–480 CE, see *Constance de Lyon: Vie de saint Germain d'Auxerre*, ed. and trans. René Borius, Sources Chrétiennes 112 (Paris: Editions du Cerf, 1965). In *CM*, Pelagianism is briefly summarized (under 404 CE) as the belief that people can gain salvation by merit and that infants are born without original sin: St. Germanus's defeat of the British Pelagians is also described from Bede (*CM* 1:175–76, 185–86).

148 On fol. 51v of the *Alban* manuscript, the illustration has been removed and only the opening "Cist d . . ." of a rubric remains.

149 R49:270, fol. 52r **Genevieve, born in Paris** *Genovefe de Paris* [nee]: nee is an editorial emendation for the sake of the rhyme with *truvee* in the previous line. Neither Bede in *HE* nor Constantius in his life of St. Germanus says anything of Genevieve, patron saint of Paris (on Genevieve, see D. H. Farmer, *Oxford Dictionary of Saints*, 5th ed. [Oxford: Oxford University Press, 2003], s.v. "Genevieve"), but her vow of chastity is featured in R49-R50 and in Paris's illustrations to TCD MS. 177, fols. 52r and 52v, and her death is included in *CM* under 512 CE (1:232). Her presence in Anglo-Saxon litanies of the saints from the late ninth to the late eleventh centuries testifies to a cult in England (Michael Lapidge, *Anglo-Saxon Litanies of the Saints* [London: Boydell Press for Henry Bradshaw Society, 1991], Index of Saints, s.v. *Genouefa*, 310) and her French and Latin hagiographic dossier exists in a late thirteenth-century manuscript: see Lennart Bohm, *La Vie de sainte Geneviève de Paris* (Uppsala: Almqvist and Wiksells, 1955), 16–17. On her early *vitae* and the modern historiographic controversy over them, see Martin Heinzelmann and Joseph-Claude Poulin, *Les Vies anciennes de sainte Geneviève de Paris: Etudes critiques*, Bibliothèque de l'école des hautes études, IV section, Sciences historiques et philologiques, 339 (Paris: Champion, 1986). The clue to Paris's inclusion of her may lie not in early traditions of the Alban cult but in contemporary thirteenth-century realities. By making Germanus's consecration of the woman who would go on to become the patron saint of Paris incidental to the bishop's visit to England and St. Alban's shrine, this incident asserts the antiquity and standing of Christianity and its protomartyr in England. Until the Holy Blood purchase in 1247 by Henry III for his rebuilt Westminster Abbey (Introduction, 37), there had been nothing in England to match Louis IX's True Cross relic and his glorious Sainte Chapelle housing it in Paris. In the illustration on fol. 52r, Genevieve kneels before Germanus and assembled churchmen, while two people behind her, probably her parents, offer her to the bishop.

¹⁵⁰ R49:274 **she vows chastity before him** *chasteté devant lui [vue]*: such vows could be taken before a bishop (the rank of Germanus and Lupus, *li eveske* at R51:288 below) by laywomen committing to a semireligious life as vowesses; see Mary C. Erler, "English Vowed Women at the End of the Middle Ages," *Mediaeval Studies* 57 (1985): 155–203. Henry III's sister Eleanor took such a vow in 1231 before Archbishop Edmund of Canterbury (subject of both a Latin and an Anglo-Norman life by Paris, the latter dedicated to the Countess of Arundel, who was probably herself a vowess), though she later broke it to marry Simon de Montfort in 1238: see J. R. Maddicott, *Simon de Montfort* (Cambridge: Cambridge University Press, 1994), 21–22. Paris several times records Eleanor's vow, her breaking of it, and the outcry caused by her marriage (Erler points out that continence was a *votum simplex* rather than *solempne* and hence breaking it for marriage was illicit but not invalid: "English Vowed Women," 166, 173). On the papal dispensation from it, *CM* 3:471; on the quotation of Lombard *Sententiae* iv *dist*. 38 against marriage of those vowed to continence, whether veiled or not, *CM* 3:487; on Richard of Cornwall's objections to the marriage as given to the papal legate, *CM* 3:475–78; on the outcry against the marriage, *HA* 2: 404; and on Henry III's later accusations to de Montfort, *CM* 3:566–67. Paris also conspicuously praises the holiness of Cecelia de Sanford, who was vowed with Eleanor and maintained her vow till her death and burial at St. Albans in 1251 (*CM* 5:235–36). One of St. Genevieve's miracles is to discern that a woman who claims to be a consecrated virgin has in fact broken her vow (*Vita sanctae Genovefae*, ed. K. Künstle [Leipzig: Teubner, 1910], chap. 6:30; AA. SS Jan. I [under 3 Jan.], 138–43 and 143–47).

¹⁵¹ R50:277, fol. 52v a ... **metal penny** *un dener*: Harden (*Auban* 74, n. to 277r) and *AND* accept "[religious] medal" as the meaning here. Early ceremonies for consecrating virgins and vowesses involve a veil and a ring rather than a medal or a penny, but there is some evidence for seeing Genevieve's *dener* as a penny rather than a medal. Bede has the Anglo-Saxon princess Saint Eorcengota's being required to pay back the coin (here a gold Byzantine *nomisma*) with which she was "bought" on her entry into religion (*HE* 3:8, 238–39). Christina of Markyate is said to have scratched a cross on the door of St. Albans and the next day at Shillington to have offered a penny at mass while vowing herself to virginity (C. H. Talbot, ed., *The Life of Christina of Markyate: A Twelfth Century Recluse* [Oxford: Clarendon Press, 1959, repr. with additional material, 1987, repr. 2007], 38–39 and 40–41), so some kind of oblationary significance is attached to the penny. The thirteenth-century life of St. Bega of Cumbria, which alludes to St. Genevieve's encounter with Germanus, also sees the object as a coin: "we read that the holy virgin Genevieve was received as a nun by St. Germanus, bishop of Auxerre, with a brass coin [*per nummum aereum*]" (*The Life and Miracles of Sancta Bega*, ed. G. C. Tomlinson [Carlisle: S. Ferreson, 1842], 48). In Paris's illustration on fol. 52v, the figure labeled "Genouefa" holds a scroll or charter in her left hand as Germanus invests her with the penny (over col. a) and Germanus, riding off to the right, looks back toward her over col. b.

¹⁵² R51:289, fol. 53r **They run ... before a good wind** *Of bon vent curent*: Bede, following Constantius (*Constance de Lyon*, chap. 3:13, 146), has the bishops' ship assailed by devils halfway across the English channel (*HE* 1:17, 54–55). Constantius makes much of the way in which the bishops' own merits and Alban's intercession ensure a tranquil voyage back (*Constance de Lyon*, 158). Paris, who illustrates the bishops and their luggage and horses going aboard a boat to the right of the illustration, makes both voyages, out and back, auspicious.

¹⁵³ R52:291, fol. 53v **Britain** *Brettainne*: since fourth-century events are being described, Paris is historically correct in using the term *Brettaine* (cf. *Engletere* at R48:259). For debate as to whether Alban was to be identified as British or Roman, see Thomas, *The English and the Normans*, 287, and Introduction, 23–24. The illustration on fol. 53v shows Germanus and Lupus and their retinue disembarking (again toward the right).

¹⁵⁴ R52:297 **Verulamium** *Verulam*: Verulamium is not mentioned as the place of the anti-Pelagian victory in Constantius or Bede.

¹⁵⁵ R54:310 fol. 54v **authority** *Auctoritez*: this implies not only that the speech is rhetorically effective but that it is official and orthodox, "correct" and "authorized," unlike the Pelagians, who have no authority (*auctur*, R54:315) who can give them warranty for their doctrine. Paris's illustration on fol. 54v is closely related to his *CM* illustration of the pope and his bishops condemning Frederick II at the Council of Lyons (George Henderson, "Studies in English Manuscript Illumination 1," *Journal of the Warburg and Courtauld Institutes* 30 [1967]: 71–137, at 73).

¹⁵⁶ R54:313–14 **for the Gospel and prophecy surpass their thinking** *Ke euvangile e prophecie / Passe lur philosophie*: Pelagius in fact wrote commentaries on the Pauline Epistles (St. Albans owned copies of these and the prefaces to them attributed to Pelagius: Sharpe, *English Benedictine Libraries*, 530, no. 40), but Pelagianism's emphasis on human free will and merit versus grace was sometimes viewed as a denial of God's absolute power and his immutable word (these being most fully shown in the typological relation of the Old and New Testament and the validity of God's chosen prophets). In this sense the Pelagians do not know the gospel and do not ground religion on God's word and authority.

¹⁵⁷ R55:320 **whatever anyone may sing or read to them** *quei ke nuls lur chante u lise*: in addition to monastic hours and church services, Paris may be thinking of practices of instruction in ecclesiastical schools. The school at St. Albans had one of the greatest reputations in England in the early thirteenth century and was patronized by lay nobles as well as candidates for the novitiate (*GA* 1:195, 196, 397; Still, *The Abbot and the Rule*, 181–84).

¹⁵⁸ R55:323, fol. 55r **whom they now commemorate** *dunt unt memoire*: literally "of whom they now have the memory" (or "memorial"). In the illustration at fol. 55r, Lupus and Germanus ride away: Germanus carries a little reliquary containing dust mingled with St. Alban's blood, labeled as such ("Capsula co*n*tinens pulu*er*em adhuc sangu*i*ne Albani rubicundu*m*").

¹⁵⁹ R56:333, fol. 55v **King Offa** *Li reis Offes*: the series of illustrations for Offa of Mercia's foundation of St. Albans, of which sixteen remain, is initiated on fol. 55v: see further Baswell, 177–78, 185–89 below. (Some are repeated in the illustrations to the *Vitae duorum Offarum* in the Cotton Nero D. I manuscript, begun by Paris and completed by others: see Lewis, *Art of Matthew Paris*, 389–91; Morgan, *EGM [1]*, no. 87, 134–36.) Beneath the French caption on TCD MS. 177, fol. 55v, Offa, labeled as "Merciorum Rex Offa," is illustrated riding with two knights and two trumpeters: beneath the horses' feet is the head of a king labeled "Caput Etheldredi reg*is* orie*n*taliu*m*" (James, *Illustrations*, 31, suggests this should be *Ethelbert*, who was killed by Offa: see *CM* 1:355). Beneath the illustration, the Latin text on this leaf continues the *De inventione et translatione sancti Albani* begun on fol. 52v, including here a hymn to Alban. For a text of this *inventio*, see *CM* 1:356–57.

¹⁶⁰ R56:340 **the flower of chivalry** *flur de chevalerie*: on Offa, the preferred founder of St. Albans in the abbey's traditions, see Introduction, 24, n. 60. For Paris's illustration of Offa and the Saxon heptarchy in his *Abbreviatio chronicorum* (Cotton Claudius D. VI, fol. 5r), see Lewis, *Art of Matthew Paris*, 166, fig. 93).

¹⁶¹ R57:344, fol. 56r **driven off the land by the king** *Dunt li rois fait grant assart*: *assart* has a primary sense of clearing land for cultivation but a secondary sense of sweeping away, destroying. The illustration beneath the rubric on fol. 56r shows Offa defeating the Anglo-Saxon king, labeled "Boernred." A marginal hand notes "*con*federacio Offe cu*m* karolo magno." On Offa and Charlemagne, see Janet L. Nelson, "Carolingian Contacts," in *Mercia: An Anglo-Saxon Kingdom in Europe*, ed. Michelle P. Brown and Carole A. Farr (London and New York: Leicester University Press, 2001), chap. 9, 126–43.

¹⁶² R57:346 **king . . . with his native baronage** *reis of sun naturel barnage*: like many contemporaries, Paris disapproved of Henry III's preferments for Eleanor of Provence's Poitevin and Savoyard relatives (see Huw Ridgway, "Henry III and the Aliens, 1236–1272," in *Thirteenth Century England II*, ed. P. R. Coss and S. D. Lloyd [Woodbridge: Boydell Press, 1988], 89–99). The notion of *barnage naturel* appears elsewhere in his work (*History of Saint Edward the King*, trans. Fenster and Wogan-Browne, 18 and 120 n. 20). Here it seems most pointed in its contemporary reference rather than as an account of Offa (who subordinated other kings and crowned his legitimate but short-lived son as successor, rather than having bastard claimants to his throne).

¹⁶³ R58:353, fol. 56v **a beam from heaven** *Un rais du ciel*: in the illustration on fol. 56v, a magnificent angel hovers over the sleeping Offa, gesturing toward a beam of light pouring down at the foot of his bed.

¹⁶⁴ R59:359, fol. 57r **Holmhurst** *Holmhur[s]t*: the *Alban* text is lost at the relevant point in the narrative because of a lacuna in the manuscript (22:715 above), but the name is clear in the rubric.

¹⁶⁵ R59:361, fol. 57r **There the light descends** *iloec descendi la luur*: on fol. 57r, the light is shown pouring down from an opening in heaven, placed above the frame of the illustration. It is on a larger scale but with less elaboration than in its first appearance over Alban's burial place on fol. 46v, where it is accompanied by angels: see 31:1061–69.

¹⁶⁶ R60:371–72, fol. 57v **They surely resemble the men who once came from the East** *Ben semblent ceus ki d'orient vindrent*: in the illustration on fol. 57v, Offa and his two companions (one hatted and one mitered) resemble the Magi on their journey to the Christ child, though they seek rather than carry "treasure." As a monastic patron, Offa may be thought of as participating in a gift-exchange where both he and the saint offer earthly and heavenly treasure to each other.

¹⁶⁷ R61: 373, fol. 58r **The beam from heaven** *li rais du ciel*: an illustration nearly identical to the one on fol. 57r appears here on fol. 58r. James (*Illustrations*, 32) notes approvingly that in the BL, Cotton Nero D. I manuscript of the *Lives of the Two Offas* the two illustrations of the location of the relics are combined into one. The repetition of the images in the *Alban* manuscript is much more likely to be deliberate and confirmatory than to have been made in error (cf. the repetition of narrative discussed in the Introduction, 51 above and see Baswell, 188 below) and in any case works very well as an analogy to the Magi: between the two scenes of the light pouring down, Offa and attendants ride, seeking what the light reveals. For a textual example of narrative confirmation of a similar kind by Paris, see Jocelyn Wogan-Browne, "The Apple's Message: Some Post-Conquest Hagiographic Accounts of Textual Transmission," in *Late Medieval Religious*

Texts and Their Transmission: Essays in Honour of A. I. Doyle, ed. A. J. Minnis, York Manuscripts Conferences 3 (Cambridge: D. S. Brewer, 1994), 39–53, at 40–43.

[168] R61:375, fol. 58r **A city set upon a hill** *Cité en munt asise*: cf. Matt. 5:14 and n. to 29:1031 above.

[169] R62:377, fol. 58v **The king commands his people to come** *Li reis sa gent venir cumande*: the illustration beneath R62 on TCD MS. 177, fol. 58v shows only a selection of the churchmen, earls, knights, and lords commanded by Offa. The king himself is included (labeled *Offa rex*) together with *Humbertus archiepiscopus*, *Ceolwlphus episcopus*, and *Vnwona episcopus*, all labeled: on the charters claimed by St. Albans as King Offa's, Unwona is listed as bishop of Leicester (a different figure from the elderly priest Unwona of *GA* 1:26), and Ceolwulf of Lindsey and Humbert of Lichfield are cited as present at the *inventio* of Alban's relics and as witnesses to the charters (*Liber additamentorum*, *CM* 6:3: Crick, *Charters of St Albans*, no. 1,111; 3, 125).

[170] R63:393–94, fol. 59r **the treasure and the relics of the holy body** *li tresors / E le[s] reliques du saint cors*: saints' bodies are widely perceived and treated as treasure in the Middle Ages, notably in their encasement in jeweled reliquaries and shrines. The illustration on fol. 59r shows a busy scene of digging and discovery supervised by King Offa: in the foreground, smaller figures wield spades and mattocks and carry away baskets of soil; a bishop in the center of the illustration reverently holds up a skull from an unearthed coffin. Two attendant churchmen respectively utter a response of praise (the beginning of the hymn *Te deum laudamus*) and comment (*redolet*) on the odor of sanctity (the sweet smell conventionally associated with saints' bodies).

[171] R63:395–96, fol. 59r **wrapped . . . color and shape** *En[volu]pez . . . [n]e culur [ne ta]ille*: for the text here (where the lines have been cut away and the manuscript patched, TCD MS. 177, fol. 59r), the translation follows Harden's conjectural restoration (Harden, *Auban*, 74, n. to 395–96r).

[172] R64:398, fol. 59v **this very place** *en meimes ceu liu*: a strong claim for continuity was of particular importance in the abbey's propagation of the cult of Alban against its rivals: *GA* 1:18 explains, for instance, that Alban would not allow himself to be carried away from the abbey to Ely in Danish raiding (see Introduction, 12) because he had made his execution site at Holmhurst (R59:359) the place in which he would dwell forever.

[173] R64:401–2 **masons and engineers who build** *Maçuns . . . e enginnurs ki fund*: for another example of loose concord between singular and plural, see 25:819–20 above.

[174] R64, fol. 59v The illustration shows Offa with an architect (unlabeled but carrying a large pair of compasses and a square), while two men use a hand barrow to carry blocks of stone up a ladder; beneath them, another carries similar blocks in a wheelbarrow. (A later inscription in a different hand at the foot of fol. 59v [not part of the regular series of Latin inscriptions beneath the text of *Alban*, fols. 29r–50r] copies out what it says are the contents of a scroll in a later image of Offa at the abbey, celebrating his foundation as a house of peace and the mansion of God: James, *Illustrations*, 33.)

[175] R65, fol. 60r The illustration is continuous with that on fol. 59v and shows six men working with carefully depicted tools: one winching a basket of stones with a four-handled windlass, another using an adze to work a capital, a third using an axe "on a shaft laid on a trestle," a fourth up a ladder boring a hole in a pole with a cross-handled auger, another on top of a wall checking it with a level, and the sixth checking the straightness of the wall with a plummet (James, *Illustrations*, 33–34). Compare the entry "Building Trades" in the *Oxford Dictionary of the Middle Ages* (forthcoming).

¹⁷⁶ R66, fol. 60v The illustration shows Offa handing an abbatial staff of office to a kneeling Willegod.

¹⁷⁷ R67:425–28, fol. 61r **a little church... St. Alban** *Une eglisette... seint Auban*: the first church over Alban's hidden burial site is named as St. Syon only in this rubric and in a Latin inscription labeling the reliquary of Alban in the illustration on fol. 61v. Two coped monks, the first of whom holds a choirmaster's staff with a T-shaped top and says "Hic est uere martir," are processing rightwards toward the place where Alban's tomb (labeled *Feretrum Sancti Albani Anglorum prothomartiris delatum in sanctam Syon*, "the feretory of St. Alban the protomartyr of the English hidden in St. Syon") is being censed by a third monk and venerated by a fourth. Since Syon is a biblical place-name with considerable figurative extension in Christian exegesis, this may be an "invention" comparable with that of Amphibalus's name (see Introduction, 8).

¹⁷⁸ R68:433–34, fol. 61v **the third day before the feast of St. John** *Tierz jur devant la seint Johan*: the feast of the Nativity of St. John the Baptist (i.e., 24 June), with Alban's feast on 22 June. The illustration on fol. 61v shows Offa in procession with four churchmen: Archbishop Humbert, Bishops Ceolwulf and Unwona, and one unnamed bishop.

¹⁷⁹ R68:437 **feast of his invention on the fourth day before the nones of August** *De sa truvure fest... as quartes nones k'en aust venent*: this is 2 August in the Roman calendar. The ritual of invention (*inventio*) marks the discovery of a saint's relics (see further Introduction, 13) and like a saint's *translatio* (removal to a new shrine) can be given a separate feast in the calendar, as Alban's *inventio* is here.

¹⁸⁰ R69, fol. 62r A leaf is lost between TCD MS. 177, fol. 61v with its illustration of the procession for Alban's feastday and fol. 62r. As James suggests, this may have shown scenes from Offa's pilgrimage to Rome and his acquisition of charters for St. Albans from the pope: copies of these scenes are found in London, BL MS. Cotton Nero D. I (fols. 22v and 23v, James, *Illustrations*, 36). The surviving illustration on TCD MS. 177, fol. 62r shows only Offa, mounting his horse with his groom in attendance, while his sumpter carries a beautifully incised chest down the gangplank of the king's ship. The scene is thus focused not on the ceremony of a king's arrival but on the urgency and significance of Offa's bringing charters for the abbey from Rome. *GA* 1:4 claims that Offa's actions were approved by Pope Adrian I (772–795), though there is no contemporary evidence for this. Paris inserts a marginal note in *CM* beside the claim for special privileges from Adrian, stating that the words of the charter were signed by the pope's own hand (*CM* 1:359; see also *FH* 1:398–99). On the spurious status of the Offa charters, see Introduction, 15 and n. 43.

¹⁸¹ R70:449–50, fol. 62v **A feast is held at St. Albans** *A seint Auban... est feste tenue*: the illustration here is not, as might be expected, a feast: it shows Offa's horse being held by a squire. R70:451–52 **a gift of his property on the high altar** *de sun purchaz fait present / Al haut auter*: these words describe what is represented on the following leaf.

¹⁸² R71:457, fol. 63r **two hundred and eighty-six years** *Deus centisme an uittante sist*: the date given here for Alban's death is inconsistent with that in *CM*, where 304 CE is given as the year of the Diocletian persecution and immediately followed by substantial extracts from William of St. Alban's *PSA* narrating Alban's passion (*CM* 1:148: so also *FH* 1:168). The date of 286 CE given here, however, is the date that Paris assigns to the start of Diocletian's reign (*CM* 1:145) (actually 284). Germanus's anti-Pelagian mission is dated here to 449 CE (R71:460), though the saint is generally thought to have visited Britain twice in 429 and 447. The tradition of Offa's founding of St. Albans in 793 has no contemporary evidence supporting it (see Introduction, 14), but Offa did rule for

thirty-nine years in the late eighth century, from 757 to 796. In the illustration on fol. 63r, Offa presents his charter on St. Alban's altar on the left while bells are rung in a bell-tower on the right-hand side (reproduced in Lewis, *Art of Matthew Paris*, 113, fig. 61). See Plate 12 for Paris's image of Offa presenting his charter on the St. Albans altar. On the disjunction between fols. 62v and 63r, see Baswell, 177–79 below.

THE PASSION OF SAINT ALBAN
BY WILLIAM OF ST. ALBANS

Thomas O'Donnell and Margaret Lamont

Introduction

The *Passio sancti Albani*, which served as Matthew Paris's principal source for the *Life of Saint Alban*, was written by William of St. Albans sometime between 1167 and 1183.[1] A date close to 1178 is to be preferred, because William's *Passio* contains an oblique reference to the Invention (*inventio*) of St. Amphibalus in that year.[2] The work is purportedly a translation of an English-language life of St. Alban and St. Amphibalus written in the late sixth century that had recently "come to the attention" of the monastery (*PSA* 1).

The *Passio* is best seen in the context of the revival of interest in Alban and the new interest in his companion in the twelfth century (Introduction, 6, 8). William, who describes himself as "new to obedience" and his work as the "first fruits of my mouth" (*PSA* 1), dedicates the work to the same Abbot Simon who had commissioned a gold feretory for the martyr's shrine. Drawing largely on Bede, Geoffrey of Monmouth, the lives of other saints, and not least his own imagination, William developed an account of his monastery's saints detailed enough to undergird the abbey's new liturgical and artistic program.

The *Passio*'s dedication to Abbot Simon signals the narrative's essentially local and monastic character. Yet the preface to the *Passio* is also a sophisticated intercalation of the work into the monastery's historical traditions. The "book written in the English language" that William claims to be translating calls to mind the mysterious ancient book containing the "true history" of St. Alban unearthed by Abbot Eadmer (*GA* 1:26–27 and 22–23 above) at the same time as

---

[1] Reference to the *Passio* (*PSA*) is by chapter number, whether in the Latin text or in the English translation.

[2] As against arguments for a wider date range (Thomson, *Manuscripts from St Albans' Abbey 1066–1235*, 1: 67), the allusion to discovering the saints' bodies in *PSA* 44 suggests that the *Passio* was composed with the *inventio* of St. Amphibalus in mind.

it makes a riposte to the ancient British book of Geoffrey of Monmouth. This preface is also the first of two prologues that place the *Passio* proper inside a double narrative frame. After William has explained that his source for the *Passio* is an English book, he includes the English "author's" own prologue, which claims the walls of ancient Verulamium itself as a source: "The former citizens of Verulamium, in order to make known their hearts' exaltation at the suffering of blessed Alban, left behind engravings on their city walls. I found these carvings long afterward on the same walls, now ruinous and decaying" (*PSA* 2). There are three narrative layers here that correspond to the three periods of the town's occupation: William's own preface to the Anglo-Normans of his time, his English "author's" prologue to the Anglo-Saxons, and the engraved ruins to the British. Each translation into a new cultural context is furthermore a moment of augmentation: the English author consults local witnesses (*PSA* 2), and William mentions his own use of Geoffrey of Monmouth (*PSA* 1). The British contribution, meanwhile, is reduced to the mute landscape itself: a heap of stones, overgrown with weeds, conveying an ambiguous message of "exaltation" at Alban's suffering (*PSA* 2).

The successive translations of Alban's story, which ironically gain clarity the further they go from their source, are perhaps meant to mirror the movement of Alban's body from an unmarked British grave to an Anglo-Saxon tomb in the time of Offa and then to a final, glorious interment in a gold-and-silver shrine during the reign of Henry I. Monika Otter, discussing the *Passio*'s multiple narrative layers, remarks that William uses the English author's encounter with the Verulamian ruins as a metaphor for the "uncertain and even painful process" of historical recovery: the English author's frustrated fascination with British antiquity is essentially William's own.[3] William's historical project in the *Passio* is to identify the first community to venerate Saints Alban and Amphibalus and to show how, despite the interval of centuries and two different conquests, the martyrs were still present in the monastery, particularly through the recovery of their bodies (which his English narrator prophesies, *PSA* 44).

William is deeply interested in the cultural life of the ancient Verulamians and takes great pains to provide his pagans with consistent, if execrable, points of view. For example, Alban is scandalized by the "new" doctrines of the Incarnation and the Trinity (*PSA* 5); the pagans credit the miracles at Holmhurst to the sun god (*PSA* 20); and they have a clearly articulated view of the meaning of penance (*PSA* 41). Gradually the *Passio*'s focus shifts to the new Christian community at Verulamium, and the final movements of the work draw their language and events from the Acts of the Apostles, the biblical book most concerned with the growth and consolidation of ecclesiastical community.

---

[3] Otter, *Inventiones*, 51.

In William's narrative, the perspective of a preconversion English author, who looks forward to the time when "religious men, Christian men" will once again inhabit the region (*PSA* 47), is also persuasively imagined.[4] Even apparent anachronisms, like sending Amphibalus off on a preaching tour to Wales (*PSA* 10), turn out to be virtues when we consider that "Wales" is precisely what a sixth-century Anglo-Saxon *would* have called the ancient kingdom of "Kambria" described by Geoffrey of Monmouth. William clearly understands his abbey's history as the history of cultural supersession, as it is in Bede. He takes care to distinguish between Verulamium-St. Albans' different eras of occupation and even goes over Bede's head by taking his authority from a purported sixth-century historian (*PSA* 2) whose fictional researches are modeled on Bede's own.

In his *Alban*, Matthew Paris is much less concerned with the specific conditions of the Verulamian legacy. He conflates Britons and Anglo-Saxons in making his pagans "Saracens" and in having a Verulamian cry out to Alban in English (TCD MS. 177, fol. 36r, see R19 above and Plate 7). In *GA*, he suggests that ancient Brythonic and English might be the same language (*GA* 1:27). Although he distinguishes Britain and England for some purposes in his French text (Introduction, 24 and n. 59), his rubrics for William's work follow St. Albans traditions by repeatedly announcing that Alban was the "prothomartyr anglorum." In *Alban*, he retains the pagans' alternate explanations of Alban's miracles, but his heathens are the stock Saracens of romances and *chansons de geste*. *Alban* thus enlarges upon the intertextual background of the *Passio*, but at the cost of William's remarkable historical imagination. In part, this is because for Matthew Paris the royal patronage and grants of liberties provided by King Offa are a much more important moment for the abbey's foundation than the conversion of long-ago Verulamians. In his personal copy of the *Passio*, Paris even suppresses William's preface, with its dedication and claim regarding the work's source,[5] presumably because he cannot reconcile the English book translated by William in the twelfth century with the British book translated by Unwona over a hundred years earlier (*GA* 1:27 and Introduction, n. 57). Without the preface, the story loses its place in the tight historiographical chain elaborated by William, and the pagan narrator merges with the Britons who persecute Alban.

William seems to have had some ambitions for the work, since Ralph of Dunstable subsequently translated it into Latin elegiacs at his request.[6] Ralph was apparently one of William's teachers—just as, Ralph says, Amphibalus had been Alban's "in the school of faith" (*VMSA* 13–16). The *Passio* was copied

---

[4] As noted also by Otter, *Inventiones*, 47.

[5] Two witnesses to *PSA* earlier than the *Alban* manuscript (BL MS. Cotton Faustina B. IV and Oxford Magdalen College MS. Lat. 53) retain the preface, though another early copy (BL MS. Cotton Nero C. VII) does not.

[6] Ralph of Dunstable, *Vita metrica sancti Albani* (*VMSA*), 7–12, in McLeod, "Alban and Amphibal," 412.

throughout the thirteenth and fourteenth centuries at St. Albans and was used in a wide range of texts, not the least of which were Matthew Paris's *CM* and *Alban*. Nevertheless, William's version of the Alban legend does not seem to have achieved its widest circulation until the fifteenth century, when it was made the principal source (along with the fourteenth-century St. Albans text, *Tractatus de nobilitate, vita, et martyrio Albani et Amphibali*, itself based on the *Passio*) for the Alban legend in the *Gilte Legende* and John Lydgate's *Life of Saint Alban and Saint Amphibalus*.[7] John of Tynemouth also used the *PSA* in his compilation of English saints' lives printed as *Nova legenda Angliae*.

Note on the Text and Translation

At least seven manuscripts of the *Passio* survive. Of these, three (Matthew Paris's Dublin, Trinity College MS. 177 [E. I. 40] and the two fourteenth-century manuscripts BL MS. Cotton Claudius E. IV and BL MS. Add. 62777) are of St. Albans provenance, and two others (Oxford Magdalen College MS. Lat. 53 and BL MS. Cotton Nero C. VII) have some liturgical or calendrical connections to the monastery. Thomson believes that the copy of the *Passio* in the Oxford manuscript, which includes obits for the priors of the St. Albans dependency of Wymondham, was nearly contemporary with William.[8] BL MS. Cotton Faustina B. IV is also early and was in the possession of the great Cistercian abbey of Holme Cultram. The last copy, in Bodleian MS. Digby 172 pt. 2, was written in the fifteenth century.

As the basis for our translation we have chosen to use the text printed in the *Acta sanctorum* (June IV, 22) by the Bollandist Godfrey Henschen (1601–1681). Henschen probably based his text on two of the Cotton manuscripts, though he does not specify which ones. The *Acta sanctorum* edition has the advantage of being widely available and including both William's prefaces. Paris's version in Dublin, Trinity College MS. 177 (TCD) corresponds closely to the text in the *Acta sanctorum*, apart from a few minor variants. Occasionally we have supplemented the *Acta sanctorum* text with readings from another manuscript (usually TCD), for instance, in obvious cases of error. We have recorded these variants in footnotes. Otherwise the most important difference between the two texts is Paris's omission of William's preface. Additions made to William's text in TCD that might indicate Paris's process of adaptation are placed in square brackets

---

[7] For the *Tractatus* and the Lydgate *Life*, see van der Westhuizen, *John Lydgate*. For the *Gilte Legende* life of St. Alban, see *The Gilte Legende*, ed. R. F. S. Hamer, with the assistance of Vida Russell, EETS o.s. 327 (Oxford and New York: Oxford University Press for EETS, 2006), 1: 376–409.

[8] Thomson, *Manuscripts from St Albans*, 1: 141 n. 50. See also Clark, *A Monastic Renaissance at St. Albans*, 106.

within the text. Paris's rubrics for the *Passio* are given in italics and their place in the manuscript given in a footnote. Paris's preferred title for Alban, "protomartyr of the English," occurs only in these rubrics. Marginal comments of particular interest by Matthew Paris can be found in the endnotes to our translation.

The *Passio* makes copious use of rhetorical figures that typify Latin high style in the twelfth century, such as polyptoton, pleonasmus, and tricolon. In eliminating many of these, our translation has favored readability over exact reproduction. Wherever William of St. Albans alludes to the Bible, classical authors, and the liturgy we have translated appropriately and have drawn attention to such allusions in our notes, along with relevant historical and critical issues.

William of St. Albans, *The Passion of St. Alban*

To his reverend father and most dear lord, Simon, William sends greetings in the Lord.

1. When a book written in the English language and containing the Passion of the blessed martyr Alban came to our attention, you commanded me to translate it into Latin. Thinking it truly a crime not to obey you, I complied with your word, not, however, out of any arrogance, but rather so that I would not be seen to disregard your authority. I believed this work ought to be consecrated to your name, since I found no one to whom I might better offer the first fruits of my mouth than the priest of the Lord.[1] But if anything should sound less than Latin to your learned ears, excuse a translator new to an obedience that regularly takes for granted things beyond his power. It should be noted, moreover, that I have added to this work the name of the blessed priest, which I did not find in the book I am translating but in the history that Geoffrey Arthur claims to have translated from the ancient British tongue into Latin.[2] But lest my prolixity displease a busy man,[3] it now remains to hear how my author composed the preface of his work.

Here begins the Passion of blessed Alban[4]

2. Whoever attempts to call to memory the glorious struggles of the blessed martyrs will have to suffer the pagans' hatred, even if he manages to escape with his life. For any time someone begins to relate the story of the martyrs' destruction—of the saints' glory, rather—those who envy their happiness soon howl with anger and hound them to their deaths. So it is that I, passing down to posterity the Passion of the blessed martyr Alban in what style I may, place no title at the head of my work, preferring to pass over[5] my name in silence rather than to speak it and lose name and life together. Although the world is full of the snares of the treacherous, I shall not stay quiet about what I have seen, what I have heard—once my name is omitted. The former citizens of Verulamium, in order to make known their hearts' exaltation at the suffering of blessed Alban, left behind engravings on their city walls. I found these carvings[6] long afterward on the same walls, now ruinous and decaying. And I saw the crumbled battlements,

heavy with age, under whose walks the blessed Alban suffered painful bodily torments. I saw filled thick with trees the place where the unvanquished martyr long ago endured death for Christ's sake. These things, among others, I learned by the report of many: how the holy man's prayer brought forth a spring on the mountaintop, so that with its beneficial waters he could relieve his enemies, who had been tortured by thirst and were despairing of life. I have thus sought out, learned, and taken pains to commit the whole course of events to writing and to memory lest it remain hidden from posterity.

Here ends the Prologue. Here begins the Passion of the blessed and glorious P<rotomartyr> of the English[7]

3. While the persecution against the Christians under Diocletian was raging far and wide, a man called Amphibalus, distinguished for his works and learning, crossed over into Britain and reached Verulamium under the Lord's guidance. He entered the city, and, turning into the house of Alban, requested hospitality. Now, Alban was a Verulamian citizen, a prominent man in that town, who traced his origin to a famous Roman family. The glory of his riches and his rank in the world suited the nobility of his family, and because of this all the people honored him. Receiving the holy man kindly, he saw to his every need. At length Alban spoke to him in a place apart, far from the clatter of the servants. "How is it," he asked, "that although you are a Christian you were able to obtain passage across the heathens' borders and arrive in this city unmolested?" Amphibalus said to him: "My Lord Jesus Christ, son of the living God, was always with me on my journey and kept me safe amid dangers. He sent me to this province for the salvation of many, so that I might proclaim to the nations the faith that is in Christ and make the people acceptable to him."[8] "And who," Alban asked, "is this Son of God? How can someone claim that a god can be born? These things are new to me and hitherto unheard of. I would like to know what you Christians believe about this."

4. Then blessed Amphibalus began to unfold the Gospels' meaning, saying: "This is the declaration of our faith:[9] we say that God is the Father and God is the Son, and that he, namely the Son, deigned to take on flesh for the salvation of men. He did this so that he who created flesh should become flesh, and he who was creator of the Virgin should himself be created miraculously from a virgin. Therefore, when the time had come for this news to be proclaimed, a heavenly messenger was sent to the Virgin; he came to her and said, 'Hail, full of grace, the lord is with you, blessed are you among women.' When she heard his words she was troubled. And the angel said to her, 'Do not be afraid, Mary. Behold, you will conceive and bear a son, and you will call him Jesus.' And Mary said to the angel, 'How should this be when I have no husband?' And the angel

said to her in response, 'The Holy Spirit will come upon you and the power of the Most High will overshadow you, and therefore the child that shall be born from you shall be called holy, the Son of God.' And Mary said, 'Behold the handmaid of the Lord, let it be for me according to your word.'[10] In this way a virgin was worthy to bear God, a handmaid to bear her lord, a daughter to bear her father. The Virgin became a mother, but she did not lose the mark of her virginity. It was not hidden from the prophets that this was to be, but they foretold it from the beginning of time in many oracles. If you will believe these things, my host, all that belongs to the faith of Christ will be properly fulfilled in you. Once you become a Christian, you will be able to cure the lame, the diseased, and all who are sick by invoking the name of Christ. No misfortune will harm you; death will not draw near you until the Creator wills it himself. At last you will end this life through martyrdom, and blessed by exceeding joy you will pass from this world to Christ. I am to be the herald of your passion: it was for this that I have come. The good Lord of loving kindness will repay the service you enter into with the prize of heavenly life."[11]

5. Alban said to him, "What sort of reverence or honor should I pay to Christ, if I should happen to accept his faith?" And [Amphibalus] said, "Believe that the Lord Jesus, together with the Father and the Holy Spirit, is one God, and you will accomplish a great work in his eyes." Then Alban said to him: "What's this you say? You're mad, you don't know what you're talking about! What you're saying can't be understood; reasoning won't allow it. If the men of this city knew you had said such things about Christ, they would avenge your blasphemous speech by cutting off your head at once, according to the laws of the community. I am deeply concerned for you, and frightened that some harm may come to you before you leave this house." With these words he got up and left angrily. He no longer wanted to put up with Amphibalus's words, nor listen quietly to his counsel. Amphibalus remained there alone and passed the whole night in vigil and prayer.

6. As Alban slept in the upper room, however, wondrous things were shown to him by divine power. Alarmed by this new vision, and disturbed by its strangeness, he got up and straightaway went downstairs. He went to his guest and said: "My friend, if what you preach about Christ is true, don't be afraid, I beg you, to explain the meaning of a dream I've had. I was looking around me, and then I saw a man coming down from heaven. A huge crowd seized him and put him to all sorts of tortures. His hands were bound in fetters, his body torn with whips, and they hung him, terribly wounded, on a tree with his hands stretched on the cross-beam. The tortured man was naked and barefoot. His hands and feet were fixed in place with nails, and his side pierced with a spear. I dreamed that blood and water flowed from a wound in his side. They fixed a reed into his right hand and put a crown of thorns on his head. When they had exhausted all human

cruelty, they mocked him, saying, 'Hail, King of the Jews; if you are the Son of God, come down from the cross, and we will believe in you.' And though they insulted him, the young man didn't answer them at all. And when they had said to him all they wanted, he finally called out in a strong voice, 'Father, into your hands I commend my spirit,' and with these words he died. His lifeless body was taken down from the cross, with blood still gushing from its wounds, and shut up in a stone tomb. The tomb was sealed and a guard was assigned to it.[12] But then there was a miracle! The senseless body came back to life and emerged from the locked tomb with all its strength restored. I saw with my own eyes how he rose from the dead. Men dressed in snow-white garments descended from the heavens and took the man back to where they had come from. A numberless army, all in white, followed him, singing his praises all the way. And they constantly blessed some father—I don't know whom—and his son, saying 'Blessed be God the Father and his only begotten Son.'[13] There was immense joy among them, exultation so indescribable that nothing can be compared to it. These and many other things were shown to me in the dream, which I would not disclose to any living being, even if I could. Do not hide from me what these things mean, I beg you. Don't be afraid."[14]

7. When the blessed Amphibalus heard these things and perceived that Alban's heart had been visited by the Lord, he rejoiced more than anyone would believe possible. He brought out the cross he had with him and said: "Behold, in this sign you can clearly recognize what your dream means and what it portends. The man who came from above is my Lord Jesus Christ, who did not refuse to undergo the torment of the cross in order to free us with his blood from the judgment to which our first father Adam's transgression bound us. Those who laid hands on the man and tortured him in every way signify the Jews. Although God had promised that he would send them his Son from heaven, and though the one they had expected for so long did eventually come, they did not welcome him or acknowledge him as the author of their salvation when he came. Instead, they resisted him in every way, repaying his goodness with evil, his love with hatred. Finally, led by their envy, they unleashed such wickedness that they arrested, crucified, and killed him, though they found no deadly crime in him.[15] In this way the merciful Lord redeemed us at the cost of his blood; by dying he conquered death and in being raised up on the cross he drew all things to himself.[16] He descended into the dungeons of hell, and he single-handedly freed his imprisoned people and cast the devil into the lowest darkness, binding him in everlasting bonds."[17]

8. Then Alban, marveling at what Amphibalus had said, exclaimed: "True! What you tell me about Christ is true and cannot be denied in any way. For tonight I understand clearly that Christ has conquered the devil, bound him, and thrust him down into the depths of hell. With my own eyes I saw that loathsome

creature lying bound in chains. Recognizing by this that everything you say is true, I promise you that from now on I will be a most faithful listener. Therefore I beg you, since you know all things, tell me what I am to do for the Father and for the Holy Spirit, now that I enter into the service of the Son." Hearing this, Amphibalus said with great joy, "I thank my Lord Jesus Christ that you have come to know for yourself how to speak these three names, and to know the three persons, whom you have openly called by their proper names. Believe in one God, confess it steadfastly and faithfully." Alban said in response, "I do believe, and henceforth my faith will be that there is no God but my Lord Jesus Christ,[18] who deigned to take on manhood for men's salvation and endured suffering on the cross; he himself is one God with the Father and the Holy Spirit, and there is no other."

9. After this,[19] the blessed penitent prostrated himself continuously before the cross and prayed for forgiveness as if he saw the Lord Jesus himself hanging there. He caressed the feet and the wounds with ceaseless kissing, as if he were kneeling before the feet of the very Redeemer whom he had seen crucified. Tears mixed with blood rolled down his face and fell on the venerable wood [of the cross].[20] He said: "I reject the devil and I denounce all Christ's enemies and believe in him alone. I entrust myself to him who (as you claim) rose from the dead on the third day."[21] Amphibalus said to him: "Be strong in spirit: the Lord is with you, and you will never lack his grace. He will never leave you. While other mortals receive the faith by human teaching, you have learned not from or through a man, but through the revelation of Jesus Christ.[22] Because of this, I see no reason to worry about you, and I intend to go on further, in order to show the way of truth to the nations." "By no means," said Alban, "but stay with me for at least a week, and while you are here show me a teacher's care, so I can be more fully instructed in Christian worship." Seeing that Alban was taking the news of his departure hard, Amphibalus was compelled to agree. Over the next few days, therefore, as the day turned to evening, teacher and student avoided men's company and hurried off to a distant house (what is commonly called a cabin). There they spent the whole night, praising God. They did this so that their secret might not become known among the infidels, who would not follow the Christians in their faith, but rather hunt them down for it.

10. Now, after some time had passed, a certain heathen boldly approached the judge and informed him of what had been going on. He left absolutely nothing unsaid by which he might more easily attack those innocents or move the judge to fury. As soon as the judge learned these things, he was inflamed with rage, and he ordered that Alban and his teacher be summoned to his presence to make a properly reverential sacrifice to the gods. But if they would not, they should violently be seized by force and bound with fetters. In place of the sacrificial victims, their throats would be cut on the altars of the gods. But this plan did not escape

Alban's notice.[23] Wishing to hinder the judge's plots in any way he could, he urged Amphibalus to depart from the city and gave him a woollen cloak woven with gold to protect him from his enemies. For in those times, during festival days, that cloak was held by everyone to be of such dignity and reverence that, wearing it, Amphibalus could pass through the ranks of his enemies unharmed. Alban would keep his master's cloak himself, knowing that his savage enemies were sure to look upon it with hostile eyes. So, giving in to Alban's entreaties, Amphibalus fled before dawn, taking the northward road. Alban accompanied him as long as it seemed safe to them both. And when they separated from one another and said farewell for the last time, who could recall their tears with dry eyes? Thus Amphibalus hastened toward Wales and martyrdom. Alban went back, dressed in his master's clothing, hoping in this way to provoke the heathens' anger against himself alone.

11. At daybreak horsemen and a large band of foot-soldiers rushed into Alban's house without warning and unleashed their anger. They searched the hiding places and [threw the whole house into confusion] with their crashing uproar. [At length their anxious searching][24] brought them to the cabin, where they found the noble Alban barefoot and in pilgrim's clothes, kneeling in prayer before the Lord's cross. Crowding in, they interrogated him about the whereabouts of the priest whom he had housed. Alban said to them: "He is with God, and, supported by God's aid, he doesn't fear human threats. Why are you looking for him?" The man they were seeking was nowhere to be found, and so the servants of wickedness, turning their evil on Alban, next laid their hands on him. They seized him, dragged him away, and bound him tightly with cruelly biting chains; some dragged him by his clothes, others by his hair. They gave him many wounds, treated him very brutally, and brought him before their idols. The whole city had gathered there, together with the judge. Alban, to show openly to them all that he was a servant of the cross, displayed the symbol of the Lord in his joined hands. Gazing on this new and unknown wonder, the heathens were confused and terrified. Even the judge who ruled the city glared threateningly at the holy man and the symbol of salvation. It is said that Alban held the judge's anger in such contempt that he disdained to identify either his noble birth or his family name. When interrogated point by point, he revealed his first name only and said in a bold voice that he was a Christian.

12. The judge confronted him, saying: "Alban, where is the priest, sent from who knows where by Christ, who entered this city in secret to deceive our citizens? If guilt did not gnaw at his conscience and if he did not doubt the virtue of his cause, he would have made himself known to us of his own free will, so that this great teacher might have accounted for himself and his student. By his own example he discloses how much fraud and deceit lurk in his teaching. Just look how, unnerved by fear, he fled and deserted you, the very man he should

have defended in this affair. Because of this (unless I am mistaken), you must understand clearly that you were wrong to agree with this foolish man. Under his influence you have sunk into such madness that you have abandoned everything in the world and aren't even afraid to hold the great gods in contempt. Therefore, lest we appear to let this insult to the gods go unpunished, it is decreed that the scorn shown to them shall be avenged by the death of their scorner. But, because anyone can make a mistake, you may still turn aside their wrath through repentance. If you separate yourself entirely from this abominable doctrine, you will earn the gods' favor in the end. Therefore, accept this sound advice and do not delay your sacrifice to the great gods. From them you will easily obtain not only forgiveness for your sins and indulgence for your offenses, but even cities and peoples, armies, wealth, provinces, and power."

13. Unshaken by threats and unmoved by bribes, Alban answered the judge: "O judge, it is clear how empty and unfounded are these words that you have labored over for so long. For, if it had seemed good or useful, and if we had both wanted it, the priest would surely have hurried into your presence. But, knowing this people has always been prone to evil, I would have been unhappy had he come. Judges whose judgments are false would never please him. I admit I have adopted his teaching, and I don't regret doing it. Perhaps in the future you will recognize that I did not adopt this faith through the words of some ignorant or common man. The feeble and sick, having been restored to their former health, will confirm by their witness that this faith I have adopted is the true one. This faith is dearer to me than all the wealth you promise and more precious than all the honors you propose. For if anyone is wealthy, he still dies in the end, however unwillingly. Nor can the gold he kept with such care bring its guardian back from the dead. But why go on? I will not make sacrifice to your false and deceitful gods, who have wretchedly ensnared all my people. And while the people diligently worship them, these gods cosset them with false hope." When Alban said this the people were outraged; on one side wailing rose up and on the other side cries of abuse.[25] But the blessed martyr was not afraid of either the judge's threats or the uproar of the people all around him.

14. The crowd of heathens gathered quickly round and together they forced the holy man toward the demonic sacrifice, ordering him to make an offering to their gods at once. But even so great a horde could not break this one man's resolve and make him consent to their unspeakable rites. Then, arrested by the judge's order, he was laid out to be whipped. Even though he was pitiably lacerated, he turned to the Lord and said smilingly: "Lord Jesus Christ, I beg you to keep watch over my soul so that it will not waver or fall from the resolution to which you have brought me. I long to make my soul a willing sacrifice to you, Lord, and by spilling my blood to become your witness." These words resounded among the lashes. And though the lictors' hands tired, the whipping had no effect. Still, the people

hoped that the martyr might renounce his purpose, especially because the resolve of the human mind tends to weaken over time. They put him in the custody of the judge for over six months.

15. Meanwhile the heavens bore witness to the offense against the martyr. From the time of Alban's arrest up until the day he was released from the prison of the flesh, neither dew nor rain refreshed the land, and no winds blew. Instead the fiery sun scorched the whole region every day. At night, too, the heat was excessive and unbearable. Neither the fields nor the trees brought forth their yield. The whole world battled against the wicked on behalf of the righteous. Then the citizens of Verulamium, unable to bear this plague, came together and said: "Overpowered by Alban's sorcery, nothing sprouts and every green thing perishes. That Christ whom Alban worships has arranged it so that there aren't even any seedlings, much less crops." Messengers were dispatched from every part of the province to summon wise, honorable, and resourceful men to consider how they might be saved. When at last they assembled, the most blessed Alban was released from his filthy prison. He walked barefoot into their midst. And when they had seen him, the wise men consulted together and all agreed that Alban was to be judged innocent. They sympathized with his wrongs and lamented over his chains. But even then Alban's family and his powerful relatives in the town were stirring mad dissension and revolt.[26] They could not suffer calmly the wrongs that had been done to such a noble man: namely that a freeborn man should stand in the presence of a judge loaded down with iron as if he were a thief when there was not even so much as a whisper of suspicion about his character. Moreover, Alban was considered the most upstanding among them all and had always studiously avoided crimes of this sort. While grave sedition was brewing among the people, and the outcry growing, the blessed man was released from his prison by the judgment of all, so that he might stand, free of his chains, to render his account before the judge.

16. Alban received this mercy gloomily and greatly feared that he would be spared martyrdom though he was ready to be martyred. Standing in the midst of the crowd, he looked up to the sky and groaned. Then, taking out the Lord's cross, he venerated it and said: "Lord Jesus Christ, don't let the devil's spite prevail so that through his cunning machinations, and with this people's assent, he can stand in the way of my suffering. I beg you that his efforts may be turned to scorn, his audacity be curbed, and his power fall away into nothingness." Then, turning toward the people, he said: "What are you waiting for? Surely you see that time will be lost by this delay. If you do not know what sentence to pass, consult your laws and look into the customs of your city. They will teach you what you ought to do. Why suffer delays? You all know that I am still an inveterate enemy of your gods. Are those gods worthy of sacrifice who visibly have no divinity in them, being the work of human hands? You are witnesses that they

see nothing, hear nothing, and understand nothing.[27] Does any one of you wish to see or hear in the manner of the gods he worships? By no means. What should we say of such gods, whose followers would consider it a humiliation to resemble them? O, most detestable vanity! To hope for life from these objects that never lived, to offer prayers to these objects that never heard, and to seek good health from these objects that were never well! Therefore I declare without reservation that whoever worships such gods is completely insane. Who, I ask, is unhappier than a man ruled by such fantasies? Woe therefore to idols, and woe to the worshippers of idols! What do you think of that?"

17. After hearing this, the heathens spoke among themselves and, having gathered advice from all sides, they unanimously pronounced a sentence of death on the holy man, and they ordered it to be carried out right away in the place the people called Holmhurst. But a disagreement arose among them because they could not decide how they should kill their enemy. Some proposed that, because he was the follower of one who had been crucified, he should be crucified. Others proposed that, because he had declared himself an enemy of their gods, he should be buried alive. And many proposed that they pluck out his eyes and then send him to look for his teacher. At last, the judge, together with all the people of the city, decreed that Alban be decapitated. Thus Alban, once more bound in chains, was dragged from the court to his execution. Leaving the judge behind in the city, the people then eagerly rushed out to see the spectacle. They pursued the holy man with constant abuse: "Get out, get out, enemy of the city and foe of all the gods! Go where your crimes have called you, and may the reversal of your fortune be exactly what you deserve." But the blessed martyr Alban did not respond to them at all.

18. Such a horde streamed together there that the place, which before had seemed so large and spacious, now appeared extremely narrow on account of the great press of people. Furthermore, the sun's strength was so great that the earth was burning up under their feet as they walked. As they went on their way, they came to the halt on the banks of a swift river. There was no small trouble for those needing to cross. In the disorderly rush, each person tried to get in front of the other, and the narrowness of the bridge prevented anyone's crossing easily. So some people, not tolerating any delay, entrusted themselves to the deep flood and swam quickly over to the farther bank. Others dared the same feat but were snatched by the roiling waters and died wretchedly under the waves.[28] Seeing this, the people grieved and lamented greatly.

19. Alban saw these things too, and he groaned and wept over the loss of the dying. Moved with pity for the people, he knelt on the ground, directing his eyes toward heaven and his mind toward Christ. "Lord Jesus," he said, "from whose holy side I saw blood and water streaming, I beg you to make the waters subside

and the flood recede so that, safe and unhurt, this entire people may witness my suffering." Behold, just as Alban bent his knees, the riverbed dried up. As long as Alban's tears poured down, no water remained in the river. The power of his prayer drained the river and opened a way for the people among the waves. Marvels piled up as miracle followed upon miracle, and Alban's mighty works shone brightly before the people. Those whom the river's current had snatched up, pulled under, and destroyed just a short while ago now reappeared unharmed and with no trace of death upon them.

20. Then the soldier who was dragging Alban to his execution at last merited his salvation through Alban. For when the soldier saw the wonders gloriously performed by Alban, he was led to repentance. He flung away his sword, threw himself at Alban's feet, confessed his error, and begged forgiveness. Bursting into tears, he said: "Alban, servant of God, truly your God is the true God, and there is no other. Know that I believe in him and claim him for my God just as you do. It is as if this stream, which by your prayers was reduced to nothing within a moment, speaks and testifies that there is nothing on earth as mighty and wonder-working as him." When the servants of wickedness heard this, their anger grew. Their envy was stirred up, and the cruelest of men became still crueler. With savage hearts they turned to the soldier and said: "The stream has not disappeared so suddenly because of Alban, as you claim. Rather we, on whom the gods' benevolence has conferred the knowledge of secret things, can reveal how this came about.[29] We worship the sun god, and we accord more reverence to him than to any other. Mindful of our devotion, he consumed the river's water with his powerful heat, so that we, healthy and with no one missing, could see our enemy killed before our joyful eyes. But because you would attribute the gifts of the gods to others, you will pay the penalty befitting such blasphemy." With these words they seized upon the soldier and knocked out his teeth, so that the holy mouth that had testified to the truth was horribly maimed. And when this one part did not suffice for so many hands, they turned to his remaining limbs and broke his bones[30] to pieces. But even though every part of his body was bruised, nevertheless the faith burning in his heart could not be diminished. Thus, moving from one evil deed to another, they left the man half-dead on the bank, his whole body shredded.

21. Who would not weep to recall how these bloodthirsty men now led Alban back and forth through rocky terrain, wild places, and briars, how thorns and exposed roots gouged his feet, how his precious blood stained the rocks? At last they reached the summit of the hill, where God's champion Alban was to bring his struggle to an end. A huge crowd of men lay there sweltering under the burning sun, already drawing their last breaths. When they saw Alban, they howled at him, saying: "See what's happened! Overwhelmed by his sorcery and so oppressed by misfortune, we have no hope left for our survival. Our days are

cut off by the magic that this Alban never ceases to practice, and we are fading away." Alban, deeply affected, pitied their wretchedness. Burning with the grace of charity, he did not neglect them, but poured out prayers for his persecutors.[31] "God," he said, "who created man out of the slime, I beg you not to allow your creatures to be brought low for my sake. Temper the air, grant waters in plenty, and let gentler winds blow, so that this heat, under which the people suffer, may swiftly be quenched by your goodwill." Even as he spoke, behold, a spring burst forth at his feet in the midst of the crowd. O wonderful power of Christ! Though the earth was scorched by the sun's great heat, a cool spring gushed out of the dusty earth of the mountaintop, flowing from the veins running underground. The river descended in a swift rush and the people ran forward to revive themselves in the waters, escaping at last the affliction that tormented them. They drank, and thus by one man's merit everyone's thirst was allayed. But still they thirsted for human blood. Though the heat that had afflicted their bodies was relieved, the fire of their raging souls burned undiminished. The sick had been saved but did not recognize the author of their salvation. Indeed, blaspheming Christ, they said, "Praise be to the great god, the Sun, who has deigned to succor his servants in their extremity: a stream of water has sprung from the earth for our salvation."

22. As the people spoke, their rage for blood was inflamed. They fastened the martyr to a branch by his curly hair. An executioner was selected from among the people, one who would commit the crime for all. He was soon ready. Eagerly he raised his sword high in the air, and swinging it down with all his might on Alban's neck, he lopped off the martyr's head with one stroke. The lifeless body fell into a ditch that had been prepared beforehand. The head hung from the branch by its tangled hair. But the cross that the holy man always held in his hand (sprinkled now with Alban's blessed gore) fell into the grass. Unknown to the pagans, a man who was secretly a Christian snatched up the cross and hid it. Meanwhile the executioner, still standing by the body, was blinded when his eyes fell to the earth. The wretch could not catch his eyes as they rolled away, nor replace them once they were gone. The heathens saw this, and as they talked among themselves, many pronounced this vengeance to be completely just.

23. While this was going on, behold, the soldier whom the pagans had left half-dead a little before climbed up the mountain on his hands and knees with all the effort he could muster. Then the judge, who had been drawn there by news of blessed Alban's miracles, gloated over the man's wounds and said: "Hey, cripple! Let's ask Alban to restore your bones to their original condition! Run, hurry, put his head on the rest of his body; at once you shall merit all the healing that will come of that. Why delay? Bury the dead, perform the funeral. No doubt he will bestow a swift cure on the hands of his servant." But that man, burning with the heat of faith, said: "I believe firmly that blessed Alban shall return my

whole health to me through his merits and that he can bring me to the Savior's mercy in the end. For what you now say in mockery can easily be fulfilled in me through him." With these words, he embraced the blessed martyr's head and reverently untangled his holy hair. Then this feeble porter took up his pious load and devoutly set it on the body. Miraculously, he was cured right away and began to recover the strength of his body, of which he had despaired. Faster than words can say, the man was made new again. He preached ceaselessly the power of Christ and the good works of Alban while all the people listened. And as soon as he was strong enough, with his own hands he performed the funeral rites owed to the saint. He himself buried the body in the ground; he himself placed a mound over it.

24. When the pagans saw what was happening, they were filled with jealousy.[32] They conferred and said: "What shall we do? Iron cannot kill this man. On the contrary, we have pounded his whole body, and, look, his flesh is restored to its first strength and beauty. What more can we do? Let us take counsel how to proceed." Then one man rushed from their midst and said: "This man cannot be killed by the sword unless he is first torn limb from limb. For he is a sorcerer, and through his magic he knows how to protect himself from being wounded by iron. He dulls the sharp edge of any iron blade, and no sword dares touch his sorcerer's body." Hearing this, they ordered the soldier to be arrested and put in chains, and they ripped his holy body to pieces with terrifying tortures, finally cutting off his head with a sword. Only this blessed soldier, who in the face of death stood firm in the faith of Christ, was worthy of being raised to the crown of martyrdom on the same day as St. Alban. He accompanied Alban in his passion and kept fellowship with him in glory. When at last they had finished slaughtering the martyrs, the judge dismissed the council and gave the people permission to leave. But as they departed, they cursed the judge's severity and said: "Woe to that judge, in whom fairness has no place, who plays his part with unreasonable zeal. Woe to that judge, whose judgment is dominated by rage, not by justice; whose willfulness gives the sentence, not his reason."

25. Then when night had fallen, the Lord Jesus Christ revealed the good works of his servant Alban with clear signs. In the silence of the night, behold, a column of light[33] stretched from the holy martyr's tomb up to heaven. Angels moved up and down it, spending the whole night in hymns and songs of praise.[34] In their songs one phrase was heard more than any other: "Alban, distinguished among men, arises a martyr in glory." A crowd soon gathered around the sight, and the number gazing at it grew greater and greater. Those standing farther off were disturbed by the strange light and understood the prodigy to be a miracle.

26. As they all stood by astonished, one of them said, "These marvels that we see show clearly that Christ the Son of God is at work."

Here begins the Passion of St. Amphibalus and his Companions.[35]

[After the glorious passion of Alban, the protomartyr of the English, had been brought to an end, and when the unbelieving saw the miracles that God had done through Alban and for him, both while he was living and after his death, they felt compunction in their hearts. They condemned idolatry and began to praise the Christian religion: "Truly the God worshipped by the Christians is the Almighty and the Savior of souls.][36] We ought to see that the gods we have worshipped until now are monsters rather than divinities: indeed it is easily seen that there is no power, no divinity in them. Our works are without profit, and we have poured out our days to no purpose. Behold, the darkness of the night sky is giving way to light. Heavenly citizens come and go and constantly commend Alban's sanctity. The world is wrapped in a fog of darkness, but Alban's brilliance admits no obscurity; Alban's merits cannot be covered up. Since the religion to which we cling is of no use, let us condemn our old error; let us be converted from falsehood to truth, from faithlessness to faith. Let us go and seek out the man of God, who, as you all know, converted Alban to Christ through his preaching.[37] You can clearly see just how true the things he said about Christ were by the wonders happening through Alban. The works of the disciple ratify his master's words beyond doubt."

27. While this man was speaking about this and more, everyone welcomed his judgment as praiseworthy. They all denounced their former error at once and proclaimed the faith of Christ. They made their way in haste to Wales, where God's servant Amphibalus was thought to be. They were not mistaken, for they had not gone far before talk of his renown told them that he would be there. When they reached him, they found him preaching the word of life to the local people. They explained to him why they had come and showed him the cross he had once entrusted to his Alban. Now spattered with the gore of the blessed martyr, it clearly showed the signs of his martyrdom. The man of God thanked the Creator for all these things, bowed down in worship, and venerated the life-giving sign with fitting devotion. When he spoke of religion to his new audience, they all joined the faith straightaway. They cast aside their empty superstition and at his holy hands they eagerly received the seal of Christ.[38] After some time had passed, talk of what had happened spread through the whole region. The rumor, which over time got stronger everywhere it went, in due course filled Verulamium with conflicting opinions. It was said that certain men of the city were wholeheartedly following the man from across the sea, and that he had persuaded them to cast aside the worship of the gods and the laws of their fathers. Disturbed by the news, the city was thrown into confusion. There was an inquiry

to see who had gone away: a thousand men were found to be missing, and their names were at once recorded. Roused to a fury, the citizens prepared to pursue them with all their might. They took to the road in an uproar, armed for combat, as though they were setting out for battle.

28. Hearing the praise of Amphibalus's name, they were led to him by his notoriety within a few days. They found the men they were seeking gathered around Amphibalus, listening intently to his words. As soon as they saw this, one of the pursuers severely rebuked the holy man of God: "Wicked deceiver," he said, "why with your smooth talking do you cheat these fools, who didn't know how to guard against your snares? Why did you do this? Because of you they presume to trample the laws and despise the gods. Why aren't you afraid of provoking the great gods? You cannot profit by this act. Once the gods begin to take vengeance on you for this insult, there can be no doubt that you will quickly perish from the earth. But if you wish, you could stand blamelessly before gods and men, together with those whom you have cast into the chains of your error. Command these men to repent of their error and to return to their homes at once. For if they are so obstinate in their error that they will not agree to give it up, not a single one will remain alive. This is our final decision."

29. Then one of the Christians, afire with the heat of faith, answered on the priest's behalf: "Perhaps today you will acknowledge that this man before you worships the true God. For we are confident that you will see, as we have, that any sick person can be restored to health in the name of Christ through him. We sought his holiness so that, once we have properly performed all that belongs to the Christian faith, we might share eternal life with him. Far be it from us to commit such a crime as leaving the feet of this holy man and once more entangling ourselves with you in these empty superstitions. Rather, end this dispute! Follow our example and take up the faith of Christ. That way you can attain his joys along with us. You threaten us with death, but we willingly embrace it for Christ's sake. And may God and our Lord Jesus Christ do with his servants what he will. Why should we abandon our good and profitable pledge? Why strive so vainly and pointlessly? There's no way we will return again to what we have already renounced for Christ's sake. This is our final decision."

30. When they heard this, the pagans' rage was inflamed even more. They sprang to their weapons and, unsheathing their swords, poured out the innocents' blood. What anguish! The servants of wickedness raged against their very own bodies (so to speak). As the father slaughtered his son, so the son his father, and as brothers killed brothers, so citizens killed one another. The hard hearts of the executioners were softened neither by respect for the old nor by compassion for their kin. But the holy martyrs competed to fling their necks beneath the blades, and while the first was slaughtered, the next complained of the delay. From this

holy group there remained only one. He had been delayed along the way because of his body's frailty and could not be there.

31. St. Amphibalus, surrounded on all sides by the bodies of the slain,[39] joyfully commended their blessed souls to God. The bloodstained executioners, pouring out all their rage against him, swore that they would eat no food until they had led the enemy of their gods back to the city, dead or alive. Cruelly binding his arms with leather straps, they drove him before their horses. While they rode high on horseback, Amphibalus made the journey barefoot. Yet the closer Amphibalus approached Alban's resting place, the less he felt the journey's harshness and the injustice of his suffering. Meanwhile the executioners, constantly looking back toward the place of slaughter, were led to earnest penitence and began to weep bitterly for the relations and friends whom they had butchered in their madness.

32. As they went along, they noticed the man lying ill beside the road. Knowing that St. Amphibalus was passing by, he cried out and said: "O servant of the highest God, help me, so that I, who lie weighed down by my illness, may deserve to be raised up by your intercession. For I believe that if you invoke the name of Christ on my behalf, you can quickly return me to health." But the executioners would not tolerate the man's insistent cries and began jeering at him. And before their mocking eyes, the man lying sick got up right away and was freed from the shackles of his long sickness through a man who was himself a captive. After this they continued on their way. What happened could not be hidden for long, and news of the event soon spread through the whole region. And the executioners were so amazed that some of them gave glory to God, saying: "How great is the God of the Christians and how great is his power!" When at last they reached their native soil and could see the city walls, they rested a while in a deserted spot. Exhausted by their hunger and toil, they fixed their spears in the ground and laid down their shields. But while the others rested, Amphibalus alone had no repose, forced to stand in his fetters. And though his heavy bonds constrained him, he still did not cease to preach the word of life to his persecutors; indeed, he could not be restrained from the word of God.

33. Meanwhile it was announced in the city that the citizens had returned home and had brought with them Alban's teacher as a great and acceptable sacrifice[40] to their gods. When this news got out, the city was filled with immense joy, for it was thought that those they had gone after had been brought home safely. But suddenly, in the midst of this rejoicing, some of the executioners appeared and told them that everyone for whose sake they had undertaken their exhausting journey had fallen by the sword in a foreign land. When the citizens learned this, all their mirth and joy were at once changed into mourning and sorrow. Fathers lamented that they had been robbed of their children, citizens of their fellow citizens; this one weeps for the loss of a brother, that one for a kinsman.

Mothers too, learning of their sons' deaths, tore at their hair and clothing and straightaway roused the sorrowful city with their cries. Everywhere there was groaning, everywhere mourning; the enormity of their grief forced lamentation from every last person. And they said: "Alas, why have these evils befallen us? Woe to us! Why drag out our unhappy lives any further? Those we thought would succeed us have preceded us in death. Alas for our children! What have you done? Because of you we are disgraced among all the nations of the earth.[41] In our misfortune we can henceforth no longer look on the faces of men, for we will often be reminded that our children abandoned their gods and for that reason perished wretchedly in a foreign land, far from their friends. You lie dead, scattered through the fields; you lie unburied, food for birds and prey for beasts.[42] What anguish! Have we been kept alive for this? Have we survived only so that we as parents will bear the blame for what our children did? Oh misery! Our hope has died; the repose of our old age has been taken away. Woe to that sacrilegious and deceitful man whom Alban took into his home and who first brought the accursed name of Christ to our city just a short while ago. He has overturned everything: clearly, he is the cause of all their deaths. Immortal gods, if ever we have served you, destroy that unspeakable man and turn this great plague away from our lands. Avenge our losses and the insults to you and hurl the evils he inflicted on us back onto his own head!"

34. When the executioners saw that the people were consumed by unbearable grief, they leapt into their midst, and said: "Citizens, do not weep, do not grieve beyond measure. Hold back your tears and take comfort, lest we seem to begrudge our children's joy. There is no need to mourn the loss of the dead so much; their death is followed by life, and grief by joy. Nothing is crueler than when parents are separated from their children by the suddenness of death. How could we deny this? But for all that, when they die, they bequeath to posterity a great reason to rejoice. Those who will reign forever as blessed conquerors in heaven with Christ are not at all to be mourned, but rather rejoiced over. Therefore do not be pained, but give thanks to Christ, who has deigned to take to himself such a multitude from our city and to establish them in heaven. Those who live happily with Christ in heaven should not be lamented as if they were dead in the ground. To weep over your loss is human indeed, but to refuse to place a limit to your grief is close to madness. Listen to how they died, and perhaps you will understand the pointlessness of your lamentation."

35. Then, swearing that they would keep their story free of lies, the executioners addressed the whole crowd: "Having set out, as you know, to look for our relatives and friends, rumor finally led us to Wales. And there we found the priest exhorting the Welsh, the Picts, and our citizens to the faith of Christ. Then, eager to separate our relatives from the others without making a scene and to bring them back with us, we set about gathering them together, now

admonishing, now threatening. But so great was their obstinacy that no effort of speech could separate them from that man's company even for an instant. We then turned to anger and leapt for our weapons. And because they scorned us, we avenged our wrongs in a massacre of our citizens. But they crowded one another to be first to fling their necks beneath the blade, and they met death willingly for Christ's sake. And that was a horrible sight, when sons raised their hands against their fathers and fathers against their sons, and laid them low and killed them. There was no pity or reverence for old age then. We cannot say what happened next without sighing heavily. Alas! When a son would have bound up his father's wounds, a brother appeared to cut off his hand. Thus our kindred were lost and our dear ones butchered. The fields, hidden beneath corpses, overflowed with blood. While this was going on, behold, Jesus himself, for whose sake they were laying down their lives, looked down from heaven and said in a clear voice: 'Cross over to me, my soldiers: behold, the gates of paradise are opened to you. Blessedness that shall not diminish has been made ready for you, and joys that shall know no ending.' When we, who were committing this slaughter, heard this, we were filled with indescribable joy; we understood that our friends were departing from this world into heaven, from death to Christ. We considered ourselves fortunate to have such kindred. Now angels were their fellow citizens, and Christ himself deigned to meet them.[43] All the same, hearing this strange divine voice shook and terrified us.

36. "Wanting to know how many were destroyed in that carnage, however, we set about counting the dead, and nine hundred and ninety-nine were discovered to have been butchered in the name of Christ. Every one of them lay trampled by the horses' hooves. And they could not be recognized because of their wounds and the amount of blood that had been spilled. But while the holy man poured out prayers to his God in thanksgiving for this, suddenly all the wounds of the dead were made whole beyond any imagining. Their blood was turned into the likeness of milk, and their skin was restored to its former beauty, so that not even the trace of a wound was visible. So it was that the righteous man's prayer restored their human appearance, which our cruelty had taken away. Then the people of that land, twisting Christ's beneficence by malicious interpretation, entirely rejected the divine miracles. They violently refused to have those who had accepted the faith of Christ buried within their borders. The deceased were denied the last debt to nature, and they were exposed to be devoured by beasts and birds. But the grace of God attended them, glorifying his servants even after death; it softened the hard hearts of the mad and made the foreigners[44] better disposed toward the dead. To make it clearly understood that Christ's worshippers shall never want for divine protection, behold, a wolf and an eagle, coming out of nowhere, took their places by the bodies of the dead. The wolf drove the wild beasts away, and the eagle the birds, so that human understanding could perceive that they had been sent to guard the dead.

37. "Seeing these things, the Picts marveled and the Welsh trembled. Human wildness was tamed and no longer attacked those protected by the right hand of God. People from the whole vicinity poured in from all sides in their eagerness to see. They embraced the relics of the martyrs with pious devotion and honored them with fitting rites. Those whom they held in derision a little earlier, and would not suffer the earth to receive, now, by contrast, they extolled with marvelous praise and wished to possess.[45] They gave thanks to the creator of all, who had deigned to consecrate their region with the blood of so many great men. Furthermore, in order to keep their memory fresh, the number and names of those who were killed were written down by the inhabitants themselves. Before they returned to their homes, the whole assembled crowd saw and heard these things. Together with us, they remain as witnesses to it all." While the executioners were saying these and other things, the people's tears were allayed and their sadness soothed. Many in the audience joined the executioners in praising Christ's power. They rejoiced in the glory of their kindred and said: "Great is the God of the Christians, who thus glorifies his servant. No sinful man would have been able to make the wounds of dead men whole. Truly he is a good physician who so quickly restores his wounded servants to health. From this we see clearly how much favor that priest has with God and how much we ought to embrace the teaching of a man who could obtain by prayer alone all the things that we have heard."

38. When the judge heard such talk, however, he burst out furiously, wishing to please the pagans: "Just how long will we bear this outrage? This man, whose words destroy the innocent, is not from God. This priest knows how to deceive the eyes of onlookers with enchantments so that they take false things as true. Through his beguiling words our city's best citizens have died. Therefore, I command that all who follow this man or who admire and esteem the words of the executioners be put to the sword, no matter where they are found." Afterward he gave orders to all the people and said: "Let us all march forth and engage our enemy at once, so that the man who (as we know) offended all may feel for himself the vengeance of all. Let everyone say what he will, we ought not to ignore or leave unavenged the harm done to our city." After this command had been announced through the city, the heathens rushed to assemble. The madmen snatched whatever weapons came to hand. Each man urged the next to go faster, and they roused one another against their enemy. Taking the northward road, they left the town empty.[46] But the number of people was boundless, and the streets could not contain the streaming multitude. And they were compelled by the thick press of the crowd to make their way at a slow pace.

39. Meanwhile some of them, not standing for delay and led by their high spirits, turned aside from the rest. They entered an alley and took a shortcut to avoid going the long way by the public road, and they reached the man of God in his chains far ahead of their companions. They seized him at once and, mauling him

horribly, stripped him. They opened up his guts with their swords and fastened them to a stake fixed in the earth. Then, falling on the holy man of God with many whips, they made him walk in a circle around that same stake.[47] While the martyr was beset with so many torments, by God's favor he gave no sign of pain. They became even bolder and set him up like a target, piercing what was left of his body with knives and spears. But the man of the Lord smiled and stood even firmer, as if he were suffering no harm. He displayed the signs of his martyrdom on every part of his body and offered himself as a wondrous spectacle to everyone — he who, after such torments and so many kinds of death, still lived.

40. Meanwhile many who sheltered God in their hearts were touched by compunction. They renounced idols and submitted to the Christian faith. They prayed to the martyr that through his intercession they might deserve to share in the eternal blessedness that God had prepared for him and that they professed to see already. For this reason they were not afraid to lay down their lives. When the prince learned of this, he quickly called for his spearmen and ordered that all those who had cast aside the worship of their gods and followed the priest's teachings be killed. Carrying out his deadly decree, the spearmen put a thousand men to death at once, while the blessed Amphibalus looked on and commended the souls of the dead to God.

41. Then one who seemed bolder than the rest addressed Amphibalus first: "Cruelest of men, why did you deceive these fools with your fraudulent arguments? Why did you compel them to abandon the worship of the gods, snared by your perverse and deadly teachings? How did our city sin against you, that you rob it of its citizens? Consider carefully, my good man, what you have done: by the subtlety of your words our family and friends are gone away into perdition. You are the cause of all their destruction; you drove them into the snare of death. Thus we pursue you with a just hatred. Justice demands with greatest justice that we oppose the opponents of justice. Where do you think you are now, wretch? You are surrounded on every side by enemy forces, with no chance of escape. But although you have provoked gods and men to wrath beyond measure, nevertheless you could earn their grace by repenting. Indeed, it would be a sign of your complete repentance if you abandoned that sect to which you have clung up until now and began to worship those unvanquished gods whom perhaps you offended unwittingly. And you won't regret it, because [your whole body will be restored by their heavenly medicine and][48] you will instantly attain riches of all kinds. Moreover, our gods, through the power of their divinity, will call back from the dead all those you have just handed over to destruction."

42. Amphibalus said to him: "While you strain to extol your gods, pagan, you should know that it is you who have offended by your speech. For only the Lord Jesus Christ raises the dead and restores them to life. Those you judge to be gods

and powers in heaven are suffering powerful torments in hell. The abode and eternal dwelling of your gods is there: there, weeping and gnashing of teeth; there, the worm that does not die and unquenchable fire.[49] The unjust, the adulterous, the slanderous,[50] and others who, while they lived here, made themselves like demons by their despicable behavior, shall be made their partners and companions in suffering. Thus those who have followed the demons' wills in sinful conformity will not lack demonic company in suffering torments. Indeed, this is a fitting payment for the offenses of the worshippers of such deities. Even you, pagan, you who worship idols like the rest will suffer under these same pains, unless you leave behind your heathen error and quickly convert to the faith of Christ. While you have the chance, let vanity be cast aside and error condemned. The mercy of our God is great; none of you should despair. Repent of your evil ways and flock to the grace of baptism. Hear what baptism confers: in baptism sins are forgiven and heaven is opened to humankind; old age is put aside, so to speak, to make a new creation. For those who before were sons of the devil through guilt are now made sons of God through grace.[51] Therefore fly to this grace, so that you may escape eternal punishment."

43. When they heard these things, they came at him from all sides, their cruel hands loaded with stones. The impious burned for the destruction of the innocent man, and they strove with all their power to cast out his blessed spirit. But although God's martyr was everywhere cut open by the hailstorm of rocks, nevertheless he continued to speak without faltering. He did not move from the spot, nor did he flinch even for an instant. Finally, when he was about to give up his unvanquished spirit to heaven, he lifted his eyes and saw Jesus standing at the right hand of the Father.[52] And he heard the choirs of angels in heaven, and he recognized his own Alban among them. Calling Alban to his aid, he said, "St. Alban, I beseech you to ask the Lord we share to send a good angel to meet me, lest the savage robber waylay me or one of the wicked obstruct my way." Hardly had he finished speaking when, behold, two angels shining with celestial brightness came to him from above. And a voice spoke to him from heaven in these words: "Amen, I say to you, for today you will be with your disciple in Paradise."[53] When the pagans heard the heavenly sound, they stood speechless.[54] Then the angels bore up the blessed man's soul, glowing with the whiteness of snow, and with hymns and songs of praise carried him with them into heaven.

44. But the men's spirits were still inflamed, and they continued to bury the chained and lifeless body under stones. Their leaders and noblemen, weakened by hunger and weariness, could not bring help to the dying man or wrest him from the hands of the madmen. Then serious dissension arose among the pagans, followed by an unspeakable brawl, finally leading to a clash of swords. Each side attacked in close ranks, and a terrible battle was begun above those most blessed limbs. But Almighty God neither willed nor permitted that the enemies of truth, who had

sworn a short while earlier that they would bring the holy man to the city dead or alive, be made into truth-tellers. For while the uproar was growing, and the pagans were thrown into confusion among themselves, a certain man faithful to Christ secretly carried off the body of the holy martyr and carefully hid it underground, where it will be brought to light eventually, as we trust, by divine mercy.

45. At that moment a heavenly retribution fell mercilessly upon the people; lips were distorted, faces were seized by strange deformities, fingers stiffened, and muscles would not do their work; their tongues, with which they had insulted the holy martyr, burned. More than that, their arms, hands, and all their supple limbs suddenly went completely rigid, so that they might never lift a stone from the earth again. Thus overcome[55] by their different punishments, they rested at last from the fighting. The judge, however, having lost all reason, was driven mad. There was no one who could boast that he had committed outrages against the Lord Jesus and his Amphibalus and still had escaped danger: for all who had raised a hand against the Lord received the vengeance they deserved from a just judge.

46. These events could not be hidden for long. Alerted by rumor, the people of the neighborhood hurried to the place and confirmed with their eyes what they had learned with their ears. Soon the whole city received the faith of Christ and praised as one the God who is just in his judgment. Moved by divine love, many left their goods behind and went to Rome. They lamented what they had done, confessed their errors, and went looking for the water of salvation. Thus from that day forward, all the people of the city, realizing that the gods they had revered were false, strove ever afterward to worship Christ the Son of God and to fear him.

47. These things and many others that God's mercy did not want hidden from mankind I have carefully put into writing. Blessed be God. That whole company of infidels that once imposed a sentence of death on the blessed Alban has departed, and men no longer think or talk much about them. The memory of Alban will not be rubbed away; rather, his praiseworthy merit—if my songs can do anything[56]—will be spread far and wide through the world. There will be a time, as we believe, when religious men, Christian men, will come to Britain to preach to the nations. When they come, they will find the miracles of God declared thus in books. They will read them and bring them to the attention of many others. Then when the truth is known the island will rejoice; then the heathen will be released from the chains of error and filled with great joy. I am not certain when the moment of this prophesied[57] visitation and grace will come. But lest men in the future worry too much about my name, let them know this: if they want to record my true name, they will call me miserable, and the worst of sinners. I, however, will set out for Rome, so that I might merit forgiveness for my sins once I have put aside pagan error there and received the water of renewal.

And I will carry this little book in my hands to be examined by the Romans, so that anything in it that happens to be improper may be exposed. May our Lord Jesus Christ deign to change it for the better through them: He is God, who lives and reigns forever and ever. Amen.

Here ends the History of the Passion of the blessed Alban, Protomartyr of the English, of blessed Amphibalus, and of his Companions.[58]

Notes

[1] **the first fruits of my mouth than the priest of the Lord**: cf. Lev. 23:10.

[2] **Geoffrey Arthur**: i.e., Geoffrey of Monmouth, the author of *The History of the Kings of Britain*. He signed five charters, though one of them may be a thirteenth-century forgery, as "Galfrido Artur" (or "Arturus," "Artour"), and his contemporaries Robert of Torigni, Henry of Huntingdon, William of Newburgh, and Gerald of Wales all knew him by that name. For a fuller discussion, see J. S. P. Tatlock, *The Legendary History of Britain: Geoffrey of Monmouth's* Historia Regum Britanniae *and Its Early Vernacular Versions* (Berkeley: University of California Press, 1950, repr. 1974), 438–39.

[3] BL MS. Cotton Faustina B. IV, fol. 3r, 6b–7b *ne uerborum prolixitas homini displiceat occupato*; AA.SS *ne uerborum prolixitas hominis displiceat occupato*, "lest the prolixity of (human) words displease a busy man."

[4] TCD fols. 20r, 7a-8a. Paris begins his copying of *PSA* with this rubric, having omitted all that precedes it in William's text.

[5] TCD fol. 20r, 18a *ommittere*; AA.SS om.

[6] TCD fols. 20r, 24a *sculpturam*; AA.SS *scripturam* "writing."

[7] TCD fol. 20r, 36a-3b.

[8] **"for the salvation of many"**: the phrase *pro multorum salute* is a favorite of the Fathers; "make the people acceptable to him" is an echo of the Vulgate version of Titus 2:14.

[9] **"This is the declaration of our faith"**: Ambrose, *De fide (ad Gratianum Augustum)*, ed. Otto Faller, Corpus Scriptorum Ecclesiasticorum Latinorum 82 (Vienna: Hoelder-Pichler-Tempsky, 1962), 1:1.6 (also PL 16.530 A).

[10] **"he came to her. . .'according to your word'"**: William is paraphrasing and quoting verbatim from Luke 1:26–42.

[11] **"The good Lord of loving kindness"**: cf. Titus 3:4.

[12] **"'Hail, King of the Jews'. . . a guard was assigned to it"**: the language of Alban's dream draws largely on the Crucifixion narratives in Matt. 27 and Luke 23. For the Ascension, see Acts 1:9–11.

[13] **"'Blessed be God the Father and his only begotten Son'"**: cf. the offertory for Trinity Sunday in the later Use of Sarum: see Francis Procter and Christopher Wordsworth, *Breviarium ad usum insignis ecclesiae Sarum* . . . (Cambridge: Cambridge University Press, 1879; repr. Farnborough, Hants.: Gregg, 1970), 2: 503.

[14] **"Don't be afraid"**: Alban reassures Amphibalus with the words (*Noli timere*) that God frequently uses to address his chosen servants; cf. Gen. 15:1 (God's covenant with Abraham), Matt. 1:20 (the angel's instructions to St. Joseph), Luke 2:10 (the Annunciation to the Shepherds), and Acts 18:9 (the Lord's words to Paul in Corinth).

[15] **"they found no deadly crime in him"**: Pilate uses almost exactly the same phrase to object to the persecution of Jesus by the Sanhedrin in the (notably anti-Jewish) Gospel of John. See John 18:38, 19:4, and 19:6.

[16] **"raised up on the cross he drew all things to himself"**: cf. John 12:32.

[17] **"He descended into the dungeons of hell . . . everlasting bonds"**: Amphibalus repeats the popular story of the Harrowing of Hell from the apocryphal *Gospel of Nicodemus*. According to early Christian tradition, on Holy Saturday Jesus descended into hell to release the Patriarchs and other holy men and women who had died before the Cruci-

fixion. See Z. Izydorczyk, "The *Evangelium Nicodemi* in the Latin Middle Ages," in *The Medieval Gospel of Nicodemus*, ed. idem 43–101. For the devil's chains see Rev. 20:2.

[18] **"there is no God but my Lord Jesus Christ"**: this is an echo of 1 Cor. 8:4 ("there is no God but one"). The verse is part of Paul's discussion of food offered to idols, but it was frequently used in patristic writing (particularly by Ambrose and Augustine) to defend the doctrine of the Trinity.

[19] TCD fol. 21r, 20b *post haec*; AA.SS *his dictis*, "after saying these things."

[20] TCD fols. 21r, 25b *crucis*; AA.SS om.

[21] In the margins of TCD fol. 21r, Matthew Paris has added: "And when he confessed this resolutely again and again, Amphibalus, under the guidance of the Holy Spirit, baptized him in the name of the same Trinity, and he became a Christian with his whole heart." Paris may be supplying missing text here.

[22] **"you have learned . . . the revelation of Jesus Christ"**: an echo of Paul's boast in Gal. 1:12.

[23] Here someone, probably Paris, has written in the margin: "Indeed he would have had noble friends at court, inasmuch as he was noble." This remark draws on a detail from *Alban* (15:452–453) to make sense of a potential plot-hole in *PSA*. It reflects the reimagining of Alban as an aristocrat in a late medieval mold, a development already visible in Paris but culminating in Lydgate's fifteenth-century *Life* of the saint. Just below this annotation another has been added: "An argument for Alban's nobility," TCD fol. 21v.

[24] TCD fols. 21v, 11a–12a *permiscent tandem quaerendi sollicitudine*; AA.SS om.

[25] Here Paris has written: "*This comes from the book of John Mansel:* for he was the leader and master of the army [*militie*] of all Britain" (TCD fol. 22r). Like the annotation in n. 23 above, this remark reflects the monastery's developing sense that Alban had held a tremendously high rank in society. A man named John Mansel was a senior counselor to Henry III. He was a visitor to St. Albans and was apparently Paris's informant. See Vaughan, *Matthew Paris*, 12, 14, 196. For Mansel's life, see Robert C. Stacey, "Mansel, John (d. 1265)," in *Oxford Dictionary of National Biography* (Oxford: Oxford University Press, 2004), 36: 530–33. When Lydgate came across the similar title "prince of the army [*miliciae*] of all Britain" in the *Tractatus de nobilitate, vita, et martirio sanctorum Albani et Amphibalo*, he took it to mean that Alban was the leader of the *knighthood* of all Britain, a rather different proposition. Given that this is Paris's hand, this note, like Mansel's book, must be a source for the late fourteenth-century *Tractatus*, rather than vice versa (see "Tractatus de nobilitate, vita, et martirio Sanctorum Albani et Amphibali," in van der Westhuizen, *John Lydgate*, 277–85, at 280, and George F. Reinecke, *Saint Alban and Saint Amphibalus* [New York and London: Garland Publishing, Inc., 1985], xxix–xxx).

[26] In the margin of TCD fol. 22v: "Note that blessed Alban was born and bred [*fuit natus et genitus*] a citizen and native of Verulamium, for it says that the people of the city were ultimately derived from the ancient Romans, the same way the Welsh were derived from the Trojans." In *Alban* 17:563–64, the Prince emphasizes Alban's Roman ancestry. Vaughan has identified this hand, which also wrote the annotation in note 39, as Paris's (Vaughan, *Matthew Paris*, 196).

[27] **"they see nothing, hear nothing, and understand nothing"**: cf. Ps. 115:4–6 [113:12–14] and 135 [134]: 15–17 and Wisd. 15:15.

[28] TCD fol. 23r, 1b *inter undas*; AA.SS om.

[29] "A perverse interpretation," Paris opines (TCD fol. 23v).

³⁰ TCD fols. 23v, 18a *ossa*; AA.SS *membra*, "limbs."
³¹ **he . . . poured out prayers for his persecutors**: cf. Matt. 5:44.
³² **they were filled with jealousy**: cf. Acts 5:17 and 13:45.
³³ TCD fols. 24v, 5a *lucis*; AA.SS *Crucis*, "of the cross."
³⁴ **Angels moved up and down it**: the pillar of light is a combination of Jacob's Ladder in Gen. 28:10–15 and the pillar of light that reveals the sanctity of King Oswald to the skeptical monks of Bardney in *HE* 3:11.
³⁵ TCD fols. 24v, 17a-18a.
³⁶ TCD fols. 24v, 18a-25a; AA.SS om.
³⁷ **"Our works are works without profit . . . through his preaching"**: the people's repentance is a pastiche of scriptural quotations and imagery (darkness, fog, dawning light) drawn largely from Isaiah (e.g., 59:6, 9:2, 29:18). For Christian commentators Isaiah's prophecies of deliverance referred specifically to the birth of Christ, and so the crowd's final resolution "Let us go" aptly connects them to the shepherds of Luke 2:15.
³⁸ **the seal of Christ**: i.e., baptism; cf. Rom. 4:11 and Eph. 2:11–14.
³⁹ On TCD fol. 25v, Paris has added in the margin: "This happened in Lichfield. For this reason it is called 'Lichfield,' or 'Field of Corpses,' since in English a corpse or the body of a dead man is called 'lich'." Vaughan says this note reflects "Paris's interest in etymologies" (*Matthew Paris*, 196).
⁴⁰ **acceptable sacrifice**: cf. the offertory of the Mass found in the later Use of Sarum: "Orate fratres et sorores pro me: ut meum pariterque vestrum acceptum sit Domino Deo nostro sacrificium" (Pray for me, brothers and sisters, that my sacrifice, and yours, might be accepted by the Lord our God), in Procter and Wordsworth, *Breviarium ad usum insignis ecclesiae Sarum . . .*, 2: 485. See also 1 Pet. 2:5 and Phil. 4:18. This ironic allusion to the Mass is yet another parallel between the pagans and Christians.
⁴¹ **"all the nations of the earth"**: cf. Jer. 44:8.
⁴² **"food for birds and prey for beasts"**: cf. Jer. 16:4 and 19:7, Deut. 28:26, and Ps. 79(78):2.
⁴³ **"Christ himself deigned to meet them"**: cf. Wisd. 6:16 and Eph. 2:19.
⁴⁴ Presumably the foreigners (*hostes*) here are the same Welsh and Picts referred to in the beginning of chapter 35. Here and throughout the *PSA*, William transposes the contemporary geography of twelfth-century Britain into Roman Britain. The territory of Wales came into being only after the Anglo-Saxon conquests, when the invaders pushed British culture into the western hinterland; the Anglo-Saxons called the country's inhabitants *waelisc*, a derivation of the Old English word *wealh* meaning "foreigner." The people encountered by Amphibalus in Wales are thus in some sense ethnically identical to the Britons he left behind in Verulamium. Though Geoffrey of Monmouth also mentions Wales in his *Historia Regum Britannie* ("Kambria," also called "Gualia"), the "foreignness" attributed to its people here is in fact a twelfth-century attitude projected back into the Romano-British past. Consequently Amphibalus appears to traverse time as well as space, when he departs on his mission. Since the Verulamians occupy the same space and are defined against the same outsiders, as the twelfth-century English, William can claim them as forerunners to his Anglo-Norman monastery.
⁴⁵ The bodies are not taken back to Verulamium, but the funeral rites here serve to acknowledge them as part of Verulamian society. For medieval attitudes to the dead, see Patrick Geary, *Living with the Dead in the Middle Ages* (Ithaca and London: Cornell Uni-

versity Press, 1994), esp. 87–92; Paul Binski, *Medieval Death: Ritual and Representation* (Ithaca and London: Cornell University Press, 1996), 11–15; Christopher Daniell, *Death and Burial in Medieval England, 1066–1550* (London: Taylor & Francis, 2005); and cf. R63:393 above and n.

⁴⁶ This line is corrected to "almost empty" in the margin of TCD fol. 27r. This correction tries to close an apparent hole in the *PSA*'s plot; namely, how were there any citizens left in Verulamium to convert to Christianity if they had all left the city to kill Amphibalus? A note in the same hand has tried to give the "leaders and noblemen" sympathetic to Amphibalus in chapter 44 clearer motivation by saying that "they were recently converted to the Lord" (TCD fol. 28r).

⁴⁷ Paris notes in the margin of TCD fol. 27r: "An innovative kind of torture." Indeed this torture has few parallels in the Middle Ages, though St. Elmo's intestines were said to have been extracted with a windlass, and in some traditions Alfred Atheling, the brother of Edward the Confessor, is said to have been tortured at Earl Godwin's command in the same way as Amphibalus: see, e.g., *The* Gesta Guillielmi *of William of Poitiers,* ed. R. H. C. Davis and Marjorie Chibnall (Oxford: Clarendon Press, 1998), 1, 4.4; Geffrei Gaimar, *Estoire des Engleis,* ed. and trans. Ian Short (Oxford: Oxford University Press, 2009), vv. 4833–4839. For a late fourteenth-century version of this story, see Friedrich Brie, *The Brut, or the Chronicles of England,* EETS o.s. 131 (London: Oxford University Press, 1906), 127–28. The closest parallel, however, seems to be with the reports of Pope Urban II's preaching of the crusades at Clermont in 1095: see Introduction, 9 above.

⁴⁸ TCD fol. 27v, 6b-8b *eorum medicamine celesti toto corpore redintegratus*; AA.SS om.

⁴⁹ **"weeping and gnashing of teeth . . . unquenchable fire"**: this traditional description of hell is based on, for example, Matt. 8:12 and 13:42 and Luke 13:28. For the worm and the fire, see Mark 9:43, 45, 48.

⁵⁰ TCD fol. 27v, 22b-23b *maledici*; AA.SS *maledicti*, "the accursed."

⁵¹ **"old age is put aside . . . sons of God through grace"**: cf. Col. 3:8–11. The adoption of believers as the "sons of God" through grace is one of Paul's favorite themes: e.g., Rom. 8:10–17 and Eph. 1:3–2:3.

⁵² **Jesus standing at the right hand of the Father**: cf. Acts 7:54–60. Most of William's biblical allusions in the second half of the *Passio* come from Acts. The details of Amphibalus's martyrdom, including the stoning by which he is finally killed and his vision, are borrowed directly from the martyrdom of St. Stephen. Acts is the book of the Bible that tells the history of the church after the Ascension, and William's dependence on it here is surely meant to reaffirm the many parallels between Christ and Alban. Yet insofar as the life described in Acts was seen as a model for medieval monastic communities, William's allusions to Acts also allow him to present the converted city of Verulamium as a precursor to his own house of St. Albans.

⁵³ **"Amen, I say to you . . . Paradise"**: cf. Luke 23:43, where Jesus comforts the Good Thief.

⁵⁴ **they stood speechless**: cf. Acts 9:7.

⁵⁵ TCD fol. 28v, 5a *afflicti*; AA.SS *afflati*, "blown up."

⁵⁶ **if my songs can do anything**: *Aeneid* 9.446. This final allusion to the *Aeneid* is just one of a number of Virgilian motifs throughout the *Passio*. Others include the prophecies of a coming salvation, the ekphrasis (as at Carthage or at Cumae), the exemplary friendship of Alban and Amphibalus (as with Nisus and Euryalus), and the strange, almost

superfluous violence at the work's end. The effects of these resonances are subtle but cumulatively powerful. For details, see Thomas O'Donnell, "Monastic Literary Culture and Communities in England, 1066–1250" (Ph.D. diss., University of California, Los Angeles, 2009), 193–97.

[57] TCD fols. 28v, 11b *praedictae*; AA.SS *praedicatae*, "preached."
[58] TCD fols. 28v, 27b-29b.

The Manuscript
(Dublin, Trinity College Ms 177)

The Manuscript Context

Christopher Baswell

A Work in Progress? The Making of the Manuscript

Despite growing scholarly and critical attention to Matthew Paris's *Vie de seint Auban*, the unique manuscript that contains it, Dublin, Trinity College MS. 177 (formerly cited by its earlier shelfmark E. I. 40, but nowdays, as in this volume, cited as MS. 177), remains an enigma.[1] We are uncertain when it was written and for just which users it was intended. The two Latin *vitae* with which it begins, with no accompanying illustrations, suggest a learned, mostly monastic audience. They are followed, though, by a text in French vernacular that could appeal to both monks and laypeople, and the book was lent to women of the highest aristocracy (see Introduction, 32–35). The drawings that illustrate the *Vie de seint Auban* (henceforth *Auban*) and the Latin texts that follow it (all explained by French rubrics) could extend the manuscript's appeal to those who did not read Latin or even French. Matthew Paris lavished some of his most expressive work on these painstaking illustrations, which consistently feature aristocratic and royal men. The manuscript was kept at various times in the abbot's study and on the high altar of the church, an object of respect and even veneration (see Introduction, 17). Yet it is rather small (242 × 165 mm, about 9½ × 6½ inches); its parchment is of mixed quality, some of it quite poor; and many of its leaves are assembled from multiple scraps, some showing signs of prior use.[2] Its production, then, is scarcely in keeping with the respect it received in the abbey or the status of some of its lay readers. Further, it is not altogether clear in what order the

---

[1] I am most grateful to Dr. Bernard Meehan, Keeper of Manuscripts, and to his staff in the manuscripts room at Trinity College Dublin, for making it possible for me to study Dublin, Trinity College MS. 177 in person.

[2] See Patricia Quinn, "*Alban* Disbound," 195–211 below. On fol. 45r–v, there are traces of red ruling incompletely scraped off, and prick marks for those rules remain visible at the bottom of the leaf. Paris is reusing a page designed for a larger book, originally meant to be used at a 90-degree rotation from its current orientation. See also Quinn, 205 on the apparent prior use of fol. 2.

manuscript's contents were produced; and it is even uncertain, in places, whether text or illustration came first.

The incomplete state of the Trinity College manuscript, with many leaves missing, the loss of pasted-in illustrations, the currently limited consultation due to its fragile condition, and the lack of a color facsimile or digitized images all combine to preserve its mystery—a situation that may help us experience today something of the fascination that the manuscript clearly held for its medieval users. Nevertheless, the painstaking studies by experts like Patricia Quinn and Richard Vaughan, abetted by careful attention to the several scribes who worked on the manuscript along with Matthew Paris and the order of Paris's interventions as corrector, annotator, and illustrator, may allow us to form conjectures about the production of the manuscript and, I propose, its evolving purposes and audiences.

Compared with the better-documented instances of Bury St. Edmunds, Canterbury, or Durham, we know rather little about the medieval library of St. Albans or the practices of its scriptorium.[3] Certainly books must have continued to be produced there after the major efforts of the twelfth and earlier thirteenth centuries,[4] or the fifteen scribes known to have assisted Matthew Paris in his many and varied productions would not have been available there.[5] On the other hand, as at other monasteries in the thirteenth century, there is increasing if sparse evidence of books acquired at St. Albans by gift or purchase in the thirteenth century and after, rather than being produced in the abbey.[6]

Whatever the activities of the St. Albans scriptorium, however, it is difficult to fit the practices of Matthew Paris—at once author, illustrator, and (in great part) copyist of his own books—with other books that do survive from St. Albans in his time.[7] As a maker of books, he merits the description that Nigel Morgan assigns him as an artist: "a talented amateur whose work contrasts with the professional, but not necessarily any the more interesting, work of these contemporaries."[8] Despite his prestigious position as the abbey's official histo-

---

[3] R. W. Hunt, "The Library of the Abbey of St Albans," in *Medieval Scribes, Manuscripts and Libraries: Essays Presented to N. R. Ker*, ed. M. B. Parkes and Andrew G. Watson (London: Scolar Press, 1978), 263–68.

[4] Thomson, *Manuscripts from St Albans Abbey 1066–1235, Part I: Text*.

[5] Richard Vaughan, "The Handwriting of Matthew Paris," *Transactions of the Cambridge Bibliographical Society* 1 (1953): 376–94, at 384.

[6] Hunt, "Library of the Abbey of St Albans," 263–68.

[7] Lewis, *Art of Matthew Paris*, 20–21. For surviving thirteenth-century books associated with St. Albans, see Neil R. Ker, *Medieval Libraries of Great Britain: A List of Surviving Books* (London: Royal Historical Society, 1964), 164–67, and Andrew G. Watson, *Medieval Libraries of Great Britain: A List of Surviving Books, edited by N. R. Ker. Supplement to the Second Edition* (London: Royal Historical Society, 1987), 59–60.

[8] Morgan, *EGM [I]*, 132.

rian from 1236 onward, Paris sometimes resorted to parchment of poor quality (as already noted) and wrote on leaves of varying size within one manuscript. He often used leaves glued together from smaller scraps in the *Chronica majora* as well as in TCD MS. 177.[9] And he appears to have held onto some of his works (the original manuscript of the *Chronica* certainly until the end of his life), amending, enlarging, and annotating them and, in the case of the *Chronica*, radically rearranging their order and distribution across one, then two, then three separate volumes.[10] We will encounter signs of similar production in TCD MS. 177.

Date of the Manuscript

The date of the manuscript remains a minor but significant controversy. Working from his unparalleled acquaintance with the varied hands of Matthew Paris, Richard Vaughan argued that Paris's neat, simple, but careful text-hand in most of the manuscript reflects early production, "perhaps before 1240"; elsewhere he suggests that it could have been Paris's first book, "written and decorated in the third, or even the second, decade of the thirteenth century."[11] Throughout his study of Paris's handwriting, however, Vaughan tended to align quality of writing and chronology rather too neatly. While there is no question that Paris's writing declined to some extent in the very last years of his entries in the *Chronica majora*, for much of his life he could, like any practiced scribe, alter his script to the formality of its occasion. Indeed, scribes working with Paris were aware of how varied his scripts were. The monk who completed work on the *Chronica majora* in BL Royal 14. C. VII after Paris's death noted, "Et licet manus in stilo varietur, modo tamen composicionis eodem servato, eidem totum ascribitur" (And though his script may vary in appearance, nonetheless, it keeps to the same writing style, and the whole work is written by the same man).[12] The care of Paris's text script throughout TCD MS. 177 may be an indication of the manuscript's importance to him, rather than a way of determining its date. As Morgan notes, "the special nature of the text as an illustrated life of the patron saint of the Abbey" may account for its accuracy and control.[13] It might also be suggested

---

[9] Lewis, *Art of Matthew Paris*, 21–22. Mary Rouse informs me, though, that this was not unusual in thirteenth-century monastic books.

[10] Now Cambridge, Corpus Christi College MSS. 26 and 16 and London, BL Royal 14.C.VII. BL Cotton Nero D. I, the *Liber additamentorum*, contains largely documentary material, some of it originally inserted in earlier arrangements of the *Chronica*. See Vaughan, *Matthew Paris*, 49–77, and Gransden, *Historical Writing in England, I: 550–1307*, 367.

[11] Vaughan, "The Handwriting," 389; idem, *Matthew Paris*, 177.

[12] Fol. 218v: see S. Harrison Thomson, *Latin Bookhands of the Later Middle Ages, 1100–1500* (Cambridge: Cambridge University Press, 1969), pl. 92 and discussion.

[13] Morgan, *EGM [I]*, 132.

that the small scale of the hand in TCD MS. 177 is simpler and easier to control than the slightly larger writing in Paris's *Chronica* manuscripts and might hence be less affected if written in his later years.

By contrast with Vaughan, most art historians see in the illustrations a developed, nuanced style "nearer 1250 than 1240."[14] Suzanne Lewis has offered the provocative if speculative suggestion that the manuscript may have been produced in two stages, first in the 1240s and then again c. 1249–1252, divided by the period Paris spent reorganizing the affairs of the monastery of St. Benet Holm, on Nidarholm in Norway.[15] Despite Vaughan's claims, some of Paris's own writing in the manuscript may support the arguments of these art historians. In addition to copying the main texts, Paris constantly intervenes in the manuscript with rubrics, marginal notes, text corrections, and reminders to himself about illustrations. He does so in scripts that range from fairly formal to the hurried, cursive note-hand he often used in the margins of the *Chronica*.[16] His script in the frequent corrections that he entered in the work of his scribal assistant, Hand 2 (see "Appendix: The Hands of TCD MS. 177" below), often displays the rather open, lax aspect that Vaughan notes in his late handwriting. The variations among these scripts suggest that the manuscript was created across a period of time (like the *Chronica*) and open the possibility, mentioned above, that its intentions equally evolved across that time.[17]

The importance of Paris's own writing and illustrations, further, has diverted attention from the help he received in producing TCD MS. 177. Paris copied the bulk of the manuscript. Twenty-three leaves (fols. 50v-72r), however, are identified by the manuscript's most recent cataloguer, Marvin Colker, as written by "a different hand."[18] In fact, a careful review reveals that there are three scribal assistants at work in this portion of the manuscript. All three seem to be non-professionals like Paris; they share a rather ponderous look and are all (though differently) inconsistent in their graphs. Hands 2 and 3, though, seem to be at least slightly later in style than Paris's rather old-fashioned hand, which could

---

[14] Morgan, *EGM [I]*, 132. For a fuller survey of art historical arguments, see Nigel Morgan, "Matthew Paris, St Albans, London, and the Leaves of the 'Life of St Thomas Becket'," *Burlington Magazine* 130 (1988): 85–96.

[15] Lewis, *The Art of Matthew Paris*, 381–87. For Paris's time at Nidarholm, see Vaughan, *Matthew Paris*, 4–7.

[16] A particularly striking instance occurs in the right margin of fol. 21r.

[17] For instance, the marginal note on the name of Lichfield, fol. 25v upper left, (p.163, n. 39) has the exaggerated sway-back ascenders typical of Paris's later hand. Such marginalia and corrections are too brief to invite systematic dating, however.

[18] M. L. Colker, *Trinity College Dublin: Descriptive Catalogue of the Mediaeval and Renaissance Latin Manuscripts* (Aldershot: Scolar Press for Trinity College Dublin, 1991), 177.

have had its first training before he joined St. Albans in 1217.[19] The first of these scribal assistants (Hand 2), moreover, shows practices that can point well past Vaughan's suggested dates before 1240; indeed this scribe is more consistent with Lewis's and Morgan's dating around 1250 or even later (see "Appendix: The Hands of TCD MS. 177" below).

This range of scripts by Paris himself and his assistants, particularly Hand 2, suggests a manuscript quite likely copied later in his life, and thus consistent with the judgment of art historians. Equally, though, the variety of Paris's own scripts in the book raises the possibility of a manuscript produced across a period of time, with an evolving form and intentions. A particularly notable instance occurs at fol. 28v. Here a rubric toward the bottom of the second column announces the end of the manuscript's second, prose Latin life of St. Alban ("Explicit historia beati albani . . ."); the script has the predominant small scale and neatness that led Vaughan to argue for a rather early date in Matthew Paris's life at St. Albans. It is immediately followed by the rubric announcing the start of another text ("Incipit historia . . ."), apparently intended to begin on the next leaf. We will return to this rubric; what matters here is its script, which is clearly in the idiosyncratic style of Matthew Paris but shows all the characteristics that Vaughan associates with his maturity, even aspects of his late hand: the slightly larger scale; the sway-back, almost broken-back appearance to the ascenders of *h*, *l*, and especially tall *s*; the emphatic shoulder stroke also seen on tall *s*; and the open, trailing-headed *a*, here with a lax quality that evokes Paris's latest handwriting.[20] The possibility of a manuscript produced across some period of time may be reinforced by the variable quality of the parchment, which nonetheless, as Quinn has noted (see 204-5 below) is often consistent within quires.

Format

Further signs also suggest that TCD MS. 177 may have been produced in an improvised fashion across a period of time. Variation of production is perhaps clearest in the format of individual pages across the manuscript. Matthew Paris used up-to-date formats but was inconsistent in the layout of individual sections in TCD MS. 177. For Ralph of Dunstable's Latin verse life of St. Alban with which the book opens (fols. 3–20), Paris consistently uses a quite standard two-column format for poetry, with three vertical lines marking the left edge of each column; the capital letters of each line are bounded by the outer two of these ver-

---

[19] Paris, for instance, uses both the uncrossed "tironian" abbreviation for *et* and the usually later crossed form; two of the three scribal assistants use only the crossed form. (Though Hands 2 and 3 also occasionally use the typically earlier ampersand, and Hand 4 uses it exclusively.)

[20] See Vaughan, "Handwriting," 386, 392–93, and plates XVI d (of 1251), XVII b (1253), and XVII d (1259).

tical lines; a single vertical line bounds the outer edge of the right-hand column (3–3–1). He rules fol. 20r the same way, for the end of the verse life, and begins the prose life of William of St. Albans in that format. But on the verso of the same leaf Paris shifts to a standard prose layout, with single vertical lines at the innermost and outermost margins and double vertical lines separating the two columns at the center (1–2–1); he uses this format for the rest of the prose life. The French *Auban* is presented in a new and somewhat variable verse format, with two vertical lines at the outermost written edges and three (or sometimes two) vertical lines dividing the two columns (2–3/2–2); this involves a different arrangement of capital letters, written directly over the left vertical rule in the left-hand column. Paris uses this page layout across the entire poem (with two exceptions, discussed below) but varies the way in which he uses the three center rules to align his capital letters.

The second scribe of the manuscript (Hand 2) continues this same format in the liturgical lessons and responses about the *inventio* of St. Alban that follow the French life (fols. 50v–62v).[21] At fol. 63r, though, as Hand 3 begins copying a group of royal charters, the pages move to yet another prose format: 2–2–1 on recto pages, 1–2–2 on verso; Hand 4 continues with the same format, as does Hand 2 when he reenters at fol. 66v (hence abandoning his earlier 2–3–2 layout). With the beginning of the Latin prose miracles of St. Amphibalus (and the return of Paris's own hand) at fol. 73r, the format switches back to the 1–2–1 format that Paris had used for the prose life of St. Alban composed by William.

Notably, with the one exception of the surviving start of *Auban*, all these changes of format occur within quires, sometimes from one side of a leaf to another. This suggests that the pages were ruled one by one, with quires already assembled if not sewn, rather than the more typical procedure of ruling across a whole open bifolium. (The format change at fol. 20v is part of a surviving bifolium, fols. 14/20. Format also changes across another original bifolium, fols. 62 [2–3–2] and 69 [2–2–1/1–2–2], and similarly fols. 72 [2–2–1/1–2–2] and 76 [1–2–1]; all were divided in some later rebinding.)[22] This in turn further suggests that the manuscript was created in a somewhat improvised fashion, despite the apparent careful planning of those pages that include images.

Rubrics

Other aspects of physical layout also point to evolving intentions on Paris's part and resulting improvisation in the placement of text. In most manuscript production of this period, rubrics were typically added on blank lines, after the writing of the main text in the less costly dark brown or black ink. In the case of

---

[21] This could be intended to accommodate places such as fol. 61r, where verse and prose occur on the same page.

[22] See Quinn, "Alban Disbound" ("Structure and Collation"), 197–201 below.

TCD MS. 177, however, there seems to have been persistent poor planning of the spaces to be left blank for rubrics; or they were added awkwardly as the manuscript itself evolved and Paris developed new ideas for its possible uses. In Ralph of Dunstable's verse *Passio*, Paris often places his rubrics where expected, on lines in the text column left blank for that purpose. Even where he does leave such blank lines, though, they often prove inadequate to the (perhaps increasing) ambition of his topic headings or comments, and his rubrics spill into extra text-column space above or below the original blank lines. But especially on early folios (although elsewhere as well), he often fails to leave blank lines at all and inserts his narrative rubrics by squeezing them into column space left blank by the short verse lines. He then increasingly shifts to adding briefer rubrics in the outer margins.[23]

In *Auban*, verse rubrics, also in French, accompany the illustrations, appearing most often on lines ruled above the images; but these were sometimes not planned in the initial ruling or proved to be longer than anticipated and are therefore squeezed far into the inner, outer, and occasionally uppermost margins.[24] In one case, the rubric is inserted within the framed image (at fol. 30v, Alban's dream of the crucifixion, see Plate 1). The French rubrics continue to accompany illustrations to the Latin materials that follow *Auban*, again squeezed in above the images; the rubrics continue to be written by Paris even on pages whose main text is copied by Hand 2 or Hand 3.[25] All these problems of placement suggest that the French rubrics (and to some extent, the Latin) were an idea that developed after the initial planning and ruling of the pages, probably even after the illustrations were entered. This has to have been the case at fol. 30v, mentioned above.

---

[23] It may be a further sign of an evolving project, produced across time, that Paris sometimes provides variants of certain words, suggesting access to a second exemplar of Ralph of Dunstable's poem at a later date; for instance "magistri" has the marginal variant "uel potentes" (fol. 3r col. 2); "figurabant," marginal "uel futurabant" (fol. 4r col. 2); "iam specialiter," marginal "connubialiter" (fol. 5v col. 1); "dira," marginal "uel dura" (fol. 6r col. 2); "deinde," interlinear "uel moxque" (fol. 8v col. 1); "reddunt," marginal "uel redibent" (fol. 9r col. 2). The first of these may be intended as an explanatory gloss; others are clearly variants.

[24] This is especially obvious at fols. 33r (see Plate 4) and 34r. In other cases, such as fol. 29v, by contrast, the text, rubrics, and illustration are all nicely integrated within the page's initial layout.

[25] At fol. 55v, a triumphal image of King Offa, the rubric fills the space above the image and spills down into the left margin (see Plate 11). The same problem occurs at fols. 59r, 60v, and 61v, all parts of Paris's illustrations of King Offa and his role at St. Albans.

The Order of Writing and Illustrations

In the preparation of text and illustrations as noted the common procedure was to enter text first (in the less costly brown or black ink) and the costlier and more time-consuming rubrics, letters decorated with red or blue flourishes, and illustrations later. Here too, however, there are signs that TCD MS. 177 was not consistently produced in that typical fashion. Instead, Paris seems to have varied his practices from leaf to leaf. This may reflect the special circumstances of a book largely copied, entirely drawn, and mostly colored by one man, whose time was simultaneously occupied (whatever the date of TCD MS. 177) by monumental projects such as the *Chronica majora*, *Historia Anglorum*, and *Flores historiarum*.

At some points, it is clear that Paris produced his pages in the traditional order. Fol. 30v, for instance, has an image of Alban's dream in its upper right column (see Plate 1). A vertical line that borders this image is interrupted at one point, to avoid crossing the end of the word "despent" (7:200) to its left. That word, then, must have been in place before the drawing and its border were added. A similar interruption of a border line occurs on fol. 34r, again an instance of a one-column illustration.[26]

Other pages, though, were produced in more eccentric fashion. Typically, in thirteenth-century manuscripts, flourished decoration of text initials was entered before the even more costly and time-consuming illustrations. On fol. 36r of TCD MS. 177, though, the illustration appears to have been made before the text initials were flourished (see Plate 7). The two-column image (Alban's banishment from the city) clearly limits the pen-drawn flourishes of the capital letter *L* in the right column just below it.

Even more unusual are the occasions in TCD MS. 177 when the illustration appears to have been drawn before any text was written on the page. On some of the pages with single-column illustrations, the column of writing next to the image is compressed in a way that suggests the illustration was produced first. This is most exaggerated at fol. 33v (see Plate 5), whose illustration of Alban venerating Amphibalus's cross is in the left-hand column but takes up some of the right-hand column space as well. This obliges Paris to rule that part of the right-hand text column out of alignment with the rest of the page, compress his script, and extend his text well into the right margin at three points. Further, an architectural detail at the bottom right of the illustration forces the initial letter to its right even farther out of alignment with the rest of the page layout. It is difficult to explain these features unless the illustration preceded the ruling and writing of the right-hand column.[27] A more modest version of the same effect is seen at fol. 47v, where a slight crowding of the first seventeen lines in the left

---

[26] The line lifts to avoid crossing "ee," 16:529.
[27] See also Lewis, *Art of Matthew Paris*, 383.

column makes space for the illustration in the right column, which thus was presumably entered before the text.[28]

Further, on eight leaves extra rectangles of parchment were pasted in to receive the illustrations, presumably because the illustration on the opposite side had bled through the thin parchment. These paste-ins (and their valuable illustrations) were all removed at a later date, with the exception of one pasted-in fragment, not a full rectangle, on fol. 57r. Since some details from the outer edges of the illustrations survive, though, it appears that the paste-ins were decorated only after they were glued to the pages. (For further detail, see below, 198, 203.) In seven of the eight cases, the lost paste-ins were on the verso page, as one might expect. That is, the recto side was illustrated first, and bleed-through of that image required that a paste-in be added to the verso before it could be illustrated. In all those instances, then, the book was being illustrated in consecutive order. On one leaf (fol. 43), however, the lost paste-in was on the recto side. This suggests strongly that, in one case at least, Paris was not illustrating consecutively but rather decorated the verso of a leaf before the recto, again reflecting a rather improvisatory production practice.

Scribal Confusion at Fols. 63r–66r

A startling moment of scribal confusion occurs in the text of TCD MS. 177 at the transition from fols. 62v to 63r, which again may be best explained by illustrations being entered before the text.[29] It again reflects the improvisatory way in which the manuscript appears to have been produced. From fols. 52v to 62v, and again from 66v to 68v, Paris's primary assistant scribe (Hand 2) copies a Latin narrative of King Offa's discovery and translation of the long-lost remains of St. Alban.[30] This text is suddenly interrupted, in the middle of a sentence, at the end of fol. 62v ("Quos namque predicatorum lingua ad"), and a second assistant (Hand 3) begins copying, on fol. 63r, a series of early charters, in the first of which King Offa donates lands to the monastery of St. Albans, which (according to the charter and other texts in the manuscript) he founded (see Plate 12). The

---

[28] On fol. 29v, a somewhat eccentric ruling at the middle of the page (three vertical hard-point lines rather than the two, in plummet, that are typical in these pages) is best explained by their coherence with an architectural division in the illustration at the top of the page. This would suggest that on this page too the decorative plan is being made page by page, and the page ruling made to accommodate it, even if the illustration is entered later.

[29] For a discussion that leads to slightly different conclusions, see Crick, *Charters of St Albans*, 45–48.

[30] For textual relations between this section and Paris's *Vitae Offarum* (*Historia duorum Offarum*), perhaps relevant to dating, see Lewis, *Art of Matthew Paris*, 384–85.

later section of these charters is copied by the third scribal assistant, Hand 4.[31] At some point in the copying of the charters, Matthew Paris seems to have noticed the mistake being made. The copying of the last charter is interrupted, just as suddenly, in the midst of a sentence at fol. 66r, most of the page is left blank, and Hand 2 resumes the interrupted narrative of Alban's relics on 66v. Paris helps confused users of the manuscript by inserting a note (in his swift, informal hand) at the bottom of fol. 62v, instructing readers to "turn over the following four leaves to this sign o—" ("verte iiii folia sequentia ad hoc signum o— "); the symbol then duly occurs again at the top of 62v where the text recommences.

This truly confusing sequence is somewhat more easily explained now that we realize that there were three assistants at work in these pages, not one, as previously thought. But it still does not account for one scribal assistant suddenly interrupting another's work. The confusion would make better sense if, here again, Matthew Paris had made his illustration on fol. 63r before his assistant copied in the text. At this point in the manuscript, the illustrations and their accompanying French rubrics have only a loose connection to the accompanying text; indeed the illustrated story of King Offa continues for four leaves, and seven images, beyond the point where the Latin text turns to King Henry I and his successors at fol. 59v.[32] Offa's journey to Rome and the support of Pope Adrian would be known to Matthew Paris and much of his immediate audience through the work of his predecessor as the abbey's historian, Roger of Wendover.[33] The illustration on fol. 63r shows Offa presenting a charter to a monk at an altar (presumably inside the church whose construction he has been depicted supervising), with a man ringing celebratory bells at right. The preceding rubric is explicit that the image represents Offa's gift of land (by charter) to the monastery. The earlier Latin narrative at fol. 59v, however, emphasized Pope Adrian's eager confirmation of the monastery's privileges during Offa's visit to Rome; the image might initially have been intended to represent Offa delivering a papal confirmation at the altar.[34]

---

[31] For superb analysis of these charters and their dependence on a recently identified St. Albans cartulary, see Crick, *Charters of St Albans*, esp. 39–48.

[32] The increasing gap between text and illustrations may further account for the French rubrics that Paris added to these images, perhaps after original page layout, since most are squeezed at the top of the page even more than most in *Auban*; some (as noted above) push into the extreme margins. In these rubrics he tells a story in French ever more separate from the Latin text below.

[33] Crick, *Charters of St Albans*, 64; Paris himself retells the story in his *Historia duorum Offarum*.

[34] Certainly the rubric at fol. 63r was added after the image; it is arranged around architectural details that rise above the ruled space: see Plate 12. The same claim cannot be made, though, for the rubric at fol. 62v, where Offa's gift of land is mentioned.

If Hand 3 knew that charters were intended to be entered somewhere in the book, then such an illustration, already in place, and whatever its original purport, might easily suggest to him that they were meant to begin at this point.[35] All this appears to give us a glimpse of the manuscript being produced now by four people, working in some proximity but without the constant oversight of their busy director, who finally spots the assistant's error and sets it right as best he can. At the very least, along with the aspects of format and rubrication discussed above, this vexed moment in the manuscript suggests a rather amateur, *ad hoc* procedure of production. Along with the variety of Matthew Paris's own scripts in the manuscript, ranging in appearance possibly from his early years and certainly to his late maturity, these codicological and scribal phenomena may further reflect a manuscript produced across a considerable period of time, and open therefore to an evolving, perhaps increasingly ambitious range of intentions, well beyond just the three versions of the life of St. Alban with which it begins today.[36]

An Evolving, Unfinished Manuscript

Indeed, TCD MS. 177 shows a number of signs of evolving or unsettled arrangement of its texts, and parts of it remain incomplete. As noted above, the fifth in the series of charters on fols. 63r–66r is interrupted in the middle of its first column. It was never completed, and the rest of the page remains blank. On fol. 65v, the spaces left for flourished initials and line fillers in the charter are also left blank.[37] Apparently, the intent of including the charters was abandoned, or their ultimate disposition in the manuscript after their misplaced start was never

---

[35] This error might be especially easy to make if (as would be likely) the quire was still unsewn at this stage in production, and the bifolium beginning with fol. 63r (or an original singlet) had been separated for some reason from the bifolium beginning with fol. 62. Quinn's examination of the unbound manuscript shows that fols. 62 and 69 were originally the outer bifolium of what she has re-assigned as quire XIII. It is unclear whether fol. 63 was originally a singlet or part of a bifolium divided in later rebinding.

[36] Any suggestion of how long the period of production was can only be speculative. What I propose here is consonant, however, with the evolution of Paris's visual style in the manuscript, noted both by Lewis (*Art of Matthew Paris*, 385–96) and by Morgan ("Matthew Paris," 89).

[37] An initial *A* is also absent at fol. 70v. Other colored initials late in the manuscript appear to have been added at a later date (e.g., fol. 69r). Once Paris resumes copying at fol. 73r, though, all initials are present in the flourished style characteristic of the manuscript. Sonia Patterson has argued that Matthew Paris did not provide the flourishes of secondary initials in his manuscripts but was instead helped by two assistants: "An Attempt to Identify Matthew Paris as a Flourisher: His Pen Flourishes and Initials," *The Library* 32 (1977): 367–76. It is notable, however, that flourished initials replace unfilled spaces exactly where Paris's hand again begins copying in TCD MS. 177.

resolved. The very last text in the manuscript (miracles of St. Alban), copied once again in Paris's own hand (though in a less scrupulous style than the first three texts in the manuscript), also ends incomplete on fol. 77r. The verso is blank. Finally, while all the illustrations were drawn by Matthew Paris, "the tinting and gilding from f. 51 onwards seem to be by another hand."[38]

There is also a suggestion that at some point Paris contemplated but abandoned a reordering of some of the Latin texts. A peculiar *incipit* at the very end of fol. 28v (already discussed above in relation to Paris's own hand) immediately follows the ending (and rubricated *explicit*) of the Latin prose life of St. Alban: "Incipit historia de inuencio eiusdem sancti Amphali sociorumque eius." In fact, no surviving Latin text follows here; rather, the manuscript moves directly to Paris's *Auban*, imperfect at the start and probably missing its first leaf.[39] This situation has led students of the manuscript to conclude, not unreasonably, that as much as a quire has been lost at this point.[40]

This *incipit* demands further consideration, however. First, its grammar is wrong ("de inuencio" instead of "de inuencione"), unless the wavy abbreviation over the last two letters is meant to stand in for both a missing *i* and final *ne*: "de inuenc(i)o(ne)." Second, as others have noted, it makes an odd gaffe in the genitive form "Amphali." While all students have taken this to be a slip for "Amph[ib]ali" — probably rightly — the absence of a syllable could reflect some uncertainty as to whether the text would now turn to Amphibalus or to Alban. Both are mentioned, in the genitive form, in the *explicit* that immediately precedes. Third, it has not been noted that while the *incipit* is clearly in Matthew Paris's hand, it is (as mentioned above) written in a style distinctly different from and later than his small firm script in the preceding *explicit*.[41] Given that this *incipit* is so clearly a late addition, the possibility should be considered that it does not announce a text (and leaves) now missing but rather a Latin text about one of the manuscript's two key saints, to be shifted from elsewhere to this position — an intention that, like others in the manuscript, was not fulfilled, though the incipit itself was never later expunged. Indeed, apt texts occur later in TCD MS. 177, and the Latin Invention of St. Alban begins its text on the recto of a new (hence potentially movable) quire, XII in Quinn's collation.[42] It would be

---

[38] Morgan, *EGM [I]*, 131.

[39] See above, 173.

[40] Colker, *Descriptive Catalogue*, 339, assumes a missing "Inuentio S. Amphibali"; Quinn too posits a "missing tract on the invention of Amphibalus" (see below, 196); see also Crick, *Charters of St Albans*, 48. Crick incorrectly records the name in the incipit as "Amphili."

[41] It is fair to speculate whether two such slips in just two lines reflect Paris working in haste and with unfocused attention, amid the multiplying demands of his later years.

[42] The text itself begins on fol. 53r. The rubricated *incipit* crosses the end and beginning of two quires (fols. 52v col. b, last 3 lines-53r col. a, first 2 lines). This would have

much more difficult to shift the Latin Invention of St. Amphibalus, which begins mid-page on fol. 68v. If this explanation of the *incipit* at fol. 28v is accepted, we have yet another, still more dramatic instance of the shifting and evolving history of TCD MS. 177, a history quite consonant with what we know of Matthew Paris's repeated adaptations of his *Chronica majora*.

A Maquette for Later Fair Copies?

The loose ends of the manuscript and its occasional poor planning are further aspects of the general modesty and improvisation of its textual production, in contrast with the delicacy and care of its illustrations. We have noted too the relatively small size of TCD MS. 177, its often poor parchment, and the many leaves assembled from scraps. Given the manuscript's considerable ambitions—a variorum edition of lives of its eponymous saint, a narrative of the abbey's royal foundation, and a record of its lands and privileges—why would Paris produce it in so modest, even shabby, a fashion? A good possibility is that Paris intended TCD MS. 177 to function as a scrappy model, a maquette, from which finer "fair copies" could later be made.

We possess just such a carefully made copy in the surviving manuscript of Paris's French verse life of Edward the Confessor, *La Estoire de seint Aedward le Rei*. This manuscript (Cambridge University Library Ee. 3. 59) is dated around 1250–1260, hence probably in Matthew Paris's lifetime.[43] It is a larger manuscript than TCD MS. 177, carefully written and lavishly decorated with illustrations clearly influenced by Paris's style but not by his own hand. It was probably made at London or Westminster, perhaps for Eleanor of Castile, the wife of the future Edward I and daughter-in-law of the queen to whom the text was first dedicated. Certainly, we know from notes scribbled by Paris on the opening leaves of TCD MS. 177 that he lent that book and his other saints' lives out to women of great wealth, who could have commissioned finer copies.[44]

We lack the earlier copy of the *Estoire* and so can make no comparison between the surviving copy and Paris's original. In other cases, though, we do have working copies of Paris's texts as well as fair copies made in his lifetime, once with his own participation. The key example is Manchester, Chetham's Library MS. 6712, a skilfully written and nicely illustrated copy of Paris's *Flores historiarum*, initially produced in the mid-1250s. Most of it was copied by hands

---

been added, typically, after the main text and would have been easy enough to efface or alter had the following quire actually been moved. Indeed, the rubric at the bottom of fol. 52v is rubbed and challenging to read, as if some such effort did take place at some point.

[43] See Morgan, *EGM [II]*, no. 123, 94–98.

[44] For complete digitized images of the manuscript and a brief introduction by Paul Binski, see http://www.lib.cam.ac.uk/MSS/Ee.3.59/. See above, 32.

that Neil Ker described as "professional" and "expert," perhaps at Westminster, but it came into Paris's hands at some point, so that he could add his newer materials (fols. 173v-202v) covering the years 1241–1249. Except for Paris's own copying, the manuscript is almost entirely copied with the text below the top line of the page layout, a recent development at the time. In decoration and production, then, Chetham's Library 6712 is a quite up-to-date, disciplined production in fair-copy style.[45]

Paris himself apparently supervised a fair copy of the portion of the *Chronica majora* covering 1189 to 1250 (London, BL, MS. Cotton Nero D. V, Part II), written by a scribe who also contributed to Paris's own working copy of the *Chronica*, Cambridge, Corpus Christi College MS. 16, famous for its frequent marginal additions and occasional added scraps of parchment to hold yet more material. Cotton Nero D. V, Part II, incorporates such marginal additions from Paris's own evolving copy and straightens out a few errors there. Paris must have supervised its production (there are a few marginal notes in his hand) but had no other interest in it, "so that it remains to this day a more or less untouched copy of his *CM* as he originally intended to leave it."[46] After Paris's death, in the late thirteenth century two scribes made fair copies of the earlier section of the *Chronica majora* up to 1188: BL Cotton Nero D. V, Part I, and BL Harley 1620.[47] Given these instances, and the well-studied signs of ongoing revision in the surviving rough holograph manuscripts of the *Chronica majora*, TCD MS. 177 may also have been assembled as a maquette, to be reproduced by others in more finished copies.

Reading the Manuscript

A Dossier of Abbatial Antiquity and Rights

In her recent edition of the charters of St. Albans, Julia Crick offers a summary of the ambitions of TCD MS. 177: "Even in its incomplete state, the manuscript presents a powerful case for the status and privileges of the house, celebrating in compact and concise form the history and miracles of the patronal saint and his newly translated peer, Amphibalus."[48] Those privileges included exemption from episcopal control and from most secular duties connected to the abbey's land-

---

[45] N. R. Ker, "From Above Top Line to Below Top Line: A Change in Scribal Practice," in *Books, Collectors, and Libraries: Studies in the Medieval Heritage*, ed. Andrew G. Watson (London: Hambledon Press, 1985), 71–74. For the ten illustrations of royal coronations, see http://www.bridgeman.co.uk/search/s_results.asp?search=chetham's+library+manchester&order=0&page=&view=1&stype=all.

[46] Vaughan, *Matthew Paris*, 110.

[47] Vaughan, *Matthew Paris*, 110 and 153, n.2.

[48] Crick, *Charters of St Albans*, 45–46.

holdings. One can add to Crick's list the important presence of the abbey's own putative founder, the Mercian King Offa, both in the Latin text and (even more emphatically) in Paris's illustrations. This powerful combination of saintly martyrdom, foundation by a triumphal king, and ancient legal claims helps explain the reverence in which TCD MS. 177 was later held, even in its unfinished, working form.

TCD MS. 177's combination of materials, however, does have intriguing precedents in other monastic books, which provide a context and springboard for its own ambitions. As early as the years around the Norman Conquest, the community of St. Cuthbert produced a *Historia de sancto Cuthberto* that mixes stories of the saint's life with information about the Lindisfarne community's history and property, including entire charters, such as that attributed to King Æthelstan. In its earliest manuscript (Oxford, MS. Bodley 596, c.1100) the text is associated with Bede's prose and verse lives of Cuthbert.[49] These materials overlap tellingly with the content of TCD MS. 177. Cartularies of Peterborough Abbey from the twelfth to the fourteenth centuries also combine the expected charters with local chronicles that include lives of saints important to the abbey.[50] Clearly one can speak, if not of a genre, then of a widespread pattern of texts collected in books by which monasteries both narrate and document their joint claims to sacred power and secular position.

TCD MS. 177 may have had a more direct model or at least a more tightly analogous manuscript, with both sacred and aristocratic themes, both saints and kings: a lavishly illustrated "miscellany" on the life of St. Edmund, produced at Bury St. Edmunds between 1124 and 1130 and now in the Morgan Library.[51] As in TCD MS. 177, the Morgan manuscript's core texts are the miracles and passion of the abbey's founding saint, Edmund, king and martyr. Like TCD MS. 177, it also includes liturgical offices for the saint. More striking yet are the analogies between the thirty-two full-page miniatures in the Morgan manuscript, almost an independent visual narrative, and the illustrations in TCD MS. 177. There are even more detailed parallels between the two manuscripts, such as the depictions of a head restored to a body or a corpse guarded by a wolf.[52] More than analogy may be at work here, moreover. The Morgan manuscript was decorated by the "Alexis Master" who also decorated the St. Albans Psalter around

---

[49] *Historia de sancto Cuthberto*, ed. Ted Johnson South, Anglo-Saxon Texts 3 (Woodbridge: D. S. Brewer, 2002), 1–5, 15–16, 65.

[50] Janet D. Martin, *The Cartularies and Registers of Peterborough Abbey*, Northamptonshire Record Society 28 (Northampton: Northampton Record Society on behalf of the Dean and Chapter of Peterborough, 1978), 1–23.

[51] New York, Morgan Library, MS. 736. For discussion and images, see Hahn, *Portrayed on the Heart*, 216–48, 336–37; also eadem, "*Peregrinatio et Natio*: The Illustrated Life of Edmund, King and Martyr," *Gesta* 30 (1991): 119–39.

[52] Hahn, *Portrayed on the Heart*, 127–28.

the same time. While we cannot know whether Matthew Paris would have had direct knowledge of the Morgan manuscript, Bury St. Edmunds was the other great Benedictine house in southern England in his day, at once a competitor and peer, and members of each abbey did a certain amount of traveling outside their walls.

If modeled on an earlier, dossier-like abbatial book such as the Morgan manuscript, TCD MS. 177 would also be a reply to it and to the pretensions of other great and ancient monasteries like Bury St. Edmunds. Both the texts and illustrations of the Dublin manuscript emphasize Alban's far greater antiquity—reaching back both to late Roman rule and to early Welsh Christianity—compared with the Saxon Edmund. The many depictions of King Offa in TCD MS. 177 may also suggest that it is a triumphalist response to the Morgan manuscript, answering Bury's prestige as the foundation of a royal saint with St. Alban's own pious, and earlier, royal founder.

At the same time, TCD MS. 177 may have drawn some of its inspiration from cartularies like those of Peterborough, which combine historical material along with copies of charters. The urge to include at least a visual evocation of official charters and cartularies is particularly clear in the five charters copied into the manuscript, perhaps (as discussed above) not exactly where Matthew Paris intended them. Whatever intermediate copy provided the text of these charters, the decorator of their opening page in TCD MS. 177 had some knowledge of the monograms (combinations of multiple letters in a single graph, often used as a visual invocation of God or Christ) that were frequent in Anglo-Saxon charters. The first charter (fol. 63v, Crick charter 1) begins with a large "Pax Rex" monogram, elaborately decorated with red pen-drawn flourishing. The second charter (fol. 63r, Crick charter 1; see Fig. 3a.2 below) is also preceded by a decorated monogram, possibly a form of the chrismon, a combination of *chi* and *rho*.[53] Although both charters are largely forgeries, they reveal knowledge of the visual presentation of authentic early Anglo-Saxon charters and make an effort to evoke authentic form, intriguingly combined with elaborate, up-to-date flourishing.

Mixed, Evolving Audiences of Monks and Aristocrats

In one key fashion, TCD MS. 177 shows ambitions considerably beyond those of the monastic books mentioned just above. Rather than restricting itself to Latin, and to strictly monastic concerns, it reaches out to a far wider secular audience, both through its programmatic illustrations (also seen in the Bury St. Edmunds manuscript) and through its extensive use of the French of England—even, once, its evocation of early Middle English. Whenever the bulk of its production took

---

[53] Crick, *Charters of St Albans*, 41, 48.

place, the manuscript seems to have been in stages of revision and improvised evolution across a considerable period, as we have seen. If the current ordering of texts and images represents Matthew Paris's maturest intentions, there seems to have been a progressive (though irregular) expansion of the manuscript's interests, audiences, and ambitions: that is, from the initial, largely monastic audience of the two Latin *vitae*, to include and attract as well the aristocratic, even royal, agents who were so much a part of the life and power of St. Albans. This was effected by the illustrations, of course, but also by the French *Auban* that follows the Latin lives and the French verse rubrics that persist along with the illustrations that accompany the later Latin narratives of the rediscovery and translation of St. Alban.

Especially important is the emphatic visual presence of King Offa, depicted both as triumphal warrior and as pious patron of the new abbey. Despite the confusion leading to a textual interruption of the invention of St Alban and translation of his remains, the sequence of images is coherent: the final image in the manuscript provides the climax to a visual program of the saintly and then royal origins of the abbey, with the depiction of King Offa presenting his charter (fol. 63r, see Plate 12). Offa is shown first as a great warrior, then as a great patron and protector of the abbey. The manuscript's core as presently constituted (*Auban* with its twin martyrdoms of Alban and Amphibalus, the invention of Alban and Offa's role therein, and the royal charters in favor of the abbey, fols. 29r-66r) gives considerable attention to lay, aristocratic virtue and good works, especially in the persons of Alban, Heraclius, and Offa. Although its main text is in Latin, that core is accessible to laypeople through the illustrations and their French rubrics. Even the later Latin miracles of both saints (fols. 68v-77r) record a sequence of mostly laypeople, including women and knights, cured by the relics of the two saints.[54]

Folded within these stories, however, is also a sequence of secondary narratives that serve at least in part to link its main lines to an aristocratic audience below the level of royalty, even simpler knights, as well as women: the conversion and martyrdom of Heraclius (subtitled in Paris's *Auban* as a free-standing "passiun seint Aracle"),[55] the growing number of Roman citizens of Verulamium who convert, and Germanus's encounter with St. Genevieve. Alban himself, of course, while a high aristocrat, is not royal either. Paris also had ramified connections with aristocrats, a wide range of noble acquaintances and informants.

---

[54] In a further and probably later move, Latin notes in leonine couplets were added at the bottom of most of the pages with images in *Auban* and once on a page without illustrations. This seems to be a reciprocal gesture, adding a layer of slightly exclusive, learned appeal to the images and vernacular language of *Auban*.

[55] Harden, *Auban*, 26, 29.

And he was personally known to King Henry III, who visited the abbey nine times during Paris's life there and once summoned him to court.[56]

The Aristocratic Arc of Narrative and Illustration

The great arc of the manuscript's illustrations and the bulk of its French rubrics reach from a pagan aristocrat to a great Christian king and what the penultimate set of French rubrics calls "la estoire" of King Offa. The very last set of rubrics starts again with Alban, then closes with a mention of Offa's thirty-nine-year reign.[57] This textual and visual arc across the illustrated core of the manuscript is rendered all the denser and more powerful by Matthew Paris's careful creation of visual continuities and rhythms.[58] Sometimes the effect is at the level of fine detail, not necessarily always conscious in its deployment, such as fabric patterns that reappear in different contexts but nonetheless echo one another. Heraclius's clothing is always of one notable pattern. Fabric with a bird pattern dresses Alban's executioner (fol. 38r, see cover image) then reappears, almost with the force of a relic, on the altar to which Offa presents his charter (fol. 63r, Plate 12).[59] A similar impact occurs when the bundle of twigs—possibly recalling Roman fasces—held by Amphibalus's chief tormentor (fol. 45r, Plate 9) is echoed by a similar bundle (perhaps for asperging) held by the priest who baptizes the citizens of Verulamium en masse, in the closing image of *Auban* (fol. 50r). Other effects provide an almost cinematic sense of continuity among the illustrations. A door represented on one page is seen again, ripped off its hinges, as "Saracens" arrest the converted Alban (fols. 33r and 33v, Plate 5). Alban's cap, repeatedly shown in early images, topples from his head on the latter page. He is shoeless when arrested and stays so for the remaining images of him. Matthew Paris carefully depicts Alban's increasingly bedraggled appearance as he is arrested, imprisoned, tortured, and finally martyred.

Certain repeated objects and postures have greater narrative and religious significance. The shaggy cloak and cross of Amphibalus are emphasized throughout *Auban*, moving across both time and place, and Paris carefully and consistently depicts how the cross has been bloodied during the martyrdom of

---

[56] Paris's aristocratic and royal connections are ably surveyed by Simon Lloyd and Rebecca Reader, "Paris, Matthew," *Oxford Dictionary of National Biography*, 42: 620–28.

[57] Harden, *Auban*, 65, 15:449–56, 457–64 (R70 and R71 in translation above).

[58] On the strong rightward movement of the illustrations, see George Henderson, "Studies in English Manuscript Illumination, Part I: Stylistic Sequence and Stylistic Overlap in Thirteenth-Century English Manuscripts," *Journal of the Warburg and Courtauld Institutes* 30 (1967): 71–104, at 78.

[59] Paris's appeal to his secular audience is not always a friendly one. Suzanne Lewis points out that the fabric worn by one of Auban's tormentors (fol. 37v) evokes an emblem of an enemy of St. Albans, Fawkes de Breauté; see Lewis, *Art of Matthew Paris*, 115–21.

Alban (fol. 38r, see cover image); from this point onward it is always depicted with blood on it.[60] The pagan "Saracens" often break through the frame of illustrations at the moment of violence: for instance, at the martyrdom of Amphibalus (fol. 45r, Plate 9).[61] By contrast, Christians or agents of heaven break through the frame of illustrations much less, and only slightly when they do so.[62] Even if such repetitions derive from visual convention, they still serve to link moments in the manuscript, even allowing them to comment quietly on one another.

The impact of Paris's visual rhythm and repetition is clearest at the level of a sequence of pages, even an individual opening (as for instance at fol. 31r and the subsequent facing pages, fols. 31v and 32r, Plates 2 and 3). Amphibalus, kneeling in prayer on fol. 31r (see Figure 3b.1), has a mirror image on fol. 31v in Alban, at the point of conversion, who now kneels to the seated Amphibalus. In the opening fols. 31v-32r, the rather static, spacious scenes of Alban's kneeling and baptism, both under round arches, contrast with the crowded mobile bodies, bracketed by busy, vertical urban architectural details, when a spy reports the conversion to the Roman "judge." Throughout the manuscript, there is often a contrast between crowded, violent scenes among the pagans and opener, less angular drawing around holy men.

The Translation of Dominion: Roman Prince, English King, and Converted Knights

Alban's Verulamium is ruled by "a wicked prince" (*un prince felun*, 14:414). When faced with Alban after conversion, he becomes irrationally angry, changes color, and reacts with "ill will" (*mautalent*, 17:543, often a term for a ruler's extra-legal acts of hostility).[63] It is this prince (called a judge in *PSA*) who initiates Alban's testing, torture, imprisonment, and eventual martyrdom. He is also a figure of rhetoric, using his best persuasion to convince Alban to leave his new faith. In two illustrations (fols. 32r, 34v, Plates 3 and 6), the prince's Roman *gravitas* seems to be more emphasized than his irrational anger. In both he is calm and alert, gesturing with his right hand. In both, however, he is the recipient of whispered bad counsel; and his acts lead to a sequence of disasters for his city.

By contrast, the English king Offa's role as a secular conqueror both visually echoes and one might say sacralizes the earlier Roman prince and the crowded violence of his pagan soldiers. Offa is depicted as a figure of vision and good

---

[60] For discussion of the cloak and the cross see McCulloch, "Saints Alban and Amphibalus," esp. 781–83.

[61] The same visual gesture appears when Alban is captured while in prayer (fol. 33v) and in Alban's execution scene (fol. 38r).

[62] Heraclius's feet notably break the frame at the moment of his martyrdom (fol. 46r), as does Amphibalus's right foot at his martyrdom (fol. 38r).

[63] J. E. A. Jolliffe, *Angevin Kingship* (London: Black, 1963), 87–109.

counsel, battle and building. Where the prince is advised by spies and bad counselors, Offa appears consulting with bishops and archbishops. He is first depicted (fol. 55v, Plate 11) in martial triumph and in full profile, crowned, dignified, and almost static, one of Paris's "monumental figures with large, expressive heads."[64] His soldiers' horses trample the head of the conquered King Ætheldred behind him. Around his crowned head, in red and blue rustic capitals, appears the phrase "MERCIORUM REX OFFA." The trumpets and spear of his soldiers explode well beyond the ruled frame of the illustration, again recalling and answering similar images among the pagan soldiers. This is royal violence, but violence celebrated in service to the church that Offa serves and the abbey he is soon to found. Indeed, the horses in this image may echo the horses of the departing St. Lupus and St. Germanus on the preceding page (fol. 55r). Soon after (fol. 58v), Offa (crowned, as always) appears in council with archbishops and bishops, seated on a decorated stone bench reminiscent of that used by the Roman prince in both his depictions. Later Offa appears enthroned, as he makes Willegod the first abbot of St. Albans (fol. 60v).

Offa has a second important visual predecessor in the manuscript. In TCD MS. 177, Offa's almost sacred role in the founding of St. Albans is most powerfully figured in the illustration of the dream in which an angel reveals to him the location of Alban's remains (fol. 56v). In this image, Paris repeats almost exactly the posture, bed, and pillow in which Alban has his own confused dream of the Annunciation, Passion, and Resurrection of Christ (fol. 30v, Plate 1), which, when explained by Amphibalus, leads to Alban's conversion. While these visual repetitions could well result from pattern books or from the mental formulae of a highly practiced draftsman like Matthew Paris, they nonetheless serve to draw together moments across the manuscript that have no close narrative or chronological connection; and they further serve to draw secular characters like Offa into a story of sacred vision and foundation. Over Offa there hovers an angel as large as Offa himself whose open wings span almost the whole image. Again, in red rustic capitals, Offa is identified as "REX OFFA," with a blue cross at left.

We may end this discussion by noting another figure in the first, triumphant image of King Offa: a nobleman immediately behind him, with a coat of arms of rampant lions and carrying a long spear (fol. 55v, Plate 11). His horse is one of those trampling on the head of Ætheldred. Noble help does not compete with Offa's centrality here, but neither is it far away. The same is true across the visual program of the entire manuscript. Between the Roman prince and King Offa, we encounter the two pagan aristocrats—Alban and Heraclius—whose conversions occupy so much of *Auban*. If royal models (negative and positive) occupy attention at the start and close of the manuscript's visual program, Alban and Heraclius play crucial roles between the two; their roles, moreover, help make

---

[64] Lewis, *Art of Matthew Paris*, 386.

Christian behavior among lay aristocrats central to the broadening ambitions of TCD MS. 177. As noted earlier, Matthew Paris carefully tracks Alban's visual transformation from a well-dressed nobleman in a comfortable house to a suffering martyr.[65]

Heraclius is perhaps even more intriguing in this context and crucial to the manuscript's potential appeal to aristocratic viewers. The appeal to the nobility of "St. Heraclius's" story lies in its shape as a romance hagiography featuring a Roman, pagan knight—essentially the figure of a secular, military aristocrat—who was inspired and converted as he led Alban to his death. This finally results in Heraclius's own martyrdom. Apparently not quite at Alban's social level, Heraclius is the first of the flood of Roman converts inspired by Alban, then by Amphibalus. But it is Heraclius's story, already expanded in Paris's poem, which receives emphatic illustration among the text's stories of conversion. Paris's text announces a "passiun d'Aracle," but the illustrations repeatedly name him as well (indeed, twice on fol. 37r, Plate 8). The episode occupies a little over a hundred of the poem's 1,846 surviving lines (vv. 936–1052), just over six percent of its length. Visually, though, it is much more emphatic. It begins and closes with the rubrics that make it a separate narrative segment; and Heraclius appears in five images which name him in rubrics within the picture frame. These latter carefully depict Heraclius's conversion, kneeling in front of the living Alban (fol. 37r), his removal of Alban's severed head from the tree (38v), service to Alban's corpse by restoring its head (47r), his beating by other pagans (47v), and his martyrdom (46r). Together, in another instance of Paris's powerful use of visual repetition, these echo events and images in the immediately preceding life of Alban.[66] Attention to Heraclius is further focused by the very consistent pattern of crosses and small circles on his tunic, most prominently when he helps arrange Alban's body for entombment (fol. 47r), and at his own beheading (fol. 46r). It is the illustrations of Heraclius, perhaps more than those of any other figure in TCD MS. 177, that exemplify the entire manuscript's evolving ambi-

---

[65] Paris's attention to Alban as an aristocrat of ancient lineage is already marked in some of his marginal glosses to his Latin source, William of St. Alban's prose *PSA* (e.g., fol. 21v, at *PSA* cap. 10: "Argumentum nobilitatis Albani"). At fol. 22v, his note to the *PSA* (cap. 15, "Sed et per parentes . . .") emphasizes Alban's ancient Roman ancestry: "Nota quod beatus albanus ciuis et indigena fuit Uerolami natus et genitus. Debet enim quod g(enu)s in ciuitate habuit. Ab antiquis t(ame)n romanis deriuatum. Sicut Walenses a troianis" (Note that blessed Alban was born and bred a citizen and native of Verulamium, for it says that the people of the city were ultimately derived from the ancient Romans, the same way the Welsh were derived from the Trojans).

[66] Alban and Heraclius kneel in comparable poses (fols. 31v, Plate 2, and 37r, Plate 8); the two scenes are further linked by the presence in each of the woolly cloak and cross of Amphibalus. Alban is beaten in a one-column drawing (fol. 35r), Heraclius in a drawing of the same size (fol. 47v); the grotesque figure at left in each image is particularly similar.

tion to open itself beyond an immediate audience and to attract the Christian aristocrats who had become the guarantors of the monastery's religious prestige and secular prosperity.

Appendix: The Hands of TCD MS. 177

Matthew Paris's own handwriting (for convenience here called Hand 1) has been the object of intense study.[67] Paris wrote the bulk of the manuscript himself (fols. 3–50r and 73–77). Fols. 50v–72v, however, were copied by three assistants.[68] All four hands continue the practice of writing "above top line" of their ruling. Many expert English scribes were writing "below top line" by around 1240; however, St. Albans was fairly old-fashioned in these practices.[69] None of the assistants is especially disciplined or consistent; this renders dating somewhat speculative.

Hand 2 makes the largest contribution among the assistants: fols. 50v-62v, 66v-72r (72v is blank). He writes a somewhat ponderous early gothic textualis semiquadrata, with notably narrower proportions than the hand of Matthew Paris. Like the script of all three assistants, his script uses a good deal of "biting" (*de, do, pp, dco*). Of all the hands in the manuscript, his appears to reflect the latest training and is consistent with a date around 1250. Most notably, without exception he pulls down the head of the minuscule *a* to form two chambers, consistently above the x-height of the line, a form that is not frequent or consistent until the mid-thirteenth century. He also uses the tironian *et* far more often (over 190 times) than the ampersand (22 times); the latter is concentrated (12 times) in the last two leaves of his stint. Further, his tironian *et* is always crossed, another habit more typical of the later end of the manuscript's possible dates. He uses round *d* almost exclusively. Ascenders to his *l*, *h*, and *b* are thickened, sometimes slightly split at the top, and ascenders to his round *d* are short. He consistently ticks *i* where surrounding minims make it ambiguous. Nevertheless, like the other assistants, Hand 2 has some vestigial old-fashioned practices; he almost always uses the tall final *s* and at least nine times uses a rustic capital terminal *R*.[70]

It may be significant that Matthew Paris proofread and corrected this scribe's work with care. Numerous marginal (and some interlinear) corrections appear in Paris's less formal note hand throughout the stint of Hand 2, whose errors are not always controlled by grammar or sense. At fol. 60v, the scribe either could not

---

[67] See Vaughan, "The Handwriting."

[68] I am grateful to my colleague Richard Rouse for examining these hands with me. The conclusions are of course my own.

[69] Ker, "From Above Top Line to Below Top Line," esp. 73–74.

[70] Compare the script of the marginalia in Cambridge, Trinity College B. 11 extra 1, c. 1255, which on at least one occasion also uses the rustic capital terminal *R* (see Pamela Robinson, *Catalogue of Dated and Datable Manuscripts c. 737–1600 in Cambridge Libraries* [Cambridge: D. S. Brewer, 1988], 1, no. 112); and Oxford, MS. Douce 137, c. 1260 (see Andrew G. Watson, *Catalogue of Dated and Datable Manuscripts c. 435–1600 in Oxford Libraries* [Oxford: Oxford University Press, 1983], 1, no. 114); both, like Hand 2, move between tall and round terminal *s*, though they use the round form rather more than does Hand 2.

FIGURE 3a.1. Hand 2, TCD MS 177, fol. 60v, col. A, lines 1–5. Note 2-chamber a, thickened and split tops to ascenders, crossed tironian *et*, *de* and *do* "biting," and tall final *s*. Matthew Paris has supplied the name "albani" in a script characteristic of his later maturity.
Copyright Board of Trinity College. Reproduced by permission.

read his exemplar and left blanks for names or made errors that Paris scraped off and corrected: *Albani, Alexander, Robertus, Waltero* (similarly, *Stephanus*, fol. 61v): see Figure 3a.1. If Hand 2 reflects the latest training of the three assistants, one might imagine a young scribe with still limited Latin.

Hand 3 (fols. 63r–64r) uses the most old-fashioned script of the three assistants (see fol. 63r, Figure 3a.2 and Plate 12). His minuscule *a* is consistently open-topped. He uses the ampersand about a third of the time; consistently uses tall terminal *s*; and uses upright medial *d* almost half the time. On the other hand, he uses round terminal *s* rather more often than does Hand 2 and shows "biting" between letters not seen in Hand 2 (*ho, he, ha, be, bo, ba*). In general, he is more disciplined than Hand 2 in keeping letters to x-height.

In the list of testators in the charter copied by Hand 3, Anglo-Saxon graphs are used with confidence: ash, thorn, yogh, wynn.

Hand 4 (fols. 64v–66r) is very mixed in his forms. He uses ampersand almost exclusively and occasional initial and medial upright *d*, both old-fashioned forms; yet his terminal *s* is more often round than in any of the other hands, and he finishes it with a narrowing convex top stroke. The head of his *a* sometimes pulls down, almost forming a second chamber, but not as firmly or as consistently as that of Hand 2. He ticks his *i* consistently and shows biting in even more letter combinations than do Hands 2 or 3. His minims are slightly more angular than those of the other assistants as well, often forming neat diamonds at the top, and his script takes on a slightly prickly look from some hair-strokes at the top of *t* and occasional horizontal strokes over the top of upright *d* and double *ll* (see Figure 3a.3, fol. 66r).

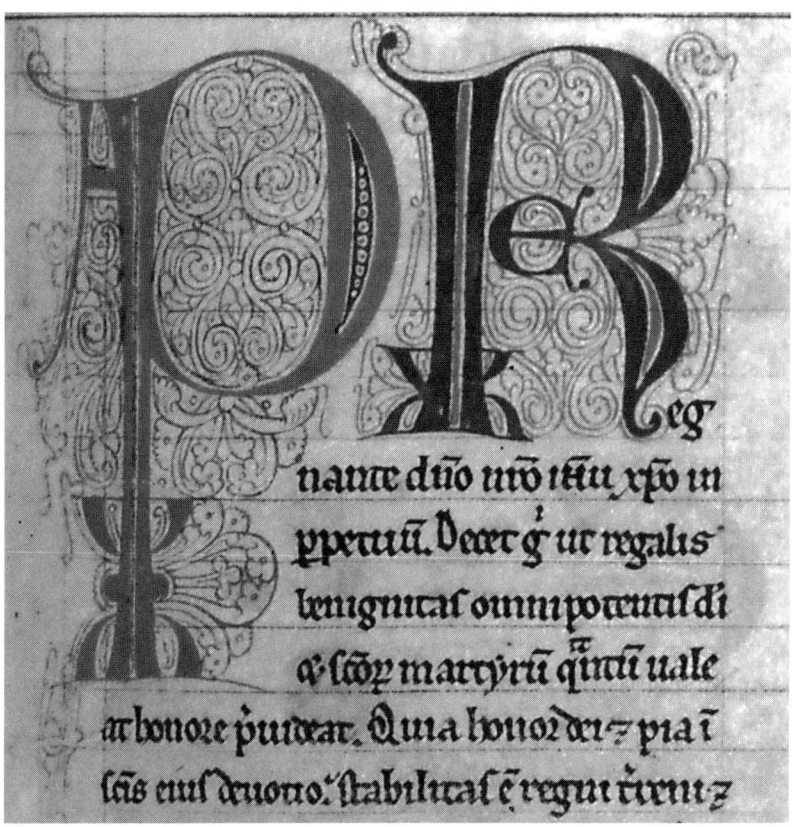

FIGURE 3a.2. Hand 3, TCD MS 177, fol. 63r, col. A, lines 1–7. Note "Pax Rex" monogram, single-chamber *a*, upright and curved *d*, short final *s*, *be* and *po* "biting," use of both ampersand and tironian et.
Copyright Board of Trinity College. Reproduced by permission.

This scribe tends to avoid Anglo-Saxon graphs (writing, for instance, *unuuona*, *ceoluulfus*, *heothored*, fol. 65r). When he uses Anglo-Saxon graphs, they are awkward compared with those of Hand 3, especially yogh. Hand 4 does try to imitate something like the Anglo-Saxon *r* and *f*, though the effect is laborious.

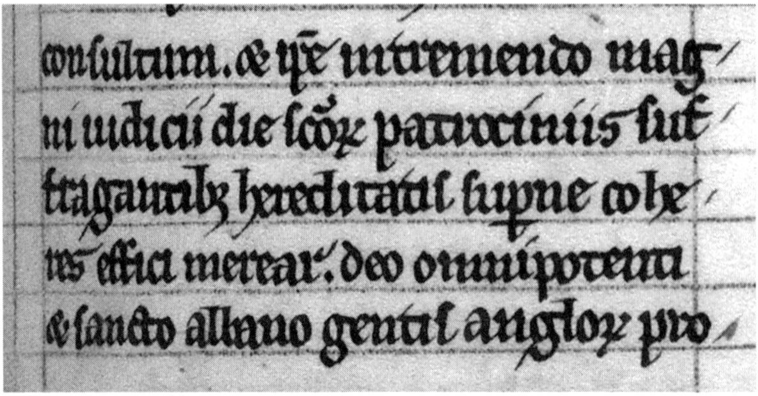
consultam. & ipe interveniendo mag
ni iudicii die scor patrociniis suf
fragantib hereditatis supne cohe
res effici mereatr. deo omnipotenti
& sancto albano gentis anglor pro

FIGURE 3a.3. Hand 4, TCD MS 177, fol. 66r, col. A, last 5 lines. Note ampersand, upright and curved d, hairstrokes on many ascenders, diamonds on minims, short final *s*, *do* and *he* "biting."

Copyright Board of Trinity College. Reproduced by permission.

Alban Disbound: Codicological Remarks on Matthew Paris's *Life of St. Alban*

Patricia Quinn

Introduction

Matthew Paris's illustrated life of St. Alban (Dublin, Trinity College MS. 177, former shelfmark E. I. 40) was disbound, repaired, and rebound in the conservation workshop at Trinity College Library between November 1983 and May 1984.[1] This provided the first opportunity to examine its structure since it was rebound in the nineteenth century.[2] The observations made in 1983 have remained unpublished, despite a reference to them in M. L. Colker's 1991 catalogue of the TCD Latin manuscripts.[3] This essay is designed principally to present physical and textual evidence in support of the collation analysis provided in the accompanying charts (see Appendix: Collation Maps). The opportunity has also been taken to correct inaccuracies found in the publications by which the manuscript (henceforth TCD MS. 177) is generally known. In particular, the manuscript is less than well served by the collotype facsimile published in 1924, which is imperfect in several respects: it reproduces only those folios where the illustrations are intact. Even these do not show the full leaf, with edges and marginalia lost in reproduction. Folios without illustrations and, more importantly, those with fragments of illustration are not reproduced, and the introduction by M. R. James is misleading in several respects.[4]

---

[1] I am grateful to Anthony Cains, former technical director of the conservation workshop, and to Dr. Bernard Meehan, Keeper of Manuscripts, for many helpful suggestions and comments. The editors of the present volume thank Bernard Meehan for his work in preparing this essay for publication.

[2] The nineteenth-century binding was of full blind-tooled vegetable tanned calf over rope millboards. It was sewn on five recessed cords, with silk endbands and plain machine-made endpapers. It had a modern overlaid calf reback.

[3] Colker, *Trinity College Dublin: Descriptive Catalogue*, 1: 341.

[4] James, *Illustrations*. More recently see Morgan, *EGM [I]*, 130–33.

The composite nature of many of the leaves is a remarkable feature of TCD MS. 177 that also occurs, for example, in Cambridge, Corpus Christi College MSS. 26 and 16 (Matthew Paris's *Chronica majora*). Here, however, the proportions and the shapes of composite fragments tend to be less regular than those of TCD MS. 177. Vaughan indicated that the "private nature" of the notes on fol. 2 of MS. 177 shows it to be one owned by Matthew Paris himself.[5] It may be suggested that the nature of the makeup of the volume explored in this essay further identifies it as one personal to Matthew Paris and probably put together physically by him. As Suzanne Lewis has commented, some of the vellum that he used "would have been rejected as unsuitable for a scriptorium artist."[6] There is a striking contrast between the artistic quality of the manuscript and the utilitarian (not to say scrappy) nature of its physical makeup.

Contents

TCD MS. 177 is made up of 77 folios. For convenience, a modified version of the table of the manuscript's contents (see also Introduction, 16–17 above) is given here:

a 1r-2v flyleaves.
b 3r-20r: Latin poem in elegiacs by Ralph of Dunstable based on William of St. Albans' prose life of St. Alban (*VSMA*).
c 20r-28v: Latin prose life by William of St. Albans (*PSA*), the source of Paris's *Auban*.
d 28v: rubric to missing tract on the invention of Amphibalus.
e 29r-50r: Anglo-Norman *laisses* by Matthew Paris (*Auban*) about St. Alban and St. Amphibalus.
f 50v-52v: lessons for the feast of the invention and translation of St. Alban.
g 52v-62v, 66v-68v: treatise on the invention and translation of St. Alban.
h 63r-66r: charters of foundation of the Abbey of St. Albans purportedly issued by King Offa and his son Ecgfrid.
i 68v-69v: about the invention of Amphibalus.
j 69v-70v: about the miracles of Amphibalus.
k 70v-72r: about the translation of Alban (72v blank).
l 73r-77r: about the miracles of Amphibalus.

---

[5] Vaughan, *Matthew Paris*, 170.
[6] Lewis, *Art of Matthew Paris*, 21.

Structure and Collation

A binder's error that resulted in the miscollation of fols. 46 and 47 has been corrected in the course of conservation so that the sequence now reads fols. 38, 47, 46, 39, 40, 41, 42, 43, 44, 45, 48, 49, as given by Morgan.[7]

The manuscript is rather crudely foliated in black ink in a modern hand at the center of the tail margin on the recto of each folio. In addition, there is a lightly penciled series in the tail corner of the fore-edge margin of some leaves. These are on fols 3, 11, 21, 31, 41, and 51, and the penciled numbers are 2, 10, 20, 30, 40, and 50, respectively.

The illustrations are also numbered in another modern hand in ink—usually in the lower horizontal of the frame, although the first seven have numbers in a blank space in the body of the illustration. The series begins at fol. 29v, which is the first extant drawing and is numbered 3; it continues in an unbroken sequence up to and including fol. 54v (numbered 39), correcting the misbinding of fols. 47 and 46 and assigning no number to the missing illustrations, perhaps suggesting an early date for the loss of illustrated fragments and a more recent one for the loss of the first two illustrations and the miscollations of fols. 47 and 46. The numbers stop at fol. 54v, although there are seventeen more illustrations.

For ease of reference the gathering numbers I-XIV have been assigned. It should be noted that some of the gatherings are "real" or original ones; some are "made," probably returning certain single leaves to their original gatherings; and others are purely notional and result from the technical requirements of rebinding the manuscript. It is not possible to conjecture a complete collation map when so little is known about the lost material.

Folios	Gatherings
1–2 :	I
3–4 :	II
5–9 :	III
10–13 :	IV
14–20 :	V
21–22 :	VI
23–28 :	VII
29–38 :	VIII
47–46 :	IX
39–45 :	X
48–52 :	XI
53–61 :	XII
62–69 :	XIII
70–77 :	XIV

(For a map of the collation, see Appendix: Collation Maps.)

---

[7] Morgan, *EGM [I]*, 131.

The text is written in two vertical columns throughout with the exception of fols. 1 and 2, which are of a different skin from the rest of the manuscript (sheep or kid as opposed to calf) and which have cropped text.[8] Fol. 2v, a mutilated drawing of the Virgin and Child, is illustrated in Morgan complete with the strips of parchment by which the mutilated leaf was framed in a modern repair.[9] The removal of these strips has resulted in a text gain at the head, tail, and fore-edge verso. There are illustrations on fols. 29v, 30v, 31r/v, 32r, 33r-35r/v, 36r, 37r/v, 38r/v, 47r/v, 46r/v, 39r, 40r-45r/v, 48r-62r/v, and 63r.

The illustrations all occupy roughly half of the text area (with the exception of fols. 30v, 33v, 34r, and 35r, which are quarter-page) and are headed by a descriptive rubric in French. James refers to a number of illustrations that were executed on separate pieces of vellum and pasted in place at the head of the text, which are now lost. These illustrations are lost from fols. 40v, 42v, 43r, 45v, 48v, 49v, 50v, and 51v. James was not correct in observing that they were "painted on pieces of finer vellum and pasted into the blank space left for them."[10] Nor is it true that the only remaining evidence of the subject matter of the missing illustrations is "an explanatory notice in French at the top of the page and a rhyming Latin distich or quatrain at the bottom."[11]

The reconstruction of the original collation of the manuscript was made simpler by a number of factors: the unusual range in weight and color of the vellum used, the survival intact of the spine edges of some single leaves, and the distinctive patchwork construction of several bifolia. The disposition of hair and flesh sides was determined by microscopic examination, usually on the basis of flesh sides being less disturbed by pumicing than hair sides. Along with this evidence, the originally conjoint pairs were realized on the basis of the color, weight, and texture of the vellum, with additional evidence as follows.

Fols. 6/9 were originally composed of two horizontal strips of vellum, the elements of which aligned perfectly when reattached.

Fols. 14/20 originally consisted of three elements, one of which (the fore-edge vertical strip on fol. 20) is now lost. The remaining horizontal strips align perfectly.

Fols. 53/61 were identified as a conjoint pair by the color and texture of the vellum, which has a pronounced nap on the hair side and which tapers in density toward the tail of both leaves at the spine edge. There is also pronounced veining of the skin in the tail margin of both leaves.

Fols. 54/60 were identified as a pair by a vein line in the vellum on the flesh side which runs across the spine fold. In addition, fol. 60r bears a very clear profile of the edges of the patch on fol. 54, where the pounced surface has been

---

[8] Described in James, *Illustrations*, 15, 16.
[9] Morgan, *EGM [I]*, pl. 279.
[10] James, *Illustrations*, 19.
[11] James, *Illustrations*, 19: on the missing illustrations see further 203–4 below.

congealed by paste, which is not to be seen on fol. 55 and which probably resulted from the drying under pressure of the patched bifolium, separated from the rest of the gathering.

Fols. 56/57 can be united by the rectangular patch that forms the lower half of fol. 56 and a vertical strip at the spine edge of fol. 56.

Fols. 55/58 could be identified as a pair by the color and texture of the two leaves, which match very closely and which vary uniformly along the spine edges of both leaves. The leaf signatures that remain on fols. 55v and 56v confirm the reconstruction of gathering **XII**.

Fols. 62/69 were also matched on the basis of the quality of the vellum, especially on the other clear pattern of follicle debris that can be seen—almost uniquely in this manuscript—across the spine edges of both leaves on the hair side.

Fols. 71/77, like the other leaves in this last extant gathering, are somewhat narrower than the average width of the rest of the text block (by about 3–5 mm) and perhaps for this reason escaped the trimming of spine edges that was the fate of many of the single leaves in the rest of the volume.

The conjoint pairs of both fols. 71/77 and 72/76 could be identified by the spine profiles, whose indentured edges fit together perfectly.

The manuscript bears the evidence of at least two previous sewings. The earlier and possibly original sewing was on four cords, to judge from the holes that can be seen in the spine folds. These holes tend to be long and slit-like in character. The book was rebound in the nineteenth century, from which time the overcasting and sewing on five sewn-in cords probably dates. The damage to the text-block caused by this nineteenth-century binding was considerable. The overcasting has perforated the spine edge in many places, and the process of rounding and backing was probably responsible for the horseshoe-shaped tear around the spine at the tail of many of the leaves toward the back of the block. Considerable quantities of hot animal glue that had been used on the spine covered the spine edges of some leaves to a depth of some 3–5 mm, often obscuring rubrication and other marginalia.

It is not possible to say whether the nineteenth-century binder was responsible for the trimming of many of the spine edges. Some single leaves were untrimmed at the spine edge, and their profiles offered the strongest evidence for rejoining conjoint pairs; but in many cases spine edges were almost certainly trimmed with a knife, and in this way marginalia have occasionally been cropped.

Of the single leaves that constituted more than half of those in the manuscript as it was received, five had stubs that were designed to hook around the adjoining gathering (another leaf, fol. 17, has a stub to which fol. 16 is glued, but this should be regarded as a "made" conjoint bifolium, rather than a single leaf). In addition to these identifiable hooked single leaves, a narrow strip of vellum was found attached to fol. 77v, possibly the stub of fol. 70 but impossible to identify because of its degraded and friable condition.

Of these five stubs, four were intact and functioning: fols. 23, 40, 43, and 44. The stub of fol. 52 had become detached from the leaf at the spine edge and was held in place on fol. 48r by glue and overcasting. The stub width is usually less than 10 mm, and the edges appear to have been trimmed freehand with a knife. On fols. 40, 43, and 44 three hooked singles occur close together and may originally have been pasted in place, to judge from the clear impression of each stub on the adjoining leaf. That these are original stubs is further proved by the text on the stub of fol. 44 where it hooks, with fol. 43, around the spine-edge of fol. 40r. The second line of rubrication at the head of fol. 40r begins *D'[Auban]*, which is written, along with the left edge of *A*, on the recto of the stub of fol. 44: the rest of the phrase *[D']Auban* is on fol. 40r.

In contrast, in the case of fol. 23, it would appear that the stub that hooked around fols. 24–27 or 28 is a canceled leaf, since the marginalia on the verso of a notional conjoint leaf are cropped. Fol. 23 is certainly not the conjoint leaf of fol. 28, and this might tend to confirm the general opinion that there is a lacuna between fols. 28 and 29. (James describes the Anglo-Norman poem as lacking its first leaf,[12] and Harden refers to the loss of the first folio of the poem.)[13]

Internal evidence, however, points to another distinct lacuna at the beginning of gathering **VIII**. This is one of only two gatherings in the manuscript that preserve leaf-signatures (the other is fols. 53–61, gathering **XII**) which are clearly visible in red ink on the tail verso of fols. 29, 30, 31, 32, and 33. These are signed **ii, iii, iv, v,** and **vi**, respectively, and since the character of the vellum in this section differs uniformly from that before fol. 29, and there is no signature on fol. 28v, it seems likely that this section lacks its first folio: **i** in the series, possibly the conjoint folio of either fols. 46 or 47 (formerly misbound). The verso of fol. 28 contains an *explicit* at the foot of the second column that was probably added during or after the assembling of the separate component texts of the manuscript. Evidence was found of an indented ridge along the spine edge of fol. 28v of a kind made elsewhere by a hooked stub: for example, fols. 40, 43, 44 when the spine edge was being cleaned of its adhesive layer, and there was no evidence of a lacuna in the text between fols. 27 and 28 (which is the only other possible location for the notional conjoint leaf of fol. 23).[14] Hence it seems possible that this leaf may have been canceled at an early stage, perhaps at the point when the texts were being assembled, and that the *explicit* refers not to the text lost from the conjoint leaf of fol. 23 but to the lost first leaf of the gathering fols. 29/38. There is no physical evidence for a lost folio between fols. 35 and 36, as suggested

---

[12] James, *Illustrations*, 19.

[13] Harden, *Auban*, 66 n. 1.

[14] Compare with the variant text in J. Bollandus, *Acta sanctorum* (Antwerp, 1701), June 22, 4: 149–59.

by Atkinson,[15] the leaf signatures of their conjoint fols. 32 and 31 reading v and iv, respectively.

The other gathering with leaf signatures is XII. Fol. 56v is signed "IIII^{us}" in the tail margin below the second column of text; fol. 55v has the cropped remnants of "III^{us}."[16] Fol. 54, whose tail edge appears to have been trimmed with shears, has cropped text at the foot of the verso, with what may be the top fragment of the normal terminal abbreviation for *us* in the center of the tail edge. This numeral is notably different from those on fols. 29–33v; it is in brown rather than red ink and in a majuscule hand as opposed to minuscule.

Exceptionally for this manuscript, fol. 56v also bears the number *XIII* in red in a thirteenth-century hand, possibly that of Matthew Paris himself, at the center of the tail margin, very similar to the quire signatures in Cambridge, Corpus Christi College MS. 26. If it is a quire signature, this is unexpected, as most such signatures occur not at the center but on one of the outside leaves. The other evidence for the reconstruction of this gathering, however, is quite unambiguous.

A lacuna is generally held to exist between fols. 61 and 62; since fols. 62 and 69 were originally conjoint, and the text is said by Hardy to end imperfectly on fol. 69,[17] it seems likely that gathering XIII lacks its outer bifolium or bifolia. The absence of a green-tinted border frame on the spine edge of the otherwise intact illustration on fol. 61v may be noted; this suggests that the procession depicted might originally have been carried directly across to the next leaf, fol. 61r[a].

As will be seen from a description of the contents of the volume, gathering XIII includes a self-contained interruption of the text, covering four folios. The reader is directed to turn four folios to the sign by a footnote on fol. 62v: *verte iiii folia sequentia ad hoc signum o*—; the sign is made again at the head of the fore-edge margin on fol. 66v (see also Baswell, 178 above).

Marginalia

In many cases the collotype facsimile introduced by James does not show the edge of the leaf, and in no case does it reproduce the marginalia at the foot of many of the illustrated leaves. These are usually in brown ink (on fol. 56r, exceptionally, in red), in a hand that may well be that of Matthew Paris himself, and briefly describe the subject of the illustration. The marginalia are mostly in Latin, though on fol. 49v at least part of the footnote is in French. Many are imperfect

---

[15] *La Vie de seint Auban: A Poem in Norman-French, Ascribed to Matthew Paris*, ed. Atkinson, 23 n.

[16] The standard abbreviation has been expanded here for these two signatures.

[17] T. D. Hardy, *A Descriptive Catalogue of Materials Relating to the History of Great Britain and Ireland to the End of the Reign of Henry VII*, vol. 1 (London: Longman, Green, Longman and Roberts, 1862), 17, no. 30.

where the leaf has been trimmed at the tail, and it is possible that such a note was made at the foot of every leaf to be illustrated, as a direction to the illustrator (even if he and the scribe were identical, as is generally believed),[18] and that the remaining ones have accidentally escaped the process of excision by trimming.[19] If, as it appears, Matthew Paris himself was the author of the captions, and if the captions were in place prior to the execution of the drawings, it may be possible to resolve the disparity between the early date for the script proposed by some scholars and the maturity of the drawings as observed by others.[20]

The marginalia are to be found on approximately one-third of the illustrated leaves: 41r, 42r, 43v, 45v, 49v, 50v, 51v, 53v, 54r/v, 56r, 57r/v, 60r/v, 61r/v, and 62r/v. On fol. 49v, the note refers to a missing illustration, where the rubric is the only other evidence of its subject-matter, and the notes at the foot of fols. 50v and 51v are the only remaining evidence of the subject, the illustrations and their rubric both being almost entirely lost.

Those parts of the marginal notes that can be established with confidence are given below, with contractions silently expanded and with questionable readings underlined.[21]

41v occisio uersus/usus . . . udetur (uidetur?)
42r lupus et aquila
43v lamenta ciuium
45v tribulacio (?)
49v sarrazan cunuers ki esteit presenz A tute cestes est auentures et tut mist escrit ki puis fu translate en latin E de latin en franceis[22]
50v xlii. Pagine de pertractura de passione. Incipit
51r Inuencio, papa cum suis, sanctus germanus, sanctus lupus [commas supplied]
51v episcopi tres in Anglia
53v episcopi applicant
54r Inuocatur albanus in auxilium disput . . .
54v [only one ascender visible]

---

[18] On the question of Paris and assistant scribes see now Baswell, Appendix: The Hands of TCD MS. 177, above, 191–94.

[19] Vaughan (*Matthew Paris*, 231) describes "similar legends for each picture written by [Paris] on the lower margins" of the *Vitae Offarum* (London, BL, MS. Cotton Nero D. I), many of which "have been cut off by the binder."

[20] See Morgan, *EGM [I]*,132. Lewis, *Art of Matthew Paris*, 381–87, summarizes the arguments and suggests that Paris's work on MS. 177 was interrupted. See also the essay by Baswell in this volume, 169–94.

[21] I am grateful to Professor M. L. Colker and to Mr. Stuart O Seanóir for their assistance in reading these notes.

[22] This is very similar to the rubric on the same page; see p. 218, item 5, below.

56r tres reges uicti. unus perfossus. tres fugitiui
57r [only one ascender visible]
57v [heavily cropped and illegible]
60r [heavily cropped and illegible]
60v [heavily cropped and illegible, apart from the upper portion of probably the word "Offa"]
61r mônachi feretrum . . .
61v Processio, Rex cum suis. Abbas [comma supplied]
62r applicacio
62v [heavily cropped and illegible]

Missing Illustrations

These details are relevant to the sequence in which the manuscript was produced. It is impossible to say why some of the illustrations were made on separate pieces of vellum and why these fragments have all been lost. The only remaining pasted-down fragment of illustration that is not a vellum repair is on fol. 57r, a gilt stream of sunlight, which is almost identical to the illustration on fol. 58r and which conceals a red line drawing and also the outlines of the cloud, which are represented on the imposed fragment. Although the lost pieces of vellum almost certainly bore the illustrations (as described by James), it is not clear, as he suggests, that they were completed before being stuck to the page; nor is it simply the case that blank spaces were left for illustrations that were never made, since imperfect rubrics and fragments of illustration remain at the edges of some blank areas. It is possible that the illustrator pasted fresh scraps of vellum (before beginning his drawings) on leaves where the show-through of the image on the other side of the leaf, described below, was particularly intrusive (see also Baswell, 177 above). This speculation is supported by the fact that nowhere is any one leaf treated in this way on both sides. Descriptions of what remains of each lost illustration follow.

Folio 40v: the rubrics at the head are intact, and there is a regular rectangular blank below them where the illustrated piece has been removed, but to the right of the page the brown-tinted border remains (with two hands around the pole of a red banner with oxidized silver detail and, below that, a dog's head thrusting out of the frame).

Folio 42v: the lower horizontal green-tinted border and the beginning of the two verticals remain, with the lines of what may be feet, two to the right and one to the left of the blank area, just above the border. The rubrics are perfect.

Folio 43r: part of the outermost black outline of the frame remains, and the rubrics are perfect.

Folio 45v: nothing whatever remains of the illustration and the rubrics also are missing, except for traces of a blue and a red initial at the head. This leaf, like some others, bears very faint traces of vertical rulings in red, at the tail margin and over the left half of the blank area.

Folio 48v: the black outline of the frame is almost intact except for the right-hand vertical, and the rubrics are perfect.

Folio 49v: the lower green tinted border and the upper black horizontal remain. Fragments of black line, which may be feet, are visible above the green border, as on fol. 42v, and the black line at the head is broken and of uneven thickness. The rubrics are perfect.

Folio 50v: nothing whatever remains of the illustration or its border, and the rubrics also are lacking. The top of the first line of both columns of the text is imperfect, suggesting that the text was written after the pasted fragment was applied.

Folio 51v: only the trace of a blue initial and the beginnings of both lines of rubric remain on the left-hand side. The lower line begins *Cist d*...

Although James ascribes his conjectures as to the subject matter of lost illustrations to the rubrics at the head and tail of the text, he does not remark on the additional loss of the French rubrics at the head of fols. 45v, 50v, and 51v, where they were written on the lost fragment instead of the leaf. He does not describe the imperfect lines of text at the head of both columns on fols. 50v and 51v, where the main text was clearly written after the piece of vellum with illustration was put down; nor does he refer to the fragments of illustration and green-tinted border that remain on fols. 40v and 42v.

These details are noted by Atkinson in his earlier edition of the poem.[23] From his many references to the condition of the manuscript, it is clear that Atkinson worked directly from it in the production of his edition, whereas it seems likely that James worked chiefly from photographs and notes that he had taken "thirty-two years earlier... while visiting Ireland."[24] For example, James's description of fol. 57r does not mention that the gilt fragment is superimposed on the illustration, an important detail that is immediately obvious on examining the manuscript but almost imperceptible in the collotype facsimile.

Skins Used

The quality and appearance of the skins used vary considerably throughout the volume. Since the quality and preparation of the material for writing often changes quite uniformly with new gatherings of texts, tending to confirm collation and perhaps suggesting the passage of time in the assembling of the volume, it seems useful to give some indication of the range of vellum used.

---

[23] Atkinson, *La Vie de seint Auban*, 56 and n.
[24] R. W. Pfaff, *Montague Rhodes James* (London: Scolar Press, 1980), 296–97.

Fols. 1 and 2 are quite different from the rest. Fol. 1 is a very horny, thick piece of sheepskin parchment, with the spine of the animal running diagonally off the vertical of the leaf. There is no text on it to show that it is contemporary with the manuscript; it may be a wrapper added in the late medieval period. The shelfmark of a previous owner, James Ussher, archbishop of Armagh (d. 1656), is on the verso of the leaf. Fol. 2, which is a great deal more sensitive than the rest to variations in relative humidity, is of fine kidskin, quite soiled and crumpled. It is creased in a horizontal line across its center with two symmetrical lines of pricking on either side, in a way that bears no relation to the text or drawing, which suggests that the leaf had been prepared or intended for some other use.

Fol. 3 is relatively horny and scored on the recto, but the vellum of fols. 4–19 is quite fine and light in color. The color is darker and the weight is heavier in fols. 20–28, and there are corrugations and distortions on most leaves. Over fols. 29–45 the vellum is browner in color, the weight varying quite considerably, but the surface on both the hair and flesh sides tends to be fairly smooth. Fols. 48–52 are particularly dark and horny. Fols. 53–69 are heavy, but with quite a pronounced nap on both the hair and flesh sides. Fols. 70–77 are somewhat lighter in color and texture and of a uniform weight. The verso of fol. 77 is heavily soiled and discolored, suggesting that the manuscript existed for some time in an unbound state.

Many of the leaves have natural lacunae, usually no more than a couple of millimeters in diameter, which were repaired by the vellum-maker or the scribe with small patches of the same material. In many cases these original patches and the text they contained have been lost and later replaced with blank patches. An example is the patch on fol. 31r, now removed, which can be seen clearly (Figure 3b.1). Occasionally these later repairs concealed text; as a general rule they have now been removed and replaced with more sympathetic repairs only where structurally necessary.

The composition of a number of leaves from smaller strips of vellum stuck together is one of the distinctive features of this manuscript, as noted above. The character of the vellum in these composite leaves is usually homogeneous, and the fact that the individual elements sometimes bear pricking and ruling marks unrelated to either the ruling or text of this manuscript suggests that some could have been cannibalized from the margins of larger, presumably discarded, leaves of manuscript waste. Where the individual pieces are attached, the overlap is usually less than 5 mm and the adhesion is generally good, although imperfect register in some cases suggests that joins may have been re-glued at some time after the manuscript was produced.

Fol. 13 bears two sets of copper-stained pin-holes, where the corner fragment of the composite folio had clearly become detached at some time and was pinned for safekeeping to its appropriate leaf and subsequently re-adhered (Figure 3b.2).

In the course of conservation, joins that were becoming detached, usually at the edges, were re-adhered using gelatine, but no attempt was made to reconstitute composite leaves for the purposes of perfecting register. In fols. 20, 54, and 59, one of the elements of each of these composite leaves is lost, and the text is imperfect in each case.

Pigments

There is some off-setting of rubrication onto the adjacent folio, usually in spine margins, which may have resulted from dampening of the spine or severe pressing by a later binder (there is no other evidence of water damage), and occasional "show-through" (invariably of green and sometimes of blue pigment).

The predominant color of the illustration was described as a "thin unpleasant green" by Atkinson. James also referred to the use of green in the tinting of illustrations,[25] but he did not describe the grey/black, yellow/brown, red, and blue tinting that is also present. What Atkinson described as "slate" appears to be an oxidized silver (or alloy of silver).[26] This is blue-black and metallic in appearance and is used typically for sword-, spear-, and axe-heads (for example, on fol. 52v, which shows through very prominently and somewhat confusingly in the illustration on the recto). This metallic color is also present in the fragment of illustration on fol. 40v and on fols. 53v, 55v, 56r, 57r, 57v, 58r, 59r, and 60r. It is less commonly used than gold, which appears first on fol. 51r and is used on almost every illustrated folio thereafter.

The extent to which the pigments, but especially the green, show through on the obverse has not generally been remarked. This show-through has the typical shadowy green appearance of basic copper acetate through slightly gelatinized vellum, and the effect may have been enhanced by the additional pouncing of the illustrated areas, which are often quite noticeably whiter and finer than the rest of the leaf. This green show-through is particularly pronounced on the verso of fols. 45, 48, 49, 50, and 51, where illustrations are now lacking.

Another distinctive feature of the illustration that has not been described, and is not obvious on the collotype facsimile, is the modeling of the surface of the uncolored vellum. This creates a fine relief effect, chiefly on the folds of draped clothing, the necks and haunches of horses (fol. 49r, Figure 3b.3), the brickwork of the abbey church (fol. 60r, Figure 3b.4), and the laths of the boat (fol. 62r). This effect, which is visible to the naked eye assisted by raked lighting, has perhaps been contrived by Matthew Paris. The variegated surface textures may, however, result from the congealing of the surface of the vellum that follows the

---

[25] James, *Illustrations*, 18.
[26] Atkinson, *Vie de seint Auban*, x.

selective application of a clear or colored wash (from which, if that is the case, all traces of color have subsequently disappeared).

Conservation and Binding Note

For the purpose of conservation the manuscript was carefully disbound, and glue and thread debris was removed from spine edges. Wax and ink stains were reduced where they obscured text. The blank patches of the nineteenth-century repair were recorded photographically and removed. Edges were given a light dry-cleaning, and tears and lacunae were repaired using calfskin vellum (from Elzas and Zonen, Celbridge, County Kildare) and goldbeaters' skin (from Long and Long, Belleville, New Jersey), using the method developed by Anthony Cains.[27]

Single leaves were guarded to each other or to stubs where appropriate, using edible gelatine, and the manuscript was sewn on five double cords (from Barbours of Lisburn, "Best Blake"), using the nineteenth-century sewing positions with a paper "zig-zag" guard (from Tim Barret, Kalamazoo, Michigan), vellum endleaves, and primary linen head and tail bands over a rolled tawed goatskin core with secondary decorative endbands in blue and white linen. It was laced onto "cushioned" boards of quartered oak and covered full in Italian tawed goatskin (from Gentili, Rome), using flour paste. The manuscript is stored in a dropback box with a linen-padded chemise to maintain gentle pressure.

---

[27] See Anthony Cains, "Repair Treatments for Vellum Manuscripts," *The Paper Conservator* 7 (1982/1983): 15–23.

Appendix: Collation Maps

Folio	Gathering	Collation as found	Collation as conjectured	Text
1	I	——	——	Fols 1r–2v
2		——	——	Notes concerning the loan of certain of Matthew's saints' lives to titled ladies
3	II	——	——	Fols 3r–20r
4		——	——	Latin poem in elegiacs by Ralph of Dunstable, based on William of St. Albans' prose life of St. Alban.
5	III	——	——	
6		——	——	
7		——	——	
8		——	——	
9		——	——	
10	IV	——	——	
11		——	——	
12		——	——	
13		——	——	
14	V	——	——	
15		——	——	
16		——	——	
17		——	——	
18		——	——	
19		——	——	
20		——	——	Fols 20r–28v Latin prose life of William of St. Albans, the source of Matthew's Poem.

Folio	Gathering	Collation as found	Collation as conjectured	Text
21	VI			
22				
23	VII			
24				
25				
26				
27				
28				Fol 28v Rubric to missing tract on the invention of Amphibalus
29	VIII			Fols 29r–50r Anglo-Norman verses by Matthew Paris about St. Alban and St. Amphibalus
30				
31				
32				
33				
34				
35				
36				
37				
38				
47	IX			
46				
39	X			
40				
41				
42				
43				
44				
45				

Folio	Gathering	Collation as found	Collation as conjectured	Text
48	XI			
49				
50				Fols 50v–52v
51				Lessons for the feast of the invention and the translation of St. Alban
52				Fols 52v–62v Treatise on the invention and translation of St. Alban
53	XII			
54				
55				
56				
57				
58				
59				
60				
61				
62	XIII			
63				Fols 63r–66r Charters for the foundation of the Abbey of St. Albans
64				
65				
66				Fols 66v–68v Treatise on the invention and translation of St. Alban (cont'd.)
67				
68				Fols 68v–69v About the invention of Amphibalus
69				Fols 69v–70v About the miracles of Amphibalus

Folio	Gathering	Collation as found	Collation as conjectured	Text
70	XIV	—	—	Fols 70v–72r
71		—	⎤	About the translation of Alban
72		—	⎥	
73		—	⎥	Fols 73r–77r
74		—	⎥	About the miracles of Amphibalus
75		—	⎥	
76		—	⎥	
77		—	⎦	

Appendix
Passages from *La Vie de Seint Auban*

1. Amphibalus inducts Alban into heavenly relationships and loyalties (*laisse* 12, fol. 32v)

	12 "Amis" dist Amphibal, "ne vus serra celé;	
340	Seint Esperitz ad tun quor eslumé.	
	Par humme sunt li autre apris e endoctriné,	
	Mes vus par Deu meimes en es revisité,	
	E par sa revelaciun a lui es acointé.	32c
	Ore vus pri e sumoin pur Deu en croiz pené,	
345	Soiez amis verais e hem de lealté;	
	Kar eschoisi vus a e vus lui de bon gré.	
	Ja ne vus en partez par nule vanité.	
	Trespassable est li mundz e tute sa beuté,	
	Cum est la flur du champ u cum l'erbe du pré.	
350	Mes ki sert Deu e fait la sue volunté	
	E murt en sun servise, a bonure fu né.	
	Cist regnera eu ciel sanz fin, curuné.	
	Mes li felun cheitif ki Deu unt ublié,	
	Li las dolerus, hai! tant sunt maluré!	
355	U est Alexandres li princes alosé?	
	Cesaires li riches e li reduté?	
	E li autre prince tant riche e tant feffé	
	Ki tant urent tresor e tant nobilité?	
	N'unt ore plus de tere fors saet pez mesuré.	
360	Mes l'alme tuz jurs viit santz mortal[it]é;	
	Mansiun truvera sanz nule fauseté	
	Sulum les faitz du cors k'eu mund ad esté.	
	Li guereduns est grantz as bons aturné.	
	Ne soiez esmeuz pur nule adversité	
365	Ke hem vus face au cors u au quor maufé,	
	Kar a la fin serras martir par Deu pruvé;	
	Le regne averez du ciel ki vus est estué."	
	De l'ewe atant demande e hom li ad porté,	

	E Auban baptize a grant humilité	
370	Eu nun de la veraie e haute trinité.	
	En l'amur Deu l'a par sermun confermé,	
	De la fei Deu la summe apris e demustré.	
	E aprés ço ke il out trestut cest achevé	
	Le cungé li ad requis e demandé;	
375	Si li dist: "Amis, ne soiez esnuié.	
	E[n] mun pais m'en vois u oi einz purposé;	
	E vus soiez, beus ostes, a Jesu cumandé.	
	De vus croi estre seur e tres bien acerté,	
	Despuis ke Deu meimes ad tun quor saelé.	32*d*
	E[n] mun pais m'envois, asez ai sujurné,	
	Sarracins cunvertir dunt tant i a plenté."	

2. The prince tries to convert Alban back to his class beliefs (*laisse* 17, fol. 34r–34v)

	17 Quant li princes l'ad veu en cel estrange atur	34*a*
	Ke il ad de sun maistre retenu par amur,	
	De ire e mautalent tut mue la culur,	
	E puis li a dit par curuz e irur:	
545	"Ki es tu ki nus as fait si grant deshonur,	
	Qui guerpi as ke tindrent ti gentil ancesur?	
	Ne fuissez citoien de parenté majur,	
	Ja fuissez a mort livrez e a dulur.	
	De vus s'esmervellent li grant e li menur,	
550	Ki sages es de aprise e d'age estes maur,	
	E deussez estre as autres essample e mireur.	
	Ore croiz ke va prechant un estrange tafur	
	Ki s'en va, vaivez, par terres sanz sujur,	
	E ore s'en est binnez en tenegre devant jur	
555	Cum luz u cum gupilz escriez de pastur.	
	Entenc cum sa doctrine folage est e errur.	
	K'a fause fust pruvee, ben pert k'il out pour.	
	Venuz dust estre ci devant nus a baudur	
	Cum maistre e avoué e cum certein prechur,	
560	E estre a sun deciple e guarant e sucur.	
	Mais ben l'ad ore pruvé ke il est boiseur.	34*b*
	'Fauseté se soille' dit hom 'au chef de tur.'	
	Pens de tun lingnage, ki grant conquesteur	
	De Rumme nez, ki furent du mund cumandeur,	
565	Sarrazins nobiles de grantz terres seingnur,	
	Ki en noz deus tuz crurent ki tant sunt de valur;	

	A eus sunt entendant roi, duc, empereur.
	Repent toi de tun maisfait, n'en serras le pejur.
	Engettez ces drapeus! Ne vus nuit la puur?
570	E cele croiz ke tu la tens, dun'e[n] as tu hisdur?
	Ben s'en puet gabber de vus cist enchantur
	Ki ta robe enporte. Hai! queu changeur!
	Mes n'est nul tant sage, tant fort, ne tant seur,
	Ki n'est aucune feit susduit par foleur.
575	Par traisun perist meint quens, meint vavasur,
	Marcheant en feire, chevaler en estur.
	N'estes pas darreins, a tei n'est fait premur.
	N'est ki ne prent sum, fere purrez retur.
	Repentir te purras de cest[e] grant foleur.
580	En noz deus ad grant franchise e duçur, 34c
	Ki pieté unt tost de repentant pecchur.
	N'averunt vers toi plus ne ire ne rancur.
	Reni Jesu ke claimes Fiz Deu, le Sauveur,
	E noz deus poestifs desoremés aur!
585	Tu en purras consirer gueredun e honur,
	Terres e citez grant[z], fiez, chasteus e tur.
	Kar li doilz serroit grantz, ne veimes unc greinnur,
	Si tu t'en murs, ki en es de la cité la flur."

3. The execution procession, Heraclius's conversion, and the beginning of his martyrdom (*laisses* 24–25, fols. 36r–37r)

	24 Li prince e la commune ne l'unt pas otrié, [36*b*]
	Ne li parent Auban ki iluec sunt assemblé,
	Ne cist de la cité, li veillard e esné;
740	Kar Auban ert gentilz e bien enparenté.
	Sulum la lei de Rumme, hom k'a mort est jugé
	Ki est commun enemi, mes n'est leres pruvé,
	E seit de parage e gentilz e bien né,
	Custumme est e dreiture ke il seit decolé.
745	A ceste mort est Auban e livrez e damnez.
	Cele sentence unt jovre e viel confermé.
	Li grant e li petit bien sunt de ço paé
	E autres jugementz unt desdit e fausé.
	Lors l'unt de rechief de chaesnes lié,
750	Hors de la cité l'unt trait ja e mené.
	Tant lui suit grant pueple k'a pou n'est voidé
	Li temples e citez u urent ainz estez.
	Dient en reschisnant ki l'unt trait e buté:

"Va t'en, his, enemi nus deus, de la cité. 36c
755 Ke tu as deservi, luer tei est apresté.
Tu murras santz delai, tu muras, maluré!"
Tiré l'unt e saché, batu e laidangé,
E cist mot ne sune, mes les ad encliné;
Jesu ure, pur nus ki en croiz fu pené.
760 La presse ert grant du pueple ki la fu auné
Pur ver le gugement au queu chief fust mené;
Curent e poinnent a cheval e a pé.
Li uns les autres passent, enviz u a bon gré;
Estroit lur fu le champ e le chemin ferré.
765 A une ewe venent grant e parfund sanz gué;
Ne batel ne nief a passer unt truvé.
Un pund i unt truvé u sunt li uns passé;
Nus ne remaint, mes de passer s'est chescun eforcé.
Li pountz estoit estroitz, de pople i out plenté;
770 A grant estrif i passent e nun a volenté.
Mes li jovre volentrifs de force e poesté
L'ewe passent a nou ki parfund fu e lé.
Mes plusurs i perisent, dunt fu grant duel mené:
Li uns du pund en l'ewe ki en sunt trebuché,
775 E autres ki au noer se mistrent, sunt neé.
Auban ki ço regarde marriz est e grevé;
A genoilluns s'est mis e gent de pieté.
Le quor e le visage vers le ciel ad dresce
E dist: "Beu Sire Deus ki as le mund furmé,
780 Ki en avisiun vi estre en croiz posé,
Pur tue franchise e debonnereté,
Fai l'ewe descrestre par quei sunt travaillé
Cist ki ver desirent ço ke m'est aturné!"
Deu ki tut guverne regnant en majesté,
785 Ki de tut prent cure quancke il ad crié,
Hautement soudee ki de lui est privé;
La requeste Auban ducement ad granté.

25 Les oraisuns e lermes de vertu sunt tant [36d]
K'Auban a Deu presente a devociun grant,
790 Ke l'ewe ki ert parfunde e raedde a flot briant,
Retraite e[n] sun chanel, va si apetizant
Ke n'i fust nus a flote, ne batel ne chalant;
E u avant passer ne pout hom nouant,
A secches plantes passent nis li petit enfant.
795 Li mort ki noiez furent se drescent en seant;

De mort resuscitez, vifs levent e juant,
Legers, enters e seins cum geu ussent dormant.
Mut en sunt esbaiz li paien mescreant.
Uns chevalers gentilz ki ala trainant
800 Auban a martire au puier le pendant,
Ki Aracle avoit nun, e cist out le cumant
De decoler Auban receu du tirant,
Quant veit le miracle Jesu tesmoniant,
E les resuscitez ki venent Deu louant,
805 Au sabelun u nuls unc hom ala avant,
Chiet as piez Auban, si engette sun brant
E dist en haute voiz, les Sarrazins ouant:
"Cist est Deus poestifs dunt Auban va prechant;
N'est autre si il nun, cist est li tutpoissant!
810 Despendu e perdu ai trestut mun viant,
Ke ceu Deu n'ai servi; mes ore nepurquant,
Mes ke a tart, deveng sis hom e sis sergant.
Hai! Jesu debonaire, k'Auban va tant prisant,
De trestutz mes pecchez, Sire, pardun demant;
815 A vus m'alme e mun cors abandun e cumant.
Ta vertu prove l'ewe a toi obeissant,
E ço ke hem desdit, purvers recumbatant,
Tesmoine le element ke a toi est attendant.
Hem a ki Deus dune raisun a sun semblant,
820 E tei tuz jurs apele, k'alez vus demurant?
Kar guerpissez Mahom! guerpissez Tervagant!
E reclamez Jesu le verai Deu vivant!"
Atant regarde Auban a piteus semblant
E dist: "Proiez pur moi Jesu eu ciel regnant!" 37a
825 Es le vus seisi e pris de meintenant.
K'avant urent ire, ore la vunt il dublant,
Fremissent cum liuns ki vu[n]t proie sivant.
Uns paens haut s'escrie, une mace portant:
"Tu mentz apertement, vassal failli puant!
830 Mar unc le deis, mar l'alas cuntruvant.
Mes jo sai l'achesun, jo en ere voir disant:
Li solailz ke aurum, ki chautz est e raant,
La huntage de lui veit k'alum vengant;
Le flot ad tut secchi ki nus fu desturbant.
835 Ki autrement le dit, fableur est mentant,
E a ço pruver sui prest ploier le gant."
Atant le fert du poin e du bastun pesant,
Les denz lui fait voler des genzives devant;

Du niés e de la buche li sancs ist e espant.
840 Derochent e debatent du cors le remenant,
Brisent braz e gambes par lui li trespassant;
Li nierf li sunt rumpu e tut le cors doillant,   37*b*
La char noire e emflee e tut le vis senglant;
Ne remeint sein ne entier eu cors ne tant ne quant;
845 A peine chaut remeint li quors eu piz batant.
Des pez le defulent chevaler e sergant;
Pur mort le guerpissent eu sabelun gisant.
Charoinne le tenent sanz alme enfreidissant,
A luus u chiens livre e as oisseus volant.

4. The beheading of Alban (Rubric 24, fol. 38r)

Ci decole un gluz depulin   38*a* and 38*b*
Auban du brant acerin.
Nuit cumence au Sarrazin;
Au martir, clarté sanz fin.
L'un tent vers ciel, l'autre en declin;
Au vespre est l'un, l'autre au matin.
Un crestien ki est veisin
La croiz prent, teinte eu sanc rosin.

5. The Saracen narrator of Alban's story reveals his intentions (*laisse* 48, fol. 49v)

Ci parole cist Sarrazins cunvers ki estoit presenz a tutes cestes aventures e tut mist en escrit, ke puis fu translaté en latin e aprés ço fu translaté de latin en rumantz.

48 Jo ki a ceu tens estoie mescreant Sarrazin   49*d*
De ceste estoire vi le cumençail e fin
Despuis ke Auban reçut en sun palois perrin
1815 Sun oste Amphibal, trespassant pelerin,
Gesk'a tant k'il furent mis en sarcu marbrin;
Of les paens estoie de la loi Apolin,
Pallaide e Diene e Phebun e Jovin,
Ki sunt dampné diable en enfer susterin;
1820 Mes le honur Jesu crest e cist vunt en declin.
La geste ai, cum la vi, escrit en parchemin.
Uncore vendra le jur, ben le di e devin,
La estoire ert translatee en franceis e latin.
Ne sai autre language fors le mien barbarin,
1825 Mais fei ke doi porter lui ki fist d'ewe vin,

Ne i deise fauseté pur tut l'or Costentin.
A Jesu me sui rendu cum mi veisin.
Desore penant deveng e preng burdun fresnin,   50*a*
Nupez sanz chauceure de cordewon caprin,
1830 Pur esclavine eschaung mun peliçun d'ermin.
Ne dormirai au vespre u jo lief au matin,
Si la k'en nief me mette au procein port marin.
Passerai Mungiu le roiste munt alpin,
Vers Rumme la cité tendrai droit le chemin,
1835 As Romeins nuncier, le pueple cesarin,
Kancke ai veu e oi, jo peccheres orphanin,
En l'eille ke cunquist Brutus e Cornelin.
Pur Auban ki l'ad teinte premers de sanc rosin,
Ki pur Deu decolé fu du brand acerin,
1840 Musterai i mun livre escrit en veeslin.
Tesmoin averai of moi mein[t] veillart e meschin.
Jo ne me os numer pur paiens depuslin
Mes pecchur cupable, dolent, povre e frarin.
Batesme i requorai de quor verai e fin;
1845 A Jesu me abaundun, serf loial, enterrin,
E la estoire de Auban ci finis e termin.
Ci finist li rumantz de l'estoire de Seint Auban le premer martir de Engletere
e de Seint Amphibal e de ses cumpainnuns.

6. King Offa and the work of foundation (Rubrics 65, 66, 67, fols. 60, 61r)

    Mut met li reis peine e cure,   60*a* and 60*b*
    Chescuns k'en sa ovre labure,
    Charpenter, maçun, verrer,
408 Chescun sulum sun mester.
    Li uns asset, li autre taille;
    Cist coupe, cist bat, cist maille,
    Cist de hache, cist de martel,
412 Cist de maillet e de cisel.

    Li gentils rois de bone vie,   60*c* and 60*d*
    Offes, parfait sa abbeie.
    Ben veit ke Deus i cunsent,
416 Ki avance sun cumencement.
    Par cunseil de ses privez,
    Prelatz sages e ben lettrez,
    De moinnes congregaciun

420   E abbé Willegond par nun
      Met en sa bone mesun,
      E gent de grant religiun.

      Dehors Verlame la cité   61*a* and 61*b*
424   Estoit de grant antiquité
      Une eglisette fundee,
      "Sancta Syon" ki fu numee.
      Paens cunvers la firent, l'an
428   Ke decolé fu seint Auban.
      En sun honur la firent fere
      Ki premer martir ert de Engletere.
      La chasse au martir fu la mise
432   Geske faitte eient la grant iglise.

Lists of Proper Names in Matthew Paris's *Life of Saint Alban*

In the entries below, the first number refers to the *laisse* and the second to verse number(s) within *laisses*, both keyed to the Harden edition of *La Vie de seint Auban*. "R" indicates a rubric. Square brackets signal occurrences introduced into the translation for the sake of clarity, and asterisks on entries indicate textual notes.

Abel 13:399
Abraham 13:402
Adam 5:105, 13:398, 20:655
Alban, 3rd-century British protomartyr 1:21, 2:41, 3:51, 4:71, 5:104, etc.
Alexander, Alexander the Great, Alexander III of Macedon 12:355*
Amphibalus, Christian who converted Alban [1:8–9*], 4:96, 5:103, 7:199, 10:280, 13:397*, etc.
Apollo 1:14*, 3:65, 11:334, 48:1817*; *see also* Phoebus
Architriclin (*lit.* "wine steward"), medieval name commonly given to the bridegroom at the wedding of Cana 3:62*
August R68:437*
Auxerre, *see* Germanus
Belial 1:14*, 43:1623
Bethlehem 3:61, 15:484
Bordeaux (*Burdele*) 34:1265*
Britain 32:1128, R52:291*, R56:335, R68:440
Brutus (with Corineus), legendary Trojan founder of Britain 48:1837*
Caesar, Julius (100 BCE–44 BCE), Roman emperor 12:356, [48:1835]
Cain (*Caim*) 13:399
Christian(s) 7:180, 8:210, 14:420, 16:511, 27:900, etc.; Christianity 29:1028

Constantine (*Costentin*) (272–337 CE), first Christian emperor of Rome 48:1826*
Cordovan (expensive shoe leather) 48:1829*
Corineus (*Cornelin*), Brutus's Trojan companion 48:1837*
Damascus (*Damas*) 41:1498
Diana (*Diene*), goddess 34:1262, 48:1818
England 28:931, *explicit*, R48:259, R67:430; ~ king of England, R56:333
Eve (*Ewe*) 5:105
Father, God 6:167, 7:186, 9:250 (*Pere Adonai*), 27:895, 45:1706; *see also* God, High Father,
French 3:70, 48:1823*
Gabriel, the archangel Gabriel 5:125
Galilee, *see* Jesus
Genevieve (d. 500 CE), patron saint of Paris R49:270*
Germanus (c. 378–448 CE), saint and bishop of Auxerre R48:262*, R49:273, R51:283, R53:300, etc.
God 2:25, 2:29, 3:68, 4:78, 4:80, 4:84, 4:97, 4:98, 5:105, 5:108, etc.; *see also* Father, High Father
Heraclius (*Aracle[s]*), Saracen soldier who accompanied Alban to execution and was converted 25:801, 29:936, 29:945, 29:947, [29:961], 29:970, 29:975, 29:981, 29:987, [29: 1010],

29:1039, 30:1040, 32:1160, etc.; St. Heraclius *incipit* before *laisse* 29, *explicit* after *laisse* 30

High Father (*Haut Pere*), God 5:122

Holmhurst, place where Alban was beheaded; later site of abbey R59:359*

Holy Spirit 5:136, 6:168, 7:186, 12:340, 27:895

Jesus, Jesus Christ 1:9, 2:46, 2:50, 3: 54, 3:65, 4:79, 6:146, etc.; Jesus of Galilee 16:501; *see also* King of the Jews, Son, Son of God

Jews (*Giue[u], Giu, Jueus*) 6:155*, 6:161, 9:240, 10:289*, 11:307, etc.

Jove 11:335, 31:1103, 35:1362*, 42:1576, 48:1818

Judas 6:155, 28:933

King of the Jews 9:240; *see also* Jesus, Son, Son of God

Last Judgment (*paraler*) 2:39

Latin 3:70, before *laisse* 48, 48:1823*

London R52:292

Longinus (*Lungis*), Roman knight (centurion) said to have pierced Christ's side 6:158

Lupus (c383–478 CE), saint and bishop of Troyes who accompanied Germanus to Britain R48:262*, R53:300

Mary, mother of Jesus 5:102, 5:128, 33:1231, 34:1252, 39:1443; *see also* Virgin

Mercia (*Murcia*), Anglo-Saxon kingdom (c. 7th-9th century CE): *see* Offa

Messiah 5:132, 28:932

Mohammed 11:333*, 14:413, 15:447, 18:608, 25:821, etc.

Montgieu (*Mungiu*), Mount St. Bernard; pass in the Alps between Italy and Switzerland 48:1833*

Moses (*Moyseus*) 13:402, 26:872

Neptune 11:335, 31:1104

Noah 13:401

Offa (active 757 to 796 CE), king of Mercia R56:333, R57:342, R59:363, etc.

Pallas (*Pallaide, Palladie*), the goddess Pallas Athena, also known as Minerva 11:336, 34:1262, 48:1818

Paris, the French city R49:267

Pelagians, followers of Pelagius (c. 354–420 CE), considered a heretic R53:304, R54:312

Pharaoh 11:309*

Phoebus (*Febum, Phebun*) sun god, 19:622*, 31:1103, 38:1417, 42:1573, 46:1738, 48:1818; *see also* Apollo

Pluto 11:336, 31:1104

Promised Land (*terre . . . de promissiun*) 11:312

Rhine (*Rin*), river 3:69

Rome 17:564, 47:1808, 48:1834; Roman 1:23, 24:741*; Romans 48:1835

Saracens (*Sarrazins, Sarracins*) 1:13*, 3:64*, 12:381, 13:394, 14:408, 17:565, etc.

Satan 1:14*, 3:67, 5:116, 11:320, 28:930

Savior 17:583

Son, 20:659, 27:895; Son of God 2:36, 2:41, 4:80, 11:304, 14:422, 17:583; *see also* Jesus

St. Albans, Abbey of, R64:397, R66:414

St. John, feast of, 68:433*

St. Syon, church built near Verulamium, R67:426

Syria (*Sulie*) 14:427*, 16:502, 23:716, 39:1448

Tervagant, imagined pagan deity 25:821, 32:1130, 46:1738

Thetis (*Tetim*), sea goddess 11:336

Trinity 7:185, 12:370, 33:1239, 47:1805

Troyes, *see* Lupus

Verulamium, Roman city, later St. Albans 1:10*, 14:415, [22], 32:1127, 34:1243, etc.

Virgin (*Virgne*), the Virgin Mary, 47:1802

Wales (*Guales*) 2:34*, 31:1112, 32:1121, 35:1284, 46:1737, etc.

Willegod (*Willegond*), first abbot of St. Albans Abbey R66:420.

List of Proper Names in William of St. Albans, *Passion of Saint Alban*

Numbers refer to paragraphs in the translation. Items may occur more than once in a given paragraph. Asterisks on entries indicate textual notes.

Adam 7
Alban, 3rd-century British protomartyr, 1, 2, 3, 5, 6, etc.; St. Alban 24, 43
Almighty 26, Almighty God 44; *see also* Creator, Father, God, Lord, Most High
Amphibalus, Christian who converted Alban, 3, 4, 5, 7, 8, etc.; St. Amphibalus 26 (*incipit*), 31, 32
Britain 3, 47
British 1
Christ 2, 3, 4, 5, 6, etc.; *see also* Jesus, King of the Jews, Lord Jesus, Redeemer, Savior, Son of God
Christian(s) 3, 4, 9, 11, 22, etc.
Creator, 4, 27; *see also* Almighty, Father, God, Lord, Most High
Diocletian (244–311 CE), Roman emperor, 3
English, the English people, *incipit* before 3, 26, 47
Father, God 4, 5, 6, 8, 43; *see also* Almighty, Creator, God, Lord, Most High
Geoffrey Arthur, Geoffrey of Monmouth, Wales (c. 1100–55 CE), author of *The History of the Kings of Britain*, 1
God 4, 5, 7, 8, 9, etc.; God the Father 6; *see also* Almighty, Creator, Father, Lord, Most High
Gospels 4

History, History of the Passion of the blessed Alban, *explicit* of the Passion
Holmhurst, place of Alban's beheading 17
Holy Spirit 4, 5, 8
Jesus 4, 35, 43; Jesus Christ 3, 9; *see also* Christ, King of the Jews, Lord Jesus, Redeemer, Savior, Son of God
Jews 7
King of the Jews, Jesus, 6; *see also* Christ, Jesus, Lord Jesus, Redeemer, Savior, Son of God
Latin 1
Lord, God 1, 3, 4, 7, 9, etc.; *see also* Almighty, Creator, Father, God, Most High
Lord Jesus 5, 9, 19, 45; Lord Jesus Christ 3, 7, 8, 14, 16, 25, 29, 42, 47; *see also* Christ, Jesus, King of the Jews, Redeemer, Savior, Son of God
Mary, mother of Jesus 4; *see also* Virgin
Most High, God 4; *see also* Almighty, Creator, Father, God, Lord
Paradise 43
Passion (of St. Alban) 1, *incipit* before 2, 2, *incipit* before 3, 47, *explicit* after 47; Passion (of St. Amphibalus) *explicit* inserted into 26, *explicit* after 47
Picts, confederation of tribes in what is now Scotland; 35, 37

Redeemer, Jesus, 9; *see also* Christ, Jesus, King of the Jews, Lord Jesus, Savior, Son of God
Roman(s) 3, 47
Rome 46, 47
Savior 23, 26; *see also* Christ, Jesus, King of the Jews, Lord Jesus, Redeemer, Son of God
Simon, abbot of St. Albans (1167–1183 CE) Dedication 1

Son of God 3, 4, 6, 7, 8, 26, 46; *see also* Christ, Jesus, King of the Jews, Lord Jesus, Redeemer, Savior
Sun, the sun god 21
Verulamium, Roman city, later St. Albans 2, 3, 15*, 27
Virgin, the Virgin Mary 4
Wales 27, 35
Welsh, the Welsh people 35, 37
William of St. Albans Dedication 1